:ethoven's music continues to form one of the cornerstones
i the concert repertoire some 200 years after it was written,
ind its sheer ingenuity and inventiveness never cease to amaze
the perceptive listener. Knowing the context in which it was
written can aid our understanding of the music, and every
biography of Beethoven's unusual life has something new to
say. Although some aspects of his life, such as his deafness,
ind his great love for his only nephew, are well known, this
ɔook also includes many details that are less familiar. John
Suchet writes with infectious enthusiasm, and his avoidance
of technical detail makes this a biography that can be read and
understood by anyone interested in the composer.'

—Professor Barry Cooper
University of Manchester, leading authority on Beethoven

'John Suchet offers us a fascinating and touchingly human
insight into a great figure who has consumed him for decades.
By exercising a genuine authority in identifying how Beethoven,
the man, manifests himself in our appreciation of the music,
Suchet brings an incisive freshness to an extraordinary life. The
results in his "Beethovenia" are always rigorously researched
and accompanied by a passion to communicate the composer's
true essence.'

—Professor Jonathan Freeman-Attwood
Principal, Royal Academy of Music, London

BEETHOVEN
THE MAN REVEALED

CLASSIC *f*M

BEETHOVEN

THE MAN REVEALED

JOHN SUCHET

Elliott&Thompson

First published 2012 by
Elliott and Thompson Limited
2 John Street, London WC1N 2ES
www.eandtbooks.com

This revised paperback edition published in 2020

ISBN: 978-1-78396-496-3

Text copyright © John Suchet 2012
This edition © John Suchet 2017, 2020

Picture credits:
Jacket: Franz Klein bust from Beethoven-Haus Bonn, Piano Sonata in A Major, Op. 101, Allegro, from the Moldenhauer Archives at the Library of Congress, Music Division, Washington DC; Page 1: (top) iStockPhoto.com / Xiaoping Liang, (bottom) John Suchet; Page 2: (top) courtesy of Chateau Duchcov-Dux / National Heritage Institiut, Czech Republic. Photograph by Marta Pavlikova, 2012, (bottom) Getty Images; Page 3: akg-images; Page 4: (top) Getty Images, (bottom) akg-images / Erich Lessing; Page 5: iStockPhoto.com; Page 6: (top) akg-images, (bottom) Beethoven-Haus Bonn, Sammlung H. C. Bodmer; Page 7: Getty Images; Page 8: (top) John Suchet, (bottom) iStockPhoto.com / Michael Luhrenberg.

9 8 7 6 5 4 3 2 1

A catalogue record for this book is available from the British Library.

Every effort has been made to trace copyright holders of material used within this book. Where this has not been possible, the publisher will be happy to credit them in future editions.

Printed by by CPI Group (UK) Ltd, Croydon, CR0 4YY

global

For my children, grandchildren and their children, safe in the knowledge that all will know Beethoven's music

Beethoven Family Tree

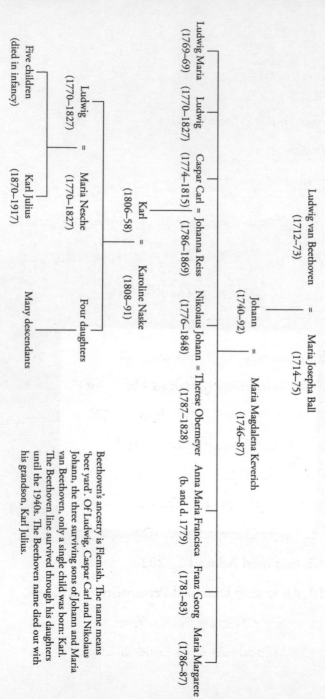

Ludwig van Beethoven
(1712–73)

=

Maria Josepha Ball
(1714–75)

Johann
(1740–92)

=

Maria Magdalena Keverich
(1746–87)

Ludwig Maria
(1769–69)

Ludwig
(1770–1827)

Caspar Carl = Johanna Reiss
(1774–1815)   (1786–1869)

Nikolaus Johann = Therese Obermeyer
(1776–1848)   (1787–1828)

Anna Maria Francisca
(b. and d. 1779)

Franz Georg
(1781–83)

Maria Margarete
(1786–87)

Ludwig
(1770–1827)

=

Maria Nesche
(1770–1827)

Karl
(1806–58)

=

Karoline Naske
(1808–91)

Four daughters

Five children
(died in infancy)

Karl Julius
(1870–1917)

Many descendants

Beethoven's ancestry is Flemish. The name means 'beet yard'. Of Ludwig, Caspar Carl and Nikolaus Johann, the three surviving sons of Johann and Maria van Beethoven, only a single child was born: Karl. The Beethoven line survived through his daughters until the 1940s. The Beethoven name died out with his grandson, Karl Julius.

Contents

Note on this Edition

Strange though it may seem to us today, given the universal popularity of his music and how well known so much of it is, Beethoven's compositions number relatively few – in comparison to his two great contemporaries, Mozart and Haydn.

Beethoven wrote nine symphonies; Mozart forty-one; Haydn an extraordinary 104. He wrote sixteen string quartets; Mozart twenty-three; Haydn sixty-eight. There are five piano concertos by Beethoven; twenty-seven by Mozart; and eleven by Haydn (including harpsichord and organ). Beethoven wrote a single violin concerto, compared to Mozart's five and Haydn's four. Beethoven wrote only one opera (albeit three versions of it), while Mozart composed more than twenty and Haydn fourteen. When it comes to sacred works, Beethoven's total of three is easily outnumbered by Mozart with eighteen masses and Haydn with eight. And those are just the most important works.

There is another distinguishing feature. Both Mozart and Haydn found the compositional process quite straightforward. Composing his first symphony at the age of eight, Mozart wrote music the way you and I might write letters or emails. He wrote music when asked to, when he wanted to, or simply to amuse himself or pass the time. Haydn was committed to a heavy workload in the employ of Prince Esterházy yet nevertheless managed to compose nearly 500 works in his lifetime, as well as organising and directing concerts. Of all his duties, composing came most easily to him.

How different it was for Beethoven! Even a cursory look at the manuscripts and sketchbooks reveals a composer who seemed to struggle at every turn. There are crossings out, angry slashings of the pen, scratching so violent the paper is torn. That struggle, of course, is manifest in the music. It is as though Beethoven tore the music out of himself and paid the price, both physically and emotionally.

What, then, is that essential quality that inhabits Beethoven's music, that permeates every bar of music he wrote? Is it enough to call it a struggle? A simple explanation would be that his music represents a journey from darkness into light. That is certainly true of his Fifth Symphony. But perhaps that is too simple. Take the famous opening bars of that work – as I have often said, surely the most famous bars in all classical music. Three short notes and a long one. That is not a theme or a melody; it is a motif. Just four notes, and yet what Beethoven goes on to do with so few notes is nothing short of miraculous. He takes us on a journey – from darkness into light – unique in music.

Most composers create a theme or a melody and then expand it. Beethoven so often does the reverse. He contracts and fragments it. The final movement of Symphony No. 3, the 'Eroica', is a perfect example. Not a conventional theme and variations, but the reverse: fragmented variations first, which finally lead to the theme. It's upside down and the wrong way round.

Beethoven was a rule-breaker. This was evident from his earliest years. Exercise books with one of his teachers are replete with red crosses where the teacher rejected what he had written. It was not that what he had written was actually wrong; it was that he was refusing to obey the rules – of harmony, counterpoint, fugue, contrabass and so on – and therefore it was inadmissible.

That refusal to obey the rules would be the hallmark of Beethoven the composer. Changes of key, stresses on the off-beat, bar lines ignored, dynamics unpredictable, soft where it should be loud, loud where it should be soft. However well you know Beethoven's music, he still takes you by surprise at every turn. To me that is the key to the enduring freshness and vitality of his music.

All that, however, misses the essential ingredient that makes Beethoven's music immortal, that has made him the greatest composer who ever lived. It is, in my opinion, a quality that no other composer possesses. And that ingredient is . . . If we could answer that question then the music would instantly be diminished. I cannot say; you cannot say; no one can say exactly what it is.

We can say that Beethoven's music lifts the spirit, that to listen to his music makes you feel you can overcome any problem life may throw at you. After all, if he can conquer the greatest affliction to befall a musician – deafness – then by listening to his music we can surely be inspired to overcome ours. That still does not give us an answer.

We know what Beethoven's music can do for us, even if we do not fully understand why. The best answer to the question, the most accurate and informative way to sum up his music, is to describe the effect it can have, in the words of those who have experienced it.

Soon after my first book on Beethoven was published back in 1996, I received a letter from a reader in his forties who told me that when he was just sixteen years of age his brother, a soldier, was killed in Northern Ireland. Six months later his mother died. He entered a spiral of misery and depression. 'Only Beethoven's music got me through,' he wrote. No further explanation, no details on which pieces of music; just a statement of fact.

Again back in the late 1990s, I was signing copies of my book after an early talk I gave on Beethoven. An elderly gentleman came up to me and said: 'I just want you to know, Beethoven saved my life. Twice.' And he walked away without another word. I can think of no other composer of whom those words could be said.

This year, 2020, we celebrate the 250th anniversary of Beethoven's birth. We can say with certainty that his birth will be celebrated for countless centuries, and by countless generations, to come.

Preface

This is an account of Beethoven's life, in accordance with current scholarship and research. Given that new facts and information emerge constantly, there are some aspects of this book that will inevitably become outdated or even prove incorrect. This is true of all biographies of great figures. I have not let it deter me from setting down the life as we perceive it today.

I make no great claim to having unearthed previously undiscovered facts about Beethoven's life. Everything in this book has been published in source material or previous biographies. But I do believe that a substantial amount of the information I have included, particularly about his childhood, has not been published for many decades, in some cases for a century or more, and I am certain never in English.

Beethoven's childhood and teenage years, I believe, were the making of him as a man and musician. For that reason I have examined them closely, and some of his experiences I have recounted in forensic detail. His trip with the court orchestra up the Rhine, for instance, rarely merits a mention in biographies, or is accorded at most a line or two, yet it provided the youthful Beethoven with a bank of memories – and a physical artefact – that he treasured for life.

Of Beethoven it is perhaps more true than of any other composer that if you know what is going on in his life you listen to his music through different ears. Beethoven's life – its dramas, conflicts, loves and losses, his deafness coupled with continuous health problems, his epic struggle with his sister-in-law for custody of her son, his nephew – is there in his music. Without such knowledge his music is still extraordinary, and I believe many people who today love it do so without any deep understanding of his life. But to know what is happening to him at the time of a particular composition puts that work on a different level for the listener. Beethoven's music is his autobiography.

My approach to the life of this great artist, as in my previous publications on him, is that of enthusiast and lover of his music, rather than musicologist. Consequently this book is aimed primarily at like-minded people, though I hope the academics will give it their approval. It is, for instance, of more interest to me that Beethoven initially dedicated the 'Eroica' Symphony to Napoleon Bonaparte than that he chose to write it in E flat. At all times I have striven to set the music into the context of his life, to explain where he was living at the time of a particular composition, why he chose to write it, the reasons behind the dedication, the state of his health, his non-musical activities, rather than present an analysis of the movement structure, key signature, thematic links.

In a nutshell I have tried to portray a difficult and complex character, struggling to continue his profession as musician despite increasing deafness, alienating friends with unprovoked outbursts of anger one moment, overwhelming them with excessive kindness and generosity the next, living in a city in almost constant turmoil because of war with France, rather than the god-like immortal portrayed in statues and paintings in heroic pose garlanded with laurel leaves.

He might have been one of the greatest artists who ever lived, but he was a still a man who had to live among fellow mortals, eat and drink, buy clothes, pay his rent. That is the Beethoven of this book.

Prologue

In the early afternoon of 29 March 1827 thousands of people flocked towards the Altes Schwarzspanierhaus, as word spread across Vienna that Beethoven had died. Their numbers grew, and soon they thronged the courtyard of the building to such an extent that the gates had to be closed. They crowded along the Alsergasse and spilled onto the green Glacis that sloped up to the Bastei, the city wall. Soon there was barely space between Beethoven's residence and the Votivkirche, where the Funeral Mass was to be held.

On the second floor of the Schwarzspanierhaus, inside Beethoven's apartment, a small group of men made final adjustments to the polished oak coffin and the corpse it contained. Beethoven's head, adorned with a wreath of white roses, lay on a white silk pillow. It was a grotesque sight, belying the identity of Europe's most revered composer. The temporal bones, along with the auditory nerves, had been removed at post-mortem for further investigation, leaving the joint of the lower jaw with no support. The famously leonine face, with strongly defined jaw-bone, was distorted almost beyond recognition.

Into the folded hands a wax cross and a large lily were placed. Two more large lilies lay on either side of the body. Eight candles burned alongside the coffin. On the table at the foot of the coffin stood a crucifix, holy water for sprinkling, and ears of corn. At 3 p.m. the coffin was closed, and the group prepared to move it down the staircase and out into the courtyard.

By this time the crowd had grown restless. Soldiers from the nearby barracks were drafted in to keep order. There was a fear that the horses could be frightened or, worse, that the coffin could be disturbed. The soldiers cleared the courtyard and the gates were again closed. As the coffin was brought out of the building, the crowd surged forward, but the gates, soldiers on the inner side, held firm. As nine priests offered blessings and the Italian court singers intoned a funeral song, a heavy pall was spread over the coffin and a large wreath laid on the embroidered cross.

When everything was ready, the gates were opened, but the crowd surged forward again, overwhelming the soldiers. They pushed against the bier, dislodging the pallbearers and chief mourners. It took several minutes to restore order. Eight *Kapellmeister*, four on each side, took hold of the pall with one hand, a candle wrapped in crepe in the other. On both sides of them stood around forty torchbearers. Behind the coffin were the chief mourners, close friends and family; in front of it musicians, civic dignitaries, and the clergy.

The order was given, the four horses took the strain, and amid a clatter of chains and a cacophony of hooves, the procession moved off. Vienna, for so many centuries capital of the

Holy Roman Empire, seat of the Holy Roman Emperor, had never seen scenes like it, nor had so many thousands of people ever thronged its streets.*

It was an appropriate tribute to a man whose music had touched people in a way that no composer's had before, who had changed the course of music, and whose compositions would speak to people down the generations and for all time. But it was also somewhat unfitting, given that Beethoven's music was not unanimously applauded in his lifetime, that his circle of friends and supporters was really quite small, that no great effort had been made in his difficult and painful final years to make his living conditions more palatable, and that on the whole there was no great stir in Vienna when it became clear their most famous resident was terminally ill.

In fact, the extraordinary homage he was accorded in death was simply the final inexplicable act in a lifetime of paradox and contradiction.

---

* The newssheet *Der Sammler* estimated the number at 10,000; Gerhard von Breuning in *Aus dem Schwarzspanierhaus* at 20,000.

Chapter 1

The Spaniard

In which a momentous life begins

It was an inauspicious start. We cannot be certain of the day on which Beethoven was born, since his birth certificate has not survived, and in the baptismal register his mother is given the wrong first name, Helena rather than Magdalena (possibly because both names share the diminutive Lenchen). The date given in the register for the baptism of the Beethoven infant Ludovicus is 17 December 1770, and the place St Remigius's Church in Bonn. It was customary for baptism to be carried out within twenty-four hours of birth; therefore it is likely that Beethoven was born on 16 December, with the lesser possibilities of the 15th in the late evening or 17th in the early hours. Given that there is a strong likelihood that the birth certificate was wilfully destroyed (as I will recount later), it is probable that we shall never know for sure the date of his birth.

More auspiciously, there is a legend that Beethoven was born with a caul, that is with part of the amniotic sac covering the face. Traditionally this carries beneficial supernatural qualities, such as protecting the individual from drowning, giving healing powers or endowing clairvoyance. He himself lent weight to the legend (or possibly created it) by writing to a publisher that he was born 'with an obbligato accompaniment'. The passage in the letter, which refers to his Septet, Op. 20, is clearly written in jest: 'I cannot compose anything that is not obbligato, seeing that, as a matter of fact, I came into the world with an obbligato accompaniment.' I have not found any other reference to it in any source.

Beethoven was the eldest, but not the firstborn, and to say that his arrival brought unbridled joy to his parents, or even to say that he was born into a normal and loving family, would be a considerable overstatement. For a start, both sides opposed the marriage of his parents, Johann van Beethoven and Maria Magdalena Leym née Keverich. It seems the reason was the same for both families: that both were thought to be marrying beneath themselves.

To take the Beethoven family first. Ludwig van Beethoven the elder, the future composer's grandfather, had established himself as the most senior, and therefore the most respected, musician in Bonn. He had left his home town of Malines in Flanders (today Mechelen in Belgium) at the age of twenty-one and settled in Bonn, where he was given a position as bass soloist and singer in the court choir. At the age of forty-nine he was appointed *Kapellmeister*, which put him in charge of music at court – in the chapel, concert hall, theatre, and court ballroom. This earned him a substantial salary and enormous prestige. In addition he ran a wholesale wine business on the side. It was probably not on any grand scale, but his income from the court, together with proceeds from the sale of wine, allowed him to rent two apartments, as well as cellars for storage. He was also wealthy enough to lend money to a number of people.

Ludwig's son Johann gained a position as tenor in the court choir. This brought him in a modest salary, which he supplemented by giving clavier and singing lessons to sons and daughters of well-off English and French families attached to the embassies, as well as to members of the nobility.

Father and son lived together in a large and well-furnished apartment at Rheingasse 934 (where, later, Ludwig van Beethoven was to spend many childhood years). In a later memoir, the child of the owner of the house, who remembered the Beethoven family living there, described the *Kapellmeister*'s apartment as being

> *beautiful and proper and well arranged, with valuables, all six rooms provided with beautiful furniture, many paintings and cupboards, a cupboard of silver service, a cupboard with fine gilded porcelain and glass, an assortment of the most beautiful linen which could be drawn through a ring, and everything from the smallest article sparkled like silver.*

But there was a cloud hanging over the Beethoven family. The *Kapellmeister*'s wife, Maria Josepha Poll, became an alcoholic and had to be moved out of the family apartment to be cared for in a special home. It is not known when this action was taken, but it was almost certainly before Johann's marriage, because at the wedding Ludwig senior was reported to have tears streaming from his eyes, and when asked about it he replied that he was thinking about his own wedding and marriage. It is known that Maria Josepha stayed in seclusion until her death in 1775.

There is no evidence that any member of the Beethoven family ever visited Maria Josepha in the home, and although Ludwig van Beethoven was nearly five when his grandmother died, he is not reported to have spoken about her a single time in his life, nor did he ever refer to her in correspondence. This is all the more remarkable since the elder Ludwig predeceased his wife by nearly two years and yet Beethoven spoke about his beloved grandfather and wrote about him time after time, and treasured his portrait (which stayed with him almost all his adult life and was in his apartment when he died).

Of course he took pride in his grandfather's accomplishments as a musician, and presumably felt shame at his grandmother's descent into alcoholism, but it seems as if he erased his grandmother's existence from his mind. This is more than likely due to the fact that he watched his own father descend into alcoholism, thus making the whole question of alcohol something that was not for discussion. But that did not stop Beethoven himself in later years consuming enormous quantities, as will become clear as the story progresses, to the extent that it brought about the cirrhosis of the liver that was the probable cause of his death.

Clearly the Beethoven family had a liking for alcohol – Beethoven's grandmother and father were both alcoholics, and he himself was probably a victim of it. It is tempting to suggest that ready quantities of wine in the household from the elder Ludwig's business sideline meant it was easily accessible for the family, and certainly early biographers attribute the family tendency to this. It is indeed likely that there was a generous supply of wine on the table, although the *Kapellmeister* kept his wine in storage in rented cellars, and there are no reports that he himself ever over-imbibed.

But alcohol and its effects aside, the Beethoven family was highly respected, thanks to the accomplishments of Ludwig senior, and lived in a certain amount of comfort. So when Johann announced to his father, as a fait accompli, that he intended marrying Maria Magdalena Leym, of Ehrenbreitstein, the *Kapellmeister* was appalled. He made enquiries and established not only that she was a widow, but had been a housemaid. The Fischers at Rheingasse 934 heard him explode to his son, 'I never believed or expected that you would so degrade yourself!'

In fact his misgivings were largely misplaced. Maria Magdalena's family included a number of wealthy merchants, as well as court councillors and senators. Her late father, Heinrich Keverich, had been chief overseer of the kitchen at the palace of the Elector of Trier at Ehrenbreitstein. True, he was 'in service', but it was a senior position, and he was in the employ of the most powerful and prestigious local dignitary, the Prince-Elector.* Furthermore, there is no evidence that Maria Magdalena was ever a housemaid.

Where Ludwig senior was correct was that Maria Magdalena was already widowed. More than that, she had experienced more sadness than a teenage woman should have had to bear. At sixteen she married a certain Johann Leym, and bore him a son. The child died in infancy, and her husband died not long after. She was thus a widow who had lost a child before she was nineteen.

Ludwig senior might have been influenced by the fact that Maria Magdalena's father had died many years before, leaving her mother as the family breadwinner, working as a cook at the court. Her mother was clearly already in fragile mental health, because she suffered a psychological breakdown soon after the marriage. She had one other surviving child, a son (four other children having died in infancy), and there was patently no prospect of a substantial dowry coming with the intended bride.

It seems an accumulation of unfortunate circumstances, combined with his own prejudices, turned Ludwig senior against the

---

* Prince-Electors were senior members of the Holy Roman Empire who had a direct role in electing the Holy Roman Emperor, head of the Habsburg Empire, whose seat was in Vienna.

marriage, to such an extent that he refused to attend the ceremony 'unless the thing were quickly over with'.

The Keverich family was apparently no more enthusiastic about the union; this, if nothing else, cemented the absence of any dowry. The evidence for this is that the wedding took place in Bonn, rather than the bride's home town, which would have been normal, and there is no evidence that any member of Maria Magdalena's family attended. One can imagine that any pride they might have had that she was marrying into the family of the *Kapellmeister* was undone by Johann's documented lack of charm (admittedly more evident in later years), and his clear obsession with money.

This latter attribute is evidenced by the fact that four months after the marriage a petition was sent to the Elector of Trier on Johann's mother-in-law's behalf, reporting that 'through an ill-turned marriage of her only daughter up to 300 Thalers disappeared'. This is a barely concealed accusation that Johann relieved his mother-in-law of the bulk of her savings, although it is likely the petition was deliberately written in an exaggerated way to increase Frau Keverich's plight. It is quite possible that this transfer of money, however it took place, occurred before the marriage, or at least that the process started then, which would be another reason for the Keverich family to be against the union.*

Exactly what took Johann van Beethoven up the Rhine to the fortress town of Ehrenbreitstein in the first place is not known, but one can imagine his father's frustration at the frequent absences as

---

* In a bizarre turn of events almost a decade later, Johann and Maria Magdalena van Beethoven took out a suit against the Ehrenbreitstein court bailiff, who was related by marriage to Maria Magdalena and who was the guardian of her mother's estate, accusing him of stealing the old lady's savings. The suit was thrown out.

he pursued a young woman with an unenviable history before she was out of her teens from another town a good thirty-five miles away. With both families set against the marriage, we can assume that the wedding of the couple who were to be the parents of Ludwig van Beethoven was a small and one-sided affair, attended reluctantly by Ludwig senior, whose tears at his own memories might have hardened his heart still further.

The marriage took place in Bonn on 12 November 1767, and it would not be long before more heartache ensued, first for Maria Magdalena and then for both her and her husband. After the marriage Johann moved out of the large well-appointed apartment he had shared with his father, and rented a small apartment at the back of a building in the Bonngasse for himself and his wife. At the same time his mother-in-law's already precarious mental health went into sharp decline. The same petition that cited the loss of her savings stated that she had begun to live a life of such penitence that she stopped eating and could not be expected to live long. Sometimes, it reported, she lay outside the church all night in the bitterest cold, wind, and rain. She died less than a year after her daughter's marriage, and it must be the case that Maria Magdalena felt considerable guilt that her choice of husband, not to mention her departure from her home town, had caused her mother so much distress.

In the weeks before her mother's death, Maria Magdalena would have realised that she was pregnant. One can only imagine what the knowledge that her mother would never see her grandchild would have done to Maria Magdalena's already damaged emotions.

Johann and Maria Magdalena van Beethoven's first child was baptised Ludwig Maria on 2 April 1769. One can envision *Kapellmeister* Beethoven's joy at the arrival of his first grandchild, augmented by the couple's decision to choose him as godfather, meaning that the child carried his name. For the couple, too, the arrival of a son after almost a year and a half of marriage must have been a cause of enormous family celebration, and one can imagine the stern grandfather melting towards the daughter-in-law he had not wanted to see become a member of the Beethoven family.

The infant Ludwig Maria van Beethoven died within a week of baptism. Even in an era when infant death was common, the loss of a child who carried so much hope for reconciliation must have been a catastrophe for the family. For Maria Magdalena it meant that she had been widowed and had lost two infants before she was twenty-three years of age.

Approximately a year later she fell pregnant again. As the months passed she must have been overwhelmed with trepidation about the child's survival. As on the previous two occasions she safely gave birth, and on 17 December 1770 the infant was baptised Ludwig after his grandfather, who was once again godfather. Like his grandfather, he was given the sole Christian name of Ludwig.

There were now two Ludwig van Beethovens in the family, and as each day passed the child grew stronger. Correspondingly there occurred a remarkable change in the demeanour of the elder Ludwig. He began to be drawn towards his daughter-in-law and soon the two had established a close and loving relationship. Unfortunately this was due at least partly to a shared disappointment in Johann.

As a boy Johann van Beethoven had shown considerable musical talent, to the extent that his father removed him from school and undertook his musical training himself (a pattern that was to be repeated when Johann, in turn, removed his son Ludwig from school to concentrate on music). He sang in the court chapel both as boy treble and after his voice had broken, and at the age of twenty-four, being proficient in singing as well as on the clavier and violin, he obtained salaried employment.

Three years later Johann was married, and things started to go downhill almost immediately. It is evident that he developed a taste for alcohol. He had no shortage of drinking companions. The fish dealer Klein lived across the street, and the two men would lounge in the window making faces at each other, prior to a night's drinking. The Fischers reported that Johann van Beethoven would spend many an evening in the tavern, often not arriving home until the middle of the night.

It cannot have helped that soon after Johann moved into his first marital home his father followed, taking an apartment just a few doors away in the same street. Ludwig van Beethoven senior was clearly a dominant, even domineering, figure, and was intolerant of his son's behaviour. He mocked him continuously. 'Johann der Läufer,' he called him. 'Johann the sprinter. Keep running, keep running. You will some day run to your final destination.'

It can't have been easy living up to his father's expectations, but whether his own inadequacies preceded his father's intolerance, or the other way around, it's impossible to say. Similarly, whether his penchant for alcohol was a cause of his father's disappointment in him, or a form of escapism from it, must also remain a matter for conjecture.

What is beyond doubt is that an event that shook the Beethoven family to its foundations offered Johann the opportunity to turn his life round. On Christmas Eve 1773 *Kapellmeister* Beethoven, who had suffered a stroke earlier in the year, died at the age of sixty-one. Johann saw himself as the natural successor and the next holder of the highest musical position in Bonn.

Unfortunately for him, he was unsuited for it in every respect. His dissolute habits were well known and unfitting to such a high office at court. There had also been a noticeable deterioration in his vocal skills, no doubt caused by alcohol, tobacco, and late nights. His skills on clavier and violin were not exceptional, and he had no compositions to his name, unlike other candidates for the office.

It is dangerous to apply modern-day sensibilities to events of more than two centuries ago, but certainly a reading of Johann's petition for the job as *Kapellmeister* suggests a confused, even negative, attitude:

> *Will your Electoral Grace be pleased to hear that my father has passed away from this world, to whom it was granted to serve His Electoral Grace(s) for 42 years, as* Kapellmeister *with great honour,* whose position I have been found capable of filling, *but nevertheless I would not venture to offer my capacity to Your Electoral Grace, but since the death of my father has left me in needy circumstances, my salary not sufficing, I am compelled to draw on the savings of my father* … Your Electoral Grace is therefore humbly implored to make an allowance from the 400 rth now saved for an increase of my salary … *[my emphasis]*

It hardly reads like an appropriate job application, seeming on the one hand to take it for granted that the job is his, and on the other pleading for a salary increase. In any event he did not get the job. There was only one *Kapellmeister* Beethoven.

Of crucial importance to the future development of his son is that these traumatic events were witnessed by the infant Ludwig van Beethoven. How much comprehension a child of three can have is impossible to determine, particularly at such a distance in time.

But, with the proviso that this is largely conjecture, we might assume the infant would at least pick up signs of distress in his mother, and probably too be aware that it is his father's behaviour that is causing it.

Ludwig was one week past his third birthday when his grandfather died, and of this at least we can be sure beyond any doubt: the loss rocked him profoundly, and it is something he never truly came to terms with. He idolised – and idealised – his grandfather and spoke highly of him for the rest of his life. Certainly when his own musical talents began to emerge, he would quickly have become aware of his grandfather's considerable achievements, at the same time no doubt witnessing the decline in his father's.

Exactly how early Ludwig's musical talents began to emerge is not known, but by the age of four he was being taught clavier and violin by his father, and so some special talent in the child must by then have been evident. There is considerable anecdotal evidence that Johann drove Ludwig hard, and more than one witness reports seeing the small boy standing on a footstool in front of the clavier in tears. Others reported seeing the father using physical violence, even shutting the child up in the cellar. These accounts were given many years after the event, by which time Beethoven had become famous throughout Europe, so it is possible some exaggeration had crept in. We can, though, be relatively sure that at the very least Johann van Beethoven drove his son hard in the quest to develop his musical talent.

By 1776 Johann van Beethoven had moved his family back into the Fischer house on the Rheingasse, where he had lived with his father before marriage, this time into a spacious apartment on the second floor. There were to be later moves, but this was the house in which Ludwig van Beethoven spent the greater part of his youth, and where he felt most at home.

On 26 March 1778 there occurred a remarkable event in the early life of Ludwig van Beethoven, one that has given rise to much myth and speculation surrounding the actions of his father.

Johann staged a public concert featuring one of his singing pupils, and his son Ludwig. Here is the advertisement he put in the newspaper:

> *Today, 26 March 1778, in the musical concert room in the Sternengasse, the Electoral Court Tenorist, Beethoven, will have the honour to produce ... his little son of six years, [who will perform] various clavier concertos and trios ... Tickets may be had at the Akademiesaal ...*

Do you spot the mistake, and, more importantly, is it deliberate? In March 1778 Ludwig van Beethoven was seven years and three months old. So why might Johann van Beethoven, on an important occasion such as this, have stated his son's age incorrectly?

There are two possible explanations, which I shall call the 'conspiracy theory' and the 'kind theory'. The conspiracy theory runs like this. Johann van Beethoven deliberately falsified his son's age because he wanted to make him appear younger than he was. This would make his musical skills all the more impressive, leading – Johann hoped – to favourable comparisons with the boy Mozart. It was well known that Mozart's father had taken him on tour as a child, to wide acclaim and the amassing of substantial payments. The fact that Ludwig's birth certificate had disappeared was no doubt because Johann had deliberately destroyed the evidence.

The kind theory absolves Johann from deliberate falsification. It points out that there was a general laxity in keeping family records at that time, that on no other known occasion did Johann make an error in his son's age, and that his own birth certificate had vanished, as well as his son's, pointing to his general careless-ness with paperwork. On this occasion he simply made a mistake.

Knowing what we know of Johann van Beethoven, it is hard to be charitable, particularly in the light of the deliberate dishon-esty that was to come a few years later. It is clear that he recognised his son's remarkable talent very early, and the fact that he put him in front of a paying audience at such a tender age is evidence of his intention to earn money through him. We know that the Beethoven family was short of funds from Johann's impassioned plea to the Elector for an increase in salary. Even if he exaggerated the poverty, which is likely, it is still beyond doubt that they were not flush, and that this situation was compounded by Johann's profligate lifestyle.

I subscribe to the conspiracy theory. Is it really likely that a father would not know how old his oldest son was? If he was in doubt, wouldn't he have checked with his wife? Or if he didn't want to do that, he could have left the age out of the adver-tisement altogether. I think it is beyond reasonable doubt that Johann van Beethoven deliberately falsified Ludwig's age to im-press the audience all the more with his talent.

Future events lend weight to this. Beethoven appeared con-fused about his age for much of his life. His second published work (of which more later) contains the words on the title page, 'composed by Ludwig van Beethoven, aged eleven years'. It was 1783, and he was in fact twelve. Well into adulthood the confu-sion remained. In his twenties there is evidence that he believed he was two years *older* than he actually was. In his mid-thirties he clearly believed he was two years *younger* than he was. Living in Vienna, he asked friends back in Bonn to send him copies of his baptismal certificate, since he was considering marriage. When the first copy arrived, he refused to accept the date, claiming his friend had mistaken him for his elder brother Ludwig, who had died at a week old. The second copy also failed to convince him – he wrote '1772' on the back of it. This in spite of the fact that he must surely have surmised that if he really had been born in 1772, just one year before his beloved grandfather died, he would have had no memories of him at all.

Was he confused, delusional, or just not interested in the facts? Or did his father's falsification so affect him that he could never quite be confident of his age? We do not know the answer.

Rather more importantly for musical history, we have no idea of how that performance in the Sternengasse concert room went. We do not know what music the young Ludwig played, nor do we have any idea of whether it was successful or not, because no one wrote it up.

There is no evidence that Johann put on any more public performances, which suggests maybe that the receipts did not justify the effort. Soon after that recital, Johann did the best thing he could possibly do for his son: he put him into school. But it was not long before he then did the worst thing possible: he took him out of school to concentrate solely on music. This was in 1780 or 1781, when Ludwig was around ten years of age. For the rest of his life he suffered from an inadequate education. His handwriting was close to illegible, his punctuation and spelling poor, and he was useless with figures – there is evidence later on that he could not add up his household bills. In later life his signatures were often so erratic that future musicologists had trouble deciding whether some were authentic.

Until Johann took his young son out of school, Ludwig led what amounted to a normal childhood. There was a sandpit on the bank of the Rhine, and he and his two younger brothers often played in it. His childhood friend Gottfried Fischer reported that Ludwig and his brothers would steal eggs from the henhouse behind the Fischer house. Once, Frau Fischer caught Ludwig crawling through the fence into the henhouse.

'Hah,' she said, 'and what are you doing there, Ludwig?'

'My brother Caspar threw my handkerchief in here and I came to get it.'

'Yes, that may well account for the fact that I am getting so few eggs.'

'But Frau Fischer, the hens often hide their eggs, and there are foxes, they steal eggs too.'

'Yes, and I think you are one of those sly foxes, Ludwig.'

'Yes, I am a musical-note fox.'

'And an egg fox too!'

Fischer adds that the two brothers ran off laughing like rogues, Frau Fischer laughing with them, unable to find it in her heart to chastise them for their monkey tricks.

On another occasion, recounts Fischer, the Beethoven brothers spotted a cockerel that had flown out of the yard and onto the top of a barn in the Fischers' backyard. They dared each other to catch him. Together they coaxed him with bread, caught him, squeezed his throat so he could not crow. Then they ran back upstairs to the attic and laughed at their prank.

Fischer also recounts how Ludwig and his brother Caspar Carl would put a target on the garden wall of the house and shoot arrows at it. A bull's-eye would earn the marksman the promise of a small coin.

These events, with the dialogue, were recorded around sixty years after the event,[*] by which time Gottfried Fischer was aware

---

[*] Gottfried Fischer, *Aufzeichnungen über Beethovens Jugend (Notes on Beethoven's Youth)*.

of the fame attained by the child who had lived in his house, so there might be inaccuracies in them and the dialogue polished. But I believe that, whatever may have passed between Ludwig and Frau Fischer, or between the brothers and the cockerel, it is very unlikely that Fischer would have invented the entire scenarios.

I find it beguiling to think that the famous composer of the 'Choral' Symphony and *Fidelio* stole hens' eggs as a child.

This is all in stark contrast to Ludwig's brief spell as a schoolboy. The school's head described him as 'a shy and taciturn boy, the inevitable consequence of the life apart which he led, observing more and pondering more than he spoke'. When, later, musicologists and biographers sought out his schoolfellows, not one related anecdotes of playing games with him, or even described him as a friend. There was no talk of trips on the Rhine or rambles across the hills. As early as his schooldays, his prodigious talent for music set him apart.

This sense of apartness was compounded by Ludwig's physical appearance. His skin was dark and swarthy, unusual in northern Germany, and Fischer recounts that from childhood on he was nicknamed 'Der Spagnol' ('The Spaniard'). It is inevitable, given how children are, that Ludwig will have been teased at school about his appearance. It might be conjecture, but it is not difficult to imagine playground taunts.

This is made more likely by one highly distressing anecdote. One of his schoolfellows, who later rose to high office in local government and the law, relates that as a schoolboy 'Luis v. B. was distinguished by uncleanliness, negligence, etc.' and he attributes this to the fact that Ludwig's mother was already dead.

Maria Magdalena van Beethoven was far from dead. She in fact gave birth to a daughter in 1779, who died in the same year, and a son in 1781, who died two years later. The implication of this, and its effect on a ten-year-old boy, are dire. At its most basic it must mean that Frau van Beethoven was never seen either to drop her son off at school, or to pick him up later. If that is excusable on the basis that Ludwig was able to look after himself, it further suggests that nothing was known among the school community about his family. That implies no casual conversations, no playground chat, which in turn points to a lonely existence for Ludwig.

Compounding that is the starkness with which his schoolmate described Ludwig's appearance. To be in such a state of neglect suggests Ludwig was paid scant attention at home by his mother, if she allowed him to attend school unwashed and dishevelled.

Finally, with regard to this brief, but portentous, anecdote, one can hardly begin to imagine the effect on a ten-year-old boy of his schoolfellows believing his mother was dead, when he knew perfectly well she was not. Given his state of disarray, and the penchant of schoolchildren to pick on a less fortunate schoolmate, it is more than likely he was the butt of playground jokes and jibes. He might even have been taunted over the (mistaken) belief that his mother was dead. It certainly seems as if Ludwig did nothing to correct matters, which in itself is puzzling.

This is conjecture, and again the anecdote was related many years later. But, as with Fischer, it is unlikely to have been wholly invented, particularly since its author rose to become Electoral Councillor and President of the Landgericht, the state court.

All in all, detrimental though it might have been to Ludwig to end his school career so soon, he might himself have welcomed it, since he could at least escape from schoolfellows with whom he had nothing in common, and devote himself to music.

A year, or possibly more, before being taken out of school, Ludwig began music lessons.* If this was a good decision on the part of his father, it was rendered unhelpful by the fact that Johann chose unsuitable music teachers for him. The first was the venerable court organist Gilles van den Eeden, who had been good friends with *Kapellmeister* Beethoven, no doubt because of their shared Flemish heritage, and was witness at his friend's marriage. Van den Eeden was over seventy years of age and had been in court service for more than fifty years when he began to teach the young boy.

To suggest a clash of generations would be an understatement, and one can easily imagine Ludwig, even at such a tender age, impatient to move faster than the aged musician from another era was prepared to go.

Details of the instructions van den Eeden gave his young pupil are unclear, as are the exact dates between which he taught him. What is certain, though, is that the arrangement, for whatever reason, did not last long, and Ludwig soon had a new teacher.

Tobias Pfeiffer was, by all accounts, an accomplished artist. He was also, as several contemporaries avow, something of an eccentric. Pianist, oboist, and flautist, he was also an actor and singer with the Grossmann and Helmuth theatre company, which accounts for his arrival in Bonn at the end of 1779. He took lodgings with the Beethoven family, and soon found himself employed to give music lessons to the young Ludwig.

He was highly accomplished on the flute, but apparently had little liking for it. Gottfried Fischer's sister Cäcilie recounts how

---

* It is impossible to be precise. The chronology of Beethoven's early years, as with the date of his birth, is uncertain.

when she asked him to play the flute, he replied, 'Oh, the flute. That instrument doesn't interest me. You waste your breath for other people, and I don't like that.' However, when he did play, with Ludwig accompanying him on the piano, the result was so beautiful that people stopped in the street outside to listen. Gottfried said he heard several people say they could listen to the music 'all day and all night'.

This anecdote is of some importance. It is the first evidence – albeit, like all the Fischer reminiscences, recalled decades after the event – of Ludwig van Beethoven performing on equal terms with an adult professional, and already establishing a reputation.

Unfortunately for the boy, though, Pfeiffer was an erratic teacher. After an evening's drinking with Johann, the two of them would arouse Ludwig late at night, drag him to the piano crying, and force him to play. Pfeiffer would then instruct him often until daylight. It does not take a lot to imagine the horror of being aroused from sleep, forced to play no doubt surrounded by alcohol fumes, and being generally bullied by two men, one your father, the other a musician whose eccentric behaviour was earning him enemies.

That eccentricity could be dangerous as well as harmless. When asked by Fischer senior, who lived on the floor below, to stop stamping up and down his room in heavy boots because it was keeping him awake at night, Pfeiffer agreed to remove one boot but not the other. On another occasion, when the barber came to tend to the men of the house, he said something to offend Pfeiffer, who picked him up bodily and threw him down the stairs, injuring him badly.

It was perhaps as much of a blessing for the people of Bonn, as for the young Ludwig, that Pfeiffer left Bonn with his theatre company after just three months.

We know from the records that Ludwig did not enter secondary school (*Gymnasium*) in the autumn of 1781. In mitigation of his father's behaviour, it should perhaps be pointed out that it was common practice for parents in Bonn to remove their children from the education system after primary, lower-grade, school, with a view to apprenticing them so they could begin to earn a living. It had happened to Johann himself, who left before secondary school to take up an appointment as court musician.

If Johann was thinking that this was an appropriate moment to test his young son's earning power, the perfect opportunity presented itself. Through a family connection in Holland, an invitation was made for the Beethovens to visit Rotterdam. Johann's court duties prevented him from going, but he sent his wife and son, with clear instructions that Ludwig should perform, and be remunerated for it.

This episode is rarely mentioned in biographies, for the obvious reason that very little is known about it, and what we do know – as with the Fischer anecdotes – was related by a neighbour many years after the event. But again, as with Fischer, it is the small telling detail that rings absolutely true. That detail in this case, I believe, throws a fascinating and intriguing light on the relationship between Ludwig and his mother.

The winter of 1781 began early with bitterly cold weather. Frau van Beethoven sat with her ten-year-old son on the deck of a sailing boat as it travelled down the Rhine towards Holland. Huddled against the wind, Ludwig became very cold. His mother coaxed him to lie on the bench, took his feet onto her lap, and rubbed them to try to keep them warm.

Could this be the same woman who allowed her son to turn up at school in such a dishevelled state that fellow schoolboys thought she was dead? If we believe the anecdotes, then there were clearly emotional complexities at work in the Beethoven family that we can only guess at.

Two years before the trip to Holland, Maria Magdalena had given birth to a baby girl who died before the end of the year. In the same year as the trip, she gave birth to a son. Would a mother leave her infant of less than a year to make the trip? What arrangements did she make for the child to be looked after? Could she have suffered from post-natal depression after the death of the baby girl? And what feelings of guilt awaited her when the baby boy she left behind died at the age of two?

Question after question, and we cannot answer any of them. But, as with the hens' eggs and the cockerel, I cannot help but be bewitched by the thought that, as titanic an artist as he was, Beethoven still got cold feet.

As for the trip, the hoped-for financial rewards were not forthcoming. The boy certainly played in the highest salons and was apparently showered with compliments, but little else. A performance before Prince Willem of Orange Nassau yielded a mere 63 florins. When his friend Gottfried Fischer asked him how it had gone, Ludwig replied, 'The Dutch are skinflints. I'll never go to Holland again.' And he didn't.

Johann also was making efforts to earn money through his son. When the Elector was absent from Bonn, and court musicians were free, Johann would take trips with his son into the countryside around Bonn and alongside both banks of the Rhine, visiting wealthy noblemen and persuading them to listen to Ludwig perform.

This afforded an opportunity not just for financial gain, but for father and son to develop a closer relationship. Although there is some evidence of the former, there is none of the latter. Neither these excursions nor the trip to Rotterdam appears to have brought the boy any closer to his parents. It is also fair to speculate that these trips, coupled with the Rotterdam experience, put him off performing 'to order' for life.

From Johann's point of view, if his son really was to be a source of income for the family, as young Wolfgang Amadeus had been for the Mozarts, then he needed to acquire more skills, and that meant finding another teacher.

Whether it was Johann, or the Elector himself, who took the next step is not clear. Whoever it was, a decision was made on Ludwig's behalf that changed his life. It was decided to employ a certain Christian Gottlob Neefe to teach Ludwig. A better man could not have been chosen. From the day he began lessons with Neefe, probably in 1781 at the age of ten, Ludwig van Beethoven began his life as a musician.

Chapter 2

The Right Teacher

This boy could become 'a second Mozart'

The small town of Bonn, on the west bank of the Rhine, then as in more recent times, punched above its weight. Surprisingly chosen as the capital of the Federal Republic of Germany in 1949, it was, in Beethoven's lifetime, the unlikely seat of the Elector, who was also Archbishop of Cologne and Münster. It was a medieval Archbishop who selected Bonn for his residence, rather than the more obvious choice of Cologne, possibly for the reason that the mighty Rhine narrowed at this point and could be blocked, thus bestowing on Bonn a crucial strategic importance. In later centuries it endowed Bonn with a certain grandeur, more than a veneer of aristocracy, a degree of wealth and prosperity, which its rival towns on the Rhine – Cologne, Mainz, Coblenz – could only look at with envy. And for the people of Bonn – fewer than 10,000 according to a survey in 1789 – it meant pleasant, well-tended surroundings and, more importantly, security and income. For a town with no manufacture or commerce, it was commonly stated that 'all Bonn was fed from the Elector's kitchen'.

Clemens August, who made his solemn entry into Bonn as Elector in 1724, endowed the town with a fine palace (now the University of Bonn) and an ornate Town Hall (today used for ceremonial functions – President Kennedy made a speech there in 1963). But, of more importance to our story, in 1733 he employed a Flemish immigrant by the name of Ludwig van Beethoven as court musician, and twenty-three years later his son Johann.

This Elector left his mark on Bonn in another way too. He danced himself to death, literally. Leaving Bonn to visit his family in Munich in early 1761, he was struck down with illness, and broke his journey to call on the hospitality of his fellow Elector in Ehrenbreitstein.* At dinner he was too ill to eat, but not it seems too poorly to take to the dance floor afterwards with the alluring Baroness von Waldendorf, sister of the Elector. She must have been exceedingly alluring, because he danced with her not once, or twice, but for 'eight or nine turns'. Other ladies, complaining of neglect, received their turn too. If his spirit was willing, his flesh could not withstand the exertion. He passed out on the dance floor, was carried to his room, and died the next day.

I recount this story, not just to raise a sympathetic smile, but because of the impact it, and subsequent events, had on the Beethoven family. Clemens August's successor as Elector, Maximilian Friedrich, had barely got his feet under the desk, as it were, when he received a petition from court bass singer Ludwig van Beethoven seeking elevation to the supreme musical position of *Kapellmeister*, the post being vacant following the death of the previous incumbent. The petition pleads with the Elector 'to grant me the justice of which I was deprived on the death of Your Highness's *antecessori*

---

* The Elector whose valet Maria Magdalena would marry some two years later.

of blessed memory', which suggests the elder Beethoven had made moves – if not in a formal petition – to be appointed *Kapellmeister* before the previous Elector's untimely demise.

We can assume the death of Clemens August, and the manner of his passing, was the predominant topic of conversation at all levels among the populace of Bonn, with varying degrees of ribald observation. Certainly, at court level, it led to immediate jockeying for promotion, in particular among the court musicians, since the top job itself was vacant.

Beethoven senior's bold approach paid dividends. By an order of the Elector dated 16 July 1761, he was appointed *Kapellmeister*, with an increase in salary, though less than he might have expected due to the fact that he was not a composer. A little over two years later he managed to secure a permanent position at court for his son Johann, as tenor and violinist. Between them, father and son (not yet married) were earning a comfortable sum.

This was particularly fortunate, for under Maximilian Friedrich things changed for the burghers of Bonn. The Elector himself was an affable and kindly man, sharing with his predecessor a predilection for the fairer sex, and court entertainment carried on much as before. But his popularity with his people was in stark contrast to that of his First Minister. Count Kaspar Anton von Belderbusch had been instrumental in securing Maximilian Friedrich's election. In return he demanded – and was granted – unrivalled political power. On examining the exchequer and discovering the previous Elector's extravagance, he came down hard on all expenditure.

Practically overnight the good life in Bonn ended. People suddenly found themselves out of work, some even losing what had previously been considered a 'job for life' at the court. At all levels there was a financial crackdown. A visitor from England was somewhat horrified to find that at dinner with the Elector, 'no dessert wines were handed about, nor any foreign wines at all', which, while it might say as much about the travel writer Henry Swinburne as it does about the Elector, at least suggests a comfortable life was expected at court, if nowhere else.

The easy-going and even-tempered Elector was not one to stand up to his First Minister, which might have something to do with the fact that Belderbusch knew rather a lot about the Elector's private life. The two men shared a mistress, a certain Countess Caroline von Satzenhofen – who happened to be Abbess of a Benedictine nunnery close to Bonn!

Once again, this is likely to have been common knowledge, at least among court employees. It is inconceivable that there were not hushed whispers when the two men were seen together, and the fact that the Elector was as much liked as his First Minister was disliked might have had something to do with resentment at the fact that Belderbusch not only behaved as if he was Elector, but even enjoyed the services of the Elector's mistress.

This, then, was the Bonn that Ludwig van Beethoven was born into, a town that had seen more comfortable days, that was nominally ruled by an ineffective Elector and governed by a strict disciplinarian First Minister, but that still boasted an enviable artistic life, with a busy calendar of performances by court orchestra and theatre, and was a desirable location for touring theatrical companies. It was this reputation for the arts, particularly music, that brought the thirty-one-year-old composer, organist and conductor, Christian Gottlob Neefe, to Bonn.

A combination of circumstances made Neefe the ideal teacher for the budding young musician, Ludwig van Beethoven. As a young man in Chemnitz in Saxony he had had serious disagreements with his father, who wanted him to follow his example and take up law. Under protest he enrolled at the University of Leipzig to study jurisprudence, but was so unhappy he apparently contemplated suicide. Against his father's wishes he gave up the law and turned to music. At the same time he immersed himself in the philosophy and ideals of the German Enlightenment, reading Gellert, Klopstock, and particularly the young Goethe.

Imagine the effect of this background on a ten-year-old boy. Ludwig's beloved grandfather was long dead, and he was watching his father descend into alcoholism and his parents' marriage come under increasing strain. Here was an adult who might well have poured out his troubles with his own father to young Ludwig, at the same time encouraging him to develop as a musician in the way he wanted, without reference to his father. He will also without doubt have filled the boy's head with radical, even revolutionary, ideas. This was the decade in which the Enlightenment was sweeping Europe, questioning the divine order of things, the God-given right of rulers to rule – ideals and philosophies that were to come to such a terrifying climax in France in just a few years' time.

Judging by an autobiographical tract he wrote in Bonn in 1782, at about the time (or shortly after) Ludwig became his pupil, Neefe believed strongly that sensual desire should be sublimated into art and the quest for ethical perfection. A more apt description of the adult Beethoven's ethics would be hard to find.

Of crucial importance, I believe, is the rarely stated fact that Neefe was a Protestant, and he had come to live in a Catholic town. True, Bonn was hardly a hive of subversive activity, but the fact that Neefe was a Protestant would certainly have been noted. He joined the local Order of Illuminati, nominally a non-sectarian organisation with branches throughout Europe, which attracted artists and literary figures such as Goethe. Members took a vow of secrecy and obedience to their superiors, and Neefe soon became one of its leaders. The movement began in Bavaria, and when it was suppressed there, the Bonn branch dissolved itself in favour of a less suspect body, called the Reading Society (*Lesegesellschaft*).

Neefe became a leading light in the Reading Society, and since his pupil was in his early teens at the time, it is not inconceivable he took him along to meetings. At any rate, it is hard to imagine a more intimate, even secretive, situation than a teacher and pupil alone in a room at the piano, and the young Ludwig would easily have come to admire the forward-thinking, radically minded, intensely musical Neefe. If evidence were needed, less than a decade later Ludwig wrote to Neefe from Vienna, rather formally, 'I thank you for the advice you have very often given me about making progress in my divine art. Should I ever become a great man, you too will have a share in my success.' I believe that the seeds of Beethoven's radicalism, both in music and in his personal and political beliefs, were sown in these early, impressionable years as Neefe's pupil.

On the death of old van den Eeden, court organist and Ludwig's first teacher, Neefe was appointed to succeed him. This was remarkable for someone who had not long since arrived in Bonn, and whose duties would require him to play at church services. It says something for the degree of religious tolerance in Bonn that Neefe's Protestant faith did not stand in his way.

The appointment gave Neefe status. Although one might suspect that his new court duties would leave him little time for instruction, Neefe was perceptive enough to recognise that his young pupil had extraordinary talents that needed nurturing. When he expressed this view, he was listened to, given his elevated position as court organist. This led to a significant development in the life of young Ludwig.

Shortly after getting the job of court organist, Neefe was committed to a lengthy absence from Bonn with the Grossmann and Helmuth company. He proposed that his young pupil should stand in for him, and play the organ at church services. Ludwig was just eleven years of age. The proposal was accepted, even if with raised eyebrows, and one can be sure that any doubts or misgivings were laid to rest when Ludwig's skill on the organ was heard.

Thanks to Neefe, Ludwig's talents were now beginning to be widely appreciated. Neefe did not stop there. It was fortunate for Ludwig that Neefe was a composer. It meant that when he expressed a desire to compose, very soon after beginning lessons, Neefe did not discourage him. A lesser teacher might well have advised him to learn to walk before he could run but, perhaps recognising something of his own early enthusiasm in the boy, he encouraged Ludwig.

It is probable Ludwig had begun making musical sketches even before beginning instruction with Neefe. Whether or not this was the case, or whether Neefe gave him direct advice on what to try his hand at, in 1782 Ludwig produced a composition for piano. It was a set of variations on a march by the recently deceased German composer Ernst Christoph Dressler. Ludwig probably wrote it during Neefe's absence. Again, a lesser teacher might have torn it to shreds, or at least criticised it heavily, even if constructively. What Neefe did, instead, was arrange to have it published.

Within a year or two of taking Ludwig on as a pupil, then, Neefe had given him the opportunity to play the organ at civic services and had arranged for the publication of his first work. Ludwig was not yet twelve years of age. Had Neefe then vanished from the scene, these services alone would have been enough to earn him his place in musical history. But there was more, much more to come.

The marriage of Johann and Maria Magdalena was drifting perilously close to the rocks. Johann, loving his drink more and more, thought nothing of walking through Bonn gulping wine from a flask, unmindful of being seen. Gottfried Fischer gives graphic accounts of the strains in the marriage of the couple living in the apartment above him, and – again with the caveats that he was a child when witnessing what he describes and that he wrote down his memoirs around sixty years later – they have more than a ring of truth to them.

Maria Magdalena, berating her husband for drinking outside in the street, draws this response: 'It is such hot weather that I have to have a drink.'

She replies, 'That's true, but you have to have a drink even without the summer heat.'

He responds, 'You are right. I agree with you. Thank you. Tell me when it's time to eat and I'll come straight in.'

Gottfried recounts how Johann van Beethoven tried to plant a kiss on his sister Cäcilie, calling her 'our patroness of music'. She replied, 'I am not the sort of girl to go round kissing people, anyway you already have a wife, go and kiss her, not me.'

'You are a clever little witch,' said Johann. 'You know exactly what to say.'

According to Gottfried, Johann chanced his luck with Cäcilie again, some years later. He made a drunken lunge at her, she deflected him with a hearty push, he knocked over the oven, pulling the stove and stovepipe from the wall. According to Gottfried's memoirs, everyone (rather surprisingly) took it in good fun, including Johann, who said, 'That taught me a good lesson', and Maria Magdalena, who appears to have been in the room at the time, told Cäcilie, 'That was the right thing to do. That's how to handle him.'

The dialogue may be stilted, the reminiscences coloured with the passage of time. But at the very least what we have here is a musician employed at court descending into alcoholism, prone to making a fool of himself in private and public, uncaring of what this might be doing to his career and reputation.

From further anecdotal evidence it is clear that Maria Magdalena had long since given up on her husband. When he received his monthly salary, or payment from pupils, he would toss the bag of money into his wife's lap and say, 'There woman, manage with that.' This is stark evidence that Maria Magdalena was in charge of the family's finances, and her husband was acquiescent. According to Gottfried, after Maria Magdalena had the money safely in her hands, she would tease her husband about his drinking, saying, 'A man cannot be allowed to return home with *empty* hands.'

'Yes, *empty* hands!' One can imagine Johann staring dolefully at his empty hands.

'Yes, *so empty*,' says Maria, 'but I know how much you would like to fill them up with a full glass.'

'Yes, yes,' as a smug grin spreads across his face, 'the woman is right, she is always right.'

Once again, if the dialogue is contrived and exaggerated, it suggests that in the early stages of their marriage at least, before Johann's drinking had a fatal effect on his career, Maria Magdalena would be content to indulge her husband's habit as long as the money kept coming in.

But this was not to last. There is anecdotal evidence from several sources as to just how unhappy Maria Magdalena was. Gottfried quotes her saying to Cäcilie, 'If you want my advice, stay single, that's the secret to having a quiet, happy life. For what is marriage? A little joy, but then a chain of sorrows.' Cäcilie in her turn is quoted as saying that she had never seen Maria Magdalena laugh, that she was always serious. Another neighbour describes her as a 'quiet, suffering woman'. She was apparently not above losing her temper, and on occasion was able to give as good as she got.

An unhappy marriage, then, although certainly in the early years not one beyond repair. But as Johann's drinking took hold, it was to lead to a disastrous sequence of events that was to throw a heavy shadow over the Beethoven household.

This is the atmosphere in which young Ludwig van Beethoven grew up. According to Gottfried Fischer, Ludwig witnessed the conversation in which his mother described marriage as 'a chain of sorrows'. He will certainly have witnessed disagreements, even rows, between his parents, and will have become aware painfully early of his father's excessive drinking.

By the time he began lessons with Neefe, he was the eldest of three sons, there was an infant in the house who died at two years of age, and a daughter born five years later who died at the age of one.* This can only have contributed to the tensions in the marriage, and the difficult atmosphere in the apartment on the second floor of the house in the Rheingasse, which Gottfried Fischer so vividly describes.

---

* Together with the daughter who was born and died in 1779, and the eldest son Ludwig Maria who died at a week, this means that in her first ten years of marriage to Johann, Maria Magdalena gave birth seven times – eight times in all, including the infant she bore her first husband.

But Ludwig had something that neither his brothers, nor anyone he knew, had. A means of escape. It must have been not just with a feeling of relief, but an overwhelming sense of excitement, that he set off each time for instruction with Neefe. An opportunity to enter the world of music, his world, where the conversation would be on a different plane from the mundanities of his home life and where, if they were discussed, they were no doubt dismissed with a wave of the hand as being too trivial to impinge on the higher calling of true art. Total escape, though, was not possible. At its most basic, Ludwig had to return to the apartment, to his mother's sadness and despair, his father's drunken antics, two younger brothers no doubt running riot, and a baby restless with ill-health.

Ludwig would not have been able to evade the knowledge that if his father's career were to implode, the full weight of caring for the family would fall on his shoulders, as the eldest son. This was customary in that era. Normally the eldest son would be apprenticed to the father's trade – as Gottfried Fischer was to his baker father – but this was not possible in Ludwig's case. He was training to be a musician, and he had not yet entered his teenage years. How on earth would he be able to earn a living as a musician at such a young age?

Once again, history – as well as a small, apprehensive boy – owes a debt of gratitude to Christian Gottlob Neefe.

In a remarkable leap of faith, Neefe wrote a piece for the *Magazin der Musik*, a musical publication owned by the German book dealer and writer on music, Carl Friedrich Cramer, in which he described the musical scene at the Elector's court in Bonn. It was published in the issue dated 2 March 1783, and is so prescient about his young pupil that the paragraph concerning him deserves to be quoted in full:

> *Louis van Betthoven* [sic], *son of the above-mentioned tenor, a boy of eleven* [sic] *years and of most promising talent. He plays the clavier very skilfully and with power, sight-reads very well, and – to put it in a nutshell – he plays chiefly The Well-Tempered Clavier of Sebastian Bach, which Herr Neefe put into his hands. Whoever knows this collection of preludes and fugues in all the keys – which might almost be called the non plus ultra of our art – will know what this means. So far as his other duties have permitted, Herr Neefe has also given him instruction in thorough-bass.* He is now training him in composition, and in order to encourage him has had 9 variations on a March by Ernst Christoph Dressler published in Mannheim. This young genius deserves support so that he can travel. He would surely become a second Wolfgang Amadeus Mozart, if he were to continue as he has begun.*

This is an extraordinary endorsement. Here is a professional musician going public in print with the belief that his young pupil is a musician of genius, not just of genius but potentially the equal of Mozart. In more practical terms it gives us a wonderful insight into exactly what Ludwig was capable of. At the age of twelve, he was proficient in arguably J. S. Bach's greatest set of compositions for the keyboard, exploring all twenty-four keys, recognised at the time as some of the most difficult keyboard music ever written. There is many a professional who fails to

---

* The harmonic embellishment of the bass line.

master 'The 48'* in a lifetime. Neefe also – and this is startling evidence of his far-sightedness – gives equal weight to the instruction he is giving Ludwig in composition.

The final two sentences stand alone as the first endorsement of Ludwig's skills to appear in print. Neefe's use of the word 'genius' and the name 'Mozart' could have made him a hostage to fortune, staking his reputation in print.† He clearly saw this as no risk, and history has most certainly vindicated him. Finally, I find it touchingly humble that Neefe is writing in the third person, almost as if to concentrate the reader's mind on Ludwig van Beethoven rather than himself.

Hardly had the piece been published before Neefe set about encouraging Ludwig in his next great enterprise – more composition. One begins to form the impression that Neefe believed there was nothing more he could teach the boy in terms of performance, that in fact Ludwig might already have been a better keyboard player than he himself was. What better course of action, then, than to encourage him in his desire to compose?

This might well have been linked to the two final sentences in that paragraph published in Cramer's magazine. In one sense they can be read as a generalised suggestion that Ludwig needed to broaden his horizons, so that he could become as good as Mozart. In another, more subtle reading, they are in effect a plea to the Elector, or failing him any moneyed aristocrat, to come up with the money that would enable Ludwig to travel to Vienna and study with Mozart.

---

* The twenty-four keys in major and minor.

† Neefe's assessment of Mozart is remarkable too, given that the composer was still only twenty-seven years of age, and had not yet composed many of his finest works.

This second reading is reinforced by the composition that Ludwig now produced. It was nothing less than a set of three full piano sonatas. If the *Dressler Variations* were impressive – the rapid runs in the final variation are intimidating even for a proficient player – the three piano sonatas are on a higher plane altogether. For a start it was extraordinarily bold and ambitious for a twelve-year-old to choose the sonata form, rather than something simpler such as a rondo, or minuet, or more variations. Secondly there are elements in all three compositions that point ahead to his more mature work. It has been convincingly argued that these three piano sonatas, although without opus numbers, should be included in Beethoven's total piano sonata output, so that we should talk of his thirty-five piano sonatas, rather than the more normal thirty-two. There might be several hundred recordings of the Beethoven piano sonatas by virtuosos over the last seventy or eighty years, but relatively few that include the first three.*

If Ludwig's choice of the sonata form was bold, the person to whom he chose to dedicate these first three sonatas showed a confidence bordering on arrogance: none other than the Elector himself, Maximilian Friedrich. And what a contrast to the dedication of the *Dressler Variations*. Those were dedicated to a noblewoman 'par un jeune amateur'. The sonatas were a gift for a scion of the House of Habsburg, the most senior aristocrat in Bonn, and the letter accompanying the manuscript shows not a shred of self-doubt:

Having become acquainted so early with the gracious Muse who tuned my soul to pure harmonies, I learned to love her,

---

* A critical edition of The 35 Piano Sonatas published in 2007 by Britain's leading Beethoven scholar, Professor Barry Cooper of Manchester University, was the first modern edition to include all thirty-five sonatas as a set.

and she, as it often seems to me, began to love me too …
Since then my Muse in hours of sacred inspiration has often
whispered to me: 'Make the attempt, just put down on paper
the harmonies of your soul!' … I was almost too shy. But my
Muse insisted – I obeyed and I composed.

And now may I dare, Most Excellent Lord!, *to lay the*
first fruits of my youthful work on the steps of your throne? …
Filled with this heartening confidence I venture to approach
you with these youthful essays. Accept them as a pure sacrifice
of childlike reverence and look upon them, Most Illustrious
Lord!, *and their young composer with favour.*

Even given the touching hint of shyness, these are hardly the words
you would expect from a twelve-year-old, and there can be no
doubt that Neefe played a significant role not just in the composition of the sonatas, but in the choice of dedicatee and wording of
the accompanying letter. And why should Neefe encourage young
Ludwig to make such a bold move? To convince the most powerful
man in Bonn that this youthful genius deserves the kind of help
that will enable him to travel, of course.

The ploy might well have succeeded, had Maximilian Friedrich
not died less than six months later. Evidence of this is the fact that
in February 1784, two months before the Elector's death, Ludwig
was appointed assistant organist to Neefe. His star was in the as-
cendant, but fate intervened.

First, in that month of February, the Rhine burst its banks.
The situation was serious, with the quarter adjoining the river
inundated. The Fischer house was on the Rheingasse, so named
because it ran at right-angles down to the river, and the house was
on the lower portion of the street. The waters quickly engulfed the
lower floors, and Gottfried Fischer wrote in his memoir that Frau

van Beethoven played a leading role in calming the panic and helping residents to safety, until she had to make her own escape over boards and down ladders. This is particularly heroic, given that she had three boys aged thirteen, ten and eight, to look after. Significantly there is no mention of their father in this episode.

It was as the waters receded and the town was struggling to get back on its feet that the Elector died, replacing one form of disarray with another. The succession was immediate, since it was the custom for all Electors to have a co-adjutor, an appointed successor. In this case, the new Elector of Bonn and Archbishop of Cologne and Münster, was one Maximilian Franz.

As Ludwig had been fortunate in his teacher Neefe, he was just as fortunate in the chosen successor as Elector. The same cannot be said for his father. In fact the months following Maximilian Franz's accession were the most difficult the Beethoven family had had to face to date.

Max Franz, as he was familiarly known, was to play a crucial role in the development of young Ludwig van Beethoven as a composer, though it did not seem that way to start with. Endowed with an acute mind and a love of the arts, he did nothing to endear himself to his people. In fact his deportment and looks made him the butt of sarcastic humour. He was described as kindly, lazy, fond of a joke, honest, amiable and affable. He had a debilitating limp, caused when he fell from his horse on campaign in Bavaria. That put paid to his short-lived military career, and so he followed the only other career path open to a member of the ruling Habsburgs: the church.

Installed in Bonn, sedentary and inactive, he quickly put on weight, and more and more weight, and was soon chronically obese, which did nothing to improve his reputation. But he had one attribute that stilled all seditious tongues. He was the youngest son of Empress Maria Theresa, and brother of the Holy Roman Emperor Joseph II. He was also brother of Marie Antoinette (Maria Antonia), wife of Louis XVI and Queen of France. In other words, he was a senior member of the most powerful ruling family in Continental Europe.

He used that power the moment he became Elector. He shut down the theatre company, depriving Neefe of a portion of his income, and ordered full and detailed reports into every aspect of government, including musical appointments and activities. The result of this investigation was to have profound implications for the Beethoven family.

Each and every court musician was investigated, and individual reports submitted. Of the three musicians directly relevant to our story, it was a disaster for Johann van Beethoven, a potential disaster for Neefe, and rather good news for young Ludwig. The reports have survived, and make compelling reading.

J. van Beethoven, age 44, born in Bonn, married, his wife is 32 years old, has three sons living in the electorate aged 13, 10 and 8 years, who are studying music. Has served 28 years, salary 315 fl.

Johann Beethoven has a very stale voice, has been long in the service, is very poor, of fair deportment and married.

Christ. Gottlob Neefe, aged 36, born at Chemnitz, married, his wife is 32, born at Gotha, has two daughters in the electorate aged 5 and 2, has served three years, was formerly Kapellmeister with Seiler, salary 400 fl.

Christian Neefe, organist, in my humble opinion might

well be dismissed, inasmuch as he is not particularly versed on the organ. Moreover he is a foreigner, having nothing in his favour, and is of the Calvinist religion.

Ludwig van Beethoven, aged 13, born at Bonn, has served two years, no salary.

Ludwig van Betthoven [sic], *a son of the Betthoven sub No. 8, has no salary, but during the absence of the* Kapellmeister *Luchesy [Lucchesi] he played the organ, is of good capability, still young, of good and quiet deportment, and is poor.*

Johann van Beethoven's 'very stale voice' was tantamount to a death sentence on his career, though it was to be a few years before the axe fell. Neefe's Protestant religion is now counting against him. Young Ludwig, it seems, has a bright future. And also a problem. If Neefe is sacked, he is the obvious successor as court organist. One can imagine the boy was torn between his natural ambition and loyalty to his teacher.

The situation was resolved by a decision to keep Neefe on, but he found his salary slashed, with a good proportion of it going to his assistant. It is the first time Ludwig van Beethoven was paid for his services as a musician. He was thirteen years of age, and it was to be the first, and almost last, salaried position of his entire life. Maybe that was the stimulus for his next grand compositional project, nothing modest: a piano concerto. But, probably realising he was not ready, he abandoned it.*

Young Ludwig, now a teenager, was acquiring a confidence that saw him start to behave in ways that drew admiration and

---

* The piano part, and some orchestral passages, have survived.

exasperation in equal measure. In Holy Week it was customary for a court singer to sing portions of the *Lamentations of Jeremiah* to Gregorian chant, accompanied on the piano. In 1785 the singer was the highly respected Ferdinand Heller, and the pianist Ludwig van Beethoven. A mischievous streak, hitherto largely hidden, emerged in Ludwig, who was piqued at Heller's self-confidence and tuneless singing.

On day two, he asked Heller for permission to try and throw him off the note by varying the piano accompaniment. Heller apparently readily agreed, stressing his experience against his accompanist's lack of it. In the service, Ludwig's fingers flew off in all directions, save for one finger which repeatedly struck the note that Heller should sing. Heller held his ground, but soon found the dazzling accompaniment too distracting. Towards the end of the passage, he lost the note completely.

Lacking a sense of humour, as well as the superior talent he believed he had, Heller entered a formal complaint against Ludwig with the Elector. Max Franz admonished Ludwig, but with a smile on his face, saying in future he had better stick to simple accompaniment. *Kapellmeister* Lucchesi, on the other hand, was a good enough musician to see that Ludwig's skill on the keyboard was a rather more important attribute than Heller's singing.

This anecdote was recorded by a young man who was to have the most profound influence on the life of Ludwig van Beethoven.

Chapter 3

Meeting Mozart

Watch out for that boy

Franz Wegeler was five years older than Ludwig, and it is not clear how and exactly when they became friends. It was certainly in the early years of 1780, when they were at opposite ends of their teenage years. How, though, is difficult to answer, because theirs was an unlikely friendship. They cannot have been school friends, given the age difference and that neither referred, in their writings or reported conversation, to their school years. Ludwig, we know, made few friends in his early years, having so little in common with other youngsters. If he looked up to the intelligent Wegeler as something of a role model, that does not explain what Wegeler saw in him. Musical talent, obviously, but again there is no evidence then or later that Wegeler had any particular interest in music – he himself admitted it – and it is unusual for teenagers to mix with youths several years younger than themselves.

There was no meeting of minds either, on intellectual matters. Ludwig was totally consumed with music, playing and composing. Wegeler, on the other hand, had scientific interests, and was to go on to qualify as a doctor. That they became close friends, though, is not in doubt, and it led Wegeler to publish, along with a future friend, his recollections of Ludwig in his Bonn years.[*] When, a little over a decade later, both were in Vienna, Wegeler wrote that 'hardly a day went by when we did not see one another'. That was clearly true in Bonn, too.

Wegeler instinctively knew how to handle the unpredictable youngster. He recalls in his memoirs how Ludwig developed an aversion to playing at social occasions, and he would often become angry when asked to do so. He would walk round to see Wegeler, gloomy and upset, complaining that he had been forced to play 'even if the blood burned under his fingernails'. Wegeler's tactic was to chat to him and amuse him to calm him down, until gradually a conversation would develop between them. When he judged the moment was right, Wegeler would walk to the writing table and tell his young friend that if he wished to continue the conversation, he had to sit on the chair in front of the piano facing outward. Soon the temptation to play became too strong; Ludwig would turn and play a few chords. Before long, he was turned fully round and then 'the most beautiful melodies would develop'.

Later, as Ludwig's skills improved, Wegeler took to leaving a blank piece of manuscript paper on a nearby stand, in the hope that Ludwig would cover it with notes. Instead he used to pick it up, fold it, and put it in his pocket. 'All I could do was laugh at myself,' writes Wegeler.

Ironically the most important service Franz Wegeler was to afford Ludwig did not come from Wegeler himself – instead it came

---

[*] Franz Wegeler and Ferdinand Ries, *Biographische Notizen über Ludwig van Beethoven*. As with Gottfried Fischer's memoirs, this account was written several decades after the event, but both Wegeler and his collaborator were educated to a much higher level than Fischer, and their accounts are regarded as largely reliable.

from a family he introduced him to. The von Breunings were a respected and highly cultured family, prominent in court and social life in Bonn. One day some time around 1784, Wegeler, who was acquainted with the Breunings, suggested he take Ludwig along to meet them. It is not an exaggeration to say that this marked a turning point in the life of the teenage musician.

The Breunings were not simply well liked, but were owed a great deal of respect due to the fact that the head of the family, Court Councillor Emanuel Joseph von Breuning, had lost his life in a fire at the Electoral Palace. In determined and frantic efforts to save as many art treasures and papers as he could, Breuning had gone back into the blazing building one time too many, and died as the structure collapsed on him.

His widow, Helene, was left to bring up four children, ranging in age from six years to an infant of four months. Finances were not a problem, and the family lived in an imposing two-storey house with dormer windows and a gated front garden in the elegant Münsterplatz in Bonn.* There, Helene von Breuning was determined to give her children as cultured and varied an upbringing as possible.

One can well imagine the trepidation Ludwig felt as he stood at the gate of the Breuning house for the first time, particularly if his appearance was as haphazard as in his schooldays. True, he had by now performed in the salons of the nobility, and was not lacking in self-confidence, but I suspect there would have been more than a twinge of nerves as he walked through the gate for the first

---

* Where today a huge bronze statue of Beethoven stands.

time, which liveried staff and the opulence within will have done nothing to dispel.

What might have persuaded Wegeler to introduce his undoubtedly rather gauche and socially inept friend to such a highborn and cultured family? The answer is obvious, even if it cannot be proved. Helene von Breuning had told young Wegeler she wanted her children to have piano lessons, and he replied that he knew just the fellow.

We can probably assume that she had seen Ludwig perform in a salon and been duly impressed, reasoning that his remarkable talent would compensate for any lack in social graces. She might also have calculated that her children would take more easily to a teenager than to an adult. Otherwise why should she not have chosen Christian Neefe, a much more highly qualified musician, for the role? Certainly he would have struggled to find the time, given his onerous court duties, but he certainly could have done with the extra income. We might even assume that he resented the fact that his young assistant was earning extra cash, though that can only be speculation.

Ludwig did more than teach piano to the Breuning children. He in effect grew up as part of the Breuning household, becoming almost a surrogate member of the family. Wegeler writes that not only did Ludwig spend the greater part of the day in the Breuning house, but many nights too. It was there, also, that he first became acquainted with German literature, especially poetry. It is beyond doubt that he will have been introduced to the works of the two emerging giants of German literature, Goethe and Schiller. Wegeler also tells us that he read Homer and Plutarch. He was trained too in social etiquette. He even went away on holiday with the family. Helene von Breuning clearly took him under her wing and made it her duty to fill in the gaps – academic and social – that early exit from school and singular devotion to music had caused.

At the same time, she was exceedingly tolerant of his some-times wilful behaviour. He was also employed as piano teacher in a count's house directly across the square – quite possibly Helene von Breuning secured it for him – and when it was time for him to go to the Count's house, she would be prepared for him to make excuses for not going, but insist he went. Then, when he left, she would remain in the doorway and watch him. Sometimes he would turn back immediately and say it was impossible to give a lesson that day, but tomorrow he would give two. Instead of scolding him, according to Wegeler, Helene would simply shrug her shoulders and say, 'He has his raptus again.' Wegeler does not elucidate on the word 'raptus', but it does not take much imagi-nation to discern its meaning.

There is no doubt Ludwig was aware of just how kind and indulgent Helene von Breuning was towards him. Later in life he referred to the Breunings as guardian angels, and said of Helene, somewhat obscurely and with maybe a touch of arrogance, 'She understood how to keep the insects off the flowers.'

In a touching passage in his memoirs, Wegeler, who mar-ried the only Breuning daughter, Eleonore, describes how many years later he, his wife and mother-in-law would get together and discuss the remarkable achievements of Europe's greatest living composer, and reminisce about how they remembered him as a gauche youth. Helene, then in her late seventies, was finding it difficult to recall the past, but still remembered young Ludwig with affection.

It is hardly surprising Ludwig escaped as often as he could to the cultured and affectionate surroundings of the Breuning household. Things at home were going from bad to worse. The unloved First Minister Count Belderbusch had died a few months after the death of his protector, Elector Maximilian Friedrich (a double blow for the Abbess). This led to a bizarre and ruinous course of action on the part of Johann van Beethoven.

He decided to put forward a claim on Belderbusch's estate, on the grounds that he had given several valuable gifts to the Count and his mistress, in return for which he had been promised promotion to *Kapellmeister*. To describe this course of action as 'bizarre' is an understatement. Johann was in effect saying Belderbusch had told him he could be bribed to give Johann the top musical job. Bribery might not have been entirely unknown in late eighteenth-century Europe, but to suggest the First Minister in a Habsburg principality who had made it his mission to end profligacy and introduce savings in the economy could be bribed to give an exalted position that was not actually in his gift to a mediocre musician who was known to like his alcohol is absurd.

It gets worse. At the bottom of the petition demanding that the Belderbusch heirs return the gifts, Johann forged the signature of a lawyer. The lawyer, one Nikolaus Phennings, swore in an affidavit, 'The above signature is not in my hand and I have not the slightest knowledge of this document, with all its vileness.'

The fraud quickly unravelled, and Johann was fortunate not to face legal action. What led Johann to embark on this doomed piece of folly is not known. Alcohol will have played its part, but this was more than a moment of madness. He must have thought about it over a period of days, even weeks. If anything, it is a sign of just how permanently addled his brain was.

His reputation, already low, now reached rock bottom. Not that it had far to travel to get there. Two years earlier, a court report on Ludwig's petition seeking appointment as assistant court organist stated, '… Your Grace has graciously provided for [Ludwig van Beethoven's] care and subsistence, his father no longer being able to do so …' Evidence that Johann remained of low standing, and was little more than a figure of ridicule, was to come on his death in 1792, when the Elector wrote to a court official, 'The revenues from the liquor excise have suffered a loss.'

Johann continued to earn a pittance, but Ludwig was in effect the family breadwinner. Given his father's alcoholism, he was also de facto head of the household. This was before he was midway through his teens. The pressure he was under must have been enormous. He held a salaried position at court, which demanded serious work. He was continuing instruction with Neefe. At home he was witnessing his father's increasing alcoholism and his mother's distress. This was made immeasurably worse by his mother's obviously declining health. She was showing all the signs of having contracted the deadly disease of consumption (tuberculosis).

And yet he found time to compose. He wrote a rondo, a song 'To an Infant' (possibly in the aftermath of his baby brother Franz Georg's death at the age of two), the aforementioned piano concerto, three piano quartets, and a trio for piano and wind.

In these early compositions the influence of one man above all others is evident: Wolfgang Amadeus Mozart. In musical circles in Bonn the extraordinary achievements of Mozart were well known. As soon as new works were published, they made their way to Bonn where they were eagerly seized on by the court musicians, and it is certain that in his lessons with Neefe, he and his teacher pored over the music, examining, deconstructing, and generally holding Mozart up as an example to be emulated.

Then there was a development that must have taken Ludwig's breath away. Four years after Neefe wrote in Cramer's *Magazin der Musik* that 'this young genius deserves support so that he can travel', it happened. How it happened, we do not know. Most likely Neefe approached the Elector directly. Maximilian Franz might have been becoming obese, his limp and the way he acquired it might have led to derisory comments, but he soon made his mark as an effective, and tolerant, ruler. He was an avid supporter of education and the arts, and over a period of time reopened the court theatre, maintained the court orchestra, and founded the University of Bonn. He would have heard young Ludwig play the organ at services, and he might well have heard him give recitals at the keyboard.

It might have been at Neefe's suggestion, or the Elector might well have made the decision himself. Either way, Ludwig's dream was about to come true. The Elector granted him leave of absence to travel to Vienna to meet Mozart, and agreed to cover the costs. It is beyond doubt that his father would have protested loudly. How could he possibly cope with the children, and a sick wife, if Ludwig was going to swan off to Vienna? But Ludwig had powerful support, and there was no stopping him.

In late March 1787, Ludwig van Beethoven, aged sixteen and a quarter, left Bonn and left his family to travel to the capital of the Holy Roman Empire, and the capital city of European music. Vienna.

When I first began researching Beethoven's life, and discovered that he and Mozart actually met, I expected to find page after page of information, documents, eye-witness accounts, letters, and so on. And what is there? Nothing but secondary accounts.

A single paragraph in a biography of Mozart written more than sixty years after Mozart's death (in fact, to coincide with the centenary of his birth), one inconclusive line in a Beethoven biography again written many years after his death, and a couple of anecdotes running to no more than a line or two each.

Why might this be, given that both composers were household names while still alive, and famous beyond words within a short time of their deaths? There really can be only one explanation, and that is that neither Mozart nor Beethoven spoke or wrote about their encounter, meaning we have no first-hand account of what happened. This alone raises more questions.

It is a similar case in the myriad of biographies of Beethoven. The encounter with Mozart barely rates more than a swift paragraph. I know of one biography, published in 2003, that does not mention the meeting at all. Their authors would no doubt justify this by pointing to the obvious: that, as with the trip to Rotterdam, we know virtually nothing. But I believe that a meeting between the two most revered, respected, admired, beloved composers in history deserves as close an examination as possible, with speculation allowed after that.

First, then, this is what we know.

On 1 April 1787 'Herr Peethofen [*sic*], Musikus von Bonn bei Kölln' arrived in Munich and checked into the tavern *Zum schwarzen Adler* ['At the Black Eagle'], according to the *Münchener Zeitung*. It appears either the newspaper knew about his musical prowess, or it did its homework while he was away, because when he checked into the same tavern on 25 April on his way home, it described him as 'Herr Peethoven [*sic*], Kurköllnischer Kammervirtuos von Bonn' ('Piano virtuoso at the Electoral Court of Cologne from Bonn'). This is the furthest that word of his musical talent had spread to date.

He reached Vienna on Easter Eve, 7 April. We do not know where he stayed or how soon after arriving he met Mozart. All we know, from the Mozart biography,* is that Ludwig was taken to Mozart, who asked him to sit at the piano and play something. Ludwig did this, but Mozart was cool in his praise, saying he had obviously prepared a showpiece specially. Ludwig then asked Mozart to give him a theme that he could improvise on. Mozart did so, and Ludwig began to improvise. His playing became more and more elaborate, because he was inspired in the presence of the master musician whom he so greatly admired. Mozart became more and more impressed, and finally, without saying anything to Ludwig, went into the adjoining room where some friends were sitting, and said, 'Watch out for that boy, one day he will give the world something to talk about.'

That is the sum total of the most comprehensive second-hand account we have. We do not even know who recounted it, only that it could not have been either of the two principals, who had both been long dead. As far as other evidence goes, Beethoven's friend and helper Ferdinand Ries (who collaborated with Wegeler on their book of reminiscences) says Beethoven told him he regretted never hearing Mozart play, but Beethoven's pupil Carl Czerny claimed Beethoven did hear him, and described his playing as 'choppy' and 'unsmooth'.

As for Beethoven himself, it appears the only recorded reference to Mozart in conversation came late in life when his deafness led him to carry a notebook, so-called 'conversation books', for people to write down their questions. His nephew Karl wrote in one of these, 'You knew Mozart, where did you see him?' And in another conversation book a few years later, 'Was

---

* Otto Jahn, *W. A. Mozart* (1856).

Mozart a good pianoforte player? It [the instrument] was then still in its infancy.'

Of course the utterly maddening, infuriating, frustrating fact is that Beethoven spoke rather than wrote his answer, so we have no idea of what he said.

Given how significant I believe this meeting, however brief, to be, I will now allow myself to put a few speculative clothes on the bare bones of what we know.

First, I believe Mozart was in no mood to see Ludwig. In fact it was the last thing he needed. His health was poor. Two and a half years earlier, at an opera in the Burgtheater (not one of his own) he was taken ill, 'sweated through all his clothes', caught a chill in the night air on the way home, began to vomit violently, and was diagnosed with rheumatic fever. His recovery was slow, and he was ill again in April 1787, the month young Beethoven came to visit.

His domestic life was in turmoil. With two small children, he had moved the family into a large apartment in the Grosse Schulerstrasse, where the rent was four times higher than in their previous apartment. He could not afford the rent, and at the time of Ludwig's visit, the family was in the throes of moving out to the suburbs.

On top of this he was worried about his father's health (Leopold Mozart was to die a little over a month later), and last but not least he was fully preoccupied with his new opera, *Don Giovanni*.

So when a sixteen-year-old boy was ushered into his apartment, presumably on the strength of a letter of introduction from Max Franz (who had met Mozart in Salzburg some years earlier),*

---

* He tried to persuade Mozart to come to Bonn as *Kapellmeister*. Mozart turned him down, saying he was too busy with his new opera, *Le nozze di Figaro*. How different the history of music might have been had he accepted!

he is unlikely to have welcomed him with open arms. One can imagine him looking the youth up and down, probably unimpressed with his attire, tousled hair with no wig or queue, the boy's Rhineland accent more guttural than he was used to in Vienna, and barking, 'Well, boy, they say you can play the piano. To me you look more like a street urchin than a musician. There's the piano, play something, and be quick about it.'

That is shameless fictionalising, I readily admit, but it gives a flavour of what I believe probably happened.

It is also more than likely that once Ludwig started improvising on the theme Mozart had given him, the older man became more and more impressed. The quote about 'watching out for that boy' is famous, and who knows how it might have become embellished in the years before it was written down? But we can safely say that Mozart was impressed with what he heard, almost certainly impressed enough to offer to take Ludwig on as a pupil.

We can make this assumption, I believe, because in the first place Mozart would have welcomed the chance to earn some extra cash, and Ludwig clearly had the Elector's financial backing, and also because he is likely to have recognised that the boy had pianistic skills well beyond his years, and this would have appealed to the virtuosic musician in Mozart. One other factor: Ludwig stayed in Vienna for almost two weeks. It was during this time, obviously, that he must have heard Mozart play. We can probably reconcile the evident contradiction between Ries and Czerny by assuming he heard Mozart play in private, but not in performance.

But the big question is: did Mozart give Ludwig lessons in the brief time he was in Vienna? That takes us back to the question I posed earlier. Given that Beethoven admired Mozart so much, performing his piano concertos on a number of occasions in Vienna, if he had received even a single lesson, would he not have trumpeted it for the rest of his life? And if Mozart was that impressed with Ludwig's playing, so much so that he immediately went into the adjoining room to tell friends, would he not have told more people, and wouldn't they also have told other people, particularly in the years following Mozart's death when Beethoven's fame was spreading across Europe?

Yet there is nothing. Even that is puzzling. If no lessons took place, you would expect even *that* fact to have been referred to by Beethoven later in life, in tones of regret.

So it remains something of a mystery. The only possible explanation I can think of – and I accept this is far fetched, even a little scurrilous – is that in both cases there were singular reputations to uphold. Mozart's family and friends did not want his legacy to be overshadowed by Beethoven, and Beethoven did not want to attribute any part of his genius to Mozart.

One last piece of speculation. What if the sixteen-year-old boy *had* taken lessons with Mozart. Might Mozart the perfectionist have smoothed off the rough edges, rounded the corners, tamed the wild spirit we know today? Impossible to answer. I suspect that could have been the case. Fiercely independent he might have been, but what sixteen-year-old boy would not have been susceptible to guidance from Europe's greatest living musician?

Enough conjecture. What we know for a fact is that within a short time of arriving in Vienna, Ludwig received word from his father that his mother was seriously ill, and that they feared for her life. He had no choice but to leave, which he did within the fortnight, arriving again at the *Zum schwarzen Adler* on 25 April.

On arriving home he was devastated to find his mother's consumption had advanced so far that she was in the terminal stages, and she died on 17 July.

If things were serious before he left for Vienna, they were critical now. He truly was head of the family, and the task of not only providing for the family, but trying to control the nominal head, Johann, fell squarely on his shoulders. There was no mother for him or his brothers to turn to when, later in the same year, their baby sister died.

The situation in the Beethoven household was indeed dire.

Not for the first time in his life, Ludwig benefited from an extraordinary stroke of good fortune. Just as Christian Neefe had been the perfect teacher to satisfy his musical ambitions, and Maximilian Franz the ideal Elector to further them, on or about 1 February 1788 there arrived in Bonn a certain Count Ferdinand Ernst Joseph Gabriel Waldstein und Wartenberg von Dux.

Count Waldstein, to give him his simple title, was a member of one of the most aristocratic families in the Habsburg Empire. His misfortune was to be the fourth son, and as such was allowed to play no role in the power politics at the Viennese court. After a couple of fruitless years in the military, he opted to join the Teutonic Order.* This led to him being summoned to Bonn by Maximilian Franz, who was Grand Master of the Order. There he was made a Knight on 17 June 1788.

Count Waldstein was in every sense Ludwig van Beethoven's most important patron in his teenage years. Max Franz might have subsidised Ludwig's abortive trip to Vienna and

---

* A prestigious – but by the nineteenth century largely ceremonial – body of German knights formed in the Middle Ages to protect and help German Christians making pilgrimages to the Holy Land.

rubber-stamped his appointment as court organist, but his interest in music beyond that was not great. Waldstein, by contrast, was himself a dilettante pianist and composer, and had a deep love for the arts, in particular music. Wegeler, in his memoir, describes Waldstein as 'Beethoven's first, and in every respect most important, Maecenas'.

It is more than likely that Waldstein first encountered Ludwig at the Breunings' house, and heard him play. He immediately recognised an extraordinary talent, and decided to make it his mission to nurture it. He did more than that. From Wegeler we learn that he visited the Beethoven family in their new apartment in a rather fine house in the Wenzelgasse, which was in a better part of town than the Rheingasse down by the river. There, after the death of Maria Magdalena, they employed a housekeeper.

Wegeler leaves us in no doubt that Waldstein gave money to Ludwig on a number of occasions, always disguised as an advance from the Elector. The move to the Wenzelgasse certainly came before Waldstein's arrival in Bonn. One wonders how long the family would have been able to remain there, and employ a housekeeper, without Waldstein's help.

There now occurred a dramatic change in the Beethoven family's circumstances. It was almost certainly brought about by an incident as humiliating for Ludwig and his family as it is possible to imagine, and it is inconceivable Ludwig would have taken the step he did without advice and guidance from Waldstein, who had the Elector's ear.

Johann van Beethoven became so drunk in public that he was arrested. Ludwig had to go to the police station, where he argued furiously with the police, before obtaining his father's release.

It was, for Ludwig, the final blow. His father's reputation was ruined once and for all. Something needed to be done, action taken. Some time in the autumn of 1789 Ludwig petioned the Elector to dismiss his father from court service, and pay half his salary over to him. The Elector went further. He not only agreed to Ludwig's demands but ordered Johann to leave Bonn and go and live in exile in a village in the country.

In the event this latter demand was not enforced. Johann remained in the Wenzelgasse house until his death. It is probable Ludwig, having taken the action he did, felt the humiliation was enough. Financially, half his father's annual salary of 200 thalers was now paid to him. As further lessening of the humiliation, Johann continued to receive the other half, but quietly made it over to his son.

Ludwig was now, at the age of eighteen, no longer just the *de facto* head of the family, but *de jure* head as well, recognised as such by the Elector. It was a turning point. The pain of his father's degradation must have been difficult to bear, but it had been going on for some time, was no secret in Bonn, and Ludwig was now at last able to acknowledge it, to have no need any longer to make excuses. The formalising of his father's disgrace was, for him, in some sense a liberation.

That immediately proved itself in his musical activity. It led to a burst of creativity. The pieces poured out of him. Among them is the most significant work that he was to compose in his first twenty-two years, and it was brought about by an unexpected, and thoroughly sad, event in the Habsburg capital, Vienna.

On 20 February 1790, Emperor Joseph II, eldest son of the great Empress Maria Theresa, died at the age of forty-nine. The Empire went into mourning. In Bonn, the remainder of the opera season was cancelled. The *Lesegesellschaft* met to discuss a way of marking the death, given that the Emperor was Max Franz's brother, and commissioned a young poet to write a text, which would subsequently be set to music. The text was duly delivered, and then the question arose of who should be asked to compose the memorial cantata.

The *Lesegesellschaft* had a number of names for consideration, all court musicians senior to Ludwig. But Waldstein was a member of the *Lesegesellschaft*, and he undoubtedly brought his influence to bear. The duty of commemorating the Emperor's death in music went to the nineteen-year-old Ludwig van Beethoven.

He certainly rose to the occasion. His *Cantata on the Death of Emperor Joseph II* is justifiably regarded as his first mature composition. For a start he is now working with full orchestral forces, solo singers and chorus. If the work has an added dimension, it is surely because he had empathy with the subject matter.

Emperor Joseph had been a reformer. He made education compulsory for all boys and girls, and brought about the freedom of serfs throughout the Empire. He completely reformed the legal system, abolished brutal punishments for minor crimes, and abolished the death penalty except for serious crimes. He ran into opposition when he tried to reform the Catholic Church – that was an ambition too far.

Of greater significance to the higher levels of society in Vienna, he was an enthusiastic patron of the arts. He was known as the 'Musical King', and championed German culture. It was he who commissioned a German language opera from Mozart,* and he ended censorship of the press and the theatre. At the same time he was intolerant of opponents to his rule, encouraging his Chancellor to establish a network of informants. He has rather

---

* *Die Entführung aus dem Serail (The Abduction from the Seraglio)*, which occasioned the famous story that when the Emperor heard it, he said to Mozart, 'That is too fine for my ears – there are too many notes', to which Mozart replied, 'There are just as many notes as there should be.'

unkindly been called the creator of the secret police. He was, to use the language of historians, an 'enlightened despot'.

In Bonn, he was a popular figure, and not just because he was the elder brother of the Elector. His reforming ideas, his 'enlightened despotism', appealed to this cultured town, which was, in some sense, an outpost of the Empire, away from the court intrigue and rigidity of life in Vienna. Without a doubt his ideas would have been debated by the Illuminati and then the *Lesegesellschaft*, and it is beyond question that the Protestant Neefe would have lauded the Emperor's praises to his young pupil.

Ludwig would have appreciated the poet Severin Anton Averdonck's text too. Although the language is highly subtle and allusory, it is an unmistakable paeon of praise to a reforming Emperor. Even if that is an exaggeration, it is undoubtedly how Ludwig would have seen it. Joseph's untimely and unexpected death would have come not just as a shock to the people of Bonn but, more than that, as very sad news indeed.

Ludwig captures this in the very first bar of his *Cantata*, a strikingly soft low note on strings, followed by a pause. The wind then echo this, followed again by a pause. Daring and original, he repeats the exchange more loudly, before leading into a fragmented mourning phrase on flute. After several more bars of fragmented, almost tortured phrases, the chorus enters with the single portentous word 'Todt' ('Dead'). The listener is hooked from the very start.

There are also elements that he was to use later in more mature works. Several passages presage the 'Eroica' Symphony, and there is a striking oboe phrase, soaring above the rest of the orchestra, that was to reappear to dramatic effect in the dungeon scene in *Fidelio*. Beethoven knew better than to waste a good idea.

And, in this case, wasted is exactly what these extraordinarily original ideas would have been. The court orchestra in Bonn –

particularly the wind – declared the piece unplayable, as it did with the sister piece that came a few months later, a *Cantata on the Elevation of Emperor Leopold II*. Neither piece was performed in Beethoven's lifetime. We do not know how the composer reacted to this rejection, but whatever he may have said, it was good practice for his later years. This might have been the first, but certainly was not the last, time in his life that musicians complained to him that his music was unplayable.

The following year another composition followed, and it could not have been more of a contrast to the two cantatas, for an extraordinary and at first sight incredible reason.

Chapter 4

Word Spreads

Young Beethoven as kitchen scullion

Ludwig van Beethoven the composer had come of age. More than that, he was an all-round musician, and was recognised as such. Assistant court organist to Neefe, he also played viola (!) in the court orchestra and he was the composer of several works. The complexities of the cantatas might have been regarded as unplayable, but for precisely that reason were judged to be highly impressive. The commission alone gave him an unrivalled reputation.

Given these factors, his decision regarding the next composition seems all the more surprising. The idea was Count Waldstein's. As a leading figure in Bonn, he was deputed to arrange a celebratory occasion to mark the end of the operatic season and the beginning of the annual Carnival in early March 1791. He decided to organise a 'ballet' in one of the grander rooms of the Town Hall, to be preceded by a procession of the town's nobility dressed in traditional German costume.

A ballet in the late eighteenth century meant in effect a series of tableaux, men (it was rare for women to take part) assuming dramatic poses on stage. For this, music was required. Waldstein asked Beethoven if he would compose it. We do not know if Beethoven received any money. It is more than likely that he did, and that it was passed to him clandestinely, for Waldstein made another request: that the music should be published under his name. And indeed it was: *Musik zu einem Ritterballet* (*Music for a Ballet of the Knights*) by Count Waldstein.

The event duly took place, and was a magnificent spectacle. Noblemen in medieval German costume, accompanied by their ladies – who, as one observer subtly put it, lost none of their charms by donning costumes of antiquity – processed across the square to the Town Hall, where in the Ridotto room more men in appropriate medieval costume took up poses from German folk legends.

We can get an idea of what this involved from the titles to the pieces composed by Beethoven: *March, German Song, Hunting Song, Love Song, War Dance, Drinking Song, German Song, Coda*. It must have been a picturesque spectacle, depicting the sort of Germanic legends a certain Richard Wagner would get hold of half a century or more later.

The music was acclaimed, later published, and attributed to Waldstein, and it stayed that way for the best part of a century, until musicologists established beyond doubt that it was composed by the nineteen-year-old Beethoven. In fact we should not be too shocked that the music was appropriated by Waldstein. Such behaviour was not all that uncommon in eighteenth-century Europe, the most notorious example being the composition, at about this very time, of the *Requiem* by Mozart, in the knowledge that it was to be presented as having been composed by Count Walsegg, the nobleman who commissioned it as a memorial to his wife.

The *Ritterballet*, to my knowledge, is never performed today, and is regarded as having no real significance, particularly when measured against the two cantatas that preceded it. But it does hold one distinction: it is the only composition for orchestra by Beethoven that was actually performed while he was living in Bonn.

There is a delightful anecdote about Beethoven that dates from around this time. It shows him in a very different light from that usually described by his contemporaries, and I cannot help believing (though there is no proof) that his unusual congeniality relates to a remarkable occurrence in December 1790, and what followed it.

The event itself happened many miles away, and did not concern Beethoven in any direct way. But indirectly it was to have the most profound musical influence on him imaginable. In September 1790 Prince Nikolaus Esterházy, great patron of the arts, died at his sumptuous palace at Esterháza. This led to freedom from a rigorous regime of musical servitude to which his composer-in-residence had been subjected for almost thirty years.

The composer was a certain Joseph Haydn, and he relished his sudden liberty. His name was well known in several European countries, and a friend of his, Johann Peter Salomon, who was a concert manager based in London, persuaded him to come to England. The two men could have chosen any one of half a dozen routes, but Salomon had been born in Bonn and had family there, and so they decided to stop off in Bonn.

This was another amazing stroke of good fortune for Bonn's young musical wunderkind, Ludwig van Beethoven. Haydn and his companion arrived in Bonn on Christmas Day 1790, and were scooped up by the musical establishment. Haydn gave his own account of what happened to an interviewer some years later. This is usually compressed into a few sentences by Beethoven biographers, but it offers such delightful insights into Haydn's character, as well as the behaviour of Bonn's senior musicians – including, without doubt, Beethoven – that it is worth recounting in some detail.

On Sunday, 26 December, Haydn and Salomon were invited to attend Mass in the court chapel. No sooner had they taken their seats than the first chords sounded, and Haydn immediately recognised one of his own works. He professed himself flattered but embarrassed. The Mass over, the two men were invited into the oratory, where they were surprised to find none other than the Elector himself, Max Franz, along with a group of Bonn's most prominent musicians.

The Elector took Haydn by the hand and presented him to the assembled company, with the words: 'Gentlemen, allow me to introduce you to the Haydn you all revere so highly.' The musicians gathered round the esteemed composer, who clearly enjoyed the adulation, but retained his natural modesty. This turned to genuine embarrassment when the Elector invited him to dinner.

The problem was Haydn and Salomon had not expected this, and had arranged for a small dinner to be served to them in their lodgings. They were committed, and it was too late to cancel. Haydn, by his own account, apologised profusely, explaining the problem, and the Elector accepted with good grace. After a suitable time, Haydn and Salomon returned to their lodgings. On entering the dining room, they discovered the small dinner had become a banquet, and there were around a dozen court musicians present. The Elector had organised a surprise party.

If Haydn, now nearly fifty-nine years of age, was feeling any weariness, he did not say, and it seems a convivial evening ensued. Was Beethoven in the company in the chapel oratory, and subsequently at Haydn's lodgings? We do not know. But I believe it is beyond doubt. He was not only Bonn's finest pianist, he was also far and away its most prolific composer, having written piano works, chamber works, ballet music, songs, not to mention two substantial cantatas commissioned by the *Lesegesellschaft*. To host a composer of the standing of Joseph Haydn in the small town of Bonn without introducing him to a homegrown young composer with an already outstanding reputation is, frankly, unthinkable.

I shall now shamelessly indulge in speculation, but in a way that is borne out a year and a half later when Beethoven's future musical course is decided in the most dramatic way. At the dinner, with musical conversation flowing easily and good food and wine being enjoyed, Haydn tells the company some home truths about being in the employ of Prince Esterházy, how he and his musicians were often treated no better than servants, made to wear uniforms, and eat in the kitchens with the staff. In return the musicians tell him about musical life in Bonn, and – singling out Beethoven – regale Haydn with tales of the two cantatas that were impossible to play.

Beethoven, probably with some pique, retaliates that the pieces were by no means impossible, all that was lacking was musicians sufficiently proficient to play them. Haydn then says, 'Look, it is a bit late now, and I have to leave early tomorrow, but I'll tell you what I'll do. On my return journey I'll make sure I come via Bonn, and I would very much like to look at the cantatas, see the manuscripts. Would that be all right?'

I confess the conversation and that last quote are drawn from my imagination, but in July 1792 that is *exactly* what happened, and it led to a life-changing decision for Beethoven. But that lies ahead.

To turn now to the anecdote that finds Beethoven in a particularly benign and co-operative mood. It was recounted nearly fifty years after the event, and the date is given as the summer of either 1790 or 1791. In the summer of 1790 Beethoven was at the height of his troubles over the cantatas. The musicians were refusing to perform the first, and he was about to embark on the second, which would meet a similar fate. In the summer of 1791, though, he was basking in the afterglow of having met the great Haydn, who had expressed a personal interest in his compositions. So let us place it at the later date.

Beethoven and a companion – likely to be either Wegeler or one of the Breuning sons – were walking in Godesberger Brunnen, a small village just outside Bonn renowned for its natural springs. They approached an older man – the source of the anecdote – and fell into conversation with him, during which he happened to remark that the church in the monastery at Marienforst, in the woods behind Godesberg, had been repaired and renovated, which was also true of the church organ, which was either entirely new or greatly improved. Beethoven's friend suggested that they go to the church, and that Beethoven should try out the new organ. The older man joined in, and soon they were urging him to play.

This is something Beethoven was by now used to. So virtuosic was he at the keyboard that he was forever being asked to demonstrate his skills. He quickly came to hate this, and in later years in Vienna, where the demands intensified as his fame spread, he would point blank refuse. On one occasion a titled lady went down on her knees in front of him in one of the most aristocratic salons in the city, and still he refused.

And on this occasion in Godesberg? 'His great good nature led him to grant our wish,' recalls the older man. The group walked to the church, but found it locked. Undeterred, they sought out the prior, who was very obliging and had the church unlocked. Beethoven went straight to the organ, tried it out, then asked his companions to give him a theme. This they did, and Beethoven improvised on it. Then another theme, and another. Always Beethoven improvised, variations flowing out of him. His playing was such that 'it moved us profoundly', recalled the older man.

Then he adds – and this is what gives the whole story an extra layer of credibility, even poignancy – workmen who were clearing up the building debris outside the church laid down their tools and came into the church to listen 'with obvious pleasure'. That more than anything, I am convinced, is what will have persuaded Beethoven to play on and on. Here was an audience of genuine music-lovers who appreciated what he was doing, not a collection of aristocrats eager to be seen to be supporting the arts.

So why do I bother recounting this anecdote, when it first appeared in print almost two centuries ago, and rarely finds its way into modern biographies? Because this is the real Beethoven, not the permanently choleric and uncooperative Beethoven of myth.

Also rarely mentioned, or given no more than a passing reference, is a trip up the Rhine that Beethoven and around twenty-five members of the court orchestra took in the late summer of 1791. Rarely mentioned because it yielded nothing in terms of composition, but with regard to Beethoven's reputation as keyboard virtuoso it was to prove very important indeed. Also, as with the Godesberg anecdote, it shines a light into the character of the young man who was to go on to become such a titan in the world of music. So, with no apologies, I intend to recount it in detail.

The trip, which Beethoven was to remember fondly for the rest of his life as 'a fruitful source of loveliest visions', was occasioned by the fact that the Elector, Maximilian Franz, as Grand Master of the Teutonic Order, was due to attend a gathering of the Order's leadership in Bad Mergentheim, which was the official residence of the Grand Master. For his and his fellow Knights' amusement, he decided that the court orchestra should join him there for a full month. Beethoven was among those selected to go.

The spa town of Bad Mergentheim lies around two hundred miles south-east of Bonn, and by far the most comfortable and practical way to make the journey two centuries ago was by boat, first up the Rhine, then along its tributary the Main, and finally the smaller Tauber. It is apparent from the few details we know that the Bonn court orchestra was under no compulsion to reach Mergentheim in the shortest time possible, probably because the boat could make only slow progress sailing against the direction of the fast-flowing water.

There is no river in Europe richer in myths and legends than the Rhine, and the portion of it that the orchestra was about to travel on, the Middle Rhine from Bonn to Mainz, with its medieval castles standing guard over villages clustered on the waterfront, is the richest in its 760-mile length.* Anyone born and brought up on the banks of the Rhine, or close to it, learns of the legends from childhood, and passes them on to their children. We know from the Fischer memoir that there were two telescopes in the attic of the Fischer house, a small one and a large one, and that with them one could see twenty miles up river, to the hills of the Siebengebirge (Seven Mountains) stretching

---

* The Middle Rhine was declared a UNESCO World Heritage Site in 2002.

away from the river on the far bank. It was Ludwig's delight to go to the attic and gaze through the telescopes, Fischer recalls, because the Beethovens had a love for the Rhine.

It is therefore beyond doubt that Ludwig learned of the legends as a child. He would have heard of how the hills of the Siebengebirge were created by dwarves digging lakes and throwing the earth over their shoulders. And he would certainly have been familiar with the legend attached to the largest of the hills, the massive rock that stood – and stands – on the east bank of the Rhine about eight miles up river, and which he would have been able to see clearly through the telescope from the attic window.

The Drachenfels (Dragon Rock) is named for the fearsome dragon that inhabited a cave halfway up the rock, whose lust for human flesh was such that it could be sated only by the annual sacrifice of a virgin. So the heathen people of the right bank of the Rhine each year crossed the river to the Christian left bank to kidnap the intended sacrifice. One day into their midst on a snow-white charger there rode a young Teutonic hero by the name of Siegfried. Fortuitously he happened to arrive on the day the heathen warriors returned to their own left bank with a bound and trembling girl intended as the annual human sacrifice for the dragon.

When challenged by Siegfried, the heathens explained that without such a sacrifice the dragon would come down into their town and devour their children. Siegfried realised that only the death of the dragon would bring an end to this awful state of affairs. Clutching his invincible sword he climbed the rock, to be met by a startled dragon who had been expecting his yearly sacrifice. It reared up at the sight of Siegfried, blowing first smoke then two jets of fire from its nostrils. Siegfried struck its neck with his sword, but it merely glanced off the scaly armour-plating. But

Siegfried saw that under the dragon's neck was a soft patch of skin. He swiftly gathered up as much dry brushwood as he could hold, and when the dragon again breathed fire at him, he thrust the bundle of brushwood into the dragon's jaws. The dry brittle wood immediately burst into flames. Roaring with pain and anger, the dragon lifted its head to shake the wood free. Its soft neck was exposed for an instant, and Siegfried rammed the sword home. The dragon fell to the ground, its blood draining fatally into the soil. The danger to the people was at last over.*

The yacht carrying the court musicians would have glided past the Drachenfels within an hour, or less, of setting off from Bonn, and I can picture them clustering onto the deck to gaze in awe at the Drachenfels, and its clearly visible cave, as the bass singer Joseph Lux – elected 'king' for the voyage – recounted the legend in tremulous tones. Is it too fanciful to imagine King Lux gazing with trepidation at the sopranos and mezzo-sopranos, urging the men to protect and shield them, as the yacht sailed past the rock?

Probably not, since before leaving Bonn the musicians had themselves held the joyful ritual of electing Lux 'Great King of the Journey'. He, in turn, then handed out duties to musicians whom he appointed senior members of his regal court, the tasks becoming more menial as he progressed to the junior ranks.

And who was youngest, and therefore most junior, of all? None other than Ludwig van Beethoven, who along with the slightly older cellist Bernhard Romberg, was appointed kitchen scullion. To me, the thought of the twenty-year-old Beethoven

---

* In another version of the legend, the chosen virgin stood naked and trembling in the mouth of the cave, suddenly holding the crucifix round her neck up to the dragon, which took fright, reared, and plunged into the swirling waters below – all without Siegfried's assistance.

being given the lowliest of kitchen duties is one of the most enchanting images from his Bonn years.

The boat, with 'mast and sail, flat deck with railing, comfortable cabins with windows and furniture, generally in the style of a Dutch yacht',* made slow progress against the current, but it would not have been long before it approached another massive rock, even richer in legend than the Drachenfels, which towers several hundred feet above the river: the Loreley.

It is true that the legend of the maiden who inhabits the rock and lures sailors to their death with the sweetness of her song achieved global fame following the publication of a poem a decade or so after the Bonn musicians' boat trip, and its musical setting some years after that. But legends have swirled around the Loreley since medieval times, occasioned by the fact that at this point the Rhine bends and narrows alarmingly.†

The current flows fast, and lethal rocks – the Sieben Jungfrauen (Seven Virgins) – lie just below the surface, creating dangerous whirlpools. Many a vessel has come to grief here.‡ As with the Drachenfels story there are several versions of the legend, but the best-known one certain to have been familiar to the Bonn musicians recounts how the lovely maiden Loreley was engaged to be married to a sailor, but he deserted her. In her grief she threw herself from the top of the rock into the swirling waters below, and in revenge lures sailors with her beautiful singing, which turns to

---

* This description dates from around ten years earlier, but reflects the kind of vessel that plied the Rhine.

† The legend that treasure was cast into the Rhine was taken and used by Richard Wagner in his epic sequence of operas, *Der Ring des Nibelungen.*

‡ As recently as January 2011 a barge carrying 2400 tonnes of sulphuric acid capsized close to the Loreley, blocking the river. Two crew members lost their lives.

mocking laughter as their vessel breaks up on the rocks and they disappear into the depths.*

As with the Drachenfels, it is certain the Bonn musicians would have gathered on deck as their yacht passed the massive rock. It is said that if conditions are right, a sevenfold echo can be heard on the southern slope of the rock. I imagine King Lux commanding silence so the musicians could listen out for it. Was it sweet singing, or scornful laughter?

In Beethoven's day, the stretch of river to the south of the Loreley became even more treacherous, narrowing to little more than a gorge, with vicious cross-currents and lethal underwater rocks. Approaching Bingen, where the Rhine takes a sharp turn east, it reached its narrowest point and was unnavigable.†

For this reason the yacht docked on the east side of the river and the musicians had to leave it, climb up to the thickly wooded hill above the bend in the river, and join it again where it widens on the stretch towards Mainz. On the heights above the small town of Rüdesheim King Lux summoned his court, and there conferred promotions on those who had earned them.‡

Step forward kitchen scullion Ludwig van Beethoven who, in

---

* Today there are markers in the river to indicate the treacherous shallows, and Rhine pleasure-boats helpfully play a tenor voice singing the song of the Loreley – words by Heinrich Heine, music by Friedrich Silcher – as the boat passes the rock. A statue of Loreley, naked and with her legs enticingly entwined, stands on an island in the river just north of the rock, and a rather unprepossessing statue of her sits outside the tourist centre on the summit of the rock, mercifully not visible from the river below.

† It was not until a century or so later that a navigable passage was blasted out of the rock.

‡ One of the most picturesque towns on the Rhine, Rüdesheim is famous today (though postdating the Bonn musicians' trip by a century) for its production of Asbach Uralt brandy.

recognition of his devotion to duty, was promoted to less menial tasks.* He must have performed extremely well, because King Lux presented him with a diploma confirming his promotion. Several threads cut from the yacht's rigging were attached to the document, and at the other end was a huge seal of pitch attached to the lid of a small box. The document folded neatly into the box. Beethoven treasured this, and kept it with him for many years after he moved to Vienna.

At Mainz, where the Rhine turns south, the musicians boarded another boat to take them east along the Main. An easy day's sailing – the Main was less turbulent and fast flowing than the Rhine – took them to Aschaffenburg, where the Elector of Mainz had his summer palace. Since their own Elector had put them under no pressure to reach Mergentheim, it was decided to make a stop in Aschaffenburg, and introduce Beethoven to one of Germany's most renowned and respected piano virtuosos, the Abbé Sterkel, who resided at the palace.

Two senior members of the orchestra took Beethoven, along with former kitchen scullion colleague Romberg, to meet the great musician, and the ensuing encounter has entered legend. The palace was an imposing four-sided structure encompassing a courtyard, standing on the banks of the Main, and it is likely that the Bonners – albeit familiar with palaces – were impressed.†
It is also probable that Sterkel played on his great reputation, no doubt dropping into the conversation how pleasant it was to be resident at the palace itself, as befits a renowned musician.

---

* We do not know what rank he was promoted to. Waiter?

† The palace was almost completely destroyed during the Second World War, but has been faithfully restored. Even today it is impressive, and is likely to have been much more so when Beethoven and his colleagues saw it.

After some polite conversation during which the visitors would surely have flattered Sterkel, they urged him to demonstrate his powers at the keyboard, and the Abbé it appears took little persuading. We do not know what he played, but we do know that Beethoven approached the piano and stood transfixed. He quite simply had never heard playing like it. Relating the story later, one of those present said that brilliant young virtuoso though Beethoven was, his playing was 'rude and hard', whereas Sterkel had a 'refined and cultivated' style, and his playing was 'in the highest degree light, graceful and pleasing'.

As the sole pianist in Bonn with virtuosic talent, it was the first time Beethoven had heard another pianist who even came close to his skills, and Sterkel's technique introduced him to a new world of grace and delicacy. He was seriously impressed, more than he had ever been before.

Sterkel finished his display to universal praise, and all eyes turned towards Beethoven – including those of Sterkel. They urged him to demonstrate his skills, but Beethoven demurred, muttering he would rather not under the circumstances. Sterkel seized the moment.

'Maybe the young gentleman from Bonn does not quite measure up to the reputation he seems to have established?'

It was, as Sterkel might well have reasoned it would be, a red rag to a bull. Seeing Beethoven's discomfort, he pressed harder. 'We have seen your latest publication, and I confess to being impressed with the complexity of the writing and the skills you require in the performer. In fact, dare I suggest, you demand more skills in the performer than maybe you yourself possess? I have an idea. Why do you not play the piece now, and put our suspicions to rest?'

Earlier that same year Beethoven had composed a substantial

piece, a set of no fewer than twenty-four variations on a theme by one Vincenzo Righini, a colleague of Sterkel in the service of the Elector of Mainz. For that reason the published work – Beethoven's first for seven years – had quickly found its way to Aschaffenburg.

Beethoven, clearly stung, his honour impugned and his ire aroused, said he would play. 'Give me the score.' Sterkel rifled through the sheet music on the piano, inside the stool, on nearby surfaces, but failed to find it. Undeterred, Beethoven began to play.

He played variation after variation, including some of the most technically demanding, from memory. Then, in the midst of playing, announcing he could not recall the remaining variations, he instantly improvised entirely new ones, of a complexity equal to the most difficult of those he had already played. To round things off, he imitated Sterkel's style of playing, exaggerating its lightness and refinement, making it appear 'almost ladylike', no doubt drawing discreet chuckles from those present.

We are not told of Sterkel's reaction, but this would not be the last time that Beethoven, his skills at the keyboard thrown into doubt, would embarrass his accuser with an unparalleled display of virtuosity.

As well as an illuminating tale regarding how easily Beethoven could be goaded into performing when his skills were impugned, this encounter in Aschaffenburg is important for another reason too. It provides evidence that, through publication, knowledge of his compositional skills had spread well beyond his home town of Bonn. Now his virtuosity was certain to achieve a similar fame.

On arrival in Bad Mergentheim, the musicians from Bonn turned their minds to musical duties. On the orders of the Elector they were given quarters in the complex of buildings that housed the Teutonic Order, and no doubt appreciated the comfort and convenience this afforded. They had a busy schedule. There were performances in theatres, ornate halls and churches, on every day of the week. There were balls, concerts, operettas and plays. Added to this were lavish receptions and banquets, with musicians on hand to entertain guests. The Teutonic Knights – Count Waldstein attended for a period – were dressed in medieval finery of white cloaks.

On the Elector's name day he presented his Bonn musicians with a bag containing one thousand ducats. Beethoven's share amounted to around forty guilders.

We would know little more about the stay in Mergentheim, were it not for the diligence of a well-known composer and music-writer of the time by the name of Karl Ludwig Junker. He visited Mergentheim and was warmly received by the Bonners. It says something of his perspicacity as music critic that he regarded the orchestra to be sufficiently accomplished to merit a lengthy report, which he published in a musical journal.

He praises the orchestra's 'surpassing excellence' in music of the utmost difficulty. He writes that the musicians were resplendent in red uniforms trimmed with gold. Beethoven played in the viola section, and it is a beguiling thought to imagine the young musician, so notoriously careless about his appearance in later years, sitting in resplendent uniform with his fellow players.

So far, so interesting, but little more than that. Indeed the name of Karl Ludwig Junker would be well and truly consigned to oblivion were it not for the paragraph that he wrote next. For reasons we do not know, he watched Beethoven improvise on the piano in a private room with no audience. More than that, Beethoven asked him for a theme, so that he could improvise on it. This is something Beethoven was consistently asked to do throughout his life, and (as I have noted earlier) he nearly always refused. On this occasion he obliged. Not only that, but he made an impression on Junker that led to a description possibly unique in all the thousands of words written by men and women who knew him. It is so extraordinary, it is worth quoting at length.

I heard also one of the greatest of pianists – the dear, good Bethofen [sic] … True he did not perform in public, probably the instrument here was not to his liking … But what was infinitely preferable to me was that I heard him extemporise in private. Yes, I was even invited to propose a theme for him to vary … The greatness of this amiable, light-hearted man, as a virtuoso, may in my opinion be safely estimated from his almost inexhaustible wealth of ideas, the altogether characteristic style of expression in his playing, and the great execution which he displays. I know, therefore, of not one thing that he lacks that is necessary to the greatness of the artist … Bethofen, in addition to his execution, has greater clarity and weight of ideas than Vogler,* and more expression – in short his playing goes straight to the heart. Even the members of this remarkable orchestra are, without exception, his admirers, and are all ears when he plays. Yet he is exceedingly modest and free from all pretension. Had I agreed, as my friend Bethofen implored me, to stay another day in Mergentheim, I have no doubt he would have played to me for hours, and the day … would have been transformed into a day of the highest bliss.

---

* A Mannheim pianist, regarded as the finest virtuoso of his generation.

This is on several levels a quite remarkable commentary. For a start here is a professional music-writer in his forties openly stating that Beethoven is a better keyboard player than the best he knows. Even if we might have expected that, it comes as a genuine shock – given what we know of Beethoven's notoriously unpredictable temperament – to learn that he is so popular with his musical colleagues. There is not one, according to Junker, who does not admire him and listen attentively when he plays. We have to deduce from this they liked him too. It comes shining through Junker's prose. Finally, what do we make of the words 'he is exceedingly modest and free from all pretension'? Well, the earliest and most authoritative of all Beethoven biographies, written by a man who interviewed many people who had known Beethoven, describes these words as 'utterly inexplicable'!*

Certainly Junker was caught up in the moment.† But if Beethoven actually tried to persuade him to stay so he could play some more for him, the two men – a generation apart in age – must have got on exceedingly well. We cannot simply dismiss Junker's words as those of a sycophant. He observed the Bonn orchestra performing, witnessed their relationships, and was given a private recital by Beethoven.

My reading of this is that Beethoven, twenty years of age, was away from Bonn, away from the tensions of family, away from the confines of court, away from anyone – and any circumstance – that was not musical. He was in the company of musicians, making music. Nothing else. I do not find it in the

---

* Alexander Wheelock Thayer, *The Life of Ludwig van Beethoven*.

† The orchestra apparently rehearsed one of the two cantatas Beethoven had composed following the death of the Emperor, and given that they considered both unplayable, it is possible there might have been a little tension in the air.

least surprising that here, in Mergentheim, for the first time in his life we see Beethoven, the innate musician.*

One can almost feel his sense of despair when the time came to return to Bonn in late October 1791.

At one o'clock in the morning on 5 December 1791, an event occurred that went largely unnoticed in Vienna, that caused much sadness in musical circles in Bonn, that would have caused Beethoven considerable grief, and that is still being mourned today. Wolfgang Amadeus Mozart died at the age of thirty-five. It is not an exaggeration to say that Beethoven, who turned twenty-one less than two weeks later, was soon being talked of as Mozart's natural successor. As performer his virtuosity was unquestioned and unparalleled.† As composer he now had a substantial number of works, in a variety of genres, to his name.

One man recognised that more than any other. He was in London when the sad news reached him, but he kept his promise to pass through Bonn on his return to Vienna. In July 1792 Beethoven once again met Joseph Haydn, now Europe's unquestioned pre-eminent musician. Haydn was now sixty years of age, and a good enough musician to recognise that he belonged to an older generation and that new blood was needed. More than that, he was prepared to do something about it.

---

* Bad Mergentheim, proud of its young visitor, today holds a regular Beethoven Festival, and conducts walking tours of locations and buildings dating back two centuries.

† In later years he would be regarded in Vienna as a finer piano virtuoso than Mozart.

A breakfast meeting was arranged between Haydn and members of the court orchestra at Bad Godesberg, close to Bonn. Beethoven was present, and no doubt remembering Haydn's suggestion at their last meeting, had the manuscript of his *Cantata on the Death of Emperor Joseph II* with him. Haydn asked to see it. He studied several pages, finally confessing himself very impressed. He urged Beethoven to continue his studies.

The meeting is recounted by Wegeler, who frustratingly gives us no further detail. However, by the time Haydn left Bonn shortly after, there was a clear commitment that if Beethoven could find his way to Vienna, he, Haydn, would give him lessons. We do not know how this was viewed by the people around Beethoven, Count Waldstein, or Christian Neefe, or most importantly the Elector, who would not only have to give Beethoven permission to take leave of absence, but also subsidise the trip. It was summer, certainly, and court duties were light, but come autumn the new opera and theatre season would have to be prepared and then got under way. There was not much Beethoven could do in the few weeks before then. But if it was to be a longer stay, how likely was it that the Elector would grant leave of absence to a young man who had by now made himself such an indispensable member of musical life at court?

Not for the first time, extraneous events worked in Beethoven's favour, though he must have been the only resident of Bonn for whom this was true. In October 1792 the French Revolutionary Army invaded German territory and marched towards the Rhine. On the 22nd they took Mainz and headed north. The towns and cities of the lower Rhine were at their mercy. Those who could fled. It was decided that the Elector and his family should leave Bonn.

In the chaos of evacuation, the question of whether or not

Beethoven should be allowed to go to Vienna paled somewhat. We do not know exactly what happened, but almost certainly Count Waldstein seized the moment to secure the Elector's agreement for Beethoven to go to Vienna, possibly for six months, maybe for a year.

Beethoven did not need telling twice. He immediately began making preparations. We do not know how he told his father, or what his father's reaction was. Probably he presented it as a fait accompli, in the knowledge that his two brothers, now in their mid- and late teens, would take over responsibility.

Before leaving, Beethoven made the rather charming decision – or maybe it was made for him – to fill an autograph book with messages from close friends. This book has survived, and is rather more surprising for what it does not contain than for what it does.

Only fourteen friends have signed it, none of them musical colleagues, many with names that do not feature in any of the literature. Christian Neefe did not sign it. It seems to give the lie to Junker's assessment of Beethoven's popularity among his fellow musicians. On the other hand, it is always possible that he had another book for musicians, or that shyness prevented him from approaching everyone he would have liked to.

One notable omission is Stephan von Breuning, one of Helene von Breuning's sons to whom he had given piano lessons. With Stephan the young Beethoven had formed an even closer friendship than with Wegeler. The two youths – Beethoven was the elder by nearly four years – spent a lot of time together. Stephan appears to feature less in this period than Wegeler, by virtue of the fact that he did not write his reminiscences down. But the friendship with Stephan von Breuning was to be the closest, and longest lasting, of Beethoven's life. It was to last, literally, until Beethoven's death. Stephan was to follow Beethoven to Vienna, and his name will feature many more times in these pages. Why, then, is he absent from the autograph book? We do not know. It might be simply that he was away at the time, because Beethoven would be gone within days.

Stephan's sister Eleonore most certainly does feature in the autograph book, and thereby, I am convinced, hangs a tale. We are in the realms of conjecture now, but I make no apologies for what follows. It is a subject that has not been accorded much space by previous biographers, but I believe that to ignore it leaves us with an incomplete picture of an adolescent Beethoven.

Where are the young women in this narrative? Conspicuous by their absence. Girls do not feature greatly in Beethoven's pubescent years, but it was not, apparently, for want of trying. According to Wegeler, 'There never was a time when Beethoven was not in love, and that in the highest degree.' In this period, in his adolescence, as well as in his entire adult life, he would fall in love with females who were simply not available. It is a consistent pattern, to such an extent that you have to wonder if it was a deliberate course of action on his part, as if he was somehow fearful of the commitment it could lead to. But in the early years, this was clearly not the case. He was certainly more than anxious to have an amorous relationship.

There was a certain Jeanette d'Honrath, from Cologne, a friend of Eleonore who would come to Bonn and stay with her. Wegeler describes her as 'a beautiful, vivacious blonde, of good education and amiable disposition, who enjoyed music greatly and possessed an agreeable voice'. She was clearly well aware of Beethoven's attraction to her, because she used to sing him a teasing little song, of which the words lamented her being separated from him, and being unable to prevent this, which was too hurtful for her poor heart. We do not know how Beethoven reacted to this. Suffice it to say she went off and married a soldier who later rose to the rank of field marshal.

Then one Fräulein von Westerholt, whom Beethoven took on as a pupil and with whom he fell in love with such a passion that Wegeler discreetly calls her just 'Fräulein von W.' and Romberg was telling tales of his friend's unrequited love forty years later. Fräulein von Westerholt became Frau von Bevervörde.

Beethoven and his friends frequented a tavern near the town hall in Bonn called the Zehrgarten, run by a certain Frau Koch, assisted by her beautiful daughter Babette. It is certain that Beethoven was attracted to her. Whether he tried to pursue this we do not know, but if he did he was clearly disappointed, since he wrote from Vienna shortly after arriving that he was hurt she hadn't replied to his letters.

It was around this time that an incident occurred that perhaps best – and most painfully – sums up Beethoven's lack of success with girls.

One evening he was in a restaurant with a number of the younger members of the court orchestra. There was a particularly attractive young waitress, and they persuaded her to tease Beethoven and flirt with him. This she did (we are not told how), and Beethoven reacted with 'repellent coldness'. They encouraged her to flirt more. Finally Beethoven lost patience and 'put an end to her importunities with a smart box on the ear'.*

This merits slightly closer examination. Why would his colleagues do this, if they did not already know of his gaucheness with girls? Had some of them previously witnessed his attempts at seduction? If so, the attempts must have failed. Clearly alcohol was flowing when they put the waitress up to her antics, but that

---

* Thayer (see above), who recounts this, does not name his source(s).

would simply have exaggerated what they all knew already – that Beethoven was pretty hopeless when it came to girls.

More importantly, can we really believe that a twenty- or twenty-one-year-old Beethoven would strike a girl? Or is the teller of the tale merely using a euphemism? We cannot be sure. But this was clearly no simple prank. It was calculated to upset Beethoven, and upset him it did. It must also have deepened a certain self-loathing he is bound to have had over his inability to acquire a girlfriend.

Which leads us back to Eleonore von Breuning, Lorchen as she was known, and the speculation I shall now indulge in. I am assuming that in order to have his autograph book signed, Beethoven went to the Breuning house on the Münsterplatz with which he was so familiar. He found Stephan out or away, but Lorchen was there, alone. He asked her to sign his autograph book.

This she did, choosing to write three lines by the German poet and philosopher Johann Gottfried Herder. They read:

Friendship with that which is good
Grows like the evening shadows
Until the sunshine of life finally sinks.

She signed it: Bonn, 1 November 1792, your true friend Eleonore Breuning.

Hardly an overwhelming declaration of affection, in fact bordering on the formal. Compare this with a birthday card she presented him with one year earlier. Two four-line verses wishing him happiness and long life, and in return asking from him, her piano teacher, kindness, patience and favour. She drew round the verses a garland of flowers, and signed it with her pet name, Lorchen.

What had happened? I am convinced Beethoven fell in love with Lorchen very soon after beginning to teach her. I believe that, at some point in his teenage years, he expressed this to her, and that later – in between the birthday card and the autograph book – he put his feelings into action with an attempted kiss, which she rejected.

Now, alone in the house with her, about to leave for Vienna, he made – I believe – one more attempt to show his affection. I imagine he made an ungainly lunge at her, which she again rejected and which left her seriously upset.

How else to explain the language he used in a letter to her written a full year after arriving in Vienna?

Although it has been a year since you have heard from me, you have been constantly and most vividly in my thoughts, and very often I have conversed in spirit with you and your dear family, though frequently not as calmly as I should have wished. For whenever I did so I was always reminded of that unfortunate quarrel. My conduct at that time really was quite detestable. But what was done could not be undone. Oh, what I would give to be able to blot out of my life my behaviour at that time, behaviour which did me so little honour, and which was so out of character for me … It is said that the sincerest repentance is only to be found when the criminal himself confesses his crime, and this is what I have wanted to do. So now let us draw a curtain over the whole affair.

Eleonore, it seems, was prepared to forgive him, to an extent. She sent him a hand-knitted neckcloth (he had asked her to send him something made by her hands). But he is still tortured by guilt, no doubt made worse by the fact that he now knew that Eleonore had formed a close friendship with his friend Wegeler, and that the two would soon be married.

> *The beautiful neckcloth, your own handiwork, came as a lovely surprise to me ... But it also made me sad, awakening memories of things long past. Also your generous behaviour made me feel ashamed. Indeed I could hardly believe you would think me still worth remembering ... I beg you to believe, my friend (please let me continue to call you friend), that I have suffered greatly, and am still suffering, from the loss of your friendship ... I know what I have lost and what you have meant to me. But if I were to attempt to fill this gap, I would have to recall scenes which you would not be happy to hear about, and I would not be happy to describe.*

I rest my case.

The most important entry in Beethoven's autograph book, without question, is that written by the man who had done more to further Beethoven's musical ambitions in Bonn than any other, Count Waldstein. In fact his entry has earned him a certain immortality. For the first time in Beethoven's life, his name is linked in writing with music's two greatest contemporary names (though the reference to Haydn is a trifle barbed).

> *Dear Beethowen!* [sic]
>
> *You journey now to Vienna in fulfilment of your long frustrated wishes. The Genius of Mozart is still in mourning and she weeps for the death of her pupil. With the inexhaustible Haydn she has found refuge but no occupation. Through him she now wishes to be united with someone else.*

With persistent hard work you shall receive: <u>Mozart's Spirit through Haydn's Hands.</u>

Beethoven left Bonn at six o'clock on the morning of Friday, 2 November (the morning after the encounter with Eleonore von Breuning), carrying a large amount of musical scores, finished and unfinished, and little else. The journey was not without danger. At one point the coach driver whipped the horses into a gallop and drove right through the Hessian army.

The coach drove south along the river, turning east at Ehrenbreitstein, the home town of Beethoven's mother. He would certainly have taken a last look at the Rhine, expecting to see it again in six months or a year.

He never saw the Rhine, or Bonn – or, indeed, Eleonore von Breuning – again.

Chapter 5

Impressing the Viennese

But Haydn feels the wrath of an angry young man

Vienna, capital city of the Holy Roman Empire, seat of the Holy Roman Emperor, formal, correct, proper. Into its midst there arrived in November 1792 a young man just one month short of his twenty-second birthday, from Bonn in the Rhineland several hundred miles to the north-west, who had never worn a wig in his life, let alone a powdered one, whose clothes were ill fitting and in need of repair, and whose accent was rough and harsh on the sophisticated ears of the Viennese.

And what of the city in which he had arrived? At the crossroads of Continental Europe, Vienna could lay claim to being Europe's most exotic city. Less than a decade before Beethoven's arrival, a traveller had written that the streets of Vienna teemed with …

Hungarians in their close-fitting trousers, Poles with their flowing sleeves, Armenians and Moldavians with their half-Oriental costumes, Serbians with their twisted moustaches, Greeks smoking their long-stemmed pipes in the cof-

*fee-houses, bearded Muslims with broad knives in their belts,
Polish Jews with their faces bearded and their hair twisted
in knots, Bohemian peasants in their long boots, Hungarian
and Transylvanian wagoners with sheepskin greatcoats, Cro-
ats with black tubs balanced on their heads.*

And everywhere there was music. It went from the very highest social strata to the lowest. In the 1790s every member of the
Emperor's immediate family had taken music lessons and was
proficient either on an instrument or in singing. The late Emperor
himself was capable of directing an opera from the harpsichord,
with his sisters singing the main parts and performing in the ballet sequence. There was a first-class court orchestra, court choir,
and court opera company. The same traveller wrote:

*One cannot enter any fashionable house without hearing a
duet, or trio, or finale from one of the Italian operas currently the rage being sung and played at the keyboard. Even
shopkeepers and cellar-hands whistle the popular arias …
No place of refreshment, from the highest to the lowest, is
without music. Bassoonists and clarinettists are as plentiful
as blackberries, and in the suburbs at every turn one alights
upon fresh carousing, fresh fiddling, fresh illuminations.*

Vienna could lay claim to being the most easy-going, even friv-
olous, city in Europe (a mantle that Paris would assume in later
decades), where enjoyment came before anything else. An English
traveller wrote that 'good cheer is pursued here in every quarter,
and mirth is worshipped in every form'.

A famous Viennese motto was that 'matters are desperate,
but not serious'. There was street entertainment, dancing was

everywhere, and cafés and *Weinstuben* were full late into the night. Prostitution was rife, and if the Emperor himself is to be believed, reached into every corner of the city. When it was proposed to him that brothels should be licensed, he replied, 'The walls would cost me nothing, but the expense of roofing would be ruinous, for a roof would have to be constructed over the whole city.'

Another British visitor neatly caught the twin themes that ran through Vienna, when he wrote, 'No city can at the same time present such a display of affected sanctity and real licentiousness.'

There was, however, a dark side to the city. Just as, a century later, the Viennese would waltz towards the oblivion of the First World War and the end of the seemingly indestructible Habsburg dynasty, so in the 1790s the carousing masked deep fear and tension. No one, though, could have foreseen that within a few short years the Holy Roman Empire and its Emperor would have been consigned to historical oblivion by a certain Napoleon Bonaparte.

Three years earlier the people of Paris had invaded the Bastille, and the French Revolution had begun. Three months before Beethoven's arrival in Vienna, the French King had been found guilty of treason, and would mount the scaffold in January of the following year. Before that year was out, his Queen would follow him. To the people of Vienna she was not Marie Antoinette, but Maria Antonia, youngest daughter of the 'mother' of their nation, the great Empress Maria Theresa, and they were aware of how she had been vilified by the French, who called her the 'Austrian whore'.

What had seemed impossible – the downfall of the oldest hereditary monarchy in Continental Europe – had happened. How safe was the Habsburg Emperor in Vienna? As the French Revolutionary Army under its inspired young commander began to rampage across Europe, the threat became ever more real. Time and again Austria entered into alliances with other European powers to take on Napoleon; time and again it suffered humiliating defeat. The old officer class of the Habsburg Empire, the cavalry still wielding lances, were no match for the revolutionary cannon of the French.

So outward frivolity masked an underlying tension. The least-safe commodity in Vienna was words. Increasingly spies proliferated, ears pricked in cafés and taverns, and above all in the back of horse-drawn fiacres. And when words were dangerous, what was the commodity that was safest of all? Music. That is how Vienna became Europe's capital city of music.

Beethoven was to live in Vienna for just over thirty-four years until his death. For the first half of that time, roughly, Vienna was a city at almost permanent war; for the second half it was what today would be called a police state, as Foreign Minister and later Chancellor Metternich clamped down on political freedom.

Cataclysmic events were taking place across Europe. Beethoven absorbed the drama, the tension, the danger, and it all left its mark on his music.

Beethoven's life in Vienna began in the humblest of ways. He was given an attic room in a house owned by a Viennese aristocrat who was a distant relative of Count Waldstein. His name was Prince Karl Lichnowsky, and he was no ordinary aristocrat. He happened to be one of the wealthiest in the city, and one of the greatest patrons of the arts, in particular music. His salon was home to the leading artists of the day.

Initially, though, Beethoven was on his own. One can almost sense his loneliness – coupled undoubtedly with a feeling of freedom – as he made a shopping list days after his arrival: 'Wood, wig-maker, coffee … overcoat, boots, shoes, piano desk, seal, writing desk …'

He was aware too that he would have to cut a figure in keeping with the elevated class that he hoped to penetrate, but that his small allowance from the Elector would be sorely stretched. Another shopping list reads: 'Black silk stockings, 1 ducat. 1 pair winter silk stockings, 1 florin 40 kreutzers. Boots, 6 florins. Shoes, 1 florin, 30 kreutzers.' One suspects these domestic issues were a distraction from the real task at hand: to become a part of the sophisticated, very formal, very aristocratic, musical scene in Vienna.

He began lessons with Haydn immediately, and then six weeks after arriving he received the worst possible news from home – or what *should* have been the worst possible news. On 18 December his father died.

There is no reference to this sad event, as far as I can tell, in anything he said or wrote down at the time, and no indication of any inner struggle over whether he should return to Bonn for the funeral. Maybe the fact that central Europe was at war made the journey inadvisable. I suspect, though, it merely hardened his resolve to get on with his new life without interruption. He did not return. It was a symbolic putting of the past behind him. His new life as professional musician in Vienna had begun.

He most certainly threw himself into it. His musical life had three strands. He was studying intensively with Haydn; he was composing new works, and through Lichnowsky's contacts he was performing at salon soirées. This total immersion in musical activity alone made him something of a rarity in Vienna, but of the three pursuits the one that truly singled him out was salon performances.

There was an undercurrent of collective guilt among the city's aristocrats that the musical genius who had died so recently, the greatest musical genius the city, indeed Europe, had seen, had not been better looked after. It was as if there was an unspoken determination among them not to let that happen again. In one sense Beethoven made it rather easy for them. He was quite simply, even in his early twenties, a piano virtuoso unlike any this city had seen, not excepting Mozart. If Lichnowsky was the key that unlocked the doors to the highest salons in the land, once Beethoven sat at the piano, his extraordinary and boundless talent ensured he would be accepted in whatever company he mixed, however elevated.

Without Lichnowsky's patronage, it is doubtful any salon doors would have opened at all for the young man from Bonn. He simply did not look like a musician. He had no sophistication about him, no refinement, no air of the artist. Thayer describes him as:

Small, thin, dark-complexioned, pockmarked, dark-eyed ... with looks of the Moor about him ... His front teeth protruded, owing to the extraordinary flatness of the roof of his mouth, and this thrust out his lips. His nose, too, was rather broad and decidedly flattened, while his forehead was remarkably full and round ... in the words of Mähler, who twice painted his portrait, a 'bullet'.

The word 'thin' is perhaps surprising, since all images of the adult Beethoven show a powerful, stockily built figure. But this did not come until later. Early portraits show none of the suppressed power of his middle years.

Once his fame was established, the word most often used to describe him – and frequently used today – was 'leonine'. This implies more than just a large powerful head and body. The lion is the king of beasts, unchallengeable, undefeatable. He had, contemporaries noted, a strong jaw, with a deep cleft in the chin, and he was powerfully built, despite his short stature, with wide shoulders, strong hands with tufts of hair on his fingers, which were short and thick.

His eyes were noticed and commented on. 'His eye is full of rude energy,' wrote one observer. Another noted that 'his fiery eyes, though small, are deep-set and unbelievably full of life'. Rossini recorded, albeit when Beethoven was in his early fifties, that 'what no etcher's needle can express is the indefinable sadness spread over his features – while from under heavy eyebrows his eyes shine out as if from caverns, and though small, seem to pierce one'.

He was, once he had become Vienna's pre-eminent musician, beyond trivial criticism for having wild hair, or being unshaven, or wearing ill-fitting clothes, or even being ill-mannered. But in his early years in Vienna, people were shocked by his sheer lack of physical grace, and were not afraid to say so.

One noblewoman wrote after encountering him, 'His entire deportment showed no signs of exterior polish. On the contrary he was lacking in manners in both demeanour and behaviour.' Hardly the kind of appearance that would fit easily in the noblest salons of Vienna, particularly when coupled with his notoriously unkempt appearance (despite the shopping list). But the moment he sat at the piano, everything changed. In fact at that point his social gaucheness worked in his favour. It increased the admiration he was accorded. How could a man so clearly unsuited to the refined pursuit of the highest of the arts be such an accomplished practitioner of it?

Word, which began in the salon of Prince Lichnowsky, raced round the aristocracy of Vienna. The city had lost Mozart, but another young genius – a truly remarkable virtuoso who looked more like a street seller – had found his way to the city. The aristocrats, patrons of the arts, flocked to see and hear him.

'I took lessons from Haydn, but never learned anything from him.' Beethoven is quoted as saying this in later years by Ferdinand Ries in the memoir he co-wrote with Wegeler. It was not as simple as that. In fact there is evidence Haydn worked hard to improve his pupil's knowledge of musical theory, particularly counterpoint. But it is true that the older man had a great deal of call on his time, not to mention his emotions.

He was deeply affected by the death of Mozart at such a young age, as well as the sudden death of another close friend. He was living through a disastrous marriage, openly writing in envy to a friend whose wife had died, 'Perhaps the time will come ... when four eyes shall be closed ... Two are closed, but the other two ...', and was juggling two mistresses, a widow in London, and an Italian mezzo-soprano who had moved to Esterháza with her husband. On top of that there was the small matter of six new symphonies he was planning for a return trip to London.

So if he had less time to give than his pupil wanted, it was perhaps understandable. But Beethoven clearly bore a rather long-standing grudge against his teacher. Ries recounts that the reason for this was that Haydn, aware of just how promising Beethoven was, asked him to put on the title page of his first works – *any* first work – 'Pupil of Haydn'. He might have understood his pupil's musical prowess, but this anecdote shows he was less understanding of Beethoven's character.

Beethoven refused point blank. This was more than a refusal, it was a gesture of defiance, an insult almost, to the older and much venerated composer. Haydn was to wreak small revenge before too long, but in early 1794 he unwittingly did Beethoven a great favour by leaving for London. It was a kind of liberation for the young man. There is some evidence that he took secret lessons with another composer, but of more importance is the fact that he began to compose in earnest.

He completed his first major work, a set of three piano trios which he would publish the following year as his opus 1. He wrote two full piano concertos, and began serious work on a set of three piano sonatas, which would become his opus 2. There were several other smaller works as well.

Beethoven had, by late 1794, been in Vienna for less than two years, yet he was already – at the age of just twenty-three – far and away the city's most accomplished all-round musician, performing regularly in salons and publishing substantial works. There was only one thing missing, and that was where Prince Lichnowsky came in.

Using his considerable influence, the Prince secured for Beethoven his first public performance. The venue was the highly prestigious Burgtheater, the largest and most important of the imperial court theatres, which stood adjacent to the Hofburg Palace, seat of the Emperor. Other works were to be performed, but the programme announced the performance of a piano concerto by Ludwig van Beethoven, who was also its composer. The last musician of consequence who had performed his own piano concertos in Vienna was Mozart.

Things did not go smoothly. In fact they could hardly have gone worse. Beethoven, all his life a chronic rewriter, completed the slow movement only two days before the concert. He was suffering from severe stomach pains and diarrhoea while he was composing. His old friend from Bonn, Franz Wegeler, now a qualified doctor, was in Vienna and did what he could with various potions. So tight was time that four copyists sat in the hallway making fair copies as Beethoven handed over barely decipherable manuscript sheets one by one. His notation was notoriously difficult to decipher at the best of times. The copyists are likely to have helped each other out with difficult passages, rather than risk the wrath of the ailing composer by querying what he had written.

Worse than this, at the rehearsal the following day, the eve of the performance, Beethoven discovered the piano was a semitone flat. With no apparent difficulty he transposed the piano part up a semitone, but it would have done nothing to improve his mood.

Frustratingly we have no eyewitness account of how the concert went. But the fact that it was repeated the following day suggests at worst a satisfactory performance, at best a success. Just as frustratingly, it is not known for certain which of his first two piano concertos Beethoven played.*

Extraordinarily, on the third night, at a concert arranged by Mozart's widow, Beethoven performed a Mozart piano concerto. Three concerts, on three consecutive nights, in front of a paying audience. Beethoven the performer had arrived.

Four months later, in what was turning into something of an *annus mirabilis* for Beethoven, his Op. 1 Piano Trios were published. Within a matter of weeks, Joseph Haydn returned from a triumphant London tour. Beethoven, putting aside any resentment he might have felt towards his erstwhile teacher, asked Lichnowsky to arrange a soirée at which he would perform the three piano trios in front of Haydn.

---

* The concerto we know as 'No. 1' was in fact the second he composed, and the one we know as 'No. 2' the first, because they were published in that order.

Haydn was now sixty-three years of age; he had been abroad for something over a year and a half, had performed, composed, been wined and dined and fêted practically every night. We can assume he was weary. We can also assume that musical friends had told him that the set of piano trios was enormously impressive. I do not think it is far-fetched to suggest that Haydn, as a musician, wanted to hear them, but that at the same time he was apprehensive. Would they represent such a major leap forward in composition that his own works would be rendered old-fashioned, out of date? He knew what his pupil was capable of. He probably feared the younger man would eclipse him.

The three works are substantial, grand and expansive, and in four movements each. They are almost pared-down symphonies. To hear all three in a single sitting makes for a lengthy, intense, evening – particularly for a man in his sixties for whom the previous eighteen months had been so demanding. There was the added element that Prince Lichnowsky had not done things by halves. He had invited the city's top music-lovers and artists. All knew and respected Haydn, all were keen to shake his hand, ask him about London … and at the end of the evening ascertain his thoughts on Beethoven's piano trios.

None more so than their composer, who, no sooner had the final chord of the final movement of No. 3 sounded, leapt up from the piano and made straight for his teacher to ask his opinion.

This is where Haydn exacted revenge of a sort on the eager, and uncooperative, young man. He began by praising the works in a general sort of way, and then had the temerity, the gall, to suggest that No. 3 needed more work, and his advice to Beethoven was to revise it before sending it to the publisher.

One can imagine the collective gasp in the salon as all eyes turned to Beethoven. If the guests were shocked, Beethoven was appalled. Wegeler, who recounts the incident, states diplomatically that Beethoven was 'astonished', the more so since he considered No. 3 the strongest of the set. Wegeler, writing many years after the event, adds, 'In fact to this day it is always found to be the most pleasing, and has the greatest effect.' It is true to say that to *this day*, that is the case. Of the set of three piano trios, it is No. 3 that modern musicologists rate the strongest.

Wegeler does not recount how the frosty (heated?) encounter played out. But although the relationship between Haydn and Beethoven of teacher and pupil was effectively at an end, there is ample evidence that Beethoven did not lose respect for the older man. At a soirée at Prince Lichnowsky's only a matter of weeks later, Beethoven performed his new set of three piano sonatas before Haydn, and when they were published the following year, they were dedicated to him (though without any mention of 'Pupil of Haydn'!).

Then in December Haydn staged a public concert at which Beethoven performed one of his two piano concertos.* Whatever tension there might have been between the two composers, it was clearly sublimated to the greater good of their art.

It is just as well that things were going well for Beethoven the musician, because for Beethoven the man they were not so good. An acquaintance from his Bonn years came to Vienna. She happened to be the 'beautiful, talented and accomplished' singer Magdalena Willman, who had been among the court musicians on the boat trip up the Rhine to Mergentheim just a few years before. Clearly

---

* Again, it is not certain which of the two he performed.

Beethoven had admired her from afar on that sojourn, but there is no evidence he pursued matters then. He most certainly did now.

Magdalena was accompanied by her brother and his wife, and Beethoven renewed his friendship with the family. He does not appear to have given her piano lessons, but it is more than likely he accompanied her in salon recitals. He must have seen her on a number of occasions, because he fell head over heels in love with her, and wasted no time in proposing marriage.

She turned him down flat. We know no further details, except one. Her niece, interviewed by Thayer sixty-five years later, told him her father had often spoken of how the famous musician had once proposed marriage to his sister. Thayer asked her why Magdalena had turned him down. She hesitated a moment, then said, 'Because he was so ugly, and half crazy!'

For the niece – Thayer discreetly calls her 'Madame S.' – to know this detail so many years later suggests it was common currency at the time of the proposal. Even if Beethoven never heard such words, he is certain to have known that he was the butt of humour, even ridicule. Following on rejections by several women in Bonn, not to mention the humiliation by the waitress, this must have hurt his pride considerably. He would have been grateful he had music to turn to. There, no one could laugh at him.

Something else had happened, guaranteed to darken his mood. His brothers had left Bonn and come to join him in Vienna. Caspar Carl had arrived in May 1794, Nikolaus Johann at the very end of 1795. Beethoven had never been close to his brothers. They were talentless individuals, and he was a being apart. Nikolaus Johann had at least trained in pharmacy, and soon found employment in Vienna. Caspar Carl appears to have done nothing. He was in the dire position of having a mediocre musical talent. He attached himself to his elder brother, negotiating on his behalf with publishers, teaching, even doing a little composing himself. But the two did not get on, and there were frequent disagreements. Within a very few years things were to sour deeply between them.

Escape was at hand, in the best and most exciting form possible. Prince Lichnowsky decided that Beethoven should undertake a European tour, and he chose exactly the same itinerary he had undertaken with Mozart some years earlier: Prague, Dresden, Leipzig and Berlin. In fact Lichnowsky, no doubt for business reasons, decided to accompany Beethoven no further than Prague, but he made sure through his contacts, no doubt gleaned on the earlier trip with Mozart, that his protégé would be well looked after.

That he most certainly was. In Prague, together with Lichnowsky, he was welcomed into the most noble salons. He performed, and composed several pieces. In Dresden he was received by the Elector of Saxony, who it appears persuaded him to give a solo recital for an hour and a half with no one present but the Elector himself. There is no record of his brief stay in Leipzig, but in Berlin, well, there is no other way to put this. He reached the top.

The King of Prussia, Friedrich Wilhelm II, personally received Beethoven, making him welcome at court. Beethoven was on his own, with nothing more than a letter of introduction, but it so happened the King was not merely a great lover of music, but a fine cellist. He very quickly recognised an extraordinary talent, and Beethoven more than reciprocated by composing several pieces for cello – two sonatas and two sets of variations – as well as other works too. The two sonatas were almost certainly too difficult for the King to play, but they were performed for him by a prominent cellist attached to the court, with Beethoven at the piano, and they would have no doubt inspired him to improve his skills. Beethoven curried more favour still by dedicating the two sonatas to the King.

Beethoven remained in Berlin for the best part of two months, and it is possible he began to tire of the attention and adulation. In later years his pupil Czerny recounted how, when Beethoven improvised at the piano, people in the salon would break into tears and loud sobs, so moved were they by what they heard. But at the end of the improvisation Beethoven would burst into loud laughter and chastise his audience. 'You are fools!' he would shout at them. 'Who can live with such spoiled children?' Czerny then adds, rather enigmatically, that Beethoven himself told him that it was for that reason he declined to accept an invitation the King of Prussia extended to him after one of his improvisations. He elaborates no further, but it is possible the King was offering him a permanent position at court.

It would seem, though, that if offence were intended, none was taken. On his departure Beethoven was presented with a gold snuff-box filled with coins by the King himself. This was not all he returned with. From Prague he had written to his brother Nikolaus Johann that he was earning considerable money, as well as winning friends and respect. He goes so far as to write that if his brother should need money, he could approach Prince Lichnowsky 'boldly, for he still owes me some'. It seems extraordinary that the Prince should owe Beethoven money, rather than the other way round, and it is impossible to know if this really was the case.

In the same letter Beethoven cannot resist a small word of advice from an older brother on matters of a private nature. 'I hope that you will enjoy living in Vienna more and more, but do be on your guard against the whole tribe of bad women.' This might be considered somewhat rich coming from someone who had received rejection after rejection from women. It could, on the other hand, be a veiled warning to take care when visiting prostitutes. This would suggest Beethoven had personal experience of this kind. Or the whole thing might have been a brother's jest to a brother. We have no way of knowing.

Of more significance is the fact that Beethoven was now known across central Europe. He mixed not only with aristocracy, but royalty too. He was lauded wherever he went. His talent was unquestioned, his virtuosity unchallenged. Added to this he had something few other virtuosos could offer: he was composing. Composition after composition flowed from him, in all genres, from the lightweight to the seriously heavy. Publishers were clamouring for new work. He had concertos under his belt, sonatas for a variety of instruments, trios, a quintet, a septet.

He was about to embark on a musical form considered the purest, and of which in later years he would prove to be master: the string quartet. There was one other form, considered the noblest and most elevated in all music, at which he had tried his hand, made many notes and sketches, but had not yet produced a complete work: the symphony. That was about to change.

In short, at the age of twenty-six, with a successful tour behind him, compositions to his name, a reputation already unrivalled in Vienna, he had achieved a golden start to what promised to be a long and glittering career.

What could possibly go wrong? Only the single most disastrous fate that could possibly befall a musician. When it started, how it started, is not known. All we know for certain is that in the summer of 1797 things go quiet. Beethoven attended a concert on 6 April, at which his Piano Quintet in E flat, Op. 16, was given its first performance. In the same month, bizarrely, a nobleman presented him with a horse as a thank you for the dedication of a composition to his wife. Beethoven apparently rode the animal just a few times before forgetting about it. The next positive occurrence is a letter Beethoven wrote, dated 1 October. Between the two dates, nothing.

There is anecdotal evidence that around this time Beethoven took a long walk, returned home sweating profusely, stripped to his underwear, opened all doors and windows, and stood in a chill draught. This led to the onset of serious illness.* No more is known. If it is true, it is likely that Beethoven closeted himself away. His old friend Dr Wegeler had left Vienna, and he would have been reluctant to confide in anyone else.

More credible is an account written many years later by a surgeon who knew Beethoven, that the composer earlier in life – he did not specify when – 'endured a frightful attack of typhus', and that this was the cause of the terrible fate that befell him.†

Beethoven was beginning to lose his hearing.

---

* The source is thought to be Beethoven's friend Nikolaus Zmeskall, but it is second hand, unverifiable, and gives the date of 1796, which, given that Beethoven was in Berlin, seems impossible.

† 'Typhus' in German translates today as 'typhoid fever'. We cannot be sure what range of complaints the word covered two centuries ago, hence it is impossible to be precise about what illness Beethoven suffered.

Chapter 6

My Poor Hearing Haunts Me

But there is 'a dear charming girl who loves me'

For some time he tried to hide it. There is no record of Beethoven consulting a doctor for another three years, possibly more. Undoubtedly there would have been more than an element of self-denial involved. It is easy to understand why he would refuse to accept that such an appalling fate had befallen him. Certainly to begin with he is likely to have expected it to clear, to wake up one morning and find it was nothing more than a blockage, and he could get on with his life.

Getting on with his life is what he did. He composed intensively, producing works of greater complexity than ever before. After a rather fraught creative process, he composed a set of six string quartets. His Piano Sonata in C minor, Op. 13, the 'Pathétique', was a huge leap forward from any previous piano sonata, by him or anybody else. And finally, somewhat late in life for a young prodigy, he completed his First Symphony. There were other smaller works too.

He was active on a social level as well. He met the French Ambassador in Vienna, the Napoleonic General Bernadotte (later to become King of Sweden). He gave a recital with the Italian double-bass virtuoso Domenico Dragonetti, impressed that Dragonetti was able to perform one of his cello sonatas on the double-bass.* He became closely acquainted with the pianist and composer Johann Baptist Cramer. Also during this time he met and corresponded with friends. There are countless notes to his good friend Nikolaus Zmeskall, some of them written with considerable humour, setting up drinking sessions at local taverns.

Nowhere, either in his own writing or reported speech, or in the memoirs of any of his friends, is there any mention that he might be having a problem with his hearing. This lends credence to the notion that he was in some sort of denial, or that he genuinely believed it was temporary and would pass. In the early stages of deafness it is not difficult to cover up problems – a slight leaning forward of the head, a quick look at the lips of the person talking, a request to repeat what was said, even joking about losing your hearing, or saying you really must get your ears syringed. Clearly, whatever problem Beethoven might have been having, it was not affecting his musical activities, and that was what mattered most.

This became very clear in two events in the first few months of 1800, one private, one public. Perhaps surprisingly it is the private event that did more to cement Beethoven's reputation. It has done more than that: it has entered legend.

It was customary at that time in Vienna for aristocrats to stage 'improvisation contests' in their salons. The way it would work was that two virtuosos, with their supporters, would meet in a

---

* Dragonetti was unusually tall, and had an extra tall double-bass specially made for him, with just three strings. It hangs on a wall today in the Victoria and Albert Museum in London.

salon, and display their skills before an audience. This would involve playing their own compositions, possibly with an ensemble, and then setting tasks for each other. One would play a theme he had invented, which the other could not possibly have heard before, and improvise on it. The other would then go to the piano and try to emulate this. Then this second virtuoso would set a theme of his own invention, and the first player would have to copy that. Often it would involve imitation. If one pianist had a particular style, the other would imitate it. It was an evening's entertainment in aristocratic Vienna.

Very soon after his arrival in Vienna, when aristocrats such as Lichnowsky realised what young Beethoven was capable of, they put him up against the local talent, and one by one he saw them off, at the same time steadily enhancing his reputation. Enter Daniel Steibelt, from Berlin, capital of Prussia, a renowned piano virtuoso with a fearsome reputation. Steibelt had stunned salon audiences in Berlin with his extraordinary virtuosity, enhanced by his trademark flourish, the *tremolando*.* Now on a tour of European capitals, he had arrived in Vienna to conquer that city's sophisticated musical cognoscenti. He brought with him something of a dashing reputation. He had been forced to join the Prussian army by his father, but had deserted to pursue a musical career.†

It seems some of Beethoven's friends went to hear Steibelt and were stunned at his virtuosity, to such an extent that they feared he might damage Beethoven's reputation. This is probably why Beethoven, by now sick of these showcase events designed solely

---

* The rapid alternation of notes to create tension and drive, honed to perfection a century or more later with the piano accompaniment to silent movies.

† In his lifetime he would compose several ballets and operas, eight piano concertos, and nearly five hundred chamber works.

for the amusement of aristocrats, agreed to go along to the home of Count von Fries. He decided that he would play his recently published Trio for piano, clarinet and cello, which he had dedicated to Prince Lichnowsky's mother-in-law.* Steibelt brought along four musicians to perform his Piano Quintet.

The company assembled, including no doubt Prince Lichnowsky and his family. Beethoven and his musicians played first. His Trio was perhaps a slightly odd choice, since the piano part does not call for a particularly high degree of virtuosity. The work is in three movements, is fairly straightforward, and the critics welcomed it as being more easily comprehensible than the earlier published Op. 1 Piano Trios. The final movement is a set of variations on a well-known theme from a comic opera which had recently played successfully in Vienna.

There was polite applause from the salon audience, including Steibelt, who had listened 'with a certain condescension', and made a show of complimenting Beethoven. He took his position, with his musicians, in front of the audience, confident his Quintet would put Beethoven's Trio in the shade and win the day. To make sure, he added some impressive (no doubt prepared) improvisation, and drew gasps from the audience with his audacious *tremolandos*.

At the end there was no doubt in anyone's mind who had put on the more impressive display. All eyes turned to Beethoven, who as was usual at these events had the 'right of reply'. Beethoven remained stubbornly in his seat and refused to play again. Steibelt had carried the day.

A week later it was decided to repeat the event, to stage a 'rematch'. Given that Beethoven had been reluctant to attend the

---

* Countess Marie Wilhelmine von Thun, who on one occasion got on bended knee to beg Beethoven to play for her. He refused.

earlier evening, we can only assume his blood was up. Steibelt's condescending behaviour, not to mention his ridiculously showy playing, had got under Beethoven's skin. He was out for revenge.

There must have been an air of tension and anticipation in Count Fries's salon on this second evening. Beethoven's unpredictable temperament was well known. Everybody knew he had been bested a week earlier, and they would have seen the flare in his eyes and the set of his jaw. This spelled trouble.

Steibelt went first this time. He performed another of his quintets, which again met with great approval. Then he once again improvised on the piano, in a way that put his previous performance in the shade. It was brilliant. But he made a mistake, a serious mistake. There were gasps from the audience as they realised he had chosen the theme from the final movement of Beethoven's own Trio, performed at the previous meeting, on which to improvise.

If the audience was shocked, Beethoven's friends were appalled. That was nothing to how Beethoven felt. This time he needed no encouragement. He got out of his seat, stormed to the front, and as he passed the music stands snatched up the cello part of Steibelt's Quintet. He sat roughly on the stool, all thoughts of salon etiquette gone, and made a show of putting the cello part on the piano stand *upside-down*.

He glared at the music, playing now to the audience, knowing he had everyone's attention, aware that the decisive moment in the 'Contest Beethoven v. Steibelt' had come. With one finger he hammered out a series of notes from the first bar of Steibelt's music. He made it sound exactly what it was: crude and unsophisticated. He then began to improvise. And boy, did he improvise. He imitated Steibelt's playing, he unpicked it and put it back together again, he played some *tremolandos*, emphasising their absurdity. He played in a way no salon audience had heard before, and that Steibelt could not have believed was humanly possible.

It is easy to picture that powerful head, hair untamed, clothes inappropriate, fingers moving in a blur, no doubt singing, shouting, quite possibly hurling insults at the Prussian, who was probably sitting, back erect, powdered wig in place, clothes perfectly fitting, fingers curling tighter and tighter, as he realised he was not just being outplayed, he was being humiliated – in front of the most sophisticated musical gathering in the most sophisticated musical city in Europe.

Steibelt did not sit that way for long. With Beethoven still playing, he rose from his chair and strode out of the salon. He made it clear he never wanted to meet Beethoven again, and that if ever he was invited to perform again in Vienna, he would do so only if Beethoven was not present. In fact he took even more drastic action than that. He abandoned his tour and returned to Berlin to nurse his wounds. Some years later he went to St Petersburg and remained there for the rest of his life. He never returned to Vienna, and never met Beethoven again.

As for Beethoven, he was now – if there was any doubt before – the undisputed master of the keyboard in Vienna, if not Europe. Even Hummel, greatly admired, could not touch him. And following the drubbing of Steibelt, Beethoven was never again asked to take part in an improvisation contest. His position as Vienna's supreme piano virtuoso was established once and for all.

The public event that had a profound impact on Beethoven's life took place on 2 April 1800, and, if less dramatic than the Steibelt encounter, was of much more importance to Beethoven. It marked his coming of age as a composer, and we should remember that it was as aspiring composer that the young man had come to Vienna; it was as composer that he wanted to make his name, as composer that he wished to earn his place in musical history. Demonstrating his skills at the keyboard was merely the means to that end.

After much lobbying, and a little bit of bribery (the dedication of the two Piano Sonatas, Op. 14, to his wife), Baron von Braun, manager of the imperial court theatres, allowed Beethoven the use of the Burgtheater for a benefit concert, his first in Vienna. This favour was never granted lightly, since it involved no profit for the theatre – after expenses, all profit accrued to the composer – indeed a couple of years later Beethoven was to fall out with Braun when he refused a second benefit concert (despite further similar bribes).

A benefit concert was hard work. It was customary for the beneficiary to decide the programme, naturally, but also calculate ticket prices, and even sell them from his own home. It was his job to hire musicians, arrange rehearsals, have posters and flyers printed and arrange for their distribution. As near to a full house as possible was imperative. It was unusual for a benefit concert to provide much profit, even with a full house, but it was a way of attracting the critics' attention, and – it was hoped – approval. Reputations could be made, and the reverse. All in all, a benefit concert – and this would not be Beethoven's last – was a calculated risk, but on balance worth taking.

Interestingly Beethoven, aged twenty-nine and with his reputation as the city's supreme piano virtuoso unassailably established, still lacked the confidence to stage a concert of his works alone. And so, as well as his newly completed Septet, First Symphony, and piano concerto (it's not known which of the two), he programmed a Mozart symphony, and two pieces from Haydn's oratorio *The Creation*. For good measure he threw in what he knew he was best at, a guaranteed audience pleaser: 'Herr Ludwig van Beethoven will improvise on the pianoforte.' A long concert, but not unusually so for the time, which was programmed to start at 6.30 p.m.

It was not a success, or at the best had a mixed result. Again, not for the last time in his career, there were disagreements over who was to conduct, with Beethoven favouring one, but the orchestra refusing to play under him and preferring another. There was also clearly not enough rehearsal, since in the piano concerto, according to the *Allgemeine musikalische Zeitung*, 'the players did not bother to pay any attention to the soloist, and in the symphony they became so lax that no effort on the part of the conductor could drag any fire out of them, particularly the wind instruments'.*

Consolation of a sort was that the newspaper's critic thought the piano concerto had 'a great deal of taste and feeling', and that the symphony contained 'considerable art, novelty, and a wealth of ideas'. We do not know what the critic thought of the Septet, but according to Czerny it became so popular so fast that Beethoven could not bear to hear it!

Far from being discouraged, Beethoven threw himself into more composing. He embarked on another symphony (his Second), setting that aside to work on a commission for a ballet, *Die Geschöpfe des Prometheus* (*The Creatures of Prometheus*).† He also composed more piano sonatas and a violin sonata.

---

* It was the wind players in Bonn who considered the two cantatas unplayable. What was it about nineteenth-century wind players?

† There was some disappointment that the expected lead female dancer was replaced, after causing a stir the previous time she appeared with her 'lavish display of the Venus-like graces and charms of her exquisite form'. She wore a flesh-coloured costume, which gave the impression she was naked.

But there was no escaping the cloud hanging over him, the dreadful affliction that was beginning to affect every aspect of his life, which instead of improving or magically disappearing, was worsening. What should he do? What could be done?

Suddenly, unexpectedly, Beethoven' closest friend from his Bonn days, his childhood – even closer than Wegeler – Stephan von Breuning, arrived in Vienna. It was a sad development that brought him. Elector Maximilian Franz, who had made it possible for Beethoven to come to Vienna, was in ailing health, and the Teutonic Order considered it prudent to appoint a successor, should the worst happen. This meant convening a Grand Chapter in Vienna. Stephan, now a qualified lawyer working for the Order, came to Vienna to attend the meeting. In the event he took a job at the War Ministry in Vienna and remained in the city for the rest of his life. He will feature many more times in these pages, as Beethoven's closest, and albeit with severe disruptions, most constant friend.

Although I can offer no proof of this, I believe it was Stephan's arrival in Vienna that unlocked Beethoven's denial of his deafness. At last there was someone he could confide in, and trust. If he told Stephan to say nothing to anyone, he could rely on Stephan to comply. I imagine the two old friends sitting up late into the night as Beethoven brings Stephan up to date on his musical activities, the concerts, salon recitals, the relative merits, pianistic and otherwise, of his young female pupils, and then pours his heart out over his encroaching deafness. I imagine Stephan's horror, no doubt diplomatically concealed, and even discreet attempts to ascertain how bad the problem was by speaking ever more quietly. He would soon have realised that it was serious.

We know the two men were overjoyed to meet up again, and spent a lot of time together. In a letter dated 29 June 1801, Beethoven writes:

> *Steffen* * *Breuning is now in Vienna and we meet almost every day. It does me good to revive the old feelings of friendship. He really has become an excellent, splendid fellow, who is well informed and who, like all of us more or less, has his heart in the right place.*

Ah yes, that letter. It can lay claim to being the most important letter Beethoven wrote among the thousands of letters and notes he wrote in his entire life, because as far as we know it was the first time Beethoven set down on paper that he was having a problem with his hearing.

It was written to Dr Franz Wegeler. No surprise, then, that he chose to reveal this intimate detail to an old childhood friend who was now a qualified doctor. To begin with he beats about the bush a bit, writing about how much he would love to see Father Rhine again, talking about his earnings from composition, and concerts he has given and hopes to give. Then, out of the blue, without so much as a new paragraph, this:

> *But that jealous demon, my wretched health, has put a nasty spoke in my wheel, and it amounts to this, that for the last three years my hearing has become weaker and weaker.*

He then talks of his health in general, and absurd remedies various doctors have given him – evidence that he has at least begun

---

* Diminutive of Stephan.

seeking medical advice – which might have helped his diarrhoea and colic, but has done nothing to improve his hearing, as they assured him would happen.

Then, a few sentences later:

> *My ears continue to hum and buzz day and night. I must confess that I lead a miserable life. For almost two years I have ceased to attend any social functions, simply because I find it impossible to say to people: I am deaf. If I had any other profession I might be able to cope with my infirmity. But in my profession it is a terrible handicap … As for the spoken voice, it is surprising that some people have never noticed my deafness. But since I have always been liable to fits of absent-mindedness, they attribute my hardness of hearing to that. Sometimes I can scarcely hear a person who speaks softly. I can hear sounds, it is true, but cannot make out the words. But if anyone shouts, I can't bear it. Heaven alone knows what is to become of me.*

This is absolutely remarkable. For a start he gives a graphic description of his symptoms. Secondly he acknowledges how much more devastating this is for a musician than for anyone else. Thirdly, he provides evidence he has tried to conceal the problem, and – arguably most remarkable of all – he admits not only to absent-mindedness, but to the fact that everybody knows he's absent-minded!

Only in the privacy of a letter to an old and much trusted friend could we expect someone of Beethoven's character to pour his heart out like that. It is more than a *cri de cœur*, it is an act of self-confession.

Unsurprisingly he begs Wegeler to say nothing to anyone

about his deafness, not even to Lorchen,* but urges him to write to the doctor he is currently seeing in Vienna. We do not know whether Wegeler did.

One other nice detail. Beethoven asks Wegeler to send the portrait of his grandfather, the *Kapellmeister*, to him in Vienna. This is the painting Beethoven knew as a child, and that his father pawned. This Wegeler did. Beethoven treasured it, and it hung on the wall of every apartment he lived in until his death.

We owe Wegeler an enormous debt of gratitude for preserving the letter. Sadly, Beethoven was not as careful with the letter that Wegeler wrote in reply. None survives. But we know he replied, because Beethoven wrote again to him five months later, and began by thanking him for his concern, and saying he was applying herbs to his belly, as Wegeler recommended.

This is another remarkable letter, for two very different reasons. First, taken with the earlier letter, it gives an extraordinary insight into just what the doctors in Vienna were putting him through. One prescribed cold baths, another warm baths. A third put almond oil in his ears, which made his hearing even worse. There was a suggestion that he try a new-fangled technique called Galvinism, though there is no evidence he actually did. The doctor who prescribed warm baths, a distinguished army surgeon, whose daughter Stephan von Breuning was to marry, then came up with something entirely novel.

He soaked the bark of the poisonous plant *Daphne mezereum* in water, strapped it to Beethoven's arms, and told him to allow the bark to dry. As it dried, it shrank, tightening the skin underneath and causing blisters to form. These the doctor lanced – to relieve Beethoven's deafness. It might have failed to achieve that

---

* Eleonore von Breuning, shortly to become Wegeler's wife.

(although Beethoven writes that he cannot deny the humming and buzzing in his ears was slightly less), but what it did do was cause Beethoven enormous pain in his arms, and make playing the piano impossible. He soon gave it – and the doctor – up.

The second reason this letter is important is that it contains a sentence so extraordinary, so unexpected, that you really do have to read it several times to make sure it says what you think it says. There he is, writing about his hearing problems again, when suddenly ...

> *My poor hearing haunted me everywhere like a ghost, and I avoided – all human society. I seemed to be a misanthrope, but I really am not one any longer. This change has been brought about by a dear charming girl who loves me and whom I love. After two years I am again enjoying a few blissful moments, and for the first time I feel that – marriage might bring me happiness. Unfortunately she is not of my class – and at the moment – I certainly could not marry – I really am far too busy bustling about ...*

Beethoven was in love! Despite all his problems, health and otherwise, the thought of marriage was on his mind, though the letter rambles on in some detail about his work and problems without mentioning love or marriage again.*

So who was the object of his affections, the young woman whom he considered below his class, and who he believed was as much in love with him as he was with her? The evidence

---

* It does contain one memorable passage, beloved of biographers when describing Beethoven's character: 'I will seize Fate by the throat – I shall not allow it to bend or crush me completely.'

points conclusively to one of his pupils, Countess Giulietta (Julia) Guicciardi, aged sixteen in 1801. His description of her as being beneath him socially seems somewhat disingenuous. Her father was a senior Austrian civil servant at the Austro-Bohemian court chancellery in Vienna, and her mother closely related to the aristocratic Hungarian family Brunsvik (who will feature again in these pages).

What certainly is true is that the Guicciardi family was not particularly well off, did not move in the same social strata as Beethoven's patrons, and would certainly have derived some cachet from the famous composer's obvious attraction to Julia. We know few details about the progress of the romance, or whether it really was a mutual attraction. But Thayer, who evidently spoke to people in Vienna who had direct knowledge, albeit many years after the event, states that it is his opinion that Beethoven went so far as to propose marriage, and that Julia was 'not indisposed' to accept it, that her mother was in favour of the match, but that her father forbade it on the grounds that Beethoven was

> *a man without rank, fortune, or permanent engagement; a man, too, of character and temperament so peculiar, and afflicted with the incipient stages of an infirmity which, if not arrested and cured, must deprive him of all hope of obtaining any high and remunerative official appointment, and at length compel him to abandon his career as the great pianoforte virtuoso.*

Another painful rejection, then, for Beethoven, no doubt made worse by the knowledge that his deafness lay behind it, and that his affliction was now common knowledge.

As for Julia, she went on to marry a mediocre musician by the name of Count Gallenberg, with whom she moved to Italy.* Her place in history is assured, though, through Beethoven's decision to dedicate his new piano sonata to her, a sonata published under the title 'Sonata quasi una fantasia', but known to us today – thanks to a music critic who compared it to the moon setting over Lake Lucerne – as the 'Moonlight' Sonata.

Once again Beethoven's deafness had stood in the way of his aspirations, in this case desires and longing of the most personal kind. How long would it be before this dreadful affliction began to affect his life's work, his *raison d'être*, his calling, the sole path he was capable of pursuing?

And then, in early 1802, one of his doctors, Dr Johann Adam Schmidt, came up with the only sensible suggestion any doctor ever made to him. He advised Beethoven to get out of Vienna, to leave the dust and dirt and bustle of the city behind, to free his ears of the rasping jangle of carriage wheels grinding over uneven cobbles, to distance himself from the demands of publishers, to go somewhere where his hearing loss would not be an obvious

---

* Gallenberg turned out to be impotent. For this reason he allowed Julia to take a lover, Count von Schulenburg, with whom she had one illegitimate son and four illegitimate daughters. For this information I am indebted to Lady Pia Chelwood, née von Roretz, who is the great-great-granddaughter of the illegitimate son of Julia and Schulenburg. Lady Chelwood, born into Austrian nobility whose family seat is at Breiteneich in Austria, is widow of the former Conservative MP Sir Tufton Beamish, later Lord Chelwood, and currently resides in East Sussex. She has in her home a marble bust of Julia sculpted from life. Sadly, Lady Chelwood died in February 2019 at the age of ninety-six.

problem, not lead to questioning and veiled comment. And also to allow him to put the pain of marital rejection behind him. In short, to rest, relax, and compose.

Dr Schmidt had a friend who owned a small cottage for rent in a small village north of the city, known for its warm springs, its gently meandering stream, its woodland, its calm. The name of the village was Heiligenstadt.

Chapter 7

Only My Art Held Me Back

In which Beethoven considers suicide

The Beethoven who arrived in Heiligenstadt in April 1802 was a very different man from that of two years earlier. Then, he was the undisputed supreme piano virtuoso in the city; he had staged his first benefit concert, which even with mixed results established him firmly as the city's leading composer (a mantle the ageing Haydn was quite content to cede), and he was falling in love with a girl who appeared to be reciprocating his interest. There was a problem with his hearing, certainly, but several doctors were trying to tackle it, at the same time assuring him it was only a matter of time before the problem was solved.

Two years on, and Baron Braun had reneged on his promise of a second benefit concert (despite the inducement of more dedications), his amorous ambitions had been quashed, and his deafness was worse. In fact it had become so much worse that he had finally lost faith in his doctors, and now believed nothing would stop the deterioration. If the best that medicine could come up with was a recommendation to take a break, it showed there was nothing more that science could offer.

In one sense, getting away for a break was the last thing Beethoven needed. He would be on his own in a small cottage – no one to converse with, eat and drink with, step out to the tavern with. He would have hour upon hour in which to brood, which would lead him naturally to magnify his problems. If he arrived depressed, that was likely to become worse as the weeks passed.

On the other hand, Beethoven liked solitude. There are countless anecdotes of how he would be oblivious to everything around him while composing, how his favourite activity was to walk for hours across country, beating time to imaginary sounds in his head, stopping to jot down thoughts on scraps of paper. If nothing else, he would have time to compose without distraction.

And compose he did. He brought his Second Symphony to fruition, and embarked on new piano sonatas and piano variations.*
Also, Heiligenstadt was only an hour's carriage ride from the city – it was not unreasonable to expect visits from family and friends.

That is what happened. Brother Carl, who was now handling his elder brother's business affairs – upsetting publishers with demands for ever larger amounts of money – came to see Beethoven to discuss a commission for new piano sonatas from a Swiss publisher. And Ferdinand Ries had arrived in Vienna a few months earlier and was proving himself invaluable to Beethoven.

Ries was the son of the leader of the electoral orchestra in Bonn, Franz Ries, who had given Beethoven violin lessons. He was fourteen years younger than Beethoven, and as a tousle-haired boy had been sent by his father to the teenage Beethoven for piano lessons. Their friendship thus went back a long way, and

---

* It has been suggested that the opening four notes of the Piano Variations, Op. 35, are taken from the first bar of Steibelt's music, when turned upside-down!

only the age difference prevented Ries being as close a friend to Beethoven as Wegeler and Stephan von Breuning.

With the French occupying the Rhineland, young men were being enlisted to fight alongside the French. But Ries had a problem with vision in one eye, and needed to wear an eye patch. This exempted him from service.

Ries had shown remarkable musical talent very early in life, and his father sent him to Vienna in 1801 to further his career.[*] He wrote to Beethoven asking him to look out for his son. In the event Ries, who was totally dedicated to Beethoven, did far more for him, acting as secretary, helper, assistant, and endured all his moods and vicissitudes with patient good grace. His memoirs, written with Wegeler, provide unique insights into Beethoven. Indeed it is his report of one incident, which almost certainly took place in Heiligenstadt, that provides stark and graphic evidence of just how far Beethoven's deafness had progressed.

One beautiful morning, after breakfast, Beethoven suggested he and Ries take a walk in the surrounding countryside. At one point Ries drew Beethoven's attention to a shepherd in amongst the trees who was playing sweetly on a flute made from lilac wood. Beethoven could not hear him. They stayed in the same spot for half an hour, but still Beethoven could not hear the sounds of the flute. Ries remarks that Beethoven became extremely quiet and gloomy. He assured Beethoven that he couldn't hear the flute either (which wasn't true), but it did nothing to lift his mood.

Fleshing out the bare detail Ries gives us, we can imagine that

---

[*] Ries went on to become an admired musical administrator, and as composer he wrote dozens of pieces, including symphonies, piano concertos, oratorios and chamber pieces, none of which has remained in the repertoire.

both men could see the shepherd, that Beethoven strained to hear, changed his position, walked a bit nearer, retreated again, but after half an hour of this, still nothing. Ries writes that Breuning had told him in Vienna that Beethoven was having problems, but this was graphic evidence of the seriousness of it.

In a final line to the anecdote, Ries writes that when Beethoven was occasionally really happy, he could be almost boisterous, 'but this rarely happened'.

Ries must have worried about leaving Beethoven alone in the cottage, and probably tried to persuade him to return to the city. But Beethoven was staying put. At least Ries knew he was composing, so his creativity was not being affected by loneliness or worry over his hearing. Even if he had not been able to hear the shepherd, he was still able to hear the piano in his room and the sounds of music in his head.

Also Ries knew he was comfortable. The cottage had a housekeeper and daughter who between them provided Beethoven with all his meals, and kept his room tidy. The cottage was beautifully situated, with windows looking out on a stream, fields and woods in one direction, and towards St Michael's Church in the other.* Ries knew too that Beethoven paid frequent visits to the spa, basking in the natural warm waters that welled up from below. It might not help his deafness, but it would certainly improve his well-being.

Beethoven's stay was not planned with a definite departure date, but probably no one – himself included – expected him to stay beyond the summer. In the event he stayed a full six months, not leaving until mid-October. During the final few weeks an extraordinary change came over him.

---

* A statue of Beethoven today stands outside St Michael's Church.

As summer gave way to autumn and the evenings became longer, so Beethoven withdrew within himself. He carefully and methodically weighed up where he was in life, what was happening to him, what was likely to happen in the future. It resulted in a remarkable decision, one that he could have allowed to plunge him even further into despair. Instead, it had quite the opposite effect.

He decided, at the age of thirty-one and three-quarters, to write his Last Will and Testament.

This is such an extraordinary document, raising questions as well as answering them, that it merits close analysis. It is, for biographers, scholars, musicologists, indeed for any lover of Beethoven's music who wants to understand him better, the single most important piece of writing he ever produced that was not in the form of musical notes. Here it is in full:

For my brothers – Carl – and — Beethoven
Oh all you people who think and say that I am hostile to you, or that I am stubborn, or that I hate mankind, you do not realise the wrong that you do me. You think you understand, but you do not know the secret cause of my seeming that way. From my childhood on, my heart and mind were disposed only towards tenderness and goodwill. I even knew I was destined to accomplish great deeds. But consider this: for the last six years I have suffered from a terrible condition, made worse by stupid doctors, yet hoping from one year to the next that it would improve, but finally realising that I'd been deceived, that I would have to face the prospect of <u>a lasting malady</u> (at least that it would take many years to be cured, or even that it might never be). Born with an ardent and lively temperament, from an early age I had to cut myself off from society in all its diversity and lead my own life. And if from

time to time I wanted more than anything not to have to do that, oh how hard I had to fight against the dreadful consequences of my poor hearing. And I wasn't yet in a position where I could say to people: Speak louder, shout, for I am deaf. Ah, how could I possibly explain that I was deficient in the <u>one sense</u> that should have been more highly developed in me than anyone, a sense that I was once in full possession of, to an extent in fact that few in my profession are or ever were? Oh I cannot do it, so forgive me when you see me shrink back, although I really want to mingle with you. My misfortune is doubly bad, because through it people misjudge me. For me there can be no enjoyment in other men's company, no stimulating conversations or exchange of ideas. I must be totally alone, except in cases of the direst emergency. I must live like an exile. If I go near to a group of people I am overcome with anxiety, and I am frightened I will be put in a position where my condition will be noticed. And so I was told by my one sensible doctor to spend these few months in the country, to rest my hearing as much as possible. Occasionally – albeit against my natural disposition – I have wished to have company. I have on occasions yielded to the temptation. But what a humiliation when someone next to me heard a flute in the distance and I heard nothing, or someone <u>heard the shepherd sing</u>, and again I heard nothing. Such things have brought me near to despair. Only a little more and I would even have ended my life. Only <u>my art</u>, that is all that held me back. It would have been impossible for me to leave this world until I had brought forth everything that was within me, and so I continued to eke out a miserable existence – truly miserable, my condition so sensitive, that a sudden change of mood could plunge me from happiness *into despair – <u>Patience</u> – that is what I must now let guide me, and what I have let guide me – I hope above all that I will be resolute enough to wait until pitiless fate determines to break the thread. Maybe my health will improve, maybe not. Whatever, I am prepared. Already in my 28th year I was forced to accept my fate, and that is not easy, in fact it is harder for an artist than for anybody. Divine One, you alone can see into my innermost soul. You understand me, you know that I love my fellow men and want only to do good. Oh my friends, when you read this understand that you did me an injustice, and should there exist in the world any man as unfortunate as I, let him comfort himself in the knowledge that, as I have done, he too can accomplish everything that is within his power, and be elevated into the ranks of worthy artists and great men. To you my brothers – Carl – and —, as soon as I am dead ask Professor Schmidt in my name, assuming he is still living, to describe my illness to you, and attach this document to my medical history, so that after my death, people might begin to understand just a little about me. Also I declare you both as the heirs to my small fortune (if it can be called that). Divide it fairly, be good friends and help each other. You know that whatever you did against me I have long since forgiven. You my brother Carl have my special thanks for the proven devotion you have shown me, especially of late. My wish is that you may both have a better more carefree life than I had. Teach your children <u>Virtue</u>, for it alone can bring them happiness, not money, and I speak from experience. It was Virtue which lifted me up when I was wretched. I owe it to Virtue, together with my art, that I did not end my own life. And so farewell and love one another. I thank all my friends, especially <u>Prince Lichnowsky</u>*

<u>and Professor Schmidt</u>. The instruments Prince L. gave me I wish to be kept by one of you. But do not quarrel over them, and if they can be of some use to you, go ahead and sell them. It makes me so happy to know I can help you, even from my grave – if that is to be the case, I would gladly hasten towards my death, and if it should come before I have been able to create all the art that I am capable of, then even given my harsh fate it will be too soon, and I will wish so much that it had come later – yet I shall still be satisfied, for will it not release me from my endless suffering? Come death when you will, I shall face you with courage. Farewell and forget me not when I am dead, for I deserve to be remembered, just as I so often remembered you during my life, and tried to make you happy: remain so –

Heiglnstadt [sic] Ludwig van Beethoven
on 6th October
1 8 0 2 [seal]

For my brothers Carl – and
To be read and executed after my death

Heiglnstadt [sic] on 10th October 1 8 0 2 – and so I bid thee farewell – with such sorrow – to think of the hope I had when I came here, that I might be cured even just very slightly – that hope I must now realise has abandoned me completely, as the leaves fall from the trees in autumn and fade away. Thus has – thus has my hope also withered, so that it is now no more than it was when I came here – but I will go on – even that Noble Courage – which so often inspired me in those beautiful days of summer – it has gone for ever – Oh Providence – let one last day of <u>pure joy</u> be granted me – for so long now the innermost echo of true joy has been denied

me – Oh when – Oh when Oh Divine One – shall I be able
to share it again with Nature and Mankind, –Never? – – no
– Oh that would be too cruel.*

The main body of the Will is written over two and a half pages, ending with signature and seal. The last part, beginning with instruction to his brothers, is written on the fourth page, but above the fold. It was clearly added as an afterthought, after he had finished and folded the document.

A straightforward Will, in one sense, leaving his effects to his brothers, but also a *cri de cœur*, full of self-pity one moment, defiance the next. Through it runs the single thread of his deafness. He has, finally, decided to confront it head on, to write about it, to think about it, to consider its effect on his artistic calling, to understand that for a musician it is a fatal defect. He talks about suicide, how he has considered it in the past but only his art held him back, how he holds it in reserve for the future. In his whole life, neither before or after, did he write a document of such intensely personal thoughts.

What, then, is it? One thing I am utterly convinced it is *not* is a suicide note. Yes, he talks about suicide, but he is clearly not about to commit it. His art, he says, saved him from taking his own life. 'Come death when you will, I shall face you with courage.' Not the words of a man about to take his own life. But they are the words of a man who might decide to take his own life one day. When might that be? When 'pitiless fate determines to break the thread'. And what might that mean? We have no clear answer, but I am convinced he is saying that when the day comes when he can no longer hear his own music, and to compose has become

---

* My translation.

impossible, *if* that day ever comes, then he will take matters into his own hands and obtain release from his 'endless suffering'.

We know now, of course, that that day never came, that he continued to compose to within days of his death twenty-five years later. He struggled, certainly, but he was still able to compose. That points to two factors, one intangible, one more practical. The courage that he speaks of in his Will never left him, for which he, and generations of human beings, can be grateful. It further suggests that he never totally lost his hearing. Something always got through, however distorted, right to the end.

Some commentators have seen the first line of the postscript, 'and so I bid thee farewell', where he suddenly slips into the more familiar, and poetic, 'thee', as an announcement of intended suicide. But in the original German, just as in the English translation, this is entirely ambiguous. He could just as easily be referring to the village of Heiligenstadt, which is altogether less dramatic.

There are several other points of interest concerning what is known to history as the Heiligenstadt Testament. The first, and most evident, anomaly is that he does not write his brother Nikolaus Johann's name. Those spaces are there in the original document. In fact it applies to Carl too, though he filled in the name later (it fits oddly into the space). What could this mean? Plenty, or nothing.

To take the 'plenty' explanation first. Both Beethoven's brothers, when they came to Vienna, decided to be known by their second name, thus Caspar Carl became Carl, and Nikolaus Johann became Johann. Beethoven clearly did not like this. It represented a break with the past of which he did not approve. He might also have considered it pretentious, and there might have been a twinge of jealousy in that he had only one Christian name and so could not do likewise. Also, as elder brother and head of the family, they should have consulted him first. Either they failed to do so, or if they did they ignored his objections.

Why, then, was he ultimately able to bring himself to write Carl's name, but not Johann's? Because Johann was the name of their father – the man Beethoven considered ruined his childhood, who dragged him from bed on his drunken return from the tavern and forced him to play the piano, who abused him verbally and very probably physically too by rapping him across the knuckles when he played a wrong note, who as he descended into alcoholism brought shame upon the family, whom Beethoven as a teenager had to rescue once from police jail, who made his wife's life a misery, and from whom Beethoven had finally managed to escape, and whose death probably came as something of a relief to his eldest son.

And here was his youngest brother consciously adopting the father's name! Probably because he knew the pain it would cause his eldest brother, and be some sort of revenge against the sibling who had inherited all the talent.

Given Beethoven's fraught relationship with both brothers in the years to come, this explanation, dramatic, even incomprehensible though it might seem, is not all that far-fetched.

The far simpler explanation is that since Beethoven was aware his Will was a quasi-legal document, he was not sure how to address his brothers, and would leave Johann's name out until he took legal advice on his return to Vienna.

Given the family history, coupled with Beethoven's character, I believe it is not unreasonable to subscribe to the 'plenty' theory.

A further point of interest is that, by Beethoven's standards, the document is remarkably neatly written. The handwriting is quite precise, the lines narrowly but tidily spaced. On the first page, roughly A4 size, he fits in no fewer than forty-five lines, on the second page forty-three. Despite the emotion of what he is writing, the stream of consciousness concerning intimate details of his life, the writing nowhere becomes ragged. It would be tempting to say he wrote it at several sittings, but the way the sentences flow into each other suggest a single sitting as far down as the signature. This is reinforced by the single date.

There are some ink blots at the top of page two, and one or two crossings out lower down both pages one and two, but nothing that would prevent this Will being accepted in law. It is, in fact, considerably neater than most of his musical manuscripts. He is clearly taking great care to make sure the document is legally valid.

It is very possible he tried out his wording first on other pieces of paper, and then copied them onto the final version. The punctuation, and individual sentences, suggest this. By contrast, the final paragraph on the folded page is redolent with dashes – nineteen in just fifteen lines, with only a handful of commas and no full stops – making it certain this was added at the last moment in a single unprepared sitting.

The final curiosity is that, on completing it, he folded the document twice, across the centre and then lengthways across the centre again, so that it was no wider than an envelope, and hid it. He not only hid it in his bag in Heiligenstadt, he hid it when he returned to Vienna, and kept it with him, hidden, for the rest of his life. He must have remembered it and seen it each time he moved apartment – more than sixty times, including summer sojourns, in the remaining years of his life – but he never told anybody about it, never consulted a lawyer about it, never attempted to have it enacted.

Now that really *is* curious.

These are all fascinating details, but ultimately they pale before the most important set of inferences the Heiligenstadt

Testament allows us to make about Beethoven's life. He had, at last, come to terms with his deafness. He had confronted it, and in a sense defeated it. He was now in control of it, not the other way round. He also no longer cared for it to be kept a secret. His deafness was now part of him. It was what he was. He was also now in control of his life. He would choose to end it when he thought fit. He alone would make that decision.

God gets barely a look in. The closest he comes is in the sentence: 'Divine One, you alone can see into my innermost soul.' But the word he uses is 'Gottheit', which properly translates as 'Divinity'. It is more nebulous, ethereal, than 'God'. And in the postscript he refers only to 'Providence' (*Vorsehung*), which is a spiritual power rather than a deity, and again to 'Gottheit'.

Beethoven has not only come to terms with, and therefore conquered, his deafness. He has taken control of his life. The Beethoven who arrived in Heiligenstadt six months earlier was to an extent a broken man. But the man who returned to the city had a new resolve. He still had much to give the world, and he was determined to go on doing that until it became impossible. He would no longer mourn for his loss of hearing. By writing the Testament he had buried it.

On returning to Vienna he said to Czerny, 'I am not very well satisfied with the work I have done thus far. From this day on I shall take a new way.'

And take a new way he most certainly did. He was about to embark on the richest period of his life, when the works that flowed from him were not just new, and different, but unlike anything any composer had written before. Not for nothing is it known as Beethoven's Heroic Period.

133

Chapter 8

Egyptian Hieroglyphics

Napoleon is no more than 'a common tyrant'

Beethoven, against all expectations – including his own – landed a job. In January 1803 he was appointed composer-in-residence at the Theater an der Wien, which, as the title implies, came with a small apartment in the theatre.

It's worth a brief detour to explain the background to this, particularly since it will introduce into the story – albeit briefly – one of those colourful figures that the world of the arts can occasionally throw up, and who, were it not for a fortunate set of circumstances, would have disappeared without trace. Instead they achieve a certain immortality.

Vienna, at the turn of the century, enjoyed an extremely healthy theatrical life. There were several theatres that came under imperial administration, headed by Baron von Braun; the most prestigious was the Burgtheater. There were also a number of independent theatres in direct competition with them, of which the most important (to our story as well) was the new Theater an der Wien.

Crucially, the Theater an der Wien – named for the small river that ran past it to the Danube Canal – stood outside the city wall, the Bastei. It was therefore suburban, which gave it an entirely different feel from the ambience of the imperial court theatres – more relaxed, more innovative, and favoured more by ordinary suburban people, rather than the nobility.* There were no purpose-built concert halls in Vienna as yet (London alone could boast that), and musicians had to compete with all other theatrical pursuits to secure a theatre – which is why Beethoven failed to obtain the Burgtheater for his second benefit concert.

The Theater an der Wien was built in 1800–1801 as the result of an unlikely collaboration between a wealthy businessman and a thoroughly eccentric theatre director whose elaborate and expensive productions had led to huge debts, which cost him his job at his previous theatre. The two men needed to do something quickly to establish their theatre, and they hit on works by the Paris-based Italian composer Luigi Cherubini. Just as they began to taste success, Braun travelled to Paris and signed up Cherubini exclusively to the court theatres.

And then the eccentric theatre director made the second decision of genius in his career. The first, for which the world remembers him today, was to write the libretto for Mozart's *The Magic Flute*, playing Papageno in the premiere. The second was to engage Beethoven as composer-in-residence at the Theater an der Wien – all the greater stroke of genius since what he wanted was opera, and Beethoven had not as yet composed one.

Beethoven was about to embark on the most important creative period of his life to date, producing works that would echo

---

* It remains thus today, staging mainly musicals, although it is no longer suburban and the Wien now runs several metres below the street. The fruit and vegetable market that lined the river bank opposite the theatre two centuries ago is now a covered market, offering everything from fruit and vegetables to fast food and clothing.

down the centuries. To a large extent, we owe the somewhat care-free conditions in which he was able to do this to a man who was 'a strange compound of wit and absurdity, of poetic instinct and grotesque humour, of shrewd and profitable enterprise and lavish prodigality, who lived like a prince and was to die like a pauper' – but not before the name of Emanuel Schikaneder became forever linked with two immortals of music.

There was a small downside to the accommodation in the Theater an der Wien that came with the job. Beethoven's brother Carl moved in with him. We do not know which of the two brothers was the instigator of this, but given Beethoven's antagonism towards both his brothers, it cannot have made for harmonious living. Carl was now more and more running his elder brother's business affairs, and making enemies in the process. He even managed to upset the publisher Simrock, a friend of Beethoven from his Bonn days, who described Carl's demands as 'impertinent and incorrigible'.

But whatever fraternal tension there might have been in the small apartment in the Theater an der Wien, there was no stopping Beethoven's creativity. He had now completed his Third Piano Concerto, and had composed an oratorio, *Christus am Ölberge* (*Christ on the Mount of Olives*).

An immediate bonus of his new job was a benefit concert on 5 April 1803 in the Theater an der Wien – a sort of public snub to Baron Braun and the imperial court theatres. This time he needed to do no persuading, no cajoling; the theatre was his, and he could perform any programme he wished. He did not hold back. He put together a programme so ambitious, with so little time to rehearse, it was almost doomed from the start. In fact, so ad hoc was the whole thing that the announcements in the press advertising the concert stated only that Beethoven would produce his *Christus am Ölberge*, the other pieces to be performed being announced later on posters.

No complete programme has survived, but we know that Beethoven intended giving his First Symphony, the premiere of his Second Symphony, the premiere of his Third Piano Concerto, and the premiere of his oratorio *Christus*. It is also highly likely he planned to interject some vocal pieces as well. Nothing if not ambitious. And, as was not unusual with Beethoven, preparations continued right up until the last minute.

On the morning of the concert, at around 5 a.m., he summoned Ries, who gives a compelling account of what he found. Beethoven was sitting up in bed, writing on separate sheets of manuscript paper. Ries asked him what it was he wanted. He replied that he was adding trombones to the score of *Christus*. Ries was dumbfounded. The final rehearsal was due to begin at 8 a.m. Though Ries does not say so, he must have remonstrated as tactfully as he could with Beethoven, pointing out that it was surely too late to add an entirely new instrumental section to the orchestra. For one thing, there was no time for the copyists to write out the parts, and in any case where on earth would they be able to find trombonists at three hours' notice so early in the morning?

Beethoven was adamant: he wanted trombonists, and I imagine Ries scouring the city at dawn to find them. Find them he did, and at the performance in the evening they played from Beethoven's handwritten manuscript sheets!

Before that there was the rehearsal, and it was, unsurprisingly, a disaster. Beethoven drove the musicians for hour after hour, until by 2.30 p.m. they were exhausted. Fortunately Prince Lichnowsky – possibly alerted by Ries, who sensed problems – attended the rehearsal from the start, and ordered bread and butter, cold meat and wine, to be brought in large baskets. He invited the musicians to help themselves which, according to Ries, they did 'with both hands', re-establishing good feelings – good enough, in fact, to risk one more rehearsal of the oratorio at Lichnowsky's urging.

The concert began at six o'clock, but threatened to be so long that several pieces were omitted. Definitely performed were the First and Second Symphonies, the Third Piano Concerto, and *Christus am Ölberge*.

The concert master of the theatre, Ignaz Seyfried, later wrote a fascinating account of the performance of the piano concerto, which gives a wonderful insight into the chaotic working mind of the towering genius that is Beethoven.

Beethoven asked Seyfried to turn the pages for him. But, 'as was so often the case', says Seyfried, Beethoven had not had time to put it all down on paper. Seyfried's blood ran cold when he looked at the piano part on the stand and saw almost nothing but empty sheets of paper. 'At the most on one page or the other a few Egyptian hieroglyphics which were wholly unintelligible to me, scribbled down to serve as clues for him ... He gave me a secret glance whenever he was at the end of one of the invisible passages, and my scarcely concealable anxiety not to miss the decisive moment amused him greatly, and he laughed heartily at the jovial supper which we ate afterwards.'

Which, if nothing else, demonstrates that Beethoven was capable of a sense of humour at least after the event. Seyfried lived with the memory for years to come. To this day I cannot hear the Third Piano Concerto without thinking of the hapless Seyfried and Beethoven's 'Egyptian hieroglyphics'.

The good humour at the post-concert supper probably dissipated when the reviews came out. The *Freymüthige* found the two symphonies, and certain passages in the oratorio, very beautiful, but thought the oratorio 'too long, too artificial in structure, and lacking expressiveness, especially in the vocal parts'. The *Zeitung für die elegante Welt* liked the First Symphony, but thought the Second strived too hard to be new and surprising. It also said Beethoven's performance of the Third Piano Concerto was 'not completely to the public's satisfaction'. But Ries would have been pleased to read that the paper particularly liked the Seraph's air in the *Christus*, with trombone accompaniment which 'in particular makes an excellent effect'.

Some concert-goers were harsher even than the critics, and prepared to say so publicly. Angry that the *Allgemeine musikalische Zeitung*, the most respected of the musical journals, described the *Christus* as having been received with 'extraordinary approval', even opining with remarkable foresight that Beethoven in time could 'effect a revolution in music like Mozart's', a correspondent wrote to the paper flatly contradicting this. 'In the interest of truth, I am obliged to contradict the report ... Beethoven's cantata did not please.'

Interestingly Beethoven himself somewhat rejected the oratorio and was later to make substantial changes to it. Possibly the criticism was offset by the fact that he made a clear profit of 1800 florins on the evening, a substantial sum. His residency at the Theater an der Wien had therefore got off to a solid financial start, even if the musical results were somewhat mixed.

Not one to learn from his mistakes, Beethoven again ran things very tight at a smaller-scale, but highly prestigious, recital just a few weeks later. A brilliant young violinist arrived in Vienna from England, by the name of George Bridgetower. Poor George Bridgetower. Rather like Schikaneder, his brush with the greatest living musician looked set to immortalise him too, but alas it was not to be.

Bridgetower, son of an African father and Polish (or German) mother, had established a fine reputation for himself, being employed by the Prince of Wales, and remaining in his employ when he succeeded to the throne as George IV. His letter of introduction on arriving in Vienna gained him access to the highest salons, and Prince Lichnowsky introduced him to Beethoven.

Beethoven heard Bridgetower play, almost certainly accompanying him on the piano, and was seriously impressed. A colleague of Beethoven, the Viennese violinist Ignaz Schuppanzigh (whose name will appear again in these pages), ran the summer series of concerts in the pavilion of the Augarten public park,* north of the city across the Danube Canal. The suggestion was made – it is not clear by whom, probably Schuppanzigh – that Beethoven should compose a new violin sonata, and he and Mr Bridgetower would give it its premiere at the inaugural concert of the season on 22 May.

Beethoven agreed. Bridgetower, having probably been forewarned, panicked. He pressed Beethoven to finish the violin part in good time so he could practise it. There was less than a month to the concert, and as far as he knew nothing had yet been written. Beethoven, realising time was short, decided to take the final movement from a sonata he had composed the preceding year, and make it the final movement of the new sonata. That much at least Bridgetower was able to work on.

---

* Today the pavilion, bearing a plaque stating that Mozart, Beethoven and Schubert all performed there, is a porcelain factory.

Beethoven set to work on the opening movement, beginning it with fiendishly difficult double-stopping across all four strings, possibly because Bridgetower had demonstrated he was capable of it. But the movement became ever longer and more complex. In a repeat of what had happened just before the benefit concert the preceding month, Beethoven summoned Ries at 4 a.m. and told him to copy out the violin part for the first movement.

It was clear that the second movement would not be ready in time, and the concert was put back two days, to 24 May. The Augarten concerts were held at 8 a.m. The night before, Beethoven was still writing out the second movement. It is probable Bridgetower, fearing his reputation was about to be torn to tatters, stood over Beethoven, rehearsing as he composed.

At the performance, in the first movement something quite extraordinary happened. In bar 18 of the *Presto* Beethoven had written a huge arpeggio run just for the piano, up two octaves, down two octaves, up two octaves again, with a final leap from a top note to a bass note. During this virtuosic display, the violinist can do nothing but stand and watch. But Beethoven had marked the *Presto* to be repeated, and in the repeat, when it came to the run, Bridgetower watched Beethoven's fingers fly up and down the keyboard, then he fixed the violin under the chin, and imitated it on the violin.

Beethoven looked up at Bridgetower in utter astonishment. The audience must have held its breath as Beethoven leapt up from the piano stool, ran across to Bridgetower, hugged him, shouted, 'Noch einmal, mein lieber Bursch!' ('Again, my dear fellow!'), ran back to the piano, played his run, then held down the sustaining key as Bridgetower again copied it on the violin.*

---

* This improvisation by Bridgetower did not survive in the published version of the sonata.

The audience was entirely won over, which was no bad thing since Bridgetower was compelled to play the second movement from Beethoven's hastily scribbled manuscript. This he achieved with success, and the third movement, the only movement that Bridgetower had had time to rehearse fully, was flawless.

The performance was a triumph, so much so that Beethoven dedicated the sonata there and then to the Englishman. Sadly for Bridgetower that is not the end of the story.

It might have been at the celebratory supper following the concert, or it might have been shortly afterwards, that Bridgetower made a mistake. He made the mistake of his life. He made an off-colour remark about a lady. Beethoven was appalled, utterly appalled, so much so that he withdrew the dedication from Bridgetower. Bridgetower tried to reason with him, no doubt arguing that it was just a joke, he hadn't meant anything bad by it. He might also have urged Beethoven's friends to intercede on his behalf. But it was no good. Beethoven's mind was made up. Nobody who could say such a thing was to have a Beethoven composition dedicated to him.

Soon afterwards Bridgetower left Vienna, and the two men never met again. Very many years later, Bridgetower was an old man living in poverty in Peckham, South London, where he was visited by a music researcher. He recounted the story of how he had lost the dedication of Beethoven's Violin Sonata through one off-colour remark which led to an altercation over a lady.

There are two sad codas to this story. Bridgetower died in poverty in a home for the destitute. We know this because the woman who witnessed his death signed the death certificate with a cross for her name. He is today buried in Kensal Green cemetery, west of London, his name forgotten to history.

After withdrawing the dedication, Beethoven sent the manuscript to a French violinist living in Paris by the name of Rudolphe Kreutzer, with a dedication to him. The sonata that bears his name, the 'Kreutzer' Sonata, is now acknowledged as the greatest violin sonata by Beethoven, or anyone. And do you know what Monsieur Kreutzer said when he received the manuscript and examined it? 'C'est impossible, c'est la musique du diable, on ne peut pas la jouer', and never once performed it in public, the sonata that bears his name.

Bridgetower lived with the knowledge of what he had lost for the rest of his life. Beethoven quickly forgot it. He was moving on to something on an altogether much larger scale.

First there was the matter of the opera he had without doubt committed himself to in order to secure the position of composer-in-residence. Schikaneder had just the thing: an opera based on Roman mythology to be entitled *Vestas Feuer* (*Vestal Flame*). He produced a libretto and gave it to Beethoven, who began work. He soon tired of it, finding the sentiments banal. 'Just picture a subject from ancient Rome – with language that comes out of the mouths of our local apple-women,' he wrote in a letter to a friend. There was no reasoning with Schikaneder, who was 'too infatuated with his own opinion' to allow anyone else to improve the libretto.

So Beethoven abandoned the project, a somewhat rash move since it was probable his job depended on producing an opera that Schikaneder could stage.* But he had other things on his

---

* He completed one scene, the last section of which he adapted later as the great love duet in Act II of *Fidelio*, 'O namenlose Freude'.

mind. He had begun work on a new symphony, his Third. It was a symphony that would, quite simply, set music on a new course. It is a cliché, and usually an exaggeration, to say any one thing changed the course of any other thing. In this case it is true. Beethoven's Third Symphony changed the course of music. We are talking here about the 'Eroica'.

As always with Beethoven, ideas began with fragmentary sketches and jottings, but it seems he composed the 'Eroica' in an intensive three-month period in the summer of 1803. This is all the more remarkable in that the work is longer, and more complex, than any symphony hitherto written by anybody. The first movement alone runs to almost 700 bars, anything between fifteen and twenty minutes in performance.

I could spend the next chapter and a half examining the musicological innovations and surprises in the 'Eroica', from the utterly unexpected and startling opening two chords with the descent to C sharp in bar seven, the 'false' horn entry before the recapitulation in the first movement, to the strange decision to make the second movement a funeral march, labelling the third movement 'scherzo', literally 'joke', and borrowing the main theme of the final movement from the finale of his ballet *The Creatures of Prometheus*, composed nearly three years earlier. But true to my pledge to reach the music through the man rather than the man through the music, I will limit myself to aspects that throw light on Beethoven the man.

Beethoven himself was in no doubt he had composed something out of the ordinary, nor were those close to him. Shortly after completing it, but before orchestrating it, he played it on the piano to Ferdinand Ries. Ries wrote to Simrock that a full orchestral performance would make 'Heaven and Earth tremble'. Some months later Ries was at Beethoven's side as the orchestra rehearsed it for the first time. Ries states candidly that the rehearsal was 'horrible'. In bar 394, over extreme *pianissimo* (*ppp*) first and second violins, the lone horn enters with the opening motif, before the full orchestra crashes in *fortissimo* for the recapitulation.

Ries, assuming the horn player had mistimed his entry, said, 'Can't the damned horn player count? That sounded dreadful!' Beethoven looked witheringly at Ries and muttered that the horn player had played exactly what he had written. Ries looked embarrassed and kept quiet. He wrote later that he had come pretty close to receiving a box on the ear, and that Beethoven didn't forgive him for a long time. That horn entry has exercised musicologists and put the fear of God into horn-players ever since.

By far the most illuminating aspect of the 'Eroica', in so far as it throws light on Beethoven's character, is its dedication – or, rather, non-dedication. Beethoven had made no secret of his admiration for Napoleon Bonaparte, a man of the people who had risen through the ranks and was now, as First Consul, leading the people of France in a new era of liberty, equality and brotherhood, following the French Revolution. Indeed, he approved of events in France to such an extent that he had spoken openly of leaving the aristocratic stuffiness of Vienna for good and going to live in Paris.

Ferdinand Ries said Beethoven considered Napoleon as great as the greatest consuls of ancient Rome. This is conjecture, but I can see his friends telling him to keep his voice down in taverns and restaurants as he extolled the virtues of Napoleon and France, Austria's enemy, at the same time knowing that any spies or government agents who might be within earshot would know this was just the eccentric musician who was losing his hearing – he was no harm to anyone.

At what stage Beethoven linked his new symphony with Napoleon is not clear, but he undoubtedly had Napoleon in mind as he composed, because when he had completed the autograph manuscript, he had a fair copy made, which he intended forwarding to Paris through the French Embassy. Was it intended as a gift for Napoleon himself? We don't know, but it's quite possible, since Beethoven wrote at the top of the title page, 'Buonaparte', and at the extreme bottom, 'Luigi van Beethoven'.* He probably intended to write the title of the piece in the space between.

In late May 1804 Ferdinand Ries recounts how he went to see Beethoven and gave him the news that a few days earlier, on 20 May, Napoleon had proclaimed himself Emperor of France. Beethoven flew into a rage, shouted out, 'Is he then, too, nothing more than an ordinary human being? Now he, too, will trample on all the rights of man, and just satisfy his own ambition. He will exalt himself above all others and become a tyrant!' He stormed over to the table on which the fair copy of the 'Eroica' score lay, snatched up the title page, tore it in two, and threw it on the floor.

But he did not entirely let go of his admiration for Napoleon. The title page of the copyist's score reads: 'Sinfonia grande/intitolata Buonaparte/del Sigr/Louis van Beethoven'. Still, though, he could allow his distaste for what Napoleon had done to overwhelm him. In a further fit of temper, he scratched out the name 'Buonaparte' with such force that there is a hole in the paper! And *still* he could not make up his mind. In faded pencil below his own name, he wrote 'geschrieben auf Bonaparte' ('written on Bonaparte'). He really could not – and never did – make up his mind about the Corsican. What he most certainly *did* do, though, was abandon any serious desire to go and live in Paris.

---

* Beethoven frequently wrote his forename both in French, 'Louis', and Italian, 'Luigi'.

If this behaviour conforms to the irascible Beethoven of legend, it can perhaps be mitigated slightly by the unfortunate turn of events that occurred at this time. The man Beethoven disliked so much, Baron Braun, fed up with the competition provided by the Theater an der Wien, bought it. In short order he sacked Schikaneder and terminated Beethoven's contract. With the loss of his job, the composer lost his apartment too.

Beethoven moved into an apartment in the same building as his good friend Stephan von Breuning, but Stephan suggested that he move in with him, to save rent. This Beethoven did. But Stephan soon had good reason to regret his offer. Apparently due notice had not been given to the previous landlord, thus incurring a penalty. At the dinner table in Stephan's apartment, Beethoven accused his friend of being entirely responsible. Stephan, appalled, defended himself. Beethoven, in a sudden overwhelming rage, stood up at the table, knocking over his chair, stormed out of the apartment, and went to live elsewhere.

There would, before too long, be a full reconciliation – Beethoven, as so often, having been utterly belligerent, was then overwhelming in his remorse – but it would not be the last time Beethoven would cause a severe rift with his long-suffering and loyal friend.

Beethoven's unpredictability was now well known among his circle, and on the whole they bore it with good grace since they recognised that a genius such as his could not come without flaws. But he most certainly did test their loyalty, and these were not just casual friends but people without whose help he could barely have survived.

Prince Lichnowsky had been paying Beethoven an annuity of 600 florins since 1800, purely out of the goodness of his heart. Ferdinand Ries was at Beethoven's beck and call, as we have seen, at all hours of the day and night. Perhaps two men who knew the composer so well were slightly foolish to have decided to play a practical joke on him, but that is what they did, and they suffered the consequences.

It seemed pretty harmless. Soon after completing the 'Eroica', Beethoven composed a mighty piano sonata, almost as if he needed to get back to the piano. For reasons that remain unclear, he dedicated it to his old patron from the Bonn days, Count Waldstein, so that it is known to posterity as the 'Waldstein' Sonata.* The original second movement of the sonata was considered too long, and after some persuading Beethoven agreed to remove it, publish it separately, and substitute a new, shorter, movement.

The original was published as an *Andante* in F. It became so universally popular that Beethoven himself christened it '*Andante favori*', the title by which it became known, and remains known today. When Beethoven first played it for Ries, the younger man was so delighted with it he urged Beethoven to play it again. On his way home, Ries called in on Prince Lichnowsky to tell him of the 'new and glorious composition'. The Prince made him play it, and Ries did as best as he could from memory. As he played he remembered more passages, and the Prince made Ries teach it to him. Together the two men hatched an innocent little plot.

---

* Waldstein became obsessed with defeating Napoleon, and raised an army to do so. It bankrupted him. It was reported he was in Vienna in 1805 in disguise to escape his creditors. It was possibly on hearing this that Beethoven dedicated the Piano Sonata in C, Op. 53, to him. There is no evidence the two men met.

The following day Prince Lichnowsky called in on Beethoven and said he had composed something for piano that wasn't at all bad, and he would like Beethoven's opinion on it. Beethoven said gruffly he was not interested, but Lichnowsky took no notice, sat at the piano, and played a goodly portion of the *Andante*. He played on, fully expecting Beethoven to appreciate the joke.

He miscalculated. Beethoven was livid. He ordered Lichnowsky out of his apartment, and Ries reports that his extreme anger accounted for the fact that 'I never heard Beethoven play again'. This could well be the case. Several months later Beethoven still held a grudge against the hapless Ries, reducing him to tears in front of company. Not much later Ries left Vienna, and although he returned for a brief period a little later, another row blew up between them over something entirely different. None of this, though, was to stop Ries championing his master's music when he moved to London, as we shall learn. Beethoven's friends might have been few, but on the whole they were unswervingly loyal to him.

Baron Braun was having something of a midlife crisis. In late August 1804 he reinstated Beethoven at the Theater an der Wien. He probably realised he needed that opera Beethoven had pledged to write, and would certainly have known that after abandoning *Vestas Feuer*, Beethoven had begun to collaborate with a lawyer, who had a sideline in translating French plays into German, on Jean-Nicolas Bouilly's play *Léonore, ou L'Amour conjugal*.

The lawyer, Joseph Sonnleithner, was a member of a family well connected in music and theatre, and he and Beethoven had met. Beethoven quickly realised Sonnleithner was in a different league from Schikaneder, and the two men began to make progress on a new opera, based on Bouilly's play.

Beethoven revelled in Braun's discomfort, writing to Sonnleithner, 'I am used to the fact that [Braun] has nothing good to say about me – let it be – I shall never grovel – my world is elsewhere.'

To say that Beethoven was stretched would be an understatement. But he was stretched in exactly the way he loved. He was involved in rehearsals and first performances of his colossal 'Eroica' Symphony. He also composed another new piano sonata, which was his mightiest to date. It would become one of his best known and most loved, given a name by the publisher who recognised its unparalleled intensity, a name that would stick for all time: 'Appassionata'. And now, as if that was not enough, he was making huge progress on his first opera.

Something else was happening too, something that would have a profound effect on him. He was once again in love.

Chapter 9

O, Beloved J!

Musical failure, but will Beethoven succeed in love?

It had begun a little over five years earlier when, in May 1799, a Hungarian widow by the name of Anna Countess von Brunsvik brought two of her daughters to the Habsburg capital to introduce them into society, to develop their interest in the arts, and, possibly uppermost in her mind, to find them wealthy husbands.

We owe the elder daughter, Therese, a debt of gratitude for the comprehensive memoirs she wrote later in life, providing us with considerable insight into the on-off, and ultimately off, relationship between Beethoven and her sister Josephine.

A family friend advised the mother to ask Beethoven to give the two girls piano lessons, warned her that Beethoven was unlikely to respond to a letter, but that if she and her daughters were prepared to climb three flights of a narrow spiral staircase and knock on his door, they 'might have a chance'. This they did, and it is easy to see Beethoven, hitherto so unlucky in his relationships with women, being somewhat bowled over at the sight of a no doubt smartly attired and coiffed noblewoman and her two daughters, the younger of whom was by any standards very beautiful, calling to see him.

Whether the Countess's request for Beethoven to give her daughters piano lessons was helped by the fact that they were cousins of Giulietta Guicciardi, or whether it was just that Beethoven saw this as an opportunity for an amorous relationship, we do not know. What is certain is that for a man who thoroughly hated teaching, he not only said yes, but took up the project with extraordinary zeal. According to Therese, he came to the hotel where they were staying every day for sixteen days, and from twelve noon stayed not just for the allotted hour but often until four or five o'clock in the afternoon to give the girls lessons.

Unfortunately for Beethoven, the Brunsviks also met the owner of an art gallery by the name of Müller, who saw 'the incomparable beauty which lay hidden in Josephine as in a bud, and from the moment he set eyes on her he burned with a fierce passion'. This 'Müller' had a rather colourful past, having had to flee the country temporarily after a youthful duel, and changing his name to make good his escape. He might or might not have come clean about this to the Countess, but he certainly left her in no doubt of his passion for Josephine and his desire to marry her.

He would have impressed her, too, by claiming the Emperor, no less, as a personal friend, a claim he was able to prove when he went to the Emperor and asked for a pardon for his past misdemeanour. This was granted and his title returned to him, so that he could truthfully present himself to Countess Brunsvik as the highly eligible Count Joseph Deym. Since he was the owner of a renowned art gallery, famous for its wax portraits and copies of classical works of art, there was no doubt either about his wealth.

The Countess was suitably impressed, brushing aside any doubts over the fact that the Count was forty-seven years of age, her daughter Josephine just twenty. When one morning at the end of the Brunsviks' brief stay in Vienna, Count Deym called on the Countess, requesting a private talk, no one was in any doubt as to what it was about, nor of the outcome. Therese records that,

> *after a few minutes, Josephine was called into the room, and my mother introduced her to – Count Deym. 'Dear Josephine,' she said, 'you can make me and your sisters very happy!' After a painful pause a scarcely audible 'Yes' floated from her trembling lips – and to this 'Yes' she was to sacrifice a whole lifetime's happiness, so nobly and with such courage. She had no idea what she was letting herself in for. Soon afterwards she threw her arms round my neck and shed a flood of tears.*

Within weeks Deym and Josephine were married. Any hope Beethoven might have had of a relationship with his beautiful young pupil was dashed.

Soon after the marriage, Josephine and her mother were horrified to discover that Deym's supposed wealth was a lie. He was, in fact, heavily in debt. The deception might actually have been two-way. Deym blamed his financial problems on the fact that a promised dowry from the Brunsvik family had not materialised.

There was then something of a transformation of loyalties. The Countess, realising that the marriage offered neither social nor financial advantage, pressed for a separation. Her daughter reportedly had furious rows with her mother, refusing to break her marriage vows.

Within three years of marrying Deym, Josephine gave birth to three children and was pregnant with a fourth when, at the beginning of 1804, she was widowed. Deym contracted consumption and died. Josephine suddenly found herself with four infant children, an art gallery to administer, and the letting of eighty rooms owned by Deym to manage.

Josephine's mental health was, according to her sister, already fragile. Later in the year that Deym died, she began to have attacks of fever, which were particularly bad at night. 'Sometimes she laughed, sometimes she wept, after which she suffered from extreme fatigue.'

Beethoven, despite any disappointment over Josephine's marriage, remained close to the Brunsvik family, so must have been aware of the sad events that had overtaken Josephine. At the end of 1804, now reinstated at the Theater an der Wien and working hard on his opera, he decided to press his suit.

In the period 1804–7 he wrote an extraordinary series of thirteen letters to Josephine Deym, which came to light only as recently as 1949, and were published in 1957. The majority of these letters are, quite simply, passionate declarations of love. The first letter to contain such language was written in the spring of 1805,* and suggests that his hand was forced.

In December 1804 Beethoven had composed a song entitled 'To Hope' ('An die Hoffnung'). Prince Lichnowsky saw the manuscript in Beethoven's apartment, and it appears Beethoven had written Josephine's name on the title page. Lichnowsky assured Beethoven he would remain tight-lipped. Beethoven relays this to Josephine in the letter, then writes:

> *Oh, beloved J, it is no desire for the opposite sex that draws me to you, no, <u>it is just you, your whole self</u> with all your*

---

* All thirteen letters, with one exception, are undated, but I am following the accepted dates attributed by modern scholarship.

individual qualities ... When I came to you – it was with the firm resolve not to let a single spark of love be kindled in me. But you have conquered me ... Long – long – long-lasting – may our love become – For it is so noble ... Oh you, you make me hope that <u>your heart</u> will long – beat for me – <u>Mine</u> can only – cease – to beat for you – when – <u>it no longer beats – Beloved J</u> ...

This is an unequivocal declaration of love, such as Beethoven had never before put to paper, as far as we are aware. And certainly, to begin with, Beethoven had good cause to believe the love was mutual, even if Josephine was being slightly ambiguous. She replied:

You have long had my heart, dear Beethoven. If this assurance can give you joy, then receive it – from the purest heart ... You receive the <u>greatest proof</u> of my love [and] of my esteem through this confession, through this confidence! ... Do not tear my heart apart – do not try to persuade me further. I love you inexpressibly, as one gentle soul does another. Are you not capable of this covenant? I am not receptive to other [forms of] love for the present ...

If Beethoven took this as encouragement, one can hardly blame him. It would appear he did, both in writing and probably in person, because later in the year Josephine decided to end any ambiguity:

This favour that you granted me, the pleasure of your company, would have been the finest jewel in my life, if you could

> *have loved me less sensually* – that I cannot satisfy this sensual love – does this make you angry with me – I would have to violate holy bonds if I were to give in to your desire.*

That is an unequivocal rejection of a physical relationship. More than that, it could be read as a refusal of a proposal of marriage. In her memoirs Therese wrote, 'Why did not my sister J, as the widow Deym, accept [Beethoven] as her husband?'

Beethoven did not immediately give up. From later letters to Josephine, it appears he went to her house to try to see her, but was refused admittance by the servants, which he found humiliating. This was enough to convince him that he was pursuing a lost cause. In the final letter of the thirteen, he writes:

> *I thank you for still wishing to make it appear as if I were not entirely banished from your memory ... You want me to tell you how I am. A more difficult question could not be put to me – and I prefer to leave it unanswered, rather than – to answer it <u>too truthfully</u> – All good wishes, dear J. As always, your Beethoven, who is eternally devoted to you.*

That 'eternal devotion' seems more like politeness, given what comes before it. Josephine now leaves our story, but will come right back into it when I discuss the identity of the Immortal Beloved, the one woman who as far as we know returned Beethoven's love.

---

* The German word Josephine uses is *sinnlich*, which translates as either 'sensual' or 'sensuous'.

There is an irony in the fact that in 1805, the year Beethoven was actively pursuing Josephine, he was hard at work on an opera that tells the story of how the love of a wife rescues her husband from certain death.

By the late summer of 1805 much of the work on *Leonore* had been done, but now the hard work began. Singers were hired, and although the females were adequate, some of the male singers were simply not up to the job. One in particular, chosen to sing the role of the prison governor Pizarro, had a high opinion of his own talent and told the company he believed there was no composer to touch his brother-in-law, Mozart. Beethoven decided to bring him down a peg by writing a truly tricky passage for him to sing. He found it impossible to master, dismissing it with contempt: 'My brother-in-law would never have written such damned nonsense.' It did not make for a happy company.

Rehearsals were difficult – as always with Beethoven performances – and he let small matters get to him. At one rehearsal the third bassoon failed to turn up. Beethoven was furious, and when Prince Lobkowitz made light of the matter, he felt the force of the composer's anger.*

A date was set for the first performance of the opera, Tuesday, 15 October 1805. Then things really *did* go wrong. The censor stepped in and banned it. The plot – a man falsely imprisoned by the prison governor who plots his murder, his life saved by his wife who disguises herself as a man to get work at the prison – was simply too political. Yes, the wrongdoer is hauled off to face justice at the order of the provincial governor,

---

* Like Lichnowsky, Lobkowitz was a great supporter of Beethoven; he received the dedication of the 'Eroica' after Beethoven decided against Napoleon.

but in the contemporary climate it just wouldn't do. Couldn't Beethoven write operas like Mozart and Cherubini, which by and large steered clear of political issues?

Beethoven, on the surface, was furious, but actually to an extent the ban worked in his favour. The process of composition had been enormously difficult, even by his standards. It had filled the equivalent of over three sketchbooks (in contrast to the 'Eroica', which had filled half of a single sketchbook), and had taken him longer than any other work he had hitherto composed. In one sense that is not particularly surprising. There is no musical genre that uses quite as many forces as opera. He had written works for voices and orchestra – cantatas and an oratorio – but in these works the singers are static. An opera demands drama, choreography, theatrical production, as well as singing. There are also issues such as costumes and scenery, which one imagines Beethoven could hardly be bothered with.

There is something else too. Beethoven, by his own admission, did not find it easy to compose for the human voice. He said that when he heard sounds in his head, they were the sounds of the orchestra. Singers, from his day to ours, have complained about his vocal composition, whether it be *Fidelio*, the *Missa Solemnis*, or the Ninth Symphony. All make demands on the voice that are to an extent not natural. As we shall see later, the premiere of the Ninth Symphony nearly did not happen, at least in part because of a revolt by the soloists who complained their parts were unsingable. Singers who complain today are aware, at least, of the unquestioned genius of Beethoven, and generally do their best to fulfil his demands. That was not the case two centuries ago. It really is no surprise Beethoven was never to write another opera.

So when the censor banned opening night, Beethoven realised it gave him more time to work on the score and rehearse the singers and orchestra. Sonnleithner the librettist, however, had friends in high places, and a grovelling petition to the censor did the trick. The ban was lifted.

Proof that the opera was nowhere near ready to be performed came with the decision to postpone opening night by five weeks, until 20 November. This could not have been a worse decision, due to circumstances totally outside the control of anyone in Vienna.

Earlier in the year Austria had joined a coalition to fight Napoleon. This was an annoying distraction from the French Emperor's principal aim, which was to invade Britain. But Austria was an enemy he could easily deal with, and he decided to do so. Abandoning his camp at Boulogne, he marched at the head of his army into Germany, crossed the Rhine, and then headed south-east towards the Danube. The Austrian army made a stand at Ulm in Bavaria, but on 20 October Napoleon swatted it aside and continued his march into Austria.

In Vienna there was total panic. Anyone who could left the city. This meant in effect the nobility, bankers, and wealthy merchants, those who had somewhere else to go, a residence in Bohemia or Hungary, perhaps, and who had the money and means to escape. Precisely the level of society in which Beethoven moved, those he could be certain would come to the Theater an der Wien to see his new opera.

By 10 November the French army had reached, and occupied, villages just a few miles west of Vienna. Three days later the vanguard of the army entered the city in battle order, flags flying, to the sound of martial music. Napoleon, to add insult to injury, made his headquarters in the Austrian Emperor's summer palace, Schönbrunn. The French had taken the capital of the Austrian Empire, with barely a shot fired.

Five days later Beethoven's new opera, *Leonore*, opened at the Theater an der Wien.* The timing was disastrous. The first act of the occupying French army was to close the gates of the city wall and put armed guards in place to prevent movement. This meant people from inside the city wall could not venture into the suburbs. The sort of people who lived outside the city wall were not, on the whole, enthusiastic opera-goers, nor did they like the idea of going out after dark with French soldiers on patrol, and so Beethoven's opera opened on 20 November to a handful of his friends and an otherwise empty house.

The following night there were a few French soldiers in the audience, and on the third night a few more. It is hardly a surprise that the plot of the opera – which, as well as being a love story, extols the triumph of freedom over oppression – did not exactly appeal to the soldiers of an occupying army, and after just three performances the opera was shut down.

Given the difficult gestation period, the problems with rehearsals, the intervention of the censor, the delay of opening night, Beethoven was already drained. Three unsuccessful performances put the seal on a dreadful experience. And unsuccessful the opera was musically, too, and that will have hurt Beethoven all the more.

The *Freymüthige* critic wrote:

> *A new Beethoven opera has not pleased. It was performed only a few times, and after the first performance [the theatre] remained completely empty. Also the music was certainly*

---

* There are conflicting reports as to whether the opera opened as *Leonore* or *Fidelio*. Certainly it was to become *Fidelio*, and it is generally accepted that at this stage it was called *Leonore*.

way below the expectations of amateur and professional alike, the melodies, as well as the general character, much of which is somewhat false, lack that joyful, clear, magical impression of emotion which grips us so irresistibly in the works of Mozart and Cherubini. The music has some beautiful passages, but it is very far from being a perfect, or indeed even successful, work.

The *Allgemeine musikalische Zeitung* was just as unforgiving:

Beethoven has sacrificed beauty so many times for the new and strange, and so this characteristic of newness and originality in creative ideas was expected from this first theatrical production of his – and it is exactly these qualities that are the least in evidence. Judged dispassionately and with an open mind, the whole piece is marked neither by invention nor execution.

Beethoven had experienced his first unquestionable flop and, easy though it might be to blame the French, there was more to it than that. His opera had been judged to have failed artistically.

Now this was something that was not entirely new to Beethoven. His cantatas, back in his Bonn days, had been judged unplayable by the court orchestra, and earlier in the same year as *Leonore* was staged, 1805, the *Allgemeine musikalische Zeitung* had this to say about his Symphony No. 3, the 'Eroica':

This long composition, which is extremely difficult to perform, is in reality an enormously expanded, daring and wild fantasia. It lacks nothing in the way of startling and beautiful passages, in which we recognise the energetic and talented

> *composer. But often it loses itself in lawlessness … The review-*
> *er belongs to Herr van Beethoven's sincerest admirers, but in*
> *this composition he must confess that he finds too much that*
> *is glaring and bizarre, which hinders greatly one's grasp of the*
> *whole, and a sense of unity is almost completely lost.*

Did Beethoven take criticism to heart? He most certainly did not. A reviewer's criticism or a musician's complaint was not enough to cause him to alter a single note. Which makes the next step in the difficult journey of his opera all the more remarkable.

Beethoven agreed to attend a meeting at the home of his patron Prince Lichnowsky, with singers who had taken part in the opera, and friends, to discuss ways of improving the score. This is unprecedented. The only possible explanation is that deep in his heart Beethoven knew the opera was not right. But it is still remarkable that he was prepared to discuss this with other people, some of them non-musicians, rather than repair to the privacy of his own apartment and work on it alone. This can be only because he did not feel comfortable with the operatic form, that he understood that opera, above all musical forms, was a collaborative enterprise. In short, he needed advice.

The Prince and the others must have been surprised that Beethoven agreed to the meeting, and if they expected it to be difficult, and Beethoven to be obstructive, they were not proved wrong. They obviously agreed in advance on the single most important improvement that needed to be made. The opera was in three acts, and the first act in particular was lengthy and failed to take the plot forward. The three acts needed to be fused into two. On top of that, several pieces needed to be cut entirely, and others reduced.

Lichnowsky's masterstroke was to have his wife, an extremely accomplished pianist, provide musical accompaniment, as every number in the opera was run through. The Princess, although only five years older than Beethoven, had taken a motherly interest in him when he first settled in Vienna, looking after him, making sure he was well housed and provided for. Beethoven knew he owed her an enormous debt. In recent years she had fallen into poor health, and had had both breasts removed. Although only forty years of age in 1805, she was extremely frail. In the last resort, Lichnowsky knew Beethoven would listen to his wife, even if to nobody else, and she, fine musician that she was, was as aware as everybody of the need for major alterations to be made to the opera.

That is, in essence, what happened, but not without considerable struggle. 'Not a note will I cut!' Beethoven kept shouting, as proposals for improvement were made. The entire opera was gone through, piece by piece, note by note, with frequent repetition. The group pleaded and cajoled; Beethoven resisted at every point.

It was well past midnight before the end was reached. Finally Lichnowsky, who had taken the lead throughout, said to Beethoven, 'And the revision? The cuts? Do you agree?' Everybody held their breath. Beethoven's voice was sombre. 'Do not make these demands,' he said. 'Not a single note will I cut.'

But there was no resistance in his voice, the fight had gone out of him, and those present could sense it. Lichnowsky said in a joyful voice that the meeting was over, the work done, there would be no more talk of it, and they would celebrate. He gave a signal, servants flung open the folding doors to the dining room, and everybody gratefully ate and drank.

As a nice coda to the evening, Joseph Röckel, the young tenor who was to take over the lead role of Florestan – and to whom we owe the eyewitness account of the whole proceedings – sat opposite Beethoven at the dining table. He was so ravenously hungry that he devoured his plate without pausing for breath. Beethoven pointed to the empty plate, smiled and said, 'You gulped that down like a wolf – what have you eaten?'

Röckel replied that he was so famished he had not noticed what was on his plate.

'Hah!' said Beethoven. 'That is why you sang the part of Florestan, who is starving in the dungeon, so well tonight. It wasn't your voice or your head that was on fine form, but your stomach. So, just make sure you are starving before you go out on stage, and we can be sure of a successful performance!'

There was laughter, and relief, around the table. Beethoven's unusually jovial mood was evidence, to those who knew him, not only that he had not taken offence at the evening's proceedings, but that he would comply.

The net result was a reworked opera in two acts, with practically every piece shortened and an entire aria dropped. One other major change. Beethoven's oldest friend, Stephan von Breuning (with whom he was reconciled eighteen months after their falling out over accommodation) revised the libretto. This was a somewhat surprising decision, given that Stephan had no track record in such matters, and in a letter to Sonnleithner Beethoven disguised the fact that the inexperienced Stephan was now involved. The suggestion of involving Stephan might well have been made to soften Beethoven's opposition to the rewrite. If so, it worked.

The new version complete, it needed only the irascible and uncooperative Baron von Braun, director of the imperial court theatres, to be brought on side and offer a performance date. This was achieved, but Beethoven soon raised the Baron's ire by insisting on composing a new overture, and then repeatedly missing the deadline for its completion. January and February passed and they were into early March.

Braun finally lost patience. He offered Beethoven the night of Saturday, 29 March, in the Theater an der Wien, which he said was the best night of the season since it was the final night before the theatre closed for Holy Week. If the opera were not performed on that night, Braun threatened, it would not be performed at all. There was also the promise of one night (possibly two) after Holy Week. But there was a catch. Given the failure of the previous performances, Braun was prepared to offer Beethoven only a share of receipts, not a guaranteed fee. This could, of course, work to Beethoven's advantage if the theatre was full. Beethoven was in no position to argue.

Still Beethoven was late in delivering the final score, so that there was time for only two or three rehearsals with piano and only one with orchestra. Beethoven, possibly under instructions, stayed away. The rehearsals were directed by Ignaz 'Egyptian hieroglyphics' Seyfried, who also conducted at the performances.

The first performance on the 29th was not a complete success, the theatre again being almost empty. Beethoven complained that the chorus was 'full of blunders', and that the orchestra – particularly the wind (shades of the cantata problems) – ignored all the dynamic markings. 'Any pleasure one might get in composing departs when one hears one's music played like <u>that</u>!' he wrote.

The second performance, after Holy Week, on Thursday, 10 April, fared rather better. There was a larger audience, though the theatre was still not full. But it seems Baron Braun was prepared to make the theatre available for more performances. Beethoven, though, had other matters on his mind. He was convinced that his due receipts, based on the number of tickets sold, were larger than the Baron was prepared to pay him.

Young Röckel is again our witness to one of the most extraordinary episodes in Beethoven's life. It is as if all the resentment towards the Baron came pouring out in one tempestuous encounter.

On the day following the second performance, Beethoven stormed into the Baron's office and openly accused him of withholding his just receipts, of underpaying him. There was a violent row between the two men. Braun told Beethoven he was the only composer to whom he had ever offered a share of the profits, and if there had been a larger audience, he would have received more money. Beethoven accused Braun again of swindling him out of what he was owed. Braun pointed out that although the boxes and front-row seats had all been taken, the bulk of the cheaper seats remained empty.

As a *coup de grâce*, calculated to offend, Braun said that Mozart was always able to fill these cheaper seats with ordinary people, whereas Beethoven's music seemed to appeal only to the more cultured classes.

Beethoven, stunned and shocked at Braun's words, stormed up and down the office, then shouted, 'I do not write for the multitude – I write for the cultured!'

Braun, knowing he now had the upper hand, calmly replied, 'But the cultured alone do not fill our theatre. We need the multitude to bring in money, and since your music makes no concessions to the ordinary people, you only have yourself to blame for the fact that your takings are less than you hoped.'

Beethoven saw red. The unfavourable comparison with Mozart, then the insult to his music, was too much. 'Give me back my score!' he shouted. It was the Baron's turn to be stunned. Beethoven shouted again, 'I want my score. My score. Now!'

The Baron, possibly deciding to call Beethoven's bluff, pulled a bell-rope and a servant entered. 'Bring the score of yesterday's opera for this gentleman.'

The two men stood staring at each other until the servant returned with the score. Braun tried to calm matters. 'Look, I am sorry about all this, but I believe that on calmer reflection –'

Beethoven did not listen. He snatched the score from the servant's hand and stormed out of the office, down the stairs, and away.

Röckel entered a few moments later and Braun looked visibly shocked at what had happened. He had, in effect, lost the opera. 'Beethoven got over-excited,' he said to Röckel. 'You know him, he respects you, go after him, and see if you can get him to agree to give the score back. I want to put it on the stage again.'

Röckel concludes predictably, 'I hastened to follow the angry Master … but all was in vain.'

It certainly was. Beethoven's opera did not see the light of day for another eight years, and then it was in a form substantially different yet again – a third version. Which does lead one to wonder whether the whole fracas over underpayment of box-office receipts was an elaborate charade engineered by Beethoven because deep down he knew, consciously or subconsciously, that his opera was still not right.

If that were so, he certainly did not regard it as a pressing matter that needed to be resolved. Or if he did, it was about to be supplanted by a crisis of a very different, and much more personal, kind.

Chapter 10

A Deeply Immoral Woman

Beethoven holds the most important concert
of his life, and is offered a job

Remarkably little is known about Beethoven's two brothers, other than information that links them directly to their famous brother. For one thing, we have practically no idea what they looked like. I can find no contemporary portrait of Carl, and the only physical description of him that I am aware of is terse and uncomplimentary, which is hardly surprising since it came from Carl Czerny, who hated him: 'Carl van Beethoven is small of stature, red-haired, ugly.'

There is, as far as I am aware, just one portrait of Johann, done when he was in his mid-sixties. It shows an extremely wide thin-lipped mouth, long prominent nose, and a right eye with severely drooping eyelid. There is no resemblance to his elder brother. Johann had at least one quality that Carl lacked. He had qualifications. He had trained and qualified as a pharmacist, and was later to buy a pharmacy in Linz and make a considerable amount of money. Not that this earned him his elder brother's respect. When Johann wrote a letter to him and signed it, 'From your brother Johann, Landowner',

Beethoven signed his reply, 'From your brother Ludwig, Brain Owner'.

Carl, on the other hand, had nothing but his mediocre musical talent. On arrival in Vienna he managed to get a job as clerk in the Department of Finance, which left him time to handle his elder brother's business affairs. This he did aggressively, and Nikolaus Simrock was not the only publisher who regretted having to deal with him. Ferdinand Ries, who like Czerny couldn't stand Carl, wrote to Simrock that Carl 'for the sake of a single ducat breaks fifty promises, and as a result makes bitter enemies for his brother ... All the publishers here [in Vienna] fear him more than fire, for he is a terribly coarse man.'

When Breitkopf und Härtel, concerned that they might lose exclusive rights to a composition to rival publisher Artaria & Co., wrote blaming Beethoven for not respecting the exclusivity, Carl replied on his brother's behalf, 'You have written my brother a letter which might possibly be appropriate for a schoolboy, but not for an artist such as Beethoven.' Similarly, when the highly respected *Allgemeine musikalische Zeitung* criticised the oratorio *Christus am Ölberge*, Carl wrote to them that he found it 'remarkable that you should print such garbage in your journal'.

Beethoven himself, at least to begin with, appeared none too concerned about this. If anything he had some contempt himself for publishers and critics, and if his brother was upsetting them, maybe it was no more than they deserved. But the case against Carl was building, with publishers threatening to end relationships, and friends and colleagues warning Beethoven that Carl was seriously compromising his reputation.

If Beethoven was unsure what to do next, Carl solved it for him in the most dramatic way. He announced to his brother that he intended getting married, and that the object of his affections was a certain Johanna Reiss. If he had set out to upset his brother, he could not have chosen to do it in a more effective way.

Johanna Reiss was the daughter of a well-to-do Viennese upholsterer and his wife, who, it is fair to say, had something of a reputation, even in her youth. As a teenager she accused the family's housekeeper of stealing something she had herself taken. The case actually went to court before she was forced to admit her dishonesty, and she was fortunate no action was taken against her. A curious anecdote from her childhood might go some way towards explaining her behaviour. She apparently told her son in later years that every time she had wanted money her father had said, 'I won't give you any, but if you can take it without my knowledge you can keep it.' This tendency to dishonesty did not leave her after she married, as we shall see.

It is also probably true to say that her unfavourable reputation extended to her morals as well, though there is no direct evidence of this before her marriage. Certainly it became a real issue in later years – again, as we shall see – and, given Beethoven's vehement opposition to acquiring her as a sister-in-law, it is probably a fair assumption to make. As far as he was concerned, the fact that she was already three months pregnant with Carl's child before she married him was proof enough of that.

As head of the family, Beethoven no doubt tried everything he could to prevent the marriage, but it was to no avail. Carl married Johanna on 25 May 1806. Almost immediately he stopped acting as his brother's business manager – it is not clear whether this was his decision or Beethoven's. Little over three months later, on 4 September, the couple's son Karl, Beethoven's nephew, was born. This straightforward sequence of events was to have the most profound effect imaginable on Beethoven's life.

Beethoven's relationship with his sister-in-law began badly, and became progressively worse as the years passed. Approximately a decade later it was to lead to what can only be described as a catastrophic period in Beethoven's life. It is impossible, at a distance of two centuries, to understand fully the complexities that were at work. A modern-day psychiatrist would require many sessions with Beethoven on the couch to try to get to the bottom of just why he disliked Johanna so intensely. Was it to mask a hidden desire for her? Was it more simply that he was envious of his brother's success in finding a wife? Was it that he thought she was unworthy to carry the name 'Beethoven'? We cannot know. But the vitriol he would use towards her in later years, and the extraordinary actions he would take against her, will, I have no doubt, shock readers of this book as much as they shocked Beethoven's circle at the time.

What we can be in no doubt about is that, at the time of Carl's marriage, Beethoven's mental state was precarious. He was in despair over his opera – all that effort, years in fact, the struggle to compose, arguments, tension, postponements, the failure of the premiere, the rewrite, the final showdown with Braun – and now he had what he saw as a grave domestic crisis on his hands. And yet, paradox of paradoxes (no surprise with Beethoven), he was composing at a furious pace, and these were not small compositions.

The Russian Ambassador in Vienna, Count Razumovsky – an accomplished violinist who had formed his own quartet – commissioned three string quartets from Beethoven. There is evidence he actually began writing out the score of the first of these on the day after Carl married Johanna. He started serious work on a new symphony, his fourth; he was soon to complete a new piano concerto, again his fourth, and before the year was out he would compose a violin concerto. All these are gigantic works which are staples of the repertoire today.

How did he accomplish all this, given how difficult life was for him in Vienna? By leaving the city, and that was thanks to his great benefactor, Prince Lichnowsky. Lichnowsky could see the strain Beethoven was under, having himself lived through the trauma of *Leonore*, and being aware now of the tension between Beethoven and his newly wed brother. Lichnowsky had a country estate at Grätz near Troppau in Silesia,* and he suggested Beethoven come away with him and spend some weeks there.

Beethoven acquiesced, and the two men left Vienna in late August for a trip that would last longer than planned, that would have a profoundly beneficial effect on Beethoven's compositional process – and that would end in scenes of unbelievable trauma.

It began so well. Beethoven took his manuscripts with him; Lichnowsky promised him peace and quiet; he had his own quarters with piano, and he worked with renewed energy. Within days of arriving, he received news from Vienna that Johanna had given birth, and that he had a nephew called Karl. One can imagine that momentarily disturbing his peace of mind, but it certainly did not interrupt his compositional flow.

He was also in receptive enough frame of mind to agree to travel the short distance – thirty miles or so – with the Prince to the castle at Oberglogau of another nobleman by the name of Count Oppersdorff, no doubt tempted by the knowledge that the Count maintained his own orchestra. It is likely that Lichnowsky further sweetened the pill by telling Beethoven that the Count's orchestra had been rehearsing his Second Symphony and would

---

* Now Opava, near the border between the Czech Republic and Poland.

perform it for him. This was a calculated risk, given the wrath the Prince had incurred over his *Andante favori* practical joke, but it seems all went well.

Beethoven, in fact, took a great liking to the Count, and was evidently so pleased with the performance of his symphony that he went on to assign the score of his soon-to-be-completed Fourth Symphony to the Count for six months' private use for 500 florins,* and promised to dedicate it to him on publication. Further proof of his unusually good relations with Oppersdorff came a year or so later when the Count was evidently so pleased with the Fourth Symphony that he offered Beethoven a further 500 florins for a new symphony, on the tacit understanding that he would receive the dedication of that too. Again Beethoven agreed, but when the new work was published Oppersdorff was somewhat disappointed to discover that he was not the dedicatee. And so he might be. It was Beethoven's Fifth.

But that is to leap ahead. Some weeks after the visit to Oberglogau the Count paid a return visit to Grätz. One evening Prince Lichnowsky entertained some French army officers to dinner. Both Beethoven and Oppersdorff were present. This was not a particularly tactful move. The French army still occupied Vienna – albeit peacefully – as well as large tracts of the Austro-Hungarian Empire, including Silesia. Lichnowsky must surely have known of Beethoven's fury at Napoleon declaring himself Emperor of France, and would certainly have heard Beethoven venting his fury at all things French. It is not beyond imagination that Lichnowsky, along with Beethoven's friends, would frequently have had to calm him down when spotting

---

* It was common practice, before publication, for a work to be sold to a patron for a limited period of time for exclusive use.

uniformed French soldiers in the streets of Vienna, as well as in cafés and restaurants.

It is therefore highly likely that Beethoven was a reluctant guest at the dinner, and is certain to have made his disapproval of the French clear, no doubt to the embarrassment of everyone at the table. Which makes what happened next even more inexplicable. The French officers, well aware of who Beethoven was, brushed aside any anti-French feeling he might have expressed, and asked him to play the piano for them. Beethoven was appalled. But the officers persisted, making frequent demands throughout the meal for Beethoven to play. More extraordinary still is that Lichnowsky not only made no attempt to defuse the situation but that he too urged Beethoven to play, no doubt hoping to bask in the reflected glory of having Europe's greatest virtuoso as a guest in his house, thereby currying favour with the French. Beethoven refused again and again, but neither the officers nor Lichnowsky would take no for an answer.

Finally Beethoven, his rage overflowing, stormed up from the table, hurled abuse at the company, and charged up to his room. There he bolted the door shut, while he hurriedly packed his clothes and gathered his manuscripts, stuffing them between folders. Lichnowsky was equally furious. He too hurried up the stairs, closely followed by Oppersdorff. Livid at finding the door bolted, he summoned servants, who forced the door open. Lichnowsky – all his pent-up frustration at Beethoven's always unpredictable behaviour boiling over – rushed in, Beethoven picked up a chair, and only Oppersdorff's timely intervention prevented serious damage and probable injury.

Oppersdorff persuaded Lichnowsky to leave Beethoven to work off his temper. Left alone, Beethoven scribbled a note on a scrap of paper: 'Prince, what you are, you are by accident of birth.

What I am, I am through myself. There have been and will always be thousands of princes. There is only one Beethoven.'

Beethoven then grabbed his belongings and in the darkness of night left the house, and walked in the pouring rain to Troppau, which was several kilometres away. From there he took the first coach he could find back to Vienna.

Once back in the city, he climbed the three flights of stairs to his apartment. In the hall there stood a marble bust of Lichnowsky which the Prince himself had given him. Beethoven seized it and smashed it to the ground.

Now there are several versions of this story, none of them told by direct eyewitnesses, and I confess the one I have related is the most dramatic. But the source is Ferdinand Ries, who is reliable, and all the sources agree there was a violent confrontation between Beethoven and his patron. What is also true is that, soon after, Lichnowsky stopped his annuity payments to Beethoven. It is also a fact that the autograph manuscript of the 'Appassionata' Piano Sonata, one of the manuscripts Beethoven had under his arm, and which has survived, carries clearly visible water stains.[*]

There is evidence that the two men continued to meet, but less frequently, and there was a change in the relationship. Slowly Prince Lichnowsky, who had done so much for Beethoven, providing him with accommodation when he first arrived in Vienna, gaining access for him to the most elevated salons in the city, financing him, and just generally always being there for him, slipped out of Beethoven's life.

Later Beethoven, who rarely forgot a grudge, gave orders to his servant that Lichnowsky was not to be admitted to his

---

[*] The autograph manuscript is today in the Bibliothèque Nationale de France, in Paris.

apartment. Lichnowsky, hurt beyond measure but undeterred, would sit in the ante-room near the door, where Beethoven would not see him, listen to the glorious sounds coming from within, then leave as quietly as he had arrived, content that he had played a part in the development of such genius.

In the following months, at the same time as coming to terms with the failure of his intended relationship with Josephine Brunsvik, he composed the work that alone ensured his immortality, the Fifth Symphony. And as his fame increased, and his works became more magisterial, so his life seemed to do the opposite, lurching forward with no clear sense of purpose or direction.

Not that the fault for this was always entirely his. The imperial court theatres were in trouble, no doubt hit by the French occupation. The blame was laid firmly at the door of Baron von Braun, and he was forced to retire. Beethoven no doubt enjoyed a certain *Schadenfreude* at the downfall of his old foe, and was able to take heart in the fact that the administration was put in the hands of a committee of senior patrons of the arts, including Prince Lobkowitz, who had received the dedication of the 'Eroica' and the joint dedication of the Fifth Symphony.

Beethoven seized the moment and penned a long letter to the committee, in essence asking for full-time employment with a regular salary, and containing a none too veiled threat to leave Vienna if his request was refused.

His timing, from the committee's point of view, could not have been worse. In the first place they needed to turn the court theatres' finances round, which meant putting on popular performances. Comedies, for instance, were much cheaper to stage than orchestral concerts, with more direct appeal to a wider audience. Also, with his behaviour over *Leonore*, Beethoven had cemented his reputation for being supremely difficult to work with. No reply from the committee has survived – it is possible they did not accord him the courtesy of one.

It seems though that Beethoven was at least promised a benefit concert. A date was set for the spring of 1807, then cancelled. It was reset for the following December, and cancelled again.

The committee spent the best part of a year trying to reverse the fortunes of the imperial court theatres, before giving up and putting in a new director, one Joseph von Hartl. We do not know if Beethoven made a direct approach to the new man, but Hartl was clearly not in a position to make any promises.

In April 1808 Beethoven directed several of his works at a charity concert in the Theater an der Wien, and he was to do so again later in the year. This is as likely to have been a deliberate attempt to curry favour with Hartl as for any altruistic motive. He was no longer looking for employment, just a benefit concert, and he was certainly in a strong position to do so. He was by far Vienna's most productive and respected composer, even if he had his detractors. He was publishing substantial new works at a prolific rate, and was at the same time continuing to perform in the salons of the aristocracy.

But no benefit concert was forthcoming. All this, taken with the Josephine saga and Lichnowsky debacle, his brother's appalling choice of wife, not to mention the slow inexorable loss of his hearing, meant that by the spring of 1808 he had had enough of Vienna, of musical cabals, of personal problems. He wanted to leave, go somewhere new, start again. But the question was how to do it, and where to go. He could not in his wildest imagination have come even close to predicting from where possible salvation would come.

But, before that, he decided to get away just as far as a small village north of Vienna that he had visited before. He stayed in a different house this time, but once again the peace of Heiligenstadt was exactly what his jagged nerves needed. To say that the bucolic calm of fields and pastures, the birdcalls of summer, the gently rippling stream, a sudden summer storm, then blue skies again, inspired him creatively, would be only the slightest of understatements.

Inspiring too were the inns and taverns of the villages dotted among the foothills of the Vienna Woods, such as Grinzing, Nussdorf, Unterdöbling, many with their resident groups of musicians playing the stomping dances of the country folk. In one such tavern there was a band of seven musicians. Beethoven watched, entranced, as the musicians, drinks at their elbows, would frequently fall asleep, reawaken at just the right moment, play a few notes in the right key – if their instrument hadn't dropped to the floor – then fall asleep again.

For hour after hour he strode the open fields and wooded lower slopes of the Vienna Woods, sitting by the stream, allowing the summer rain to refresh him, always sketchbook and pencils in his pocket.

By the time he returned to Vienna he had created one of his great masterpieces, the only orchestral or instrumental work he ever composed in which he told us exactly what the music represented, what feelings it should inspire, what events it portrayed. The music is stress-free; it reflects the ordered calm of nature. The babbling stream ripples over stones and along grassy banks, the birdcalls of summer are there – nightingale, quail, cuckoo – the country folk gather for a rustic dance, the drunken second bassoon repeatedly falls asleep, waking just in time for his few notes, the dark clouds gather, unleashing a summer storm, and finally the shepherds give thanks for the return of blue skies. You can almost smell the wet grass.

'Awakening of happy feelings on arrival in the country', Beethoven labelled the first movement, and that set the tone for the whole. His Sixth Symphony could not have been more of a contrast to the one that preceded it. 'No one can love the country as much as I do,' he wrote in a letter a couple of years later. This symphony was his evocation of what he loved. He called it the 'Pastoral'.

No sooner did Beethoven arrive back in Vienna than the gloom descended on him again. No word of a benefit concert, and so no opportunity to present his new works to the public. His thoughts turned once again to leaving Vienna, going somewhere new, starting afresh. With perfect timing, an exquisite opportunity presented itself.

Beethoven was offered the job of *Kapellmeister* at Kassel, capital of the Kingdom of Westphalia, on an annual salary of 600 ducats. Or as Beethoven himself put it in a letter to a friend, 'I am to be paid handsomely – I have been asked to state how <u>many ducats</u> I should like to have ...'

What had happened was that the High Chamberlain at the Westphalian court, Count Friedrich Ludwig Waldburg-Capustigall, either by letter or in person, conveyed the offer of the job of *Kapellmeister* to Beethoven on behalf of His Majesty King Jérôme of Westphalia. Or to put it another way, the universally derided and despised youngest brother of Napoleon Bonaparte, who had been stuck on the throne of a fictitious kingdom his brother had carved from the states of north-east Germany and called Westphalia, wanted to bring a bit of culture to his court and someone had mentioned the name 'Beethoven' to him.

Whichever view you take – and Beethoven took the former – it was highly flattering, and the financial incentive seriously attractive. The duties, as spelled out by the Count, were light in the extreme: Beethoven was to play occasionally for the King, and conduct his infrequent concerts. Beyond that there were no obligations. He was to have a carriage permanently at his disposal. A further plus was that this was Germany. Kassel was around 160 miles from Bonn. Beethoven, in a sense, would be going home.

He sent word that he would accept, and a contract was prepared. What do you think happened then? The long-awaited benefit concert suddenly materialised. As if out of nowhere. Hartl told Beethoven he could have the Theater an der Wien for a benefit concert on 22 December 1808.

There was a catch. On the same night, the long-programmed concert to raise funds for the Musicians' Widows and Orphans Fund would take place in the prestigious Burgtheater. The city's best orchestral players had long since been hired. To make matters worse, the organisers of the charity concert, in league with Vienna's senior musician, *Kapellmeister* Salieri, threatened any Burgtheater musician who agreed to play for Beethoven with the sack.*

It was thus a motley selection of musicians, who well knew the reputation of the man they would be working with, who gathered for rehearsals at the Theater an der Wien. Not for the first time in Beethoven's life, a musical disaster threatened.

A musical disaster was what happened, yet this was to be the single most important concert of Beethoven's life. Just the kind of paradox with which Beethoven's life is replete.

---

* Beethoven made this claim in a letter to his publisher the following January. It is unlikely his suspicions were founded.

The rehearsals went about as badly as it is possible for rehearsals to go, even by the standards of *Leonore*. The orchestral players, no doubt with the experience of *Leonore*, not to mention other encounters with Beethoven, decided to lay down ground rules. Beethoven would not be allowed to attend rehearsals, and furthermore should not conduct at the concert. Only section leaders would agree to talk to him, and if any disputes arose on which he was not prepared to give way, the players would walk out.

It seems they got their way over rehearsals. Beethoven was confined to a room at the back of the building, and the concert master Seyfried would come to him between pieces to get his view. Given that Beethoven's deafness was now serious, one can imagine how difficult this was for him. In effect he was unable to make constructive criticism – no doubt just what the players had aimed for – and clearly held back, possibly as a bargaining tool to ensure he conducted. He got his way at least on that.

When you look at the pieces Beethoven had programmed, you certainly feel a twinge of sympathy for the musicians. The concert was to be a gigantic undertaking, guaranteed to stretch the most accomplished instrumentalists, not to mention the inherent difficulties of working with this particular composer.

This is how the concert was advertised in the *Wiener Zeitung*:

On Thursday, December 22, 1808, Ludwig van Beethoven will have the honour to give a musical Academie *in the Theater-an-der-Wien. All the pieces are of his composition, entirely new, and not yet heard in public.*

First Part:

1. *A Symphony, entitled: 'A Recollection of Country Life',
    in F major*
2. *Aria*
3. *Hymn with Latin text, composed in the church style
    with chorus and solos*
4. *Pianoforte Concerto played by himself*

Second Part:

1. *Grand Symphony in C minor*
2. *Holy, with Latin text composed in the church style, with
    chorus and solos*
3. *Fantasia for pianoforte alone*
4. *Fantasia for the pianoforte which ends with the gradual
    entrance of the entire orchestra and the introduction of
    choruses as a finale*

No fewer than eight pieces, with a total running time of around four hours, depending on how long item 3 in Part II was, an improvisation by Beethoven. Clearly the two showpieces were the new symphonies, one to begin each part of the concert. And just in case you are in any doubt, these are the 'Pastoral' to open the first part, the Fifth to open the second.

This concert, as scheduled, demanded musicianship of the very highest level from the orchestral players, superlative singing from a chorus, and an audience prepared to be patient and long suffering in the extreme. With the benefit of hindsight, we can envy the audience for being present at the first performance ever of three of Beethoven's greatest works, if we include the Piano Concerto, even if the musical demands outstripped the players' competence.

To flesh out the other pieces, the Aria was 'Ah! Perfido', composed for soprano and orchestra some years earlier; the Hymn was the *Gloria* from the Mass in C, composed the previous year; the Piano Concerto was to be the newly completed No. 4; the Holy was the *Sanctus* from the Mass in C, and the final Fantasia was the *Choral Fantasia*.

Two of these other pieces presented particular problems – in each case problems of Beethoven's own making. His preferred choice to sing the aria was the soprano who had created the title role in *Leonore*, Anna Milder-Hauptmann.* She accepted immediately, but 'an unlucky quarrel provoked by Beethoven' resulted in her refusing.† Several other sopranos were tried, but found wanting. Finally he engaged the sister-in-law of his friend Schuppanzigh the violinist, Josephine Killitschky, who was both young and inexperienced.

There was potentially a much larger problem with the final piece in the programme, the *Choral Fantasia*. This had only just been composed by Beethoven, and consisted of a long solo piano introduction, joined first by the orchestra, and then the chorus. In fact so recently had he composed it, that he had not written out the piano introduction. This meant, in effect, that the orchestra had no idea when to come in. One can imagine there was some rehearsal – Beethoven being permitted into the rehearsal room for this, at least – with Seyfried assuring the orchestra that if he could turn pages for Beethoven when confronted by nothing more than a few squiggles, he could be sure to lead them in at the right point.

These incidentals, certainly in Beethoven's eye, were merely

---

* Described by Haydn, endearingly, as having 'a voice like a house'.

† They evidently made it up later, since Milder went on to sing the role of Leonore in the revamped *Fidelio* some years later.

irritants compared to the much larger issue of a successful performance of the pieces on which he knew his reputation hung, the two new symphonies.

As for the audience, they had something else to contend with too. It was a bitterly cold December evening, and the Theater an der Wien was unheated. With four hours of music to look forward to, it does not take much imagination to see them turning up in heavy coats, scarves, gloves, hats, possibly stamping their feet to keep warm and blowing into their hands. Not exactly conducive to a good evening's music-making.

Good was what it was not. Frustratingly there are no reviews of the concert – it's hard to understand why this is the case, other than the probability that the critics decided to cover the other concert that night in the Burgtheater – but several of Beethoven's friends and colleagues have left eyewitness accounts.

These accounts choose not to comment on the opening piece, the 'Pastoral', but I believe the audience will have been stunned by the birdcalls towards the close of the second movement. These are not incorporated into the music as other composers had done with birdcalls (notably Handel), but are stand-alone, and standout, solo passages for flute, oboe and clarinet.

Is it too much of an exaggeration to suggest that the birdcalls, which Beethoven repeats a few bars later, drew laughter from the audience? Possibly not, since the *Allgemeine musikalische Zeitung*, in a review of a performance of the 'Pastoral' only a few months later in the Gewandhaus in Leipzig, wrote elliptically of the birdcalls:

> *Even a few incidental imitations of certain little natural manifestations (especially towards the end), treated jokingly, can only be received with a benign smile even by those who*

otherwise dislike that kind of thing, because they are so aptly portrayed and, as previously stated, only introduced jokingly.

The aria, which followed the 'Pastoral', we can assume was pretty dreadful. Thayer writes, albeit without attribution, that poor Josephine Killitschky was so nervous, and made even more so by the nervousness of her friends on her behalf, that when Beethoven led her on to the stage and let her hand go, she became overwhelmed with fright and 'made wretched work of the aria'.

We know nothing of how the *Gloria* from the Mass went, but the Fourth Piano Concerto, directed by Beethoven from the keyboard, has left us with an image of Beethoven that has lodged in legend and coloured our thinking of him ever since.*

Early on in the first movement, at the first attacking passage, Beethoven apparently forgot he was the soloist, leapt up from the piano stool, and conducted the orchestra so vigorously, waving his arms so wide, that he knocked both candles from the music stand off the piano. The audience, not unreasonably, laughed. Beethoven saw this, lost his temper, and made the orchestra start again.

While the players rearranged their music, Seyfried hurriedly sent two choirboys on stage to stand either side of Beethoven with a candle. The boy on the right side stepped close to Beethoven so he could follow the piano part. At the same point in the first movement Beethoven flung his arms out again, hitting the boy in the face and causing him to drop his candle. The other boy, seeing it coming, ducked.

---

* The account that follows was given by the composer Louis Spohr in his memoirs published fifty years later, and he attributes it to Seyfried. Given the passage of time, and the fact that it is second hand, it is not impossible that some elements are exaggerated

'If the audience had laughed the first time, they now indulged in a truly Bacchanalian riot,' Spohr wrote. 'Beethoven broke out in such fury that when he struck the first chord of the solo he broke six strings.'

And so Part I of this historic concert ended.

Again we know, frustratingly, nothing of how the Fifth Symphony went, or the *Sanctus*, and we do not know any details of the piano improvisation. We most certainly do know what happened when it came to the *Choral Fantasia*.*

Beethoven, it appears, had agreed to the dropping of a passage that comes soon after the orchestra joins the piano, possibly as a concession to the lateness of the hour and the chill in the theatre. But in performance he forgot this, and so while the orchestra ploughed on, he played the repeat. This exposed the clarinettist, who appeared – to Beethoven at least – to come in at the wrong place.

Orchestra and soloist struggled to come together again, but it was impossible: 'Like a runaway carriage going downhill, an overturn was inevitable.' Beethoven leapt up from the piano in a fury, stormed over to the orchestra and hurled insults at the players so loudly that the audience heard every word. He stabbed at the music and demanded they start the piece again. Several musicians – including, most probably, the offending clarinettist – stood and threatened to leave the stage.

Maybe Beethoven mumbled an apology, or at least calmed down, because eyewitnesses agree the piece started again (presumably from the entrance of the orchestra) and this time went without a hitch.

---

* There are several eyewitness accounts, which I have amalgamated to give a clear narrative.

The audience went home no doubt chilled to the bone, but content that as usual a concert by Beethoven did not disappoint, even if for reasons unconnected with the supreme works they had just heard. The orchestra seethed backstage afterwards, several of them swearing they would never play for Beethoven again.

Seyfried gives a rather nice coda:

> *At first Beethoven could not understand that he had in a manner humiliated the musicians ... But he readily and heartily begged the pardon of the orchestra for the humiliation to which he had subjected it, and was honest enough to spread the story himself and assume all responsibility for his own absence of mind.*

In circumstances, therefore, bordering on the bizarre, Beethoven had given the world his Sixth Symphony, the 'Pastoral'; his Fifth Symphony, and his Fourth Piano Concerto.

Chapter 11

Under Cannon Fire

In which Beethoven once again tries his luck at love

Beethoven lived in squalor. If that seems like an exaggeration for such a supreme artist, consider this description by a senior French(!) army officer and diplomat* who visited him in his apartment only a few months after the benefit concert:

Imagine the dirtiest and most disorderly room possible. There were water stains on the floor, a rather ancient piano on which the dust struggled for supremacy with sheets of paper covered with handwritten or printed notes. Under the piano – I do not exaggerate – an unemptied chamber pot. Next to it, a small walnut table that had ink spilled on it, a large number of quills encrusted with ink ... and yet more music. The chairs nearly all had straw seats, and were

---

* An interesting comment on the unpredictability of Beethoven's likes and dislikes is that he welcomed this particular French officer, Baron de Trémont, whom he had never met before, into his apartment, despite his antagonism towards the French officers at Lichnowsky's Silesian estate.

covered with plates filled with the remains of last night's supper, as well as clothes.

It was for precisely this reason that a certain member of the Habsburg royal family decided to take action when he heard of Beethoven's intention to leave Vienna for Kassel, coupled with the composer's deafness and a general lack of social awareness.

This was no ordinary member of Habsburg royalty; this was Archduke Rudolph, youngest brother of the Emperor, no less. Rudolph had one quality certain to endear himself to Beethoven, no obvious admirer of royalty. He was an extraordinarily gifted musician. He was an excellent pianist, and a talented composer too. Beethoven met him for the first time, probably at a soirée, around 1808 or possibly earlier, and agreed to give him tuition, both on piano and in composition. In fact he was the only person Beethoven ever took on as a pupil of composition, so Beethoven must have been seriously impressed.*

In a sense it is fair to say that Rudolph stepped into the vacuum left by Prince Lichnowsky, both artistically and financially. And even more than that. As an accomplished musician, he recognised Beethoven's genius and instinctively understood and forgave his shortcomings. As brother of the Emperor, he was able to gain access for Beethoven into the highest salons in the city. Lessons with Beethoven took place in Rudolph's private quarters in the Hofburg Palace, the seat of the Emperor, and so Beethoven was able to come and go as he pleased in the heart of the royal establishment.

Rudolph, although seventeen years younger than Beethoven, took it upon himself to be, in effect, Beethoven's guardian, to

---

* Recordings of Rudolph's piano and chamber works are available on CD today, but are rarely performed.

protect him as a supreme artist from the vicissitudes of life. A word from the Archduke would instantly smooth matters over, and Beethoven was most certainly not averse to dropping his patron's name when he needed to.

Rudolph was perfectly placed to help Beethoven. Poor health had prevented the Archduke from pursuing the military career his position fitted him for, so instead he had entered the Church and taken minor vows.* This meant he was domiciled in Vienna, free to indulge himself in the city's artistic activities.

It is certain that towards the end of 1808 Beethoven would have lost no time in telling Rudolph of the offer he had received from Kassel, and his intention of accepting it. Rudolph recognised immediately that the move would be a mistake for Beethoven, potentially a fatal one. People in Kassel did not know him; they would not understand his eccentricities, and would soon tire of making allowances for his increasing deafness.

But how to persuade him to remain in Vienna? What incentive could he offer? He came up with a brilliant solution. He called in two of the city's senior aristocrats, patrons of the arts, and together they offered Beethoven a lifetime annuity of 4000 florins on the sole condition that he agree to remain in Vienna, 'or some other town situated in the hereditary lands of His Austrian Imperial Majesty'. There were no other stipulations. He did not have to agree to compose, or perform, just remain where he could be looked after and protected.

It did not take much working out, even for Beethoven, to see that this was an offer he could not refuse. Despite having formally accepted the offer from Kassel, he thought nothing of pulling out,

---

* A similar set of circumstances to Beethoven's royal patron in Bonn, Archduke Maximilian Franz.

and agreed to Archduke Rudolph's proposal. Maybe with renewed peace of mind, he began work on a new composition. It was to be his Fifth Piano Concerto (named the 'Emperor' by the publisher, despite Beethoven's objections), his mightiest by far, and in gratitude he was to dedicate it to Rudolph, along with the Fourth, and several other works, including the monumental 'Hammerklavier' Piano Sonata and the *Missa Solemnis*. In fact, Rudolph was to receive more dedications from Beethoven than any other single individual, and we can say without hesitation that he deserved it.

The renewed peace of mind led to a development in another direction as well. It appears he was ready to chance his luck once again at love. Within days of signing the contract with Rudolph, he wrote to a young male friend in terms that were unusually light-hearted, with a touch of arrogance, and which give a nice insight into his priorities:

> *Now you can help me look for a wife. Indeed you might find some beautiful girl where you are at present [Freiburg], and one who perhaps now and then would grant a sigh to my harmonies ... If you do find one, however, she must be beautiful, for it is impossible for me to love anything that is not beautiful – or else I should have to love myself.*

It was, apparently, less unusual than you might think for Beethoven to appreciate female beauty, and not always in the subtlest of ways. Ries wrote in his memoirs:

> *Beethoven very much enjoyed looking at women. Lovely, youthful faces particularly pleased him. If we passed a girl who could boast her share of charms, he would turn round and examine her through his glasses, then laugh or grin when*

he realised I was watching him. He often fell in love, but usually only for a short time. When once I teased him about his conquest of a certain beautiful lady, he confessed that she had captivated him more intensely and longer than any other – seven whole months.

Ries frustratingly gives no clue as to who this 'certain beautiful lady' might be, and there is no indication that Beethoven had any particular woman in mind in his letter to his Freiburg friend.

If Beethoven had indeed found new peace of mind, with the annuity solving any financial problems and giving him freedom to compose as and when he liked, it was to be shattered once again – and this time it really was not his fault.

Austria had quite simply not learned from its mistakes. It declared war on France *again*. Napoleon, newly returned to Paris from Spain, decided once and for all to give Austria a hiding from which it would not recover. He left immediately to take command of his army in Germany,* and began his march on Vienna.

A few skirmishes out of the way, Napoleon advanced rapidly across Germany, into Austria, and east towards the imperial capital. In scenes similar to those of three and half years earlier, there was a mass exodus from the city, amid scenes of some panic as word spread that this time Napoleon was in no mood to be benevolent.

The exodus reached right to the top. On 4 May the Empress

---

* Fatefully giving Arthur Wellesley, the future Duke of Wellington, the opportunity to gain a firm foothold in Portugal, which would ultimately lead to French defeat in Spain.

left Vienna with the royal family, including Archduke Rudolph. This had an unexpectedly beneficial – and indeed unusual – effect on Beethoven's musical output. He decided to compose a piano sonata to commemorate Rudolph's departure.

He initially composed only the first movement. It opens with three descending chords, over which Beethoven wrote, '*Le – be – wohl*' ('Farewell'). He said he would write the second movement, entitled *Die Abwesenheit* (*Absence*), while Rudolph was absent from the city, and told him he would not compose the final movement, to be called *Das Wiedersehen* (*The Return*), until Rudolph's safe return to Vienna.*

Napoleon established his headquarters at Linz, less than a hundred miles in a straight line west of Vienna, and sent his commanders to the capital to demand its surrender. It was in Linz that Johann van Beethoven, a year before, had bought a pharmacy, and the ensuing conflict was to make his fortune, as well as earning him a lifetime's contempt for having, in effect, collaborated with the enemy.

The defence of the imperial capital was in the hands of sixteen thousand soldiers, bolstered by around a thousand students and artists, and an ill-equipped and under-trained civil militia, all under the command of a junior member of the royal family, Archduke Maximilian. The Emperor, from the safety of exile, ordered Maximilian to resist the French and defend the city at all costs. Thus Maximilian rejected the demand to surrender, effectively signing a suicide note for Vienna.

---

* This he did, Rudolph returning to Vienna in late January of the following year, and the complete sonata is regarded as one of Beethoven's finest. When it was published in 1811 as Op. 81a, the publisher decided to give it a French name, 'Les adieux', by which it is known today. Beethoven preferred to call it 'Das Lebewohl'.

The French commanders unhurriedly set up their new short-barrelled howitzer cannon on rising ground in Spittelberg, a suburb a short distance west of the city wall, the Bastei. A day passed in quiet anticipation, the people of Vienna bracing themselves for what they knew was coming. A contemporary wrote that people milled around in the streets, swapping jokes and light-hearted banter to keep spirits up, and then when dusk fell retreated indoors, until no sound could be heard inside the city wall.

At nine o'clock on the evening of 9 May 1809, as daylight finally faded, twenty cannon opened fire. The bombardment continued through the night, pounding the inner city mercilessly. Any defence was rendered useless by the distance and range of the howitzers. The soldiers and militia had nothing to fight against except shells dropping onto them from the sky. Surrender was inevitable, and it was not long in coming. At half-past two the following afternoon the white flag was raised.

And where was the city's most famous resident, its leading artist, during this traumatic period? At home, in his apartment, which abutted the Bastei on the inner, city side and was therefore almost in direct line of fire.

Why Beethoven did not leave the city for the safety of the surrounding countryside, we do not know. It is even more incomprehensible given his penchant for rural calm, and his escape almost every summer to the peace of small villages. We can safely assume he had no shortage of offers. All the city's leading aristocrats left the city for the safety of their country estates, including Prince Lichnowsky. Did the Prince attempt to mend their relationship by suggesting Beethoven accompany him and his wife? We do not know.

Beethoven's brother Carl did not leave Vienna either, and we know from Ferdinand Ries that the two brothers had intimate contact at this time, despite the antagonism between them. Ries says in his memoirs that Beethoven was 'very frightened' by the bombardment of the city, and spent most of it in the cellar of his brother Carl's house, 'where he covered his head with pillows to shut out the sound of the cannon'. Carl and his family lived in an apartment building on the corner of Rauhensteingasse and Himmelpfortgasse close to St Stephansdom in the heart of the city, and so they must all have been in extreme danger. This, added to Beethoven's overt contempt for Johanna and dislike for his brother, coupled with the presence of an infant not yet three years of age, must have made for a highly tense time.[6]

After the bombardment, Vienna was a changed city. Prices soared, to such an extent that copper coins were done away with. Food, bread in particular, became expensive – always guaranteed to upset the populace – and the French demanded huge sureties, requisitioned enormous amounts of supplies, and levied a tax on all property. Never was Beethoven more grateful for his annuity, from which he had begun to receive the first payments.

There was an added element, true of all military occupations. Foreign soldiers in uniform patrolled the streets, heaping humiliation on top of other hardships on the populace. If any resident of Vienna was likely to let resentment at this boil over, it was Beethoven. And he did. A young musical colleague reported that Beethoven, seeing a French officer in a coffee-house, shook his fist at him, and shouted, 'If I, as a general, knew as much about warfare as I, the composer, know of counterpoint, I'd be able to give you a lesson or two!' One imagines that from anyone else this would have led to immediate arrest, but not from the universally known, admired, eccentric and harmless composer.

As a coda to the occupation, twenty days after the bombardment, quietly and practically unnoticed, the world lost one of its finest composers. Franz Joseph Haydn died at the age of seventy-seven.

Beethoven had more reason than the obvious to be grateful for his annuity payments. The mythical woman of his letter to Freiburg had materialised. He was once again in love, and this time he was determined to present himself as an irresistible catch, and that meant smartening up.

The lady in question was the eldest of two daughters of a family of Italian extraction by the name of Therese Malfatti. Her father had made his fortune in the silk trade, enough to branch out and establish his own sugar refinery, and owned a sumptuous house just off the fashionable Kärntnerstrasse, and a country estate in Walkersdorf about forty miles north-west of Vienna.

Therese was known to be a volatile, impetuous young lady – eighteen years of age in 1810 – and was said by those who knew her to have more of the fiery Italian temperament in her than her slightly younger sister or any other family member.

Perhaps Beethoven's friends warned him of this, but if so he paid little heed. They might have pointed out to him too that he was about to turn forty years of age, and that Therese was therefore young enough to be his daughter. If they did, he again brushed it aside.

He no doubt saw himself as a prime catch. He could now – for the first time in his courting experiences – offer financial security, thanks to the annuity. He was a friend of the Emperor's brother, and could reasonably expect court engagements. Even if

An idealised representation of Beethoven, the heroic demigod. This statue stands in the Beethovenplatz just outside the Stadtpark, Vienna.

The house at no. 515 Bonngasse. The Beethoven family rented rooms at the back on the first floor. In one of these Beethoven was born. The house is now a museum dedicated to Beethoven, with artefacts including his last piano.

Count Waldstein was Beethoven's most important patron in his formative Bonn years. Beethoven later dedicated his Piano Sonata Op. 53 to Waldstein.

Karl Lichnowsky. In every respect he was Beethoven's most important patron during his early years in Vienna. Beethoven dedicated several works to the Prince, though he later fell out with him.

By the turn of the nineteenth century an unshakeably romanticised image of Beethoven had taken hold. This is a lithograph by the German painter and sculptor Sascha Schneider purporting to show Beethoven performing the 'Moonlight' Sonata for Giulietta Guicciardi, to whom it is dedicated.

Archduke Rudolph, the most supportive of Beethoven's patrons, both artistically and financially. In gratitude Beethoven dedicated far more compositions to Rudolph than to anyone else, including many of his greatest works. Rudolph was a fine composer and pianist in his own right.

The title page of the copyist's score of the 'Eroica' Symphony. The hole in the paper where Beethoven scratched out Napoleon's name can clearly be seen. At this stage the symphony was entitled 'Sinfonia Grande'.

Beethoven in 1814, aged forty-three, in an engraving by Blasius Höfel, considered by Beethoven's friends to be one of the best likenesses of him ever achieved. Unusually in portraits of Beethoven, the dark complexion that led to his nickname 'The Spaniard' is clearly evident.

Karl van Beethoven (1806–58), the composer's nephew and the sole Beethoven of the succeeding generation. Beethoven embarked on a lengthy, turbulent, and ultimately ruinous court case to exclude Karl's mother from the boy's upbringing. Beethoven considered Karl to be his own son, and encouraged the boy to call him 'Father'.

This miniature was found in Beethoven's effects after his death. Its identity is uncertain. It has been attributed to more than one woman, including Antonie Brentano, a strong candidate for the Immortal Beloved. All we can say with certainty is that she was a woman who meant a great deal to Beethoven, since he kept the portrait hidden.

Beethoven Composing, painted by Carl Schlösser, c.1890. The image of Beethoven composing works of genius in chaotic and relatively squalid surroundings took hold even before his death. Although there may well be an element of exaggeration in this painting, it accords with eyewitness descriptions by his friends of manuscripts strewn in total disorder.

Beethoven is buried in the Musicians' Quarter of the Zentralfriedhof, the main cemetery south-east of Vienna. The obelisk-shaped headstone bears the single word 'Beethoven', no dates, no eulogy.

The massive bronze statue of Beethoven in the Münsterplatz in Bonn, facing towards the house where the von Breuning family lived.

his compositions were not universally understood, they were accepted as masterworks, and brought him unrivalled recognition. More lucrative commissions were sure to come.

So, for the first time in his life, he paid exquisite attention to his appearance – even if he admitted he found it thoroughly alien to him. He wrote to one friend asking if he could borrow his mirror – 'Mine is broken' – and to another, Ignaz Gleichenstein,* sending him 300 gulden, asking him to buy linen or Bengal cotton which the society tailor Joseph Lind would make into shirts for him, as well as at least half-a-dozen neckcloths.

Please do this at once, he added, 'since not only do I understand nothing whatever about such matters, but also such matters are profoundly distasteful to me.'

He was clearly in no doubt that Therese would agree to a marriage proposal, since he wrote to Wegeler asking him to send urgently his baptismal certificate, offering to pay all expenses, including Wegeler's travel from Koblenz (where he was now living with Eleonore and their two children) to Bonn, and cautioning him not to confuse him with his elder brother Ludwig Maria, who had died at six days old.

Beethoven had been introduced to the Malfatti family by Gleichenstein, was instantly attracted to Therese, and soon began heaping lavish (and certainly exaggerated) praise on her piano skills, offering to give her lessons. Knowing as we do how Beethoven hated giving lessons, the attraction must have been very strong indeed.

---

* It was to Gleichenstein that Beethoven had written in Freiburg asking him to find a 'beautiful girl'. Gleichenstein, a young musician who helped Beethoven in much the same way as Ries, was to marry Therese's sister Netty, who outlived him by forty years.

It did wonders for his spirits. He sent Gleichenstein another 50 gulden for neckcloths, saying in the accompanying letter that he felt whatever wickedness people had inflicted on his soul 'could be cured by the Malfattis'. As evidence of his acceptance into the Malfatti household, he teased Gleichenstein in the letter that he, Gleichenstein, was not the only person the family dog Gigons was happy to see.*

To set the seal on his amorous intent, he did what only he could do, or at least with such a degree of prestige and kudos. He composed a piece of piano music for Therese, making it deliberately simple so that she could play it.† The clincher, as far as he was concerned.

But once again, as on every previous attempt at forming a lasting relationship with a woman, he was seriously misjudging the situation.

For a start, it seems Therese had given him no clear indication of her feelings. In repeated notes to Gleichenstein, he asked him – given his closeness to Therese's sister Netty – to try to find out whether he had reason to be optimistic that a marriage proposal might meet with a favourable response. Clearly his frustration was building. Therese was certainly flattered by the attention of Vienna's most famous musician,‡ and it was possible – given her flighty nature – that she flirted with him.

It is known she had other suitors at the time, and she might

---

* One of only two references in all Beethoven's letters and papers to domestic pets.

† Thus not repeating the mistake he had made with the Piano Sonata in C sharp minor, Op. 27 No. 2, 'Moonlight', dedicated to Giulietta Guicciardi, the third movement of which is beyond the reach of any but highly accomplished pianists.

‡ In old age she boasted she had been Beethoven's pupil.

well have led Beethoven on, keen as she must have been to retain his friendship, even playing him off against the others. The point clearly came when he felt she was more than interested in him, and he decided to take things further.

Then it all went disastrously wrong. Exactly what happened we do not know, but we can surmise from surviving correspondence that Beethoven was at the Malfatti house, possibly alone with Therese, became drunk on very strong punch, and made a clumsy lunge at her. She was utterly appalled, and rejected him in no uncertain terms.

The family repaired to the estate in Walkersdorf and summoned Gleichenstein to join them. To him was given the unenviable task of writing to Beethoven to spell out the family's displeasure, and make it clear to him that they did not wish Beethoven to continue seeing their daughter in any capacity. The letter has not survived – who could blame Beethoven if he tore it up? – but his reply to Gleichenstein expressed his deep hurt: 'Your news has plunged me from the heights of the most sublime ecstasy down into the depths.' And the news that he was being barred even from continuing to give Therese piano lessons drew from him a sentence of extraordinary pathos, even self-pity: 'Am I then nothing more than a Music-Man for yourself or the others?'

Beethoven here uses the untranslatable German word *Musikus*, which carries a derisory, even insulting connotation. 'Mr Music Man' might be the closest English rendition.

Beethoven wrote one final lengthy letter to Therese. He berates her gently for her flighty nature: 'Our fickle T who treats so lightheartedly all the affairs of life.' He confesses that he is leading a lonely and quiet life. He teases her about a theme he composed for her when they were together, inviting her to find its hidden meaning, but cautioning her in a painful reference to his own indiscretion: 'Work it out for yourself, but do not drink punch <u>to help you</u>.' He even – in shades of his *mea culpa* to Eleonore von Breuning nearly twenty years before – writes, 'Remember me and do so with pleasure – Forget my mad behaviour.'

Thus another amorous adventure ended in failure, and Therese passed out of Beethoven's life. But not out of musical history. For what was the piece of music he composed specially for her, that was undemanding enough for her to be able to play, and that was found in her effects after her death forty-one years later?

It is a small piece, and Beethoven gave it the innocuous title 'Bagatelle'. But it is what he wrote at the top of the title page that has exercised musicologists and scholars ever since. This is what he wrote: 'Für Elise am 27. April zur Erinnerung an L. V. Bthvn' ('For Elise on 27 April to remind you of L. V. Bthvn').

The question is, who was Elise? One theory that gained acceptance was that Beethoven's handwriting was notoriously difficult to decipher, and that the publisher mistook 'Therese' for 'Elise'. But that stretches credulity – the two names do not resemble each other even closely. More likely is that Therese had the family nickname 'Elise'. Her sister Anna was known as 'Netty', and such nicknames were common practice.* Beethoven too had a propensity for giving people nicknames – there are numerous examples in his correspondence – so he might even have invented the name himself (though he does not use it in correspondence with her). Another possible explanation is that after the debacle of Lichnowsky spotting Josephine Brunsvik's name on the manuscript of the song 'An die Hoffnung', he deliberately disguised Therese's name. Or finally, maybe this is not the piece that he composed for her at all. He composed it for a woman

---

* Josephine Brunsvik was known to her sisters as Pepi or Pipschen.

named Elise about whom we know nothing, and she passed it on to Therese.

What we *do* know is that the Bagatelle known around the world today as 'Für Elise' is quite possibly the single best-known piece of piano music ever written by anyone,[*] and is beloved by under-talented pianists of all generations, who may well boast that they can play Beethoven. 'Für Elise' is what they play.

Did Beethoven finally, once and for all, abandon all hope of a relationship with a woman who might return his love? Most certainly not. We are now approaching the single closest and most intense relationship he was ever to have.

It did not result in marriage, it did not even last long. In fact we know far more about what did not happen than about what did. Most frustratingly of all, we do not know beyond doubt who the woman in question was. She is known to posterity simply as 'The Immortal Beloved'.

---

[*] In the 1990s it was the most downloaded mobile phone ringtone in the world.

Chapter 12

Immortal Beloved

'My angel, my all, my very self'

This is what we know beyond any doubt. On the morning of 6 July Beethoven, in a hotel in the Bohemian spa town of Teplitz,[*] wrote a four-page letter to a woman. That same evening he added two and a half more pages. The following morning, 7 July, he completed page seven and added three more pages. The letter contains declarations of love throughout, which become extremely intense towards the end, and the letter closes with an unequivocal declaration of eternal, and mutual, love. This letter was found – as was the Heiligenstadt Testament – in his effects after his death.

Here it is in full:

> *6th July, morning*
> *My angel, my all, my very self – only a few words today, and even with pencil – (with yours) only tomorrow will I know definitely about my lodgings, what an awful waste of time – Why this deep sorrow when necessity speaks – How else can our*

---

[*] Today Bad Teplice in the Czech Republic.

*love endure except through sacrifices, through not demanding
everything from one another? How can you alter the fact that
you are not wholly mine, I not wholly thine – Oh, God.*

*Look to nature in all her beauty and let her calm your
heart about what must be – Love demands everything and
rightly so, and that can only mean <u>me with you and you with
me</u> – you forget so easily that I would have to live for myself
and for you, only if we were completely united would you feel
as little pain as I –*

*My journey was terrible. I did not get here until 4 in
the morning yesterday. Because they were short of horses the
coach took a different route, but it was a dreadful road. At
the one to last stage they warned me not to travel at night,
that I would have to go through a dangerous forest, but that
spurred me on – and I was wrong. The coach, of course, had
to break down on the dreadful road.*

*Esterházy took the other more usual route and had the
same trouble with 8 horses that I had with four. Yet to a
certain extent I got pleasure as I always do when I overcome
a problem –*

*Now swiftly from external matters to internal ones. We
will surely see each other soon. There is no time now to tell
you what I have been thinking about these last few days regarding my life – if our hearts were only united I would not
have to have such thoughts. My soul is so full of things to tell
you – Oh – There are times when words are simply no use –
be cheerful – remain my only true darling, my all, as I am
yours. The rest is for the gods to decree, what is to be for us
and what should be –*

your faithful

Ludwig

Monday evening on 6 July
You are suffering my most precious one – only now have I dis-
covered that letters must be posted very early in the morning.
Mondays – Thursdays – the only days when the mail-coach
goes from here to K. – you are suffering – Oh, where I am
you are with me, with me and I can talk to you – if only we
could live together, what a life it is!!!! now!!!! without you –
Pursued by the kindness of people here and there, which I
think – which I no more want to deserve than do deserve –
humility of a human towards humans – it pains me – and
when I regard myself in relation to the universe, what I am
and what is He – I weep when I think you will probably
not receive the first news of me until Saturday – as much as
you love me – I love you even more deeply – do not ever hide
yourself from me – Goodnight – taking the baths has made
me tired – ~~*Oh go with, go with*~~ *– Oh, God – so near! so far!*
is our love not truly sent from Heaven? And is it not even as
firm as the firmament of Heaven?

good [sic] *morning on 7 July – even lying in bed thoughts*
of you force themselves into my head, my Immortal Beloved,
now and then happy, then again sad, in the hands of Fate, to
see if it will heed us – I can only live with you wholly or not at
all, yes, I have even decided to wander helplessly, until I can
fly into your arms, and say that I have found my haven there,
my soul embraced by you to be transported to the kingdom of
spirits – yes, sadly that must come – you will accept it more
readily, knowing I am true to you, that never can another
woman possess my heart – never, never – Oh, God, why do
we have to be so far apart from what we love? And yet my life
in V. now is such a wretched existence – Your love makes me

at once the happiest and unhappiest of men – at my time of
life I need stability, calmness of life – can that exist in a rela-
tionship like ours? – Angel, I have just been told that the post
leaves every day – and so I must close, so you can get the letter
immediately – be calm, only through reflecting calmly about
our existence can we reach our goal to live together – stay
calm – love me – today – yesterday – what tearful longing for
you – you – you – my Love – my all – Farewell – Love me
still – never misjudge the most faithful heart of your beloved

   L.

eternally thine
eternally mine
*eternally ours**

Now the questions begin. Let us start with the most mundane element, the date. That's clear enough, isn't it? No, it isn't. For a start
you'll notice that although he is precise about the date and time,
and in the second part the day, he does not give the year. During
Beethoven's lifetime 6 July fell on a Monday in 1795, 1801, 1807,
1812, 1818. Nineteenth-century scholars could not agree on the
year, and it was not until the twentieth century that 1812 became
accepted, as far as I am aware, without question.

But here's something else to consider. Beethoven was notoriously unreliable when it came to dates. A huge number of his
letters, including lengthy ones as opposed to mere notes, are undated. Scholars have since assigned dates to them all, but not with
certainty. Yet here he is being precise even about the time of day.
Why? There is no need for him to be so precise, since it is clear he

---

* My translation.

and the woman were together possibly on the 5th, or shortly before, and she was aware of his travel plans. This attention to detail is totally unlike Beethoven.

Is he falsifying the date, and leaving the year out, deliberately, in case the letter falls into the wrong hands? It is certainly possible he feared the letter might go astray, since it is extraordinarily free of detail. For instance, nowhere does he use the woman's name, or even give her an initial. The only two initials are for place names. 'V' is clearly Vienna, and 'K' more than likely Karlsbad,* the only town beginning with 'K' within easy reach of Teplitz and which matches the times for the mail coach.

There is a further mystery in that the letter was found hidden in his desk after his death. This means he kept it with him for the rest of his life. He must surely have been reminded of it every time his desk was moved. There are two possible explanations: either he never sent it, or the woman received it and gave it back to him. The envelope has not survived; maybe there never was one, or maybe he kept it in a blank envelope after deciding not to send it. Certainly there are no stamps or sealing-wax marks on the letter. It is a reasonable assumption that he never sent it.

But if he was worried about the letter falling into the wrong hands, so worried even that he decided not to send it, why did he keep it? Simpler, surely, to destroy it, and thereby destroy the evidence.

Unless he *wanted* it to be found after his death, to show that he did have more success when it came to love than his friends gave him credit for. After all, it is very possible he wanted the Heiligenstadt Testament to be found so that the grief his deafness caused him would be there in writing.

---

* Today Karlovy Vary, in the Czech Republic.

One theory I am certain can be discounted, that the letter was an elaborate hoax by Beethoven, that no such woman, no such love affair existed. If you are going to set out to do that, would you really put in details of an uncomfortable coach ride, problems with finding a hotel room, complications over mail-coach timings?

And this is Beethoven, remember, who once said, 'I would rather write ten thousand musical notes than one letter of the alphabet.' No, it was not a hoax.

We can, I believe, be sure that there was a love affair between Beethoven and a woman, a mutual, reciprocal love affair. Was it consummated? The letter does not make it clear for certain one way or the other. Beethoven tentatively expresses the hope that the two might live together. Some researchers have taken this as evidence of a physical relationship, others have drawn the opposite conclusion. It is almost as if Beethoven is loath to commit to paper anything that is definitive.

But all these questions pale before the single most important question of all, which has been asked by every Beethoven biographer since the first almost two centuries ago; which has been answered in many different ways; which has been considered solved time and time again, but about which whole books continue to be published, films created, documentaries made, articles written.

Who was the woman? Who was Beethoven's Immortal Beloved?

I need first to sketch in a little background, before describing how events unfolded. The period following the rejection by Therese Malfatti proved to be difficult for Beethoven. His health was causing real problems. The perennial problems of colic and diarrhoea debilitated him. One can imagine that the trauma of yet another rejection aggravated things. So did something else beyond his control.

The Austrian economy was crippled by the effects of war. After the value of the currency became weaker and weaker, it was officially devalued in March 1811. This had the effect, not only of forcing prices to rocket, but of robbing Vienna's richest aristocrats overnight of their wealth. One, our old friend Prince Lobkowitz, dedicatee of several of Beethoven's most important compositions, was bankrupted and suffered the humiliation of having his estates seized.

Of direct relevance to our story is the fact that Lobkowitz was one of the two senior aristocrats who joined Archduke Rudolph in agreeing to pay Beethoven the annuity that kept him in Vienna. In September 1811, after only two years of payments, Lobkowitz was no longer able to continue.

It got worse for Beethoven. Two months after that, the other aristocrat who contributed to the annuity, Prince Kinsky, was thrown from his horse and killed. His payments too were halted, and Beethoven began a long-running dispute with his estate to try to get the payments continued.

As ever with Beethoven, there is a paradox. He continued to compose at a furious rate: the 'Archduke' Piano Trio, music for two plays, *König Stephan* and *Die Ruinen von Athen*, and most importantly the Seventh Symphony completed and the Eighth begun.

By the summer of 1812 he needed a break – in fact, *another* break. The previous summer he had visited the spa town of Teplitz, and decided to do the same again in 1812.

On either the evening of Sunday, 28 June, or the morning of Monday, the 29th, he left Vienna for Prague. He arrived in Prague on Wednesday, 1 July, and checked into the hotel *Zum schwarzen Ross* ('At the Black Steed'). The following day he attended a meeting regarding the Kinsky annuity. The day after that, the 3rd, he failed to keep an appointment scheduled for the evening. On Saturday, 4 July, before noon, he left Prague for Teplitz. He arrived in Teplitz at 4 a.m. after a difficult journey during which his carriage lost a wheel. He found a room at the hotel *Die goldene Sonne* ('The Golden Sun'). The next morning, Monday, 6 July, he began the letter to the Immortal Beloved. He added to it that evening, and again the following morning. Later that day he moved into the hotel *Zur Eiche* ('At the Oak Tree'), where he stayed for some weeks.

A close reading of the letter, fitting it into this time frame, indicates that Beethoven met the Immortal Beloved on Friday, 3 July, probably in the evening when he failed to keep a pre-arranged appointment. How long the two were together, whether they spent the night of the 3rd together, we do not know. After this, he left for Teplitz, and she left for Karlsbad. That they met cannot be in doubt – she gave him her pencil.

While we can be relatively certain of Beethoven's movements, therefore, through the evidence of hotel ledgers and police registers, the same is most certainly not true of the Immortal Beloved, for the simple reason that we are not sure what name we are looking for.

It is surely safe to assume the woman must be someone who was well known to Beethoven in Vienna. The passion in the letter is not credible if this is a woman he met in Prague and fell in love with on the same day (or the day after). It also would be entirely out of character for Beethoven to behave like that.

Only one name that Beethoven definitely knew appears in registers both in Prague and then Karlsbad on the right dates. Her name is Antonie Brentano, and the American musicologist and

Beethoven biographer Maynard Solomon, in his exhaustive biography published in 1977,* came to the unequivocal conclusion that Antonie was the Immortal Beloved. He presented powerful evidence of an intimate friendship between them, regarding her presence in the two right locations at the right time as conclusive proof.

So certain was he that he wrote in the biography, 'The weight of the evidence in [Antonie Brentano's] favour is so powerful that it is not presumptuous to assert that the riddle of Beethoven's Immortal Beloved has now been solved.'

In that if nothing else, he was mistaken. Several names have been proposed since, some for the first time, some not, and in 2011 alone two full-length books were published arguing the case for different women.†

The argument *against* Antonie Brentano is that she was a married woman with children, and in fact was with her husband Franz and one of their children staying at the *Rothes Haus* ('Red House') hotel in Prague. Is it realistic to assume she would be able to absent herself from husband and child for a clandestine meeting with Beethoven, which might well have lasted for several hours, if not an entire night, and which was clearly emotionally fraught? And even if she had, would Beethoven, whose strong

---

* Maynard Solomon, *Beethoven* (Schirmer Books, New York, 1977; rev. edn, 1998).

† Edward Walden, *Beethoven's Immortal Beloved: Solving the Mystery* (Scarecrow Press, 2011). In a forensic examination appropriate for a trained lawyer, Walden argues the case for Bettina Brentano, whose half-brother Franz was Antonie's husband. John Klapproth, *Beethoven's Only Beloved, Josephine!* (private publication, 2011). Klapproth, a German-born government official living in New Zealand, rehearses well-worn, albeit powerful, arguments in favour of Josephine Brunsvik.

moral rectitude was beyond doubt, have entertained such a meeting with a woman who was a wife and mother?

For every argument, there is a counter-argument. For precisely that reason, it could be argued, he expressed himself so strongly in the letter, stating unequivocally that the love affair could not proceed, however much they both might wish it. There remains the question, though, of whether Antonie could have absented herself from her husband and daughter to pursue an affair, consummated or not.

The argument in favour of Antonie is further weakened by the fact that three weeks after arriving in Teplitz, Beethoven went to stay with Antonie and her husband and daughter in Karlsbad. Could that really have happened, all together under the same roof, if Beethoven and Antonie were desperately in love with each other and had met secretly in Prague?

After Beethoven left them in Karlsbad, he never met them again. But they stayed in touch, and Beethoven was to dedicate compositions to Antonie much later, very substantial compositions. There is also evidence that a decade later Franz Brentano advanced Beethoven a considerable sum of money when he was in need. If Franz knew Beethoven and his wife had had a love affair, his generosity is truly remarkable. If he never found out, he was at best naïve.

There can be no doubt that Beethoven was very close to the Brentanos, but under the circumstances outlined above – even given the fact that Antonie can without doubt be placed in Prague and Karlsbad on the right dates – I find it hard to believe he and Antonie were lovers, requited or unrequited.

Shortly after Solomon published his book, his arguments in favour of Antonie were challenged by one of Europe's leading musicologists and Beethoven scholars, the German Marie-Elisabeth

Tellenbach. Her candidate is Josephine Brunsvik. In fact, despite recent arguments in favour of other women, it is fair to say that the two leading candidates for identification as the Immortal Beloved are Antonie Brentano and Josephine Brunsvik.

Tellenbach argues against Antonie for precisely the reasons I have outlined, that although she fits the facts, emotionally as wife and mother and in the company of husband and daughter, it is not realistic to postulate a love affair.

She puts powerful arguments in favour of Josephine, not least that the letters discovered after the Second World War prove beyond doubt that Beethoven was in love with her and asked for a physical relationship. There is also the song 'An die Hoffnung', the discovery of which by Lichnowsky led to such embarrassment for Beethoven.

But there are counter-arguments. Josephine remarried in February 1810. The marriage was disastrous, and her husband, Baron Stackelberg, an Estonian, was frequently absent from Vienna. Since there is no direct evidence that Josephine was in either Prague or Karlsbad on the relevant dates, it means she would have had to absent herself from Vienna for some weeks, travel between Vienna, Prague and Karlsbad, without being seen or reported by anyone. In other words, she would most probably have had to travel in disguise. For a married woman – happily married or not – this presents almost insurmountable practical problems.

Solomon argues that with Europe at war, travellers were compelled to register with the police when crossing borders. Therefore it is impossible for Josephine to have done this incognito. Tellenbach counters that Prague and Karlsbad were both within the Austrian Empire, and so registration was not compulsory. Who is right? We cannot say.

The emotional argument regarding Josephine can be seen in

two ways. Would Beethoven, having been rejected by her while she was between marriages, want to rekindle his desires? Maybe, maybe not. Josephine was known to be emotionally unstable. How would this have affected Beethoven? It might have deterred him; it might have attracted him.

A further example of how intractable the arguments are is that it appears self-evident that the Immortal Beloved has to have been in Karlsbad, following the tryst in Prague. Not necessarily. All that we need to be able to say is that Beethoven *believed* her to be in Karlsbad. She does not actually have to have been there. In fact, if at the last moment he realised that she was not where he thought she was, maybe that would explain why he did not send the letter. This weakens the case for Antonie, and strengthens it (possibly) for Josephine.

There is a poignant coda to the candidacies of Antonie and Josephine. Both gave birth eight to nine months after the Prague encounter.

Antonie gave birth to a son, Karl Josef, on 8 March 1813. At an early age Karl suffered partial paralysis of the legs. At the age of three he showed signs of severe mental illness, and suffered from seizures. Antonie took him to a succession of doctors, who could do nothing for him. In a letter Antonie wrote, 'Oh, when one has to drink such a bitter cup of sorrow daily, hourly, how can there remain a last bit of joy and strength?' Karl died at the age of thirty-seven.

Josephine gave birth to a daughter on 9 April 1813. She named her Minona. Minona remained unmarried and lived to the age of eighty-four, almost into the twentieth century. She inherited her aunt Therese's estate, including her papers and the diary she kept meticulously in which she wrote of her sister Josephine's attachment to Beethoven. But no letters which might throw light on the events of July 1812 have survived. This has led to speculation that Minona, who treasured the memory of her mother, destroyed any evidence of an affair between her mother and Beethoven, and with it evidence that she, Minona, might have been Beethoven's daughter.

It has been pointed out that Minona is Anonim spelled backwards, 'the child with no name'. There is a photograph of Minona taken in old age. She bears a striking resemblance to Beethoven, which proves nothing.

To return to the letter, the more intricately one examines it, the more unyielding it becomes. But I believe there is a danger. It is possible to *over*-analyse its meaning. Beethoven was never subtle with words. His many hundreds of letters exactly mirror his thoughts. For profundity of thought and emotion, listen to his music.

This is a love letter, written in the white heat of passion. It is as if he is barely pausing to think. Towards the end of the letter, his writing becomes more frantic, the words more widely spaced, the lines shorter. He is emotionally wrought, quite possibly in despair. Looking at the writing, it is entirely feasible that he has drunk several glasses of wine.

What I believe the letter gives us is unequivocal proof that Beethoven was in love with a woman, a woman who returned that love in equal measure – the only evidence we have in his whole life of his love being fully reciprocated. Yet he knew their love could not endure. Circumstances prevented it. *'I can only live with you wholly, or not at all.'* Why? Because she was married? Or because he knew he could never give himself to her in the way a husband should, because of the demands of his music?

One fact I can state with total certainty, without the slightest chance of contradiction. The arguments, theories, speculation will continue. If Beethoven's letters to Josephine were discovered as recently as the 1940s, who knows what other evidence is inside a shoebox in an attic somewhere in the world?

In fact some years ago I was approached by a young Frenchwoman who said just that – that her mother, who lived outside Paris, had a letter written by Beethoven which she kept in a shoebox in her attic. She said the handwriting had been authenticated as belonging to Beethoven, and the letter proved beyond doubt that Josephine Brunsvik was the Immortal Beloved. I arranged to meet her, but the meeting was cancelled by a family member.

It is quite possible that the woman who was Beethoven's Immortal Beloved is a woman as yet unknown to history. One day new evidence will emerge. It might be in my lifetime, though I rather doubt it.

But even in the calm of Bohemia, taking the waters and musing over a lost love, the outside world intruded on Beethoven, in the shape of his own family. It sent him into a spiral of despair. His youngest brother Johann, it seemed, had succeeded where he had failed. He had found himself a woman, and he intended marrying her.

Beethoven sent Johann an urgent message, saying in effect 'over my dead body', abandoned his stay in Bohemia, packed his things, and headed as fast as he could for Linz to confront his brother. He only hoped he wasn't too late.

Chapter 13

An Utterly Untamed Personality

Beethoven turns again to his 'poor shipwrecked opera'

Before we accompany Beethoven on his mercy mission to Linz, something else happened in Teplitz that merits attention. In this small spa town in north-west Bohemia, the two greatest artists of the age met – and didn't like each other very much.

Beethoven had revered Johann Wolfgang von Goethe from his teenage years in Bonn, when he set some of Goethe's poems to music. More followed after the move to Vienna, and in 1810 he composed incidental music to Goethe's play *Egmont*. This was a commission from the Burgtheater, which wished to revive the play, and it appealed to Beethoven on two levels. The first was his admiration for Goethe; the second the subject matter of the play, which depicted the revolt of the Flemish hero Count Egmont against the Spanish occupier – thus appealing not just to Beethoven's innate belief in the triumph of freedom over oppression, but to his fondness for a true story that happened in the land of his fathers.

So pleased was he with his work, that he wrote to his publishers, Breitkopf und Härtel, in January 1812, asking them to forward the score to Goethe himself. Six months later Beethoven was in Teplitz, and found that Goethe was there too.

The two great artists met for the first time on 19 July, and what a contrasting pair they were. Goethe, elegant, sophisticated, at ease with aristocracy even royalty, at the height of his fame just a few years after the sensational success of the first part of his epic drama *Faust*; he was indisputably Germany's leading figure in poetry, drama, philosophy and science. Tutored privately from an early age, he was proficient in Latin, Greek, French, Italian, English and Hebrew, and had also been taught to dance, ride and fence. He was, in essence, Enlightenment man.

Well might Beethoven, albeit twenty-one years Goethe's junior, feel somewhat inadequate in the great man's company. He had his music, most certainly, but it was the only area in which he could claim any kind of ascendancy over Goethe.

At the time of their meeting, Goethe was sixty-three years of age, Beethoven forty-one. If opposites attract, they should have got on very well indeed, particularly since their different disciplines, combined with a substantial age difference, should have precluded any rivalry. And it seems, at first, there was indeed a mutual admiration.

After the first meeting, Goethe wrote to his wife, 'Never have I seen a more intensely focused, dynamic, or fervent artist.' Some days later Goethe called on Beethoven, and reported that he played the piano 'delightfully'.

But a famous anecdote shows an underlying tension. The two men were walking together, and the renowned Goethe attracted considerable attention. He found this irritating, and said so. Beethoven drily commented, 'Don't let it trouble Your Excellency; perhaps the greetings are intended for me.'

Then something really did go wrong between them. We do

not know for certain what it was, but an incident occurred – highly embarrassing for Goethe – that might explain it.

Goethe and Beethoven were walking in the park behind the castle in the centre of Teplitz, when Goethe spotted the imperial royal family walking towards them. Goethe caught Beethoven's arm and said they must pay their respects. Goethe took his position to the side of the path, and as the Emperor and Empress passed, arm in arm, Goethe removed his hat, swept his arm to the side, and executed a deep bow.

Beethoven, appalled at Goethe's act of sycophancy, slammed his top hat down on the back of his head, held his hands tightly behind his back, and strode defiantly in the opposite direction.

Admittedly the source for this is Bettina Arnim, née Brentano, sister-in-law of Antonie, who is widely judged to have fabricated elements of her contacts with Beethoven, but it is highly unlikely she would have invented the whole episode – even if we allow her points of exaggeration – and the two protagonists seem to confirm in letters they wrote soon afterwards that something of the kind happened.*

Goethe wrote to a friend:

I made the acquaintance of Beethoven in Teplitz. His talent amazed me. However, unfortunately, he is an utterly untamed personality, not necessarily in the wrong if he regards the world as detestable, but certainly not making it any more pleasant either for himself or others by thinking so. On the other hand one certainly has to make allowances, indeed pity

---

* In the Schlosspark in Bad Teplice there is today a small monument by the side of the path, and a plaque set into the path, commemorating the incident.

him, as he is losing his hearing, which perhaps has a less
harmful effect on the musical part of his nature than the so-
cial. By nature rather reserved, he becomes doubly so because
of this deficiency.

Beethoven, by contrast, saw it – unsurprisingly – rather differently. He wrote to his publisher:

Goethe delights far too much in the atmosphere of the court,
far more than is seemly for a poet. How can one really say
very much about the ridiculous behaviour of virtuosi in this
respect, when poets, who should be regarded as the leading
teachers of the nation, can forget everything else when con-
fronted by that glitter.

If the two men were not unhappy to take leave of each other, it
seems Beethoven's admiration for Goethe might have outweighed
the playwright's for him. Some years later he set Goethe's poems
'Meeresstille' ('Calm Sea') and 'Glückliche Fahrt' ('Prosperous
Voyage') to music, and sent the settings to Goethe. Receiving no
acknowledgement, he wrote to Goethe almost a year later, referring first to 'the happy hours spent in your company' which he
would never forget (!), then saying rather pointedly, 'I am now
faced with the fact that I must remind you of my existence – I
trust that you received the dedication to Your Excellency of *Meeresstille und glückliche Fahrt.*'

There is again no record of Goethe replying. But if his frustration with Goethe was causing him any anxiety, word from
brother Johann of his impending marriage was more than
enough to distract him. Beethoven decided to leave for Linz
straight away; it was the worst decision he could have made.

Beethoven had been in Teplitz for more than two months, and it had been a difficult time for him. There was the emotional aftermath of the Immortal Beloved affair, as well as the obvious tensions surrounding his relationship with Goethe. He had not stayed still, travelling between Teplitz, Karlsbad and Franzensbad, to take different waters on doctors' orders. When he first arrived in Karlsbad, he had forgotten his passport, and the police made him return to Teplitz for it. He had also performed at a public concert.

In August the weather turned and autumn came early. It all caught up with him. Already in poor enough health to have contacted his doctor, in September he fell ill and was confined to bed. The presence of a pretty woman did much to raise his spirits. Amalie Sebald, a singer from Berlin, seventeen years Beethoven's junior, was in Teplitz with her mother. She took it upon herself to look after Beethoven, well aware that she was tending to the needs of Europe's foremost musician.

She brought him cooked chicken and hot soup. He was flattered by her attention, and wrote her several flirtatious notes. But there was no suggestion that things went any further, and Amalie and her mother left after less than a fortnight.

Tired, unwell, and without doubt depressed – 'I am writing to you from my bed. I must tell you that people in Austria no longer trust me completely, and no doubt they are right too,' he wrote to his publisher – he should have packed his things and returned to Vienna, where he could sleep in his own bed and be tended by his doctor.

Instead, spurred on by the news of Johann's intended marriage, he threw his things together and rushed south to the central

Austrian town of Linz, via Prague and Budweis, to confront his brother. And confront him he did.

First he tried the straightforward approach of attempting to talk his brother out of marriage. Foremost in his mind was the fact that the object of his brother's affection was a woman by the name of Therese Obermeyer, whom Johann had taken on as his housekeeper. A housekeeper to be given the name of Beethoven? It was, to the head of the family, simply unthinkable. The other brother, Carl, had married an immoral woman, now Johann was intending to marry a domestic servant.

There was an oblique, and to Beethoven appalling, similarity in the circumstances of his two brothers. Whereas Johanna was already pregnant with Carl's child months before their marriage, Therese had an illegitimate daughter from a previous relationship.

Something else had happened in the Beethoven family that was an embarrassment by any standards. To Beethoven it was much, much more than that. Carl's wife Johanna had committed an act of extreme folly, which was to come back years later to haunt her.

A friend had asked her to look after a pearl necklace, valued at 20,000 florins, possibly because she was about to travel and wanted to ensure the necklace was safe. Johanna, it appears, hid the necklace and reported it stolen. It took the police five minutes to put two and two together. Johanna was arrested and put on trial for theft. She was found guilty and sentenced to the extraordinarily harsh punishment of a year's imprisonment. This was reduced to two months, then to one month, and finally to the relatively lenient sentence of one month's house arrest. But the damage was done. Johanna had a criminal record, and Beethoven was not to forget it.

His fire was up; he knew he had to take drastic action, but even Johann can hardly have been prepared for what happened next. Beethoven went to see the local bishop. We have no record of the conversation, but we can assume he told the bishop that since Therese had an illegitimate child, she was an immoral woman who could not be allowed to marry. The bishop no doubt asked whether either Therese or Johann had been married before, and on hearing that they had not, told Beethoven there was nothing to prevent the marriage.

We know Beethoven received no satisfaction from the bishop, because he then went to the local magistrates to ask for a ruling against the intended marriage. That must have failed too, because in what can only be described as an act of extreme desperation, he went to the police and demanded that they set a deadline for Therese to leave Linz, or face arrest. On what grounds is not clear, nor is the response of the police. But certainly no order was issued against Therese.

Johann, hardly surprisingly, was not simply shocked at his brother's behaviour, he was insulted and humiliated. Given Beethoven's actions, the whole town now knew of the family dispute. More than that, his intended wife saw her name being dragged through the mud. Illegitimate daughter she might have, but this she did not deserve.

According to Thayer, Johann decided to confront his brother. In the large room he had given him in his own house, he remonstrated with him, ordering him to keep his nose out of his affairs, to mind his own business. Instead of contrition over the extreme action he had taken, Beethoven argued back. Tempers flared and … 'A scene ensued on which – let the curtain be drawn,' Thayer diplomatically writes.

There can be no doubt that the two brothers came to blows. Europe's most renowned musical genius scrapping with a leading citizen of Linz, his younger brother. It is not an edifying spectacle.

If anything, Beethoven's actions not only misfired, they were counter-productive. To retain any kind of dignity at all for either of them, Johann had no choice but to marry Therese, which he did on 8 November 1812.

It would be wrong to give the impression that this was a swift visit by Beethoven to Linz, during which he took frantic measures to try to prevent his brother marrying, then left having failed. Such was Beethoven's fame by now that he was unable to move entirely as he wished.

There was huge excitement in Linz at the arrival of such a famous figure. It is quite possible that Johann let it be known that his famous brother was on his way to come and stay with him, basking in the reflected glory he knew that would bring. Even if he had misgivings about the purpose of the visit, he would most likely not have let that stop him spreading the news.

Linz Cathedral* had its own *Kapellmeister*, a certain Franz Xaver Glöggl, who announced in his music journal, the *Linzer Musik-Zeitung*, the arrival of Beethoven on 5 October. He did not disguise his elation: 'We now have the long-desired pleasure of welcoming to our city the Orpheus and greatest composer of our time, Herr L. Van Beethoven, who arrived here a few days ago. If Apollo is favorably disposed towards us, we shall also have an opportunity to admire his art.'

Glöggl in fact got less than he wanted, but was not entirely disappointed. Beethoven evidently took a liking to Glöggl,

---

* Anton Bruckner was later to be organist at Linz Cathedral from 1856 to 1868.

perhaps welcoming the company of another musician, and ate at Glöggl's house almost every day. Indeed relations between them must have been very warm indeed, for Glöggl dared to ask Beethoven to compose some funeral music, known as *Equale*, for trombones, and Beethoven agreed.*

Inevitably the nobility of Linz vied among themselves to hold soirées in Beethoven's honour. At one such occasion Beethoven's behaviour caused a mixture of consternation and amusement.

Beethoven, as guest of honour, was entertained to music by local musicians, and then some of his song settings were sung. After that his host, no doubt hoping the music had put him in benign mood, asked him if he would entertain the gathering to one of his famed improvisations on the piano. Beethoven refused.

There was some polite conversation, another attempt to cajole Beethoven into playing, then a general invitation for everyone to repair to the adjoining room where a table had been spread with food. The guests picked up a plate from the table by the door, and moved into the next room. Beethoven did not come with them. In fact he was nowhere to be seen. Some of the guests offered to go and look for him, but returned shaking their heads. Finally it was decided to sit at the table and eat.

Once the meal was firmly under way, sounds of the piano being played drifted in from the adjoining room. It was obviously Beethoven, but the guests were not quite sure what to do. They knew that if they all rushed in, he was likely to stop. At the same time, they could hardly continue eating and talking.

---

* Beethoven composed three short pieces for four trombones (*equale* signifying a piece for equal, or similar, instruments). Two of them, adapted for four male voices, were sung at the composer's funeral.

So, one by one, with extreme caution, they stepped quietly into the music room, aware they were witnessing something rare, which was to be savoured and treasured. Beethoven continued to play for the best part of an hour, exactly the sort of improvisation for which he was famous, but which he was by now so reluctant to provide.

Then, as suddenly as he had started, he stopped, realising that he had been invited to eat. He leapt up from the piano and, barely seeing anyone else in the room, dashed to the door, where he collided with the table and sent the china crashing to the floor.

There was nervous laughter, which quickly turned to relief, as the host smilingly escorted Beethoven to the dinner table.

Unbelievably, incredibly – but this is Beethoven, so maybe it is neither unbelievable nor incredible – while he was in Linz doing battle with his brother, his emotions in tatters, his health even if improved still fragile, his mood despondent, he completed his Eighth Symphony, his wittiest and most humorous symphony to date, replete with twists and turns, unconventional key changes and unexpected dynamics.

If this might be expected to lift his mood, it did not do so. He returned to Vienna in November after an absence of four months in a state bordering on despair. He wrote to Archduke Rudolph that he was 'ailing, although mentally, it is true, more than physically'. He began to keep a diary (*Tagebuch*), and the first entry, although undated, was probably written in November or December of 1812, and it indicates a tortured soul:

Submission, absolute submission to your fate, only this can

give you the sacrifices — — — for the servitude — Oh hard
struggle! — Do everything that still needs to be done to plan
for the long journey. You must — — yourself find everything
that your dearest wish can offer, yet you must bend it to your
will — Keep always of the same mind —

You may no longer be a man, not for yourself, only for oth-
ers, for you there is no longer any happiness except in yourself,
in your art — Oh God, give me strength to conquer myself,
nothing at all must chain me to life —

Whatever internal traumas he was suffering, external events could
only worsen them. It was just days after returning to Vienna that
he heard that his benefactor Prince Kinsky, one of the three sig-
natories to the annuity contract, had fallen off his horse and died.
The payments were stopped and he began a protracted, and draining, fight with the Kinsky estate to get the payments reinstated.

More likely to hurt him emotionally, he returned to the city
to find that his brother Carl was seriously ill with tuberculosis,
the disease that had killed their mother. In fact so grave was Carl's
health that in April 1813 he made a declaration in which he called
on his brother Ludwig to undertake sole guardianship of his son
Karl. The one-paragraph document was signed by Carl, Beethoven, and three witnesses. It does not mention Johanna by name,
but the obvious effect of it would be to exclude Johanna from
playing any part in the upbringing of her son.

This, on the face of it, was an extraordinary decision. Exactly
what turned Carl against his wife is not known. Most certainly Beethoven himself would have pressured his brother, and we
might find it surprising with modern eyes that three witnesses
were persuaded too. But that was nothing compared with the turn
of events that would follow.

In fact Carl's health improved in the following months, and the declaration was not enacted, but it was a foretaste of what was to come.

Beethoven's behaviour in this period was giving his friends cause for concern. He had given up caring about his appearance, or even his hygiene. Restaurants – those that would admit him – kept a solitary table at the back of the room, so that his eating habits did not deter other guests.

It is from this time that rumours began that he visited prostitutes regularly. There has been enormous controversy over this, derived from the fact that in notes and letters to his close friend Zmeskall there is nothing specific, but he uses oblique words and phrases that are capable of different interpretations. If he did visit prostitutes, as a single man in his forties it would certainly not be unusual, but for Beethoven the moralist it comes under the same category as conducting an affair with a married woman. It is possible, though highly unlikely.

That his emotions were in a dire state, though, is not in doubt. 'So many unfortunate incidents occurring one after the other have really driven me into an almost disordered state,' he wrote to Rudolph. Most important of all, he had composed nothing substantial, nor published anything for over a year.

More than anything it was his volatility, his unpredictability, that made him so difficult to be with, that made his friends, even his family, so reluctant to involve themselves with him. His brother Carl, even as his health was being sapped by tuberculosis, was not immune from his elder brother's wrath – or from the overwhelming remorse that followed it.

Carl, Johanna, and their six-year-old son Karl were at the dinner table some time in late 1812 or early 1813. Suddenly the door opened and Beethoven burst in. 'You thief! Where are my manuscripts?' Carl, physically weak, either denied he had taken anything, or told his brother he had no idea what he was talking about. A violent quarrel ensued, which threatened to come to blows, or possibly even did, since Karl recalled later that his mother had difficulty separating the two men. Carl tore himself away, with his wife's help, crossed the room, opened a drawer, took out the 'missing' manuscript pages, and threw them down in front of Beethoven.

Visible proof that his brother had not stolen the pages was enough to calm Beethoven down, who actually went so far as to apologise. In reality he had no choice, in the face of the evidence. But righteous indignation – quite possibly a culmination of smaller aggressive incidents – got the better of Carl, and he refused to be placated. He continued to hurl abuse at his elder brother, who rushed out of the room – leaving the offending manuscript pages behind. Carl continued to shout after him, saying he did not want that 'dragon' (*Drachen*) to set foot in his home again.

According to Karl, a short time after the incident he and his father were crossing a bridge over the Danube Canal, when by coincidence Beethoven was crossing in the opposite direction. Beethoven saw Carl, and gasped to see the physical deterioration in his brother. He threw his arms around Carl's neck and covered him in kisses with such passion that 'people stared in complete bewilderment'.

Beethoven's contrition might be commendable, but its excessiveness, and the fact that it was delivered so publicly, suggest a certain lack of proportion. However we look at it, we are left to struggle with the knowledge that one of the greatest artists who ever lived came to physical blows with both his brothers, and that in each case the dispute was entirely of his making.

Arguably Beethoven, in 1813, was at the lowest ebb in his life. A failed love affair, continuing ill-health, domestic tribulations, blocked creativity, worsening deafness … You begin to wonder how much more he could take, what might come along that might tip him over the edge. Those words at the end of his first entry in the *Tagebuch* – 'nothing at all must chain me to life' – take on a truly ominous ring.

However, not for the first time in life external events came, obliquely, to his rescue, and once again they concerned the adventures of the Corsican-born commander and Emperor who was rampaging across Europe at the head of the Continent's most powerful fighting force.

On 21 June 1813, Arthur Wellesley, at the head of 79,000 British, Portuguese and Spanish soldiers, routed the French army under King Joseph of Spain at the Battle of Vitoria. Joseph had been placed on the throne of Spain by his younger brother Napoleon Bonaparte three years earlier. The battle cost Joseph all his guns, supplies, treasure – and his kingdom. The loss of Spain was a devastating blow to the French Emperor, all the more so for coming less than a year after his own humiliation in Russia.

In Vienna there were wild scenes of jubilation on the streets, in the parks, along the high paths of the Bastei. No one doubted that this was the beginning of the end of Napoleonic hegemony in Europe. For a country whose army had suffered so often at the hands of Napoleon, whose capital city, seat of empire, had been shelled into surrender, it was a sweet moment.

To what did the people of Vienna turn to celebrate? Music, of course. And to whom? It was just what Beethoven needed. He gave two hugely successful concerts, at which he conducted the first public performances of his Seventh Symphony,* as well as the piece he had composed to celebrate the Battle of Vitoria, *Wellingtons† Sieg‡* (*Wellington's Victory*). This was followed by a third concert, including again the Seventh Symphony, and the first performance of the Eighth.

And what did the Emperor and the ruling elite of Austria do to celebrate? What they had done many times before: declare war on France. This time Austria joined the allies in a new coalition, which resulted in Napoleon, at the head of 195,000 men, facing 365,000 Austrian, Prussian, Russian, and Swedish soldiers at the Battle of Leipzig, known as the Battle of the Nations.

---

* The composer Louis Spohr, playing in the violin section of the orchestra, has left a vivid description of Beethoven conducting at these concerts: 'When a *sforzando* occurred, he tore his arms which were crossed across his chest with great vehemence asunder. At *piano* he crouched down lower and lower to indicate the degree of softness. When a *crescendo* entered he gradually rose again, and at the entrance of the *forte* he jumped into the air. Sometimes he shouted to strengthen the *forte* … It was obvious that the poor man could no longer hear the *piano* passages of his own music.'

† Arthur Wellesley was not, in fact, elevated to the dukedom until the following year.

‡ Beethoven composed it, remarkably, for the Panharmonicon, a mechanical instrument that reproduced the sounds of the orchestra, invented by Johann Nepomuk Mälzel, known to musical history as the inventor of the metronome. So successful was it that, at Mälzel's suggestion, he orchestrated it.

Defeat for France was inevitable, though in the event French losses were nothing like as great as those of the allies, when considered proportionately. But defeat it was. The disastrous Russian adventure, the loss of Spain, now defeat on the battlefield – the Napoleonic era was nearing its end.

The allies followed up their victory by invading France in January 1814. Less than three months later Napoleon was deposed by the French Senate, forced to abdicate in favour of his son, and was exiled to the Mediterranean island of Elba.

The question was what to do now. It was decided that, with Napoleon Bonaparte finally defeated, a Congress of European leaders would be held to redraw the post-Napoleonic map of Europe. Where would this triumphal meeting be held? In the city that had so suffered at the hands of Napoleon and his army: Vienna.

It was actually by virtue of the successful concerts, not the decision to hold the Congress in Vienna (which came some months later), that the theatre directors decided to approach Beethoven and make a rather bold suggestion. Would he consider reviving his opera *Leonore*, which had been so ill-fated eight years earlier?

Perhaps to their surprise, he agreed, on condition that the libretto be extensively revised. His choice for this was a German-born playwright and librettist, Georg Friedrich Treitschke, whose work he admired. The directors agreed.

It really is remarkable – in a way that so often characterises Beethoven's life – that, despite the extreme depression into which he had sunk so recently, and considering the traumatic events that had surrounded the first two productions of his opera, he not only agreed to rework it, but did so with gusto, apparently establishing a comfortable working relationship with Treitschke.

Beethoven clearly gave Treitschke carte blanche, and even when they disagreed he allowed himself to be persuaded. Treitschke tightened up the first act, entirely rewriting the end, so that the prison governor's anger is a natural consequence of the prisoners being allowed out into the daylight, and his order that they return to their cells bringing the first act to a satisfying close.

But Treitschke's revisions to Act II were far more far-reaching. Beginning with Florestan's heart-rending cry from his dungeon, he rewrote Florestan's aria so that a man being starved to death experiences a last blaze of life before he dies. This met entirely with Beethoven's approval. Treitschke – earning our eternal gratitude – has left a riveting account of Beethoven in the white heat of inspiration:

> *What I now relate will live for ever in my memory. Beethoven came to me about seven o'clock in the evening. After we had discussed other things, he asked how matters stood with the aria. It was just finished; I handed it to him. He read it, ran up and down the room, muttered and growled, as was his habit instead of singing – and tore open the piano. My wife had often begged him to play, but in vain. Today he placed the text in front of him and began to play wonderful improvisations, which sadly no magic could cause to remain solid in the air. Out of them he seemed to conjure the motif of the aria. The hours passed, but Beethoven continued to improvise. Supper, which he had intended to share with us, was served, but he would not allow himself to be disturbed. Finally, at a late hour, he embraced me, and declining an invitation to eat, he hurried home. The next day the admirable composition was finished.*

This is quite possibly the only eyewitness account we have of Beethoven actually involved in the compositional process – I am not aware of any other. It is made all the more precious because the aria he composed that night and completed the following morning is the aria we know today. It is one of the most famous, and poignant, moments in all opera: Florestan, starving to death in the underground dungeon, lets out a piercing cry, followed by a lament, but now ending in a kind of trance, seeing a vision of his wife Leonore as an angel leading him to freedom in Heaven. Any operatic tenor will confirm what a challenge it is, beginning with the *crescendo* cry, going through an extensive range of emotions, and ending in an extremely high register – all sung from a lying and sitting position.

With his fine sense of theatricality, Treitschke moved the final scene into the town marketplace, in other words up into the daylight – both previous versions of the opera had taken place entirely in the dungeon. This allowed the rescue to be fully celebrated, for the reunited couple to sing a joyous duet accompanied by full chorus, as well as giving the psychologically satisfying transition from darkness into light.

It was as if, this time, Beethoven's opera was pre-ordained to be a success. It went into rehearsal in April 1814, and was performed several times over the following weeks. Changes continued to be made, and on 18 July it was performed in its final version, the version we know today. Beethoven composed yet another overture, the fourth, crisper, more dramatic than its predecessors, and again that is the overture played today.

It had been around a decade in coming, and had caused Beethoven more pain and heartache than any other composition, but *Fidelio* was at last complete, and in a form he was satisfied with. Small wonder that when the organisers of the Congress of Vienna decided to arrange a gala evening for the crowned heads of Europe in September, they chose to stage *Fidelio*. Small wonder too that Beethoven henceforth turned his back on the operatic form, and never composed another.

Before we leave the Congress, which has entered history more for the entertainment it provided – *'le congrès ne marche pas, il danse'*, with the Viennese amusing themselves in a new game of spotting the King or Prince hurrying through the streets at night in disguise on the way to his mistress – than any concrete political results, it had one more direct effect on Beethoven's musical output.

To honour the presence of so many crowned heads, he set absurd lyrics to music in a composition entitled 'Der glorreiche Augenblick' ('The Glorious Moment'). The piece has survived, is rarely played today, and is usually treated as an aberration.[*]

So why did he agree to set to music the simplistic words of a certain Alois Weissenbach, Professor of Surgery and Head Surgeon at St John's Hospital in Salzburg? More than that, why did he invite Professor Weissenbach to call on him for breakfast, and greet him with a warm handshake and even a kiss? Because Professor Weissenbach was profoundly deaf. 'It was pitiful to hear them shout at each other,' wrote an eyewitness. I suspect it wasn't at all pitiful, and that they relished each other's company, two men barely able to hear a word the other said.

The frivolities and philandering were brought to a sudden end at the beginning of March 1815, when word reached Vienna that the unthinkable, the impossible, had occurred. Napoleon Bonaparte had escaped from Elba, landed in southern France, and was marching north, gathering an army around him.

But it is unlikely this impinged much on Beethoven. He had a far more serious problem to contend with, a crisis that had been in abeyance for two years, but that now returned with a vengeance.

---

[*] Sample verse: 'And Wellington, the Spanish horde/Battled against with trust in the Lord/And at Vitoria struck them he/Till home with shame they had to flee.'

Chapter 14

Into the Witness Box

How the single letter 'o' ruined Beethoven's life

Carl van Beethoven had fallen ill again with tuberculosis, and this time it was clear to everybody that it was terminal. The ramifications of this, and what followed, were to have the most profound effect on Beethoven, indeed it is not an exaggeration to say that they were to affect him for the rest of his life.

It is possible to pinpoint the beginning of it to the exact day: 14 November 1815. Carl van Beethoven lay dying. He was forty-one years of age. On that day Beethoven went to see his brother. By chance, he discovered Carl's Will lying on a sideboard. He had not known either that the Will had been written or what its terms were.

He picked it up, read it – and Clause 5 hit him like a thunderbolt: 'Along with my wife I appoint my brother Ludwig van Beethoven co-guardian [of my son Karl].'

He angrily told his brother there and then that the Will could not stand as it was. It flatly contradicted the declaration of two and half years before, when the tuberculosis first took hold, which stated Carl's wish that, in the event of his death, his brother

Ludwig should become Karl's guardian. He insisted that Clause 5 had to be changed. Carl acquiesced. He took a pen and crossed out the words 'Along with my wife' and 'co-'.

It must have been an extraordinary scene. Carl was less than twenty-four hours from death. One imagines him propped up in bed, his small frame ravaged by disease, his cheeks flushed in the characteristic sign of tuberculosis, probably racked by coughing, a handkerchief flecked with blood held to his lips, gazing in despair with feverish watery eyes … as his brother strode across the end of his bed, waving his arms and ranting against Johanna.

Beethoven himself wrote of it later, in a memorandum to the Court of Appeal, in measured tones. Having discovered the Will and read it, he realised '[certain] passages had to be stricken out. This I had my brother bring about since I did not wish to be bound up in this with such a bad woman in a matter of such importance as the education of the child.' In reality one can only envision the vitriol he poured out to his dying brother against the woman he had loathed since the day he had set eyes on her – and, given her reputation, before. Clearly the passage of time had not exactly mellowed Beethoven's antagonism towards his sister-in-law.

Thanks to his timely arrival at his brother's bedside, however, he had averted disaster. Satisfied with his efforts, he left his brother, but not for long. Some sixth sense, possibly, caused him to return just an hour and a half later. If he had suspicions, they were justified. The Will had gone. There followed yet another confrontation between Beethoven and his dying brother. We do not know exactly what was said, but we know the circumstances, and I have therefore allowed myself to presume Beethoven's words.

'What has happened to it? Where is it? Who has taken it?' Beethoven demanded to know. Carl summoned his failing strength and told his brother – haltingly, no doubt, knowing even so close to death the torrent it would unleash – that something had been added to the Will, and he had been made to sign it.

'Was it to do with Karl?' Beethoven demanded. 'It was, wasn't it?' Carl must have made the smallest nod of his head he possibly could, as he said something. Beethoven wrote later in the memorandum that his brother begged him to hurry to the lawyer's office, recover the Will and bring it back so he could change it, 'because otherwise some great misunderstanding might arise therefrom'.

'Those were his very words,' Beethoven wrote. It seems unlikely. The probability is he dragged the name of the lawyer from Carl, or if Carl was too weak to give him details, searched the room and possibly other rooms too until he found the lawyer's name and address, and hurried off.

The lawyer's office was closed. Beethoven reported that the 'lawyer could not be found that day'. But it was a Tuesday, and the lawyer had clearly been involved in whatever alteration had been made to the Will only a short time earlier. He made repeated attempts to find him, but without success. It is probable the lawyer had simply gone home.

At five o'clock the following morning Carl died. When the Will was later read, the codicil that had been added during Beethoven's short absence from the room, which Carl had signed along with three witnesses, was as devastating as Beethoven had feared.

At its heart, surrounded by legal language, this crucial sentence:

I have found it necessary to add to my Will that I by no means desire that my son be taken away from his mother, but that

> *he shall always … remain with his mother, to which end his*
> *guardianship is to be exercised by her as well as my brother …*
> *God permit them to be harmonious for the sake of my child's*
> *welfare. This is the last wish of the dying husband and brother.*

Carl cannot, in his worst fears, have imagined just how far his last wish would come from being realised.

Beethoven went on the attack. He decided to fight Johanna in every way he could, for as long as it took, whatever the cost, to exclude her from the guardianship of her son. It is difficult for us today, even at a distance of two centuries, to excuse him for what he did. His friends were equally appalled. There is virtually no mention of them in this period. It is likely they tried to broach the subject, tried to reason with him, to persuade him to drop legal action, felt the full force of his wrath, and retired from the scene.

What certainly lay behind Beethoven's determination, as well as his antipathy towards Johanna, was his unwavering belief that his nephew Karl would – alone – be 'Beethoven the musician' of the next generation. Alone, because Carl was now dead, Johann was trapped in a loveless marriage that had not produced children and was unlikely to do so, and he, Ludwig, knew he would never marry.

Karl, the sole child of the Beethoven brothers, was by now nine years old, with no evident interest in music and no obvious talent for it either. None of that altered his uncle's unswerving belief that Karl would carry the musical banner forward. And for that to happen, the boy had to be separated utterly from the malign influence of his mother so he could give himself wholly to his uncle, to his 'father'. But there was a hurdle in the way: Carl's Will. Beethoven knew he had, somehow, to get rid of it.

On 28 November, two weeks after Carl's death and one week after his Will was enacted, Beethoven appealed to the *Landrecht* to exclude Johanna from the guardianship of her son. It was a high-risk strategy. The *Landrecht* was the upper court, the court of the nobility. Only those of noble birth could have their cases heard there. Ordinary people, the 'lower classes', were obliged to use the lower court, the *Magistrat*. Beethoven was not of noble birth – far from it – but most people were not aware of this, or, more probably, in a city where everybody connected to the arts had noble rank of some kind or another, few thought to question it.

Though there is no direct evidence of this, it is more than likely that when Beethoven, as a young man of almost twenty-two years of age, arrived in Vienna from Bonn, he found himself mistakenly introduced as Ludwig *von* Beethoven, and it was therefore assumed he was a member of German aristocracy. It was an easy mistake to make: he was German, his prodigious musical talent saw him quickly taken up by the aristocratic patrons of the arts, so that he became a familiar figure in the highest salons. No doubt his very un-aristocratic mode of dress and demeanour was put down to the eccentricities of a musician. No one, therefore, thought it in any way inappropriate that Beethoven should take his case for guardianship of Karl to the court of the nobility, the *Landrecht*.

Beethoven appeared before the court on 13 December and declared that he could produce 'weighty reasons' for excluding Johanna from the guardianship of Karl. The court ordered him to do so within three days, or his case would fail. This is the moment when Johanna's folly regarding her friend's string of pearls came back to haunt her.

Beethoven applied to the City Magistrates for an official certificate detailing Johanna's conviction for embezzlement in 1811, which was to be the main plank of his argument that she was unfit to bring up her son. The Magistrates' office replied that it could not issue him personally with a copy of the judgment against Johanna, but that it would forward it direct to the *Landrecht* tribunal. This it did on 21 December.

To reinforce his case, Beethoven drew up a lengthy document outlining his argument and submitted it to the *Landrecht* on 20 December – technically the final day allowed to him by the court, given the intervening weekend. The document is written in another hand and signed by Beethoven, the assumption being that it was actually drafted by a lawyer. The key sentences state that the codicil in Carl's Will appointing his widow joint guardian of Karl was added 'when I was absent for an hour and a half, i.e. without my knowledge and behind my back', and that it can be proved easily that his dying brother added the codicil only 'because he was insistently urged to do so by his wife and was not in a condition to take an entirely free decision'.

In language clearly formulated by the lawyer, Beethoven declares he regards it as 'a sacred duty enjoined on my conscience not to abandon my rights to the guardianship ... and shall make every effort to do whatever in my strongest conviction can contribute to and promote the true welfare as well as the moral and intellectual benefit of my nephew'.

On 9 January 1816 the *Landrecht* ruled in Beethoven's favour. Ten days later he appeared before the tribunal and 'vowed with solemn handgrasp' to perform his duties as Karl's sole guardian. On 2 February Karl, nine and a half years old, was taken from his mother.

Beethoven's first act as guardian was to put Karl into a local boarding school, away from the influence of his mother. But it was not to be as simple as that. Johanna made repeated attempts to see her son – on one occasion apparently disguising herself as a man to gain admittance.

Beethoven decided the headmaster needed to know exactly what kind of woman Johanna was, to ensure he would deny her access to her son, and wrote to him in extraordinarily defamatory terms:

> *Last night that Queen of the Night was at the Artists' Ball until 3 a.m. exposing not only her mental but also her bodily nakedness – it was whispered that she – was willing to hire herself – for 20 gulden! Oh horrible!*

You can almost sense Beethoven's reluctance to commit to paper his allegation that she was prostituting herself, and his satisfaction at being able to equate her with the duplicitous character from Mozart's *The Magic Flute*, one of his favourite operas. Since there is no evidence from anyone else at the Artists' Ball to corroborate Beethoven's accusations, we must assume either that he was inventing what he saw, or at best exaggerating. Perhaps she was being overtly flirtatious, which in Beethoven's eyes equated with what he described.

Beethoven angrily went back to court to take out an injunction forbidding Johanna from seeing her son. The court granted it, but with a proviso: Johanna could see Karl in his leisure hours, and only with Beethoven's consent.

It was an unhappy situation, exacerbated by events. Later in the year Karl complained of severe stomach pains and had to undergo a hernia operation, after which he needed to wear a truss. The trauma of this brought home to Beethoven just what he had taken on, and how unsuited he was to take on the role, not just of father, but mother as well. He practically said as much in the later memorandum to the Appeal Court:

> *I once in anger pulled my nephew from his chair, because he had done something very naughty. As he had to wear a truss permanently after his operation for hernia ... my action caused him some pain <u>in the most sensitive spot</u> when he had to turn round quickly.*

In the same document he impugns Johanna's character with potentially more devastating accusations than in the letter to the headmaster:

> *Immediately after my brother's death she began to have intimate relations with a lover, and her behaviour even shocked the modesty of her innocent son. She was to be seen in all the dance halls and at festivities, while her son went without the necessities of life and was left to fend for himself in the charge of some wretched maid of hers. What would have become of him if I had not looked after him?*

There is no evidence any of these accusations were true. This is a man clearly prepared to stop at nothing to get his way, even if it meant destroying a close family member.

Beethoven began to make plans to take Karl out of the boarding school and have him live with him, but it is perhaps another indication of his growing self-doubt that this did not happen for another sixteen months.

That self-doubt was accompanied by a raft of other emotions. Beethoven was clearly disturbed by what he was doing. There is evidence his conscience was troubling him. He wrote in his diary, 'My part, O lord, I have performed. It might have been possible without hurting the widow, but it was not so … Bless my work, bless the widow! Why can I not wholly obey my heart and help her, the widow?'

One of the daughters of the boarding school headmaster quoted him in her diary as saying, 'What will people say? They will take me for a tyrant.'

Worse than anything, during the long-drawn-out legal process, Beethoven was composing – virtually – nothing. This period was to be the most barren, artistically, of his life.*

In the autumn of 1818, Johanna appealed twice to the *Landrecht* to reconsider its decision excluding her from her son's guardianship. She cited Beethoven's failings as guardian, as shown by the fact that Karl was expelled from another school his uncle had sent him to, and several instances of unruly behaviour that had been reported to her. No wonder, she told the court – he needed his mother's influence. She also argued that Beethoven's deafness seriously impeded his attempts at guardianship.

Beethoven, again with legal advice, submitted a document rebutting her arguments. On the question of his deafness, he wrote – to the surprise of his friends who surely must have made some pact to say nothing to contradict him:

Everybody who is closely acquainted with me knows only too well that all verbal communications between me and my nephew and other people are carried on with the greatest of ease and are by no means impeded by my indifferent hearing. Furthermore, my health has never been better …

---

* With one major exception, of which more later.

This at a time when, according to one eyewitness, people had to shout at Beethoven to make themselves understood, when he had begun to carry a notebook and pencil everywhere so people could write their questions down, and when in correspondence he frequently referred to his ill-health.

In an obvious boost to his self-confidence, and his belief that what he was doing was morally right, the *Landrecht* rejected both of Johanna's appeals.

By now Beethoven had taken Karl out of the boarding school to live with him. It was a fraught situation. Beethoven was aware of his eccentricities, but had never made any attempt to hide or adjust them in front of friends. With Karl it was different. He suspected Karl was ashamed to be seen out with him, because his clothes were always untidy and in need of repair.

He noted Karl's reluctance to eat in restaurants with him. Several of his favourite restaurants would keep a table apart for him and he knew why. But he could not adapt his behaviour and it undoubtedly worried him. There was also his deafness, and he was aware that Karl was frustrated at constantly having to repeat himself. Also Karl was still recovering from the painful hernia operation and still wearing a truss. Beethoven simply did not know how to handle such domestic issues.

Then, on 3 December 1818, Karl – a pawn hitherto in the prolonged battle between his mother and his uncle – took matters into his own hands. He ran away – to his mother. Beethoven was devastated. He hurried back to the boarding school whose headmaster he had befriended. The headmaster's daughter recorded in her diary, 'B. came in great excitement and sought counsel and help from my father, saying that Karl had run away! I recall that … he cried out tearfully, "He is ashamed of me!"'

Beethoven went round to Johanna's apartment the next morning and demanded she return Karl in compliance with the court order. Johanna promised to do so that evening. But Beethoven feared she would spirit the boy away, and so he called the police. They reminded Johanna of her obligations, and she – one can only imagine with what degree of anguish and heartache – handed her son over to them.

Now Johanna herself took the initiative. She used the fact that Karl had run away from his uncle to be with her as reason to petition the *Landrecht* yet again to reconsider its exclusion of her from Karl's guardianship.

The court convened on 11 December and all three parties to the case – Karl, Johanna and Beethoven – gave evidence separately.

It must have been dreadfully intimidating for Karl, just twelve years of age, to stand in the dock and give evidence against his mother, which he knew he had to do because of the court order that favoured his uncle. His answers, as quoted in the court minutes, are nervous and anxious. He speaks highly of his uncle, and when asked if his uncle has ever maltreated him, replies that it happened only once, after the police had returned him from his mother, and his uncle threatened to throttle him. He admits to making disrespectful comments about his mother in the presence of his uncle, but he did this to please his uncle.

Johanna's testimony is calm and assured. Why else would her son come to her, if not because he did not like living with his uncle? She had indeed advised him to return, but he was reluctant to do so because he feared his uncle would punish him.

Her lawyer, a relation by marriage, presented a damning indictment of the Beethoven family. He said that the Beethoven brothers were eccentric men, so often at each other's throats that they were more enemies than friends. As for Johanna's late husband Carl, he was civil towards his elder brother only when he wanted money from him.

In what has to be the most extraordinarily condemnatory statement ever made in public about the great artist whose music will enrich humanity for all time, the lawyer said, 'Johanna van Beethoven's son Karl cannot be allowed to remain under the sole influence of his uncle and guardian, because of the danger that he will suffer physical and moral ruin.'

For good measure the lawyer added that he had himself observed that Karl had frostbitten hands and feet when he ran away to his mother, that he was wearing flimsy clothes in the depths of winter, and had clearly not taken a bath for a long time.

Then came an episode of high drama that would change Beethoven's life.

Johanna, it appears without appreciating the full implication of what she was saying, told the court she believed Beethoven intended sending Karl away to a private school outside Vienna. She, on the other hand, wanted him to go to the local public seminary, where he would mix with other boys and be in the familiar surroundings of the city. Furthermore, she had been assured there was a place available for him.

When it came to Beethoven's turn to enter the witness box, the court asked him why he was against sending Karl to the seminary. Beethoven replied that there were too many pupils there and the supervision would be inadequate.

Then the court, probably like Johanna unmindful of what they were about to unleash, asked him what plans he had for the boy's education. Beethoven's reply sank him. He said he would put Karl back into the boarding school for the winter, then send him to the private seminary in the town of Melk – adding, almost as an afterthought, that he would gladly send Karl to the There-sianum Academy 'if he were but of noble birth'.

The panel of judges must have sat aghast when they heard his words, then exchanged looks of incredulity with each other. One of the judges finally asked him the obvious question. Were he and his late brother then not members of the nobility? Clearly suspecting that they were not, the judge asked Beethoven if he was in possession of documents to prove he was of noble birth.

Beethoven had in the witness box with him his friend, the journalist and librettist Karl Joseph Bernard, to help him with his deafness. One can imagine Bernard, white-faced, turning to Beethoven and repeating the judge's question loudly into his ear, writing it down as well to make sure Beethoven understood it. And one can imagine Beethoven's shock, as he must have taken in the unbearable realisation that he had demolished his own case with a few unnecessary words.

Probably without waiting for Beethoven to prompt him, Ber-nard told the court that 'van' was a Dutch predicate that did not signify membership of the nobility, and that Beethoven did not possess any documents to prove the contrary.

The judges recalled Johanna and asked her if her husband Carl was of noble birth. Her answer was devastating: 'So the brothers said, and the documentary proof is in the possession of the oldest brother, the composer.'

Under oath Johanna was testifying that the Beethoven broth-ers claimed to be of noble birth, and Ludwig van Beethoven was in possession of the documents to prove it. Johanna's record for honesty, as a convicted thief, was not good, and it is certainly possible that she was lying.

But the judges of the *Landrecht* had no need to waste their time trying to establish the truth of the matter. Beethoven had admitted he did not have documentary proof of nobility, and that was enough to allow them to wash their hands of the matter. This was not a case for the *Landrecht*, and they referred it – no doubt with some relief – to the *Magistrat*, the lower court, the court of the 'common people'.

It was, for Beethoven, much more than a disappointment; it was a public humiliation. In no time the news raced round Vienna. Beethoven, who counted the aristocracy among his friends, who could call on the Emperor's brother without so much as an appointment, who was lauded in the highest salons in the land … was himself of no higher status than the ordinary people in the street.

There was another, more practical, reason for his distress. He knew perfectly well that the *Magistrat*, the lower court, was a champion of ordinary people, with a reputation for finding in their favour when they ran into trouble with the nobility. It was certain to take a dim view of the fact that he had taken his case to the court of the nobility when he was in fact on the same level before the law as any other common citizen.

His fears were well founded. The new year had barely begun when the *Magistrat* found against Beethoven, withdrew Karl from his guardianship, and returned him to his mother. Beethoven was devastated.

But Beethoven was not finished. He was determined to win this fight. It had been going on for more than three years, and he was in no mood to give up. Five times during the year 1819 he wrote to the *Magistrat* pleading with them to reconsider. Some of the letters were brief, some rambling. He received no reply.

Then, in the autumn of that year, Beethoven took on a new legal adviser, Johann Baptist Bach. In February 1820, with Bach's help, he drew up a lengthy document – the longest piece of writing in Beethoven's hand – divided into seven parts. It details every aspect of the case, and is unstinting in its characterisation of Johanna as a wicked and immoral woman, with a criminal record, with no education whatsoever, and utterly unsuited to bringing up her son.

Bach submitted the document, not to the *Magistrat*, but to the Court of Appeal, the highest court in the land. Three weeks later, on 8 April 1820, the court ruled in Beethoven's favour. Johanna made a direct appeal to the Emperor to intervene personally. He refused.

Finally, Beethoven had won. Karl was his. Johanna had lost. Was that not proof he had been right from the start? But what on earth could have brought about this extraordinary turnaround? We shall never know. One of Beethoven's friends had told him that the *Magistrat* was known to be corrupt, and if he had used bribery he would undoubtedly have won at that earlier stage. Might he have used bribery with the Court of Appeal? There is no evidence he did, but there wouldn't be, would there?

Karl was at last Beethoven's, at the end of a four-and-a-half-year struggle. But at what a cost. He was soon to fall seriously ill, and was never again to enjoy complete good health in the remaining six years of his life.

The court case he pursued so relentlessly against Johanna is an episode for which it is hard to forgive him. One of his modern biographers writes:

> *The lawsuit over his nephew brought out the worst in Beethoven's character, and during its course he exhibited*

> *self-righteousness, vindictiveness, unscrupulousness, lack of*
> *self-control, and a wholesale disregard for any point of view*
> *but his own.*[*]

Perhaps the most we can say is that the mind of a true genius is often found to be wanting in other areas; that the balance between different parts in the brain of a genius is not always as it should be. The genius might be supreme in the area of his genius, but in other areas – which to the non-genius may seem straightforward and obvious – he is left floundering.

But what is also clear is that Beethoven had a conscience. There is evidence even he knew deep down that what he was doing was wrong. There is the quotation already cited: 'What will people say? They will take me for a tyrant!' And in his diary he wrote, 'This one thing I clearly perceive: life may not be the greatest good there is, but the greatest evil is certainly guilt.'

A little later: 'It would have been impossible without hurting the widow's feelings, but it was not to be. Thou, almighty God, who seest into my heart, know that I have disregarded my own welfare for my dear Karl's sake, bless my work, bless the widow, why cannot I entirely follow my heart and from now – the widow – God, God, my refuge, my rock …' Little wonder he suddenly enquired after Johanna's health when he heard she had been unwell, and offered her money.

What is truly extraordinary is that Johanna, despite all that Beethoven had inflicted on her, appears never to have written or spoken out against her brother-in-law during the rest of her long life, which outlived Beethoven's by forty-one years and ended in

---

[*] Martin Cooper, *Beethoven: The Last Decade 1817–1827* (Oxford University Press, 1970).

her early eighties. Nor is there any evidence that she ever tried to make money from her closeness to Beethoven – memoirs, reminiscences, what today's newspapers would call 'kiss and tell', of the great composer into whose family she married – despite ending her life in some degree of poverty.

It is all the more surprising given the macabre events that would befall her son Karl, for which his uncle was directly, if unwittingly, responsible.

Chapter 15

A Musical Gift from London

How Rossini found Beethoven 'disorderly and dirty'

Beethoven's health had caused him problems all his adult life, and it concerned his digestive system. He complained of bloated stomach, colic, diarrhoea, indigestion. Today he might well have been diagnosed with irritable bowel syndrome, or something similar. Certainly he did nothing to ease the problems. He drank excessively, mostly local red wine. He smoked a pipe when drinking in a tavern. (A pipe with its bowl filled with tobacco could be bought at the counter.)

His eating habits would appal any doctor – he ate irregularly, would miss dinner and get up in the night to eat, eat enormous quantities one day and practically nothing the next, sometimes devouring a meal so quickly it was bound to give him digestive problems. In a restaurant he was known on some occasions to skip a main course, on others to order two. Once, dissatisfied with the lamb chops put in front of him, he hurled the plate at the waiter, who reacted by pretending to enjoy the taste of the gravy as it trickled over his lips.

Eating for Beethoven was rarely a pleasure; it was simply a

means to an end. Not that he was entirely unthinking when it came to food. He employed a cook, and sacked several for not cooking to his satisfaction. It appears he was not averse to trying his hand in the kitchen himself. He sent a note to a local fish-monger, undated but probably in 1822, enclosing 5 gulden, and requesting them 'most politely' to let him have 'a carp weighing 3 or 4 lbs, <u>or better still</u>, a pike of at least 3 lbs. If you have neither of these kinds of fish, then please send me some other fish of about the same weight.'

It is possible, of course, that he was ordering the fish on be-half of his cook. But we know for certain that he did on occasion cook, thanks to his musical colleague, and Egyptian-hieroglyphic page-turner Ignaz Seyfried, who relates that on one occasion, be-ing without a cook, Beethoven decided to invite friends to supper and cook the meal himself. Their host greeted his guests wear-ing a blue apron and nightcap. After a wait of an hour and a half, Beethoven served up 'soup of the kind dished up to beggars, half-done beef, vegetables floating in a mixture of water and grease, and roast that seemed to have been smoked in the chim-ney'. Beethoven, alone, was proud of his efforts, and the situation for the guests was saved, says Seyfried, only by the 'unadulterated juice of the grape'.

Mercifully for Beethoven (and his friends), these occasions were rare, and for the most part he ate in restaurants or at friends' houses. But there is no denying his eating and drinking habits exacerbated whatever underlying health problems he had.

For one thing, he seems to have suffered from a painfully dis-tended stomach. He wrote to his tailor, 'I need a new body belt. This one is no good, and owing to the sensitive condition of my abdomen it is quite impossible for me to go out without a strong protecting belt.'

The court case made matters far, far worse. From 1816, the year it took over his life, his health deteriorated and continued to do so. In October, the month after Karl's hernia operation, he wrote that he was suffering from 'a violent, feverish cold, so that I had to stay in bed for a very long time, and only after several months was I allowed to go out, even for a short while'. He details the treatment he was prescribed: six powders daily and six bowls of tea, a healing ointment to be rubbed into his skin three times a day, another medicine, and a tincture of which he was to swallow twelve spoonfuls daily.

None of it worked to his satisfaction, so he sacked his doctor. This was the estimable Dr Malfatti, a relative of his former *inamorata* Therese. He will make a dramatic reappearance in the final stages of Beethoven's life. A new doctor diagnosed severe catarrhal inflammation of the lungs and warned Beethoven he would be ill for a long time.

On top of all this, and far more detrimental to his wellbeing, was his deafness, which now, as he approached his fifties, was severe.

But, in late 1817, a totally unexpected event occurred that was to help him turn the corner. I say 'help', because it is not clear which came first, the unexpected help or his own decision to compose a major new work.

'Major' is an understatement. 'Monumental' is better. 'Gigantic' is not an overstatement.

Some time around late November or early December, Beethoven received a visit from a certain Thomas Broadwood Esq., of the London firm of piano manufacturers, John Broadwood & Sons. We do not know how the meeting came about – Thomas Broadwood was on a tour of European capitals, probably to secure orders – but it would undoubtedly have been set up by a musical colleague who suspected Beethoven might be interested.

Beethoven's style of playing had always been markedly different from that of other pianists. He held his hands flat over the keys, using the strength of his forearms and wrists to push his fingers, with little bend at the joint, into the keys. This contrasted starkly with the established style of playing, as used for instance by Hummel, hands arched high over the keys, fingers fully bent at the joint, giving a much more delicate style of playing.

Without doubt his deafness influenced his action, as he struggled more and more to hear what he was playing, and his compositions favoured it – it is hard to imagine a pianist such as Hummel giving necessary weight to the great opening chord of the 'Pathétique' Piano Sonata, for instance. It was known in Vienna that English pianos were built with a heavier action than those in Vienna and Paris, and were thus more suited to Beethoven's style. At their meeting, Broadwood confirmed this, and in an extraordinary act of generosity – unwittingly earning his company, still going strong today, a place in musical history – he offered to send Beethoven a Broadwood concert grand as a gift from London.

He kept his promise. In late January 1818 Beethoven took delivery of a brand new six-octave grand piano, which was shipped from London to Trieste and then taken overland to Vienna. One can only begin to imagine Beethoven's excitement as he watched workmen break open the wooden shipping case reinforced with tin, at last leaving him alone to gaze at this wondrous gift.

The piano was built of Spanish mahogany with a solid steel frame, triple-stringed throughout, inlaid with marquetry and ormolu, the brass carrying-handles formed of laurel leaves. Engraved on the board above the keys were the words: Hoc Instrumentum est Thomae Broadwood (Londini) donum, propter Ingenium illustrissimi Beethoven. His own name was inscribed in ebony, alongside 'John Broadwood and Sons, Makers of Instruments to

His Majesty and the Princesses. Great Pulteney Street. Golden Square. London.' To the right of the keyboard, in black ink, the signatures of five prominent musicians active in London – among them his old friend and pupil Ferdinand Ries.*

Beethoven expressed his unbounded gratitude in a letter to Broadwood written in excruciating French: 'Jamais je n'eprouvais pas un grand Plaisir de ce que me causa votre Annonce de l'arrivée de cette Piano, avec qui vous m'honorès de m'en faire present ...'

Immediately Beethoven set about – or continued – in earnest composing a new piano sonata, which was to be the longest, most complex, most profound sonata of any he had hitherto composed, or was ever to compose. He knew it. He told Czerny, 'I am writing a sonata now which is going to be my greatest.'

The finished work, which he completed in just a few months, begins with a huge two-octave leap in the left hand, followed by seven *fortissimo* chords, with a deliberate discord in the fourth. This is Beethoven, pure Beethoven. He was composing again, and the works that were to follow the 'Hammerklavier' – the name given to the sonata by Beethoven, quite possibly in honour of his new instrument – the Piano Sonatas, Opp. 109, 110, 111, the *Diabelli Variations*, the *Missa Solemnis*, the Ninth Symphony, the Late Quartets, were to be his greatest body of work, indeed the greatest body of work any composer would ever produce.

But it was not straightforward. The 'Hammerklavier' was the single glorious exception to the barren years of the court case. In the final year of that lengthy trauma Beethoven began to compose

---

* Some years after Beethoven's death the piano was presented to his great admirer Franz Liszt, who is reported never to have played it, judging himself unfit to touch the keys played by Beethoven. Later Liszt presented it to the Hungarian National Museum in Budapest, where it stands, fully restored, today.

the *Diabelli Variations*, but set them aside, unable to make progress. He promised a new sacred work to be performed at Archduke Rudolph's enthronement as Archbishop of Olmütz, and indeed began work on a setting of the Mass to be called *Missa Solemnis*, but did not complete it until two years after the enthronement.

Why these problems? Once again domestic issues were hindering his creative process. In late 1820, shortly after the Court of Appeal's final ruling in his favour over custody of Karl, he fell ill again. But this was nothing like his usual complaints. In fact so serious was it that in January 1821 the *Allgemeine musikalische Zeitung* went so far as to report: 'Herr von Beethofen [*sic*] has been sick with a rheumatic fever. All friends of true music and all admirers of his muse feared for him. But now he is on the road to recovery and is working actively.'

'All admirers feared for him …' This is nothing less than a suggestion that Beethoven's life was in danger. *That* is how debilitating the whole protracted court case, and its concomitant problems, had become.

As for the second sentence of that report, the newspaper was either correct but the recovery did not last, or it was completely wrong. Later in January the rheumatic fever took hold again, and Beethoven was ordered back to bed, where he remained for a full six weeks.

At his lowest ebb he received news that is certain to have saddened him greatly. Josephine Brunsvik, once the object of his affections, died at the tragically early age of forty-two after a long illness. Her sister wrote that she died of 'nervous consumption', and 'suffered from want, was lacking food and assistance of any kind'.

This is unlikely, given that Therese was with her at the end, but it points to a mental collapse as well as a physical deterioration. Word of Josephine's condition is bound to have reached Beethoven some time before, so he was not unprepared, but her death can only have exacerbated his own physical condition.

That is what happened. No sooner had the rheumatic fever passed than he fell ill again, this time with jaundice. It was one thing after another. He remained unwell throughout the summer and into autumn, only writing that in November he had begun to recover his health.

It did not last. He spent the entire first half of 1822 suffering from what he described as 'gout in the chest'. At his lowest ebb he received a visitor, and what might under different circumstances have been a remarkable, even fruitful, meeting, was anything but.

Vienna was experiencing something of a craze for the operas of a certain Italian composer by the name of Gioachino Rossini, who, keen to bask in the adulation of the musically sophisticated Viennese, came to the city on his honeymoon. Once there, he insisted on paying a visit to Beethoven, whom he greatly admired.

There are two versions of what happened. One says that Beethoven, known to be less than enthusiastic about Italian opera, twice refused to receive Rossini. Rossini himself, though, insisted he did indeed call on Beethoven, and gave a fascinating account of what happened when the two composers met.

As with so many stories and legends surrounding Beethoven, Rossini's was given many years after the event – in this case nearly forty – and it is understandable that he would want to show the meeting in the best possible light. So there might well be exaggerations in his account, but – stripping it of its more obvious self-praise – it has the ring of truth in so many aspects that it is worth retelling.

Rossini was appalled at the squalor in which Beethoven lived.

He described being ushered into an attic that was 'terribly disordered and dirty'. The ceiling had cracks through which the rainwater poured down 'in streams'.

Rossini says that Beethoven, after first ignoring him, then congratulated him, particularly on *The Barber of Seville*. One might expect Rossini to say this, knowing as he did late in life that *The Barber* was such a popular work. But he has a nice line in self-deprecation as well, not too proud to relate how Beethoven damned him with faint praise.

'Do not ever try your hand at anything but *opera buffa* [comic opera],' he quotes Beethoven as telling him. 'You would be doing violence to your destiny by wanting to succeed in a different genre. In *opera buffa* none can equal Italians. Your language and your temperament predispose you for it.'

Rossini describes how the meeting was necessarily short, since Beethoven was profoundly deaf, and neither understood the other's language.

That evening Rossini was guest at a gala dinner at the palace of the Austrian Chancellor, Prince Metternich. He relates how he berated the company, made up of court members and aristocracy, for allowing the 'greatest genius of the epoch' to live in such straitened conditions, and suggested the wealthy families of Vienna should contribute a small amount each to allow him to live in some degree of comfort.

His proposal, he relates, met with little support, the general reaction being that however much you tried to help Beethoven, he would ignore your goodwill and live exactly as he wished, in whatever degree of squalor that might be.

How starkly this account contrasts with the experience of another renowned composer, a Viennese, of a rather more shy disposition than the ebullient Rossini. In the same month as Rossini's visit, Franz Schubert published his *Eight Variations on a French Song* for piano four hands, with a dedication to Beethoven. He agonised over whether he should personally give a copy to Beethoven, considering his own compositions to be unworthy. Finally he plucked up the courage to do so, but when he went to Beethoven's lodgings the great man was out, so Schubert left it with the servant.

As far as is known, Schubert, whose admiration for Beethoven was such that on his deathbed he asked to be buried in a grave alongside Beethoven's, met him only once, when Beethoven was on his deathbed, though even this is not certain.*

It was probably in the autumn of this year, 1822, that an extraordinary event occurred that has become one of the legends surrounding Beethoven's life. It was related to Thayer, again some forty years after the event, by a lithographer named Blasius Höfel for whom Beethoven sat, so as with many other tales of eccentricity it might have become embellished over the years, but as with Rossini's account there is no reason to doubt its authenticity.

One autumn evening Höfel was enjoying an early-evening drink in the tavern *Zum Schleifen* ('At the Ribbon') in the Vienna suburb of Wiener Neustadt. Among the party was the local Commissioner of Police. It was already dark when a police constable came to the tavern to find the Commissioner.

'Sir,' said the constable, 'we have arrested someone for behaving in a suspicious manner. He won't be quiet. He keeps on

---

* This deathbed wish was granted, and further honoured when both bodies were exhumed and moved to the Musicians' Quarter in Vienna's Zentralfriedhof, where they lie just a few feet from each other today.

yelling that he is Beethoven. But he's just a tramp. He's in a moth-eaten old coat, no hat. He has no identity papers, there's no way of finding out who he is. We're not sure what to do.'

'Keep him under arrest overnight,' replied the Commissioner. 'We'll speak to him in the morning and find out who he is.'

But it did not end there. As the Commissioner told Höfel later, at eleven o'clock that night he was woken at home by a policeman who told him the man in custody would not quieten down, was still yelling that he was Beethoven, and was demanding that Anton Herzog, Musical Director in Wiener Neustadt, be called in to identify him.

The Commissioner decided he had better investigate. He went to Herzog's house, woke him up, and asked him to accompany him to the police station. The Commissioner and Herzog were taken to the cell, and as soon as Herzog cast eyes on the tramp he exclaimed, 'That *is* Beethoven!'

The Commissioner, no doubt congratulating himself that he had taken the matter seriously, ordered Beethoven's immediate release. Herzog took him back to his own house, gave him the best room, assured him he would not be disturbed, and looked forward to seeing him for breakfast if he so wished, or if he preferred to sleep longer …

The next day the local Mayor came to Herzog's house to apologise in person to the renowned composer for his treatment at the hands of an over-zealous police officer, gave Beethoven his best coat and the mayoral carriage to transport him home.

By then everyone knew what had happened. The day before Beethoven had got up early in the morning, put on his threadbare old coat, forgotten to take a hat, and set out for what he intended to be a short walk. He reached the towpath on the Danube Canal and followed it. He walked on for hours.

By late afternoon he ended up at the canal basin at the Ungertor, a considerable distance from the city. He was totally lost and disorientated, and in a pitiful state having had nothing to eat all day. In this condition, tired, drawn, hungry, in tattered old clothes, he was seen by local people looking in at the windows of houses. They became suspicious and called the police.

A constable approached him and told him he was arresting him for behaving suspiciously.

'But I am Beethoven.'

'Of course you are. Why not? I'll tell you what you are. You're a tramp, and that Beethoven is no tramp.' (*'Ein Lump sind Sie; so sieht der Beethoven nicht aus.'*)

And yet through all these traumas – ill-health, personal problems, one thing after another – he continued to compose. The *Missa Solemnis* was finally completed; he composed the three piano sonatas that were to be his last; he took up the *Diabelli Variations** again, and he was making notes for further compositions.

Then, out of the blue, in November 1822, he received a letter from St Petersburg. The writer of the letter was a Russian nobleman by the name of Nikolas Borisovich, Prince Galitzin, and the request he made of Beethoven – or, more accurately, Beethoven's positive response – has earned the Prince his place in musical history. He asked Beethoven if he would consent to compose one,

---

* The music publisher Anton Diabelli, an accomplished amateur pianist, had composed a simple waltz, and asked fifty composers to compose a single variation on it. Beethoven at first refused, considering it demeaning, but eventually wrote thirty-three variations, creating his greatest set of piano variations.

two, or three new quartets, for which he would pay Beethoven whatever he, Beethoven, considered appropriate.

This was an unexpected stroke of luck for Beethoven, because in letters he wrote earlier in the year he said that he was considering composing string quartets, maybe as many as three. Now he could not only get on with composing them, he would be paid as well.

But once again – as with the *Diabelli Variations* and the *Missa Solemnis* – he put the quartets to one side, because quite simply he got a more attractive offer. There was another composition he had begun making sketches for in the autumn of the previous year. That's a slight understatement. You could say this was a composition that had been on his mind, and slowly germinating, since he briefly attended lectures on the German philosopher Immanuel Kant at the University of Bonn as a teenager, and acquired a volume of poetry by the German poet and playwright Friedrich Schiller.

He had kept that volume of poetry with him, always intending to set to music a poem that particularly appealed to him, 'An die Freude' ('Ode to Joy'). By 1822 he was beginning to think that maybe a symphony would be the appropriate way to go about it. No composer, not Mozart, Haydn, nor anyone else, had ever incorporated words – spoken or sung – into a symphony. If this was the way forward, then it was going to be a radical departure from any previous symphony, and from what a symphony was generally accepted to be.

The first indication that he intended writing a new symphony (though there is no indication yet that it would include voices), came in a letter he wrote to his friend and helper Ferdinand Ries, now based in London, on 6 July 1822: 'Have you any idea what fee the <u>Harmony Society</u> * would offer me for a grand symphony?'

Ries evidently replied with good news, because on 20 December, Beethoven wrote to Ries accepting the Society's relatively low offer of £50. There was history between Beethoven and the Philharmonic Society. In 1815 the Society had paid Beethoven 75 guineas for three overtures. He provided them with three overtures that had already been performed, whereas they were expecting new works, and the directors of the Society were disappointed with their quality.†

This time, therefore, the offer was just £50, and one suspects that even that amount was offered with some reluctance. They cannot have known that the work with which their name would forever be associated would redefine the symphony and represent the pinnacle of Beethoven's achievement.

It took Beethoven well over a year to bring his Ninth Symphony to fruition, the biggest problem being how to introduce the voices in the final movement. Aware of how ground-breaking this final movement would be, he sketched then rejected several ideas, before deciding to quote the theme from each of the preceding three movements, but rejecting it before it could be completed. A solo bass voice then articulates in words the desire to abandon these sounds in favour of more pleasing and joyful tones. The final movement therefore breaks free and takes flight. The mind of a genius at work.

---

* The Philharmonic Society of London.

† The three overtures were *Die Ruinen von Athen (The Ruins of Athens), Zur Namensfeier (Name Day)*, and *König Stephan (King Stephen)*.

By early 1824 the Ninth Symphony was complete. Now for the easy part: securing a theatre and date for the first performance. Easy, because word had spread in Vienna that its most celebrated composer was working intensively on a new symphony, his first for over ten years, and that it was going to be radically different. The theatre managers of Vienna were falling over themselves to win the concert for their theatre.

Easy? Nothing is ever easy where Beethoven is concerned. For reasons known only to him – possibly no more than a desire to spite the Viennese musical establishment – he decided he wanted his new symphony to be given its premiere in Berlin.

Berlin? That musical establishment was dumbstruck. Why Berlin? Their bewilderment was certainly laced with anger. Not only would it mean none of Vienna's musicians would be involved, but to add insult to injury it awarded the prize of a new Beethoven work to the capital of Prussia, a militaristic nation the Austrians at best treated with suspicion, at worst hated, whose army they had faced on the battlefield and would do again.

When they realised Beethoven was serious – the general manager of the Berlin Theatre was delighted to accept his proposal – they swallowed their pride and anger, and decided to write an open letter to their most famous musical son.

In wonderfully overblown language, no fewer than thirty illustrious musical names implored Beethoven, whose 'name and creations belong to all contemporaneous humanity and every country which opens a susceptible bosom to art', to recognise that 'it is Austria which is best entitled to claim him as her own', along with Mozart and Haydn, 'the sacred triad in which these names and yours glow as the symbol of the highest within the spiritual realm of tones [which] sprang from the soil of their fatherland'.

They continued:

We beg you to withhold no longer ... a performance of the latest masterwork of your hands ... We know that a new flower glows in the garland of your glorious, still unequalled symphonies ... Do not any longer disappoint the general expectations! ... Do not allow these, your latest offspring, some day to appear perhaps as foreigners in their place of birth, introduced perhaps by persons to whom you and your mind are alien! Appear soon among your friends, your admirers, your venerators!

Well, Beethoven was as susceptible to flattery as any man. '[The letter] is very beautiful! – it rejoices me greatly!' he wrote.

That small hurdle cleared, the problems really now *did* start.

Beethoven insisted on making the final decision on every aspect of the concert – the venue, the time, the programme, selection of musicians and singers, copying of the musical parts, rehearsal timings, and even the price of seats. All of which would have been fine, if he had been able to make up his mind on any of it.

Time was running short. Spring would soon give way to summer, and the concert season end. It would take at least three weeks to prepare for the concert – rehearsals and posters printed – and the single most important decision had still not been taken. The venue.

The obvious choice was the Theater an der Wien, which had seen so many of Beethoven's works premiered. Baron Braun was long since gone, and the current manager, Count Palffy, was known to be enthusiastic about Beethoven's music. It would also be simpler and quicker to arrange dates with the Theater an der Wien than with the bureaucracy of the imperial court theatres.

But there was a problem. Beethoven loathed Palffy. It dated back some years, to when Beethoven was giving a recital in the salon of one of his patrons. Palffy was in the small audience, carrying on a conversation with a lady. Beethoven, having tried several times to silence him, finally stopped playing, shouted, 'I will not play for pigs!' – and stormed out.

It was probably in revenge that Beethoven now demanded a change of conductor and leader if the concert was to be held at the Theater an der Wien. Palffy was surprisingly accommodating. He agreed to allow Michael Umlauf to conduct, in place of the theatre's resident musical director, and Beethoven's friend Ignaz Schuppanzigh to lead instead of the resident leader. On top of that, Palffy offered Beethoven the theatre, staff, musicians, as many rehearsals as he wanted, at the price of a mere 1200 florins, allowing him to keep all profits.

It was a remarkably generous offer, and Beethoven's friends and colleagues were delighted that at least the problem over the venue had been resolved.

But Beethoven turned it down. Back to square one.

There was an underlying issue that was making matters infinitely more difficult than they needed to be. There were essentially two camps operating on Beethoven's behalf. The one that was negotiating with Palffy was made up of patrons and musicians. But Beethoven was convinced they were not to be trusted, so he authorised his brother Johann and nephew Karl to make secret overtures to other theatres – Johann, who had business experience but no knowledge of the world of music, and Karl, now aged seventeen, with no knowledge of anything.

The first group, after Beethoven's rejection of Palffy's offer, entered into talks with the manager of the Theater am Kärntnertor, one of the imperial court theatres. This prompted Palffy to improve his offer, dropping the price for the Theater an der Wien to 1000 florins. He also offered a selection of dates: 22, 23 and 24 March.

This time Beethoven agreed, no doubt to a collective sigh of relief from the first group. But unknown to them, Beethoven's brother and nephew were negotiating with a *third* theatre – a totally inappropriate venue, being more a hall than a theatre and seating only five hundred people.

Days, weeks, were passing, and nobody was getting anywhere. Finally, confronted with reality, Beethoven made the only sensible decision: he abandoned the concert. There would be no performance of his Ninth Symphony.

Then he changed his mind *again*. The concert would be held in the Kärntnertor (whose resident orchestra he had described not long before as being worse than a musical clock). Palffy made one last desperate bid. Beethoven could have the Wien for nothing. But this time Beethoven's mind was made up, and he did not change it again.

His Ninth Symphony would receive its premiere at the Kärntnertor on Friday, 7 May.

Now the soloists needed to be selected, and fast. The females were relatively straightforward. Everybody agreed on the soprano Henriette Sontag, and the contralto Karoline Unger. The men were more of a problem. The preferred tenor claimed the part was too low for his voice. The bass claimed the part was too high and impossibly hard.

Choices were finally made, singers selected, chorus members named, with an orchestral force of 24 violins, 10 violas, 12 cellos and basses, and double the number of woodwind. This, by the standards of the day, was an enormous line-up, but everybody understood that with this new symphony, they were dealing with something quite out of the ordinary.

Then Beethoven dropped a bombshell. He said he would conduct. Profoundly deaf, unable to hear normal conversation, unable to hear musical sounds, even with his ear to an ear trumpet held on the piano keys, he insisted on conducting the most complex and demanding score he had ever written.

Hurriedly a plan was put into operation – a cunning ruse. Yes, said the concert organisers, of course he would conduct, who else could possibly conduct such a work but its creator? Purely, though, as a back-up, for no other reason than to make sure everything went smoothly, Michael Umlauf would be on stage with him. Michael Umlauf, the well-known conductor. But don't worry, Herr Beethoven, he won't get in your way. Beethoven acquiesced.

Given the shortness of time, there could be only two full rehearsals. The first was a disaster, the second worse. The problem was the solo singers. They complained that their parts were simply impossible. They told Beethoven he did not understand the human voice.

Beethoven was in no mood to compromise. He told them to sing exactly what he had written. Karoline Unger, the contralto, threw a tantrum. To Beethoven's face, she called him 'a tyrant over all the vocal organs', and turning to her colleagues said, 'Well then, we must go on torturing ourselves in the name of God!'

The bass soloist went one further. At the last minute, declaring his part was impossibly high, he pulled out. He was replaced, probably, by a member of the chorus who was familiar with the part from rehearsals.

In secret the four soloists made a pact. At the concert they would not try for notes they were doubtful of reaching, and they simply would not sing impossibly difficult passages. Beethoven was deaf anyway, he wouldn't know.

The stage was set for a farcical first performance of the most important, demanding, complex, innovative work Beethoven had ever composed.

The Theater am Kärntnertor was almost full, which was gratifying, but it was the wrong audience. The concert season was all but over, and Vienna was basking in early-summer warmth. The nobility, aristocrats, patrons of the arts, had left the city for their country residences.

A genuine disappointment for Beethoven was that the royal box was empty. Beethoven had personally gone to the Hofburg Palace to invite members of the imperial royal family. His most loyal supporter, Archduke Rudolph, was away in Olmütz. Beethoven rather hoped the Emperor himself, with the Empress, would attend. But the empty royal box spoke of an unwillingness to be associated with disaster.

Beethoven's small circle of close friends was there. He no doubt watched with sadness as his old friend and drinking partner Nikolaus Zmeskall was carried to his seat on a sedan chair because of crippling gout that had left him bedridden.

We can assume a ripple of laughter (no need to stifle it, he can't hear), as Beethoven, a pace or two in front of Umlauf, walked to the stage and people noticed that he was wearing a green frock coat. Black was de rigueur, but Beethoven did not own the 'correct' garment. He was otherwise appropriately dressed: white cravat with waistcoat, black breeches, black silk stockings, and shoes with buckles.

Another ripple of expectant laughter, maybe even a gasp of anticipation, as Umlauf – unseen by Beethoven – made a sign of the cross over the players.

Beethoven took his place in front of the musicians, raised his arms and brought them down. To the side of him, and slightly behind, Umlauf made sure he had their attention, raised his arms and he too brought them down.

The audience fell silent as the mysterious opening chords sounded, a floating cloud of sound, a sound world they had not heard before, yielding to huge affirmative chords from the whole orchestra. They watched, and listened, as Beethoven flailed with his arms to the sounds in his head, and Umlauf directed the musicians who were playing as if their lives depended on it.

The second movement took them completely by surprise, with its driving rhythm and totally unexpected solo section for timpani, rarely before accorded more than an accompanying role. The constantly repeated theme that emerges halfway through the movement is surely a foretaste of what is to come. By now the audience – sophisticated musically, even if not belonging to the aristocracy – knew they were experiencing something extraordinary.

The end of the second movement, quietly disintegrating before that theme is heard once more, but cut off this time, yielding to a series of final affirmative chords, brought them to their feet. The audience needed release, they needed to breathe. They leapt to their feet, shouting and applauding.

Beethoven continued to conduct the orchestra in his head. Umlauf turned to see the audience on its feet, shouts of *Encore! Encore!* reverberating around the hall. He made a judgement. He raised his arms for the third movement. The gentle chords from the wind calmed them, yielding to a theme of sublime gentleness on strings.

At the end of the third movement, Umlauf led swiftly into the huge discord that began the final movement, before cellos and basses gave their portentous sound to a hint of the great theme that was to come.

The bass singer was soon on his feet, and the words 'O Freunde, nicht diese Töne!' rang out over the audience.

Umlauf, knowing now he and the musicians were creating something extraordinary, drove the pace on, players and singers performing as if somehow knowing this was a defining moment in the history of music.

Suddenly, it all stops, total silence. A small beat on bass drum and deep wind. Syncopated dotted rhythm. Martial music. Tenor summons all forces.

In unison, in harmony, faultlessly, the music drives to its conclusion. Umlauf held it all perfectly together, singers, chorus and orchestra giving the performance of their lives.

Again, just before the end, a tremendous slowing down, almost to a stop, before full forces drive to the final flourish.

Umlauf brought his arms down for the final great chord. It was over. The audience erupted, rose to their feet, cheered and shouted, handkerchiefs and hats waved in the air. *Beethoven! Beethoven! Beethoven!*

Umlauf looked to his side. Beethoven, oblivious to what was happening, continued to wave his arms, conducting the orchestra he was hearing in his head. Karoline Unger, the contralto who had so berated him in rehearsal, stepped forward. Gently she touched Beethoven on the shoulder, nodded encouragingly at the bewildered face, and turned him to face the cheering audience.

At that moment Beethoven knew the gift he had given to the world.

Chapter 16

'I Want to Be a Soldier'

In which Beethoven gets drunk with friends

B eethoven's creative process was in full drive. Within a few weeks of the triumphant premier of his Ninth Symphony, he began serious work on the Galitzin commission for three string quartets.

This would have been remarkable if he were a much younger man in good health with no domestic problems to distract him. On all counts this was untrue of Beethoven. First, the aftermath of the Kärntnertor concert should have been a time to pause, take stock, thank the team who had worked so hard to make it possible. Instead Beethoven accused them of cheating him.

He summoned them to a lunch at the *Zum wilden Mann* ('At the Sign of the Wild Man') restaurant in the Prater, and openly accused them of withholding receipts from him. They defended themselves, pointing out that in a highly unusual arrangement Beethoven's brother Johann and nephew Karl had actually been in charge of financial arrangements for the concert at his insistence

Johann overseeing expenses and payments, and Karl collecting audited receipts from the box office.

Beethoven persisted, insisting he had been informed by an 'entirely credible source' that he had been cheated out of money that was justly owed to him. His guests knew there was no reasoning with him, made their excuses and left.

Just a few weeks after this Karl, a little short of his eighteenth birthday, dropped a bombshell on his uncle. He was about to complete his first year as a student at the University of Vienna, studying philosophy and languages. He knew how badly he was doing, so badly that he was certain to have to repeat the year's studies. He decided on a radical change of direction.

Clearly bracing himself for the storm he knew he was about to unleash, Karl wrote first in a conversation book how he would not do anything without his uncle's consent, then scribbled a lengthy preamble admitting his new choice of career was rather strange, 'not a <u>common</u> one'. Then the single word: Soldier.

Beethoven predictably exploded. Karl was the sole Beethoven of the next generation; he was an artist, and to him was accorded the highest privilege of bearing the name Beethoven. A couple of years earlier, Beethoven had instructed his pupil Czerny to give Karl piano lessons, and Czerny had reported back that the boy had no musical talent whatsoever. This did not deter Beethoven from the unshakeable conviction that Karl's destiny was as an artist. For the time being, though, Karl had no choice but to remain at university, but the seed had been sown. Almost inevitably it was not long before Beethoven fell ill again.

Extraordinarily, unbelievably, none of this hampered Beethoven's creativity, and by early the following year he had completed the first of the string quartets, Op. 127. Just as the three Piano Sonatas, Opp. 109, 110, 111, had taken the piano sonata into new territory, the Ninth had redefined the symphony, Beethoven was now doing the same with the string quartet.

Neither he, nor anyone, had ever composed a string quartet comparable to Op. 127. The second movement was the longest he had written for string quartet. The demands on all players, particularly first violin, are extraordinary. All four players are required to play to the most exacting standards imaginable. The first violin has to execute leaps across the strings, perform demi-semiquaver runs, and stop almost off the fingerboard on the top E string. Key signatures change in mid-movement – no fewer than four times in the *Adagio* – with accidentals scattered like so much confetti.

A date for the first performance was set for 6 March 1825, on earlier assurances from Beethoven that the quartet would be ready in good time. It was not, of course, leaving the musicians less than two weeks' rehearsal for the most difficult piece of music they had ever been confronted with.

Shades, again, of the Ninth Symphony, but this time there was to be no happy outcome. The performance was a failure. Beethoven, now completely deaf, did not attend. His brother Johann, known as a musical ignoramus, did, and reported back to Beethoven that it was all the fault of the quartet leader, his old friend Ignaz Schuppanzigh. Johann said Schuppanzigh was tired from too much rehearsing, did not like the quartet anyway, and would rather not have been performing it.

The truth was that Schuppanzigh had been driven to his wits' end by Beethoven's delay in completing the piece, had indeed over-rehearsed to the point of fatigue, and would rather the date of the performance had been postponed.

Beethoven summoned his friend and blamed him entirely for the failure. Schuppanzigh stood his ground, probably intentionally angering Beethoven even more by telling him he could easily master the technical demands of the piece, but was having trouble arriving at its spirit.

It was no surprise that when the quartet was performed for a second time two weeks later, it was with a different first violinist. This time the performance was a triumph, and was repeated several times in the following days.

How did Beethoven react to all this tension? In the way he had done so often, with increasing frequency. He fell ill once again. This time, though, it was far more severe than before. He was suffering from his usual bad digestion and diarrhoea. He also complained of catarrh and frequent nose bleeds. Most ominously of all, he was spitting up blood.

His doctor, Anton Braunhofer – successor to the successor of Dr Malfatti, both sacked – warned Beethoven that his condition was severe, and that he risked inflammation of the bowels and 'inflammatory attacks' if he did not strictly follow his advice, which was to consume no wine, coffee, spirits, or spices of any kind. He gave him a medicine to swallow as well.

He was strict with his obviously restive patient, writing in a conversation book:

> I can assure you that all will turn out well, but you must be patient for a while yet. An illness cannot be cured in a day. I won't bother you much longer with medicine, but you will have to stick strictly to my dietary prescriptions, which won't cause you to starve.

It was summer, and Braunhofer's advice to Beethoven to leave the city concurred with his own desire to get away, and so he left once again for Baden. To begin with, the change of air did him good. Within a few days of arriving he wrote Braunhofer a letter describing his severe symptoms, but in the form of a humorous dialogue between a patient and his doctor.

As further evidence of his good humour, he added to the letter a small sixteen-bar canon, which he said he had written on a walk in the Helenenthal (Valley of Helen, west of Baden), on the 'second Anton's bridge'.

It is a beguiling image: the great composer in obviously bad health, but never too ill to pull a scrap of manuscript paper from his pocket and, perhaps leaning on a railing watching the stream rushing underneath the bridge, compose a piece of music.

The good humour, predictably, did not last. The weather was unseasonably cold. Beethoven complained in a note to Karl that it was so cold he could hardly move his fingers to write, adding that it was 'practically impossible to produce anything in this cold and utterly dismal climate'.

The obvious target was Braunhofer, whose remedies were showing no signs of working. He even blamed Braunhofer for not warning him to avoid asparagus, which gave him diarrhoea after he ate it at an inn in Baden. Beethoven took his health into his own hands. He began to drink wine again – white wine diluted with water to begin with, then straight wine – and coffee (instead of chocolate which Braunhofer had recommended as a substitute). He wrote to Karl that Braunhofer was 'narrow-minded and a fool with it'.

As a further sign of mental strain – or rather a continuing refusal to accept reality – in letters to Karl, he addressed him as 'Dear Son!' and signed the letter 'Your faithful father'. Karl had now left university and enrolled in a business school, with Beethoven's permission, probably as an attempt to induce him to forget a military career.

He visited Beethoven several times in Baden, but entries in conversation books show that his uncle's hold over him – Beethoven's refusal to countenance his wishes, his constant demands to know how Karl was spending his time, his continued refusal to allow Karl to see his mother, his belief that he really was Karl's father – was beginning to wear Karl down in a serious way. He was becoming something of a ticking time-bomb.

And yet, and yet ... once again none of this was hindering Beethoven's creative process. Even before the unsuccessful first performance of the string quartet Op. 127, Beethoven had begun work on its successor, which would become Op. 132.* Now, in mid-May 1825, convalescing in Baden, he was about to write one of the most extraordinary of all his string quartet movements.

As if in final proof that Braunhofer was a fool, Beethoven's health suddenly took a turn for the better. The fact that he was now ignoring Braunhofer's advice, as well as having lost (probably purposefully) the medicine prescribed, was proof it had nothing to do with medical advice. No, it was divine intervention.

There are not many instances of Beethoven showing a religious side, but in his final years on occasion a degree of spirituality emerged. Now he put that to good use. He decided to compose the third movement of the string quartet as a personal offering of gratitude to God for his recovery from what he clearly believed was a life-threatening illness.

---

* None of the Late Quartets (nor any of the final three piano sonatas) were given names, and their opus numbers are non-sequential, due to their publication dates. The order of composition was Op. 127, Op. 132, Op. 130, Op. 133 *(Grosse Fuge)*, Op. 131, Op. 135.

At the top of the movement he wrote: *Heiliger Dankgesang eines Genesenen an die Gottheit, in der lydischen Tonart* ('Sacred Song of Thanksgiving to the Deity from a Convalescent, in the Lydian Mode').

The Lydian Mode was an ancient musical form used in medieval church services, and in the first thirty bars of the movement Beethoven has the four strings play solid chords in perfect imitation of a church organ. It creates a most remarkable sound, and stands alone in all Beethoven's compositions for string quartet. It then gives way to a lively section marked *Neue Kraft fühlend* ('Feeling new strength'). Beethoven is describing his illness and recovery in music.

But matters with Karl were beginning to deteriorate. Word reached Beethoven – we don't know from whom – that Karl was disobeying the court order and secretly seeing his mother. Beethoven wrote to him from Baden, at *exactly* the time he was composing the *Heiliger Dankgesang*:

> *Until now it was only conjecture, though someone has indeed assured me that you have been seeing your mother in secret – Am I to experience once more this most abominable ingratitude?*

And again, ten days later, still bitter:

> *– God is my witness, I dream only of being completely removed from you and that wretched brother and this horrible family who have been thrust upon me – May God grant my*

wishes. For I <u>can no longer trust you</u>.
Unfortunately your father
or, better still, not your father

As soon as he had completed Op. 132, he began work on the third string quartet, Op. 130, and as with the *Heiliger Dankgesang*, once again his personal problems found their way directly into his composition. This time it was not his health, but his agony over his nephew Karl's behaviour.

The fifth (of six!) movements is as extraordinary in its way as the *Heiliger Dankgesang*. Beethoven called it *Cavatina*, a word usually applied to a simple, melodious, expressive air. In this case that is something of an understatement.

The first violin takes the melody, beginning with a deep B flat on the low G string, rising a sixth. It is a lift, marked *sotto voce*, which seems to take the soul with it. After a development, the first violin then falls a sixth. It is heartrending. When you believe Beethoven cannot increase the intensity any more, he writes *pianissimo* quavers for three strings, and then the first violin … weeps. I do not know any other way to describe it.

Beethoven wrote '*Beklemmt*' over the first violin part. It is difficult to convey the meaning with a single word. It means oppressed, anguished, tortured, overcome by grief and heartache. It is a unique passage in all Beethoven. The first violin climbs, in quavers and semiquavers, off the beat, almost every note an accidental, interspersed with rests, sighs, then falls an octave, exactly as you do when you sob, catch your breath, then weep. The first violin climbs again, with demi-semiquavers, before another fall, more sobs. The passage lasts for just six bars, before the opening theme, with its rising sixth, resumes.

It is small wonder Beethoven's friend Karl Holz, a violinist, said the *Cavatina* cost Beethoven tears in its writing, and Beethoven himself confessed that nothing he had written had so moved him and that just to hear it in his head brought him to tears.

There can, in my mind, be no doubt of the inspiration for this extraordinary writing. Beethoven realised – even if he would not admit it to himself – that he was losing Karl.

Beethoven broke off writing Op. 130 to return to Vienna to attend the first performance of the earlier quartet, Op. 132. Thanks to the presence of the English conductor Sir George Smart, we have a vivid account of what happened. And thanks to the Berlin music publisher Moritz Schlesinger, who arranged the performance, we have an equally vivid account of the merriment that followed.

Schlesinger was staying in the hotel *Zum wilden Mann* in the Kärntnerstrasse, and it was in an upstairs room that the four musicians, along with Beethoven, Karl, Schlesinger, Smart, and a prestigious gathering of academics, assembled.

It seems the quartet was performed twice. Smart reports that the room was hot and crowded, Beethoven took off his coat, and directed the performers. He could not hear, because of his deafness, but his eye told him that one *staccato* passage was incorrectly played. Beethoven took the violin from Karl Holz, who was second violin, and demonstrated how he wanted it played – but played it a quarter-tone flat!

This is a fascinating little detail. We know Beethoven took violin lessons from Ries's father Franz as a teenager in Bonn, but evidently did not reach a very high standard, and I am not aware of any other evidence of him playing violin in later years. The small audience must have looked on bewitched, to see the great composer, now profoundly deaf, in effect conducting his string quartet, even playing a passage.

Probably because of this interrupted first performance, the decision was made to play the quartet a second time – the full forty-five minutes – presumably without interruption. Smart tantalisingly reported only that those present paid Beethoven 'the greatest attention', as you would expect them to do.

After the audience had departed, Schlesinger ordered a meal and wine to be served in the private room for the small gathering of himself, Beethoven, Karl, and the musicians. Beethoven took out a conversation book, put it on the table, and almost all contributed to it – unusually, it includes a written comment by Beethoven himself. Thanks again to Schlesinger, the conversation book has survived, and it gives fascinating insight into a post-performance meal involving a great composer and his colleagues.

The remarks mostly are flippant comments by a group of men relaxing, and all the more intriguing for that. Schuppanzigh, who had played first violin, is frequently referred to as Falstaff, on account of his girth. Holz, whose name means 'wood' in German, which Beethoven punned on frequently in notes and letters, is called 'the wooden friend'.

The Italian double-bass virtuoso, Domenico Dragonetti, who had so impressed Beethoven many years earlier, apparently refused to attend the first performance of the Ninth Symphony in London, and receives a sound pasting from Holz: 'Dragonetti demanded too much money for his participation, and said Beethoven had written the entire Symphony just for him.'

One can imagine Beethoven reading this and laughing out loud at Dragonetti's presumption. The great Italian composer Cherubini – a very tall man, it seems – 'has so much regard for a certain <u>Beethoven</u>, that if one mentions his name, Cherubini grows even taller out of respect –' Beethoven is certain to have chuckled again.

The music publisher Tobias Haslinger (who was not present) is teased for having a name similar to the title of Handel's oratorio *Il Ritorno di Tobia*. Schlesinger says, 'I told Tobias today, Beethoven will immortalise you and the Paternostergässl [the street where the publishing house was located].'

Beethoven at this point reached forward for a pencil, and scribbled, 'Tobias confided in me today that you are also giving the Quartet to [the publisher] Steiner.'

It is not long before the men's writing becomes a little slapdash, and their words no doubt slurred, as the wine takes hold, and no surprise that a group of men becoming drunk start to talk in ribald terms about women.

> SCHUPPANZIGH: *I asked Czerny whether he had never fallen into a hole without hurting himself.*
> HOLZ: *Also comical, like Falstaff.*
> SCHUPPANZIGH: *A slovenly fellow. A whoremonger … He is saying that Mozart drooled over [Barbara] Auernhammer's bosom, because she was the most delightful sweetie he could find.*

Beethoven's reaction is not recorded. I can see much male laughter and joshing, the language becoming even cruder, for that reason not written down, and the great composer joining in the laughter as he drank more wine.

If that is how it was, it was a fleeting moment of joviality for Beethoven. He had a major domestic problem, one of his own making. Before leaving for Baden back in May, Beethoven had given notice on his Vienna flat, and done nothing about finding new lodgings. He left his brother Johann to clear his things out. He received the newspaper in Baden, and despite being fully occupied with the string quartets, found time to scour the columns for a vacant apartment. Whenever he found one, he summoned the hapless Karl down to Baden, gave him the details – or sent the details to him in Vienna – and told him to go and look, and let him know if it was suitable.

He found an apartment in the Ungargasse, told Karl to tip the caretaker to hold it for him, but it seems it came to nothing. He dispatched Karl to look at other apartments. There was evidently one that took Beethoven's fancy, over which Karl had evidently failed to act, because Beethoven sent him a note saying, 'The apartment was in the newspaper again on Tuesday. Was there really nothing you could have done, not even through someone else?'

To describe Beethoven's lifestyle as peripatetic is something of an understatement. In thirty-five years in Vienna he moved over thirty times, rarely staying at one address for more than a few months. If you include his lengthy summer stays away from Vienna, he had well over seventy addresses in all.

There were, certainly, instances of him being expelled from a lodging because of complaints from other residents about his habit of working through the night, pounding on the piano keys to try to hear his music, banging on the apartment walls. He had to leave one apartment after getting in a stonemason to knock a hole in a wall and install a window to give him a decent view, without permission from his landlord. Other residents demanded to know why they couldn't do the same. More often, though, he simply became restless and wanted a change of environment.

So when he vacated his apartment in May, nobody was surprised. Karl, though, clearly resented the constant summonses to Baden, and being given the onerous task of finding new lodgings for his uncle.

An apartment was found, possibly the one referred to by Beethoven in his petulant note to Karl. It was a four-room apartment with servants' quarters on the second floor of a large building that was once home to an order of Benedictine monks from Spain. It stood outside the Bastei and the largest room had two windows looking out across the green Glacis towards the city wall.

The apartment had one unexpected bonus. It was directly opposite another apartment block, the 'Rothes Haus' ('Red House'), where his old friend Stephan von Breuning lived, and where, many years before, Beethoven had briefly lived with him, an arrangement that had ended with the heated argument that had led to their estrangement.

Stephan lived there now with his wife and two children, and one day in August 1825, when Beethoven was in Vienna for the performance of his string quartet Op. 132, purely by chance – in an incident reminiscent of his reconciliation with his brother Carl some time before – Beethoven was walking along a street just outside the Bastei, head down, and probably quite literally bumped into Stephan and his young son Gerhard.

Gerhard, whose memoirs[*] written many years later provide a unique and intimate insight into Beethoven's last years, recounts that a joyful reunion took place, and good relations were once

---

[*] *Aus dem Schwarzspanierhaus (From the House of the Black-Robed Spaniard).*

more finally restored between the two men whose friendship dated back to their childhood years.

Beethoven moved into the apartment in the Schwarzspani-erhaus ('House of the Black-Robed Spaniard') in mid-October 1825. No one could have foreseen it, but it was to be his final home, and the place of his death.

His actual demise might not have been foreseeable, but there was no disguising his worsening, even pitiful, condition. His behaviour, too, although always eccentric, was now seriously worrying.

Karl resisted being seen out in the street with his uncle, who would wave his arms wildly while talking unnecessarily loudly, who couldn't hear what was said to him and insisted on being shouted at, whose clothes were inappropriate to the season – heavy coat in summer, lightly dressed in winter – and in need of repair. Street urchins would follow, and taunt him.

Stephan's wife related that Beethoven's animated gestures, his loud voice, his ringing laugh, and his indifference to whoever might be near by, made her ashamed to be seen out with him because people would take him for a madman.

Beethoven clearly took a liking to Constanze von Breuning, because he frequently invited her in for a coffee. She always politely declined, because – according to her son – she found his domestic habits rather unappealing. He had a habit of spitting; his clothes were dirty, and his behaviour extravagant. He was aware he was not overly attractive to the opposite sex, because he told her he longed for domestic happiness and greatly regretted that he had never found a wife.

Constanze had reason, even, to take exception to Beethoven's inappropriate behaviour. On one occasion she left the Rothes Haus for the rather long walk to take the waters at the Kaiserbad on the Danube. Beethoven – who might well have been watching through the windows on the back of his apartment – joined her, and insisted on accompanying her for the whole way.

She spent about an hour in the bathhouse, and was rather surprised to find Beethoven waiting for her outside to accompany her home. This would have been difficult for her, given Beethoven's eccentric and extravagant behaviour, if he had been an unknown individual, but it is true to say that he was the most famous man in Vienna. Important personages, musicians, admirers came from all over Europe in the hope of meeting him. One even came especially from Quebec. Beethoven was world famous. It is likely Constanze's walk to the baths and home again was constantly interrupted, to her embarrassment.

If his behaviour was becoming increasingly bizarre, his physical condition now shocked those who knew him. He was clearly unwell. His stomach was distended and his ankles swollen. He was, in late 1825, approaching his fifty-fifth birthday. Friends remarked that he suddenly looked much older and his complexion had become permanently sallow. We can assume that his old foes – indigestion, colic, irregular bowels – were causing him increasingly acute problems.

Though the disease was not understood at the time, and with the caveat that post-diagnosis, particularly at an interval of two centuries, is dangerous, it is probably true to say that Beethoven was suffering from terminal cirrhosis of the liver.

The person closest to him, who might be expected to care for him and tend to his needs, was his nephew, his 'son', Karl. But Beethoven had by now thoroughly alienated the young man, aged nineteen by the end of 1825.

It was nearly a decade since Karl had lost his father and the nightmare of the prolonged court case had begun. Ever since, he had witnessed the conflict between his uncle and his mother. He had been a pawn in their custody struggle. He had suffered physically with a hernia, and there were even reports of violence in the aftermath of his operation. Wearing a truss and in considerable pain, he had been forced by Beethoven to take a strenuous walk with him in the Helenenthal outside Baden.

Exhausted, bleeding from his wound, he had taken to his bed, where Beethoven had continued to berate him. He snapped, lashed out, cutting Beethoven's face.

When he had run away to his mother, Beethoven had called the police to have him returned. He was suffering frostbite at the time. In living with his uncle, in his early teens, he had had to survive in the domestic chaos that was Beethoven's life. One can only imagine what mealtimes were like, or when they were. Beethoven might have employed a cook, but none lasted long.

It was as if Beethoven refused to allow Karl to make a single decision for himself, not least over the matter of wanting to join the army. Karl had no desire to enrol in the university, no wish to go to business school, no ambition to learn music. He wanted to be a soldier. But Beethoven was not having it.

There was no let up. Summoned to Baden time and again, his life interfered with and his schedule disrupted, ordered to find lodgings; he was being used more and more by Beethoven to run his domestic affairs. His professional affairs too. Possibly as a further inducement to Karl to follow a musical career, or more likely simply because he was mistrustful of anyone outside immediate family, Beethoven asked Karl to write to publishers, copy musical parts, buy him essential equipment such as manuscript paper, quill pens and pencils.

If Karl had been ten years older, and his life free of tension, he might have relished living in the same apartment as the world's greatest composer, assisting him in practical matters. Instead he was turning into a bitter, pathetic, resentful young man. It is not an exaggeration to say Beethoven was destroying the person he loved most in the world.

We know now, at a distance of two hundred years, that Beethoven at this time was composing his greatest works, that this was no ordinary composer, this was one of the greatest creative geniuses who ever lived. It can be argued that allowances could be made for his behaviour.

But Karl did not see it that way. And things were about to get a great deal worse.

Beethoven wanted to know *exactly* what Karl was up to. He knew Karl was clandestinely seeing his mother, and he probably realised he was powerless to stop it. But what else was Karl spending his time doing? Beethoven had a weapon: he held the purse strings. He frequently gave Karl money – in fact he had gone out of his way to ensure legally that his estate in its entirety would go solely to Karl after his death. He wanted the boy to live comfortably, but to live according to *his*, Beethoven's, precepts.

So he took action. He asked his young friend, the violinist Karl Holz, who was only seven years older than Karl, to spy on him, and report back. Holz, it seems, not only saw nothing wrong in this, but pursued his instructions with some relish. We can, in this instance, be grateful for Beethoven's deafness, which necessitated the use of conversation books, for giving us a glimpse into these surreptitious activities.

Holz reported back to Beethoven:

I have lured [Karl] into going to a beer house with me,

because I [wanted] to see if he drinks too much, but that does
not appear to be the case. Now I will invite [him] at some
point to play billiards, then I will be able to see immediately
from how good he is whether he has been practising a lot –

Holz, being that little bit older, took it upon himself to offer Karl
a little moral advice:

I told him also that he is not supposed to go too often into the
Josephstadt [suburb]* –
   His reason is that he goes because it doesn't cost him any-
thing.
   I also told him that his uncle would be more inclined
to give him money if [he] went to some concerts in the
Burg[theater] a few times each month and listened to some
classic pieces –
   I told him also that I would speak with you about this.
He didn't want that.

That last entry is particularly revelatory. If Karl had had any doubt
that Holz had been put up to these social activities – drinking,
playing billiards – by his uncle, he did not doubt it any longer.
Holz had admitted it. *He didn't want that.* The fact that Karl does
not want Beethoven to know whatever it was that Holz was referring to, shows the strain, and guilt Karl was living under.

He had been a pre-teen when all this had started. He was
about to become an adult, and there had been no let up.

Karl had had enough. He made a fateful decision.

---

* A red light district of Vienna.

Chapter 17

Two Pistols and Gunpowder

An invitation to get away from it all

Problems were once again mounting for Beethoven – over and above any issues with Karl. His health was deteriorating. It is truer to say that ill-health was constant, with occasional improvements, than that he kept falling ill. It was, as before, his usual complaints of indigestion and irregular bowels – severe diarrhoea would be followed by acute constipation. There was also a recurrence of the eye problems that had first surfaced nearly three years earlier, causing him to sit in a darkened room by day and put a bandage over his eyes at night. This time an eye lotion was prescribed. He complained, too, of back pain. There was also the swelling of his stomach and ankles, which was now very apparent and showed no signs of abating.

Dr Braunhofer once more came onto the scene, and made his familiar recommendations of no coffee or wine, advised Beethoven to eat as much soup as he could, and prescribed small doses of quinine. Beethoven's health was poor enough for his friends to insist he stay indoors, follow the doctor's advice, and try to take things a little more easily.

Utterly extraordinary as it is to report (I know, I am repeating myself, but this is Beethoven), his appalling health did not stunt his creativity. That – again – is the smallest understatement. As his health plummeted, he began work on a new string quartet, which was to become Op. 131, and which musicologists today rate as the greatest of them all. He was to continue work on this quartet throughout the turbulent months that were to follow.

Propitiously, in March his health did seem to improve slightly, at just the time his String Quartet in B flat, Op. 130, was being rehearsed for its first performance. Schuppanzigh was back in favour, and led the quartet in the inaugural performance on 21 March 1826.

It was a qualified success, but very qualified. The second and fourth movements were liked enough to be repeated, but the final movement left the audience in a state of shock. This is the piece known today as the *Grosse Fuge* (*Great Fugue*). It is a massive fugue of 741 bars, which can take anything up to twenty minutes in performance, and leaves players and listeners drained.*

After the first performance, opinion was divided. There were those that said the movement was simply too long, too mighty, for what had gone before. They said the piece was substantial enough to be published separately, as a work in itself. Others – mostly Beethoven's friends – leapt to its defence, arguing it had been misunderstood and would be accepted after more hearings.

The publisher Matthias Artaria bravely approached Beethoven, and suggested he publish the *Grosse Fuge* separately, in a

---

* I once heard a performance of the *Grosse Fuge* by the Lindsay Quartet at the Wigmore Hall in London. At the end the leader Peter Cropper, his shirt soaked with sweat, stood, and had to steady himself on the chair. His face was grey and he was close to collapse.

version for piano four hands, and that Beethoven compose a new final movement for the quartet.

Beethoven, predictably, would have none of it, and then, unpredictably, agreed. He even made the arrangement himself. For that reason – that Beethoven himself agreed to hive it away from Op. 130 – the *Grosse Fuge* is most often performed today as a separate work, and the string quartet performed with the new final movement that Beethoven was to write later in the year.

What neither he, nor anybody else, could have foreseen, was that the new final movement was to be the last complete piece of music Beethoven was ever to compose. He wrote it fairly quickly in October and November of 1826, and it is uncharacteristically light, even to a degree optimistic.

This is all the more remarkable, given that Beethoven had just lived through what were undoubtedly the tensest, most traumatic, most numbingly dreadful four months of his life.

In the spring of 1826 matters with Karl came to a head. Karl asked his uncle for more money. Beethoven went round to his lodgings on a Sunday and confronted him. It appears there was a third, unidentified, person in the room. Beethoven demanded to see the receipt of payment to Karl's landlord Matthias Schlemmer for the previous month's rent. Karl said he had already given it to his uncle. Beethoven denied it. Karl then searched his room but could not find it. He wrote in Beethoven's conversation book that it would surely show up, and if it didn't Schlemmer could give him another one.

Beethoven evidently then demanded to know from Karl how he spent his money, because Karl wrote, 'I go out walking and have a drink and that sort of thing. I don't have any other expenses.'

There are no further entries in the conversation book, but we know that an angry scene ensued, because a few days later Beethoven again went round to Karl's lodgings, and Karl wrote:

You accuse me of insolence if, after you've shouted at me for hours when I haven't deserved it, I can't just switch off the bitterness and pain you have caused me and become jovial. I am not the wastrel you accuse me of being. I can assure you that since that embarrassing scene in front of another person on Sunday, I have been so upset that everyone in the house has noticed it. I now know for certain that I gave you the receipt for the 80 florins I paid in May. I told you that on Sunday. I have searched my room and it is not there, so it has got to turn up.

Karl then told his uncle to leave him alone, because he had an inordinate amount of work to do for the upcoming exams. Beethoven accused him of appearing to have work to do only when he came to see him, and of being idle and dissolute for the rest of the time.

Karl denied it, and then in turn accused Beethoven of believing tittle-tattle and gossip from other people. It is not written down, but Karl then seems to have made some kind of dire threat.

Tempers were flaring on both sides. Karl suddenly exploded and grabbed his uncle by the chest. At that moment Holz came in, and separated them. We know this from an entry by Holz in the conversation book: 'I came in just as he took you by the chest.'

Beethoven was deeply upset, and spent a sleepless night. But by the next day he felt remorse and forgiveness. He wrote to Karl:

If for no other reason than I now know you obeyed me, all is forgiven and forgotten. I will tell you more when I see you. I have calmed down now. Do not think I have any other thought on my mind but your well-being. That is how you must judge my actions. Do not take any course of action which would cause <u>you</u> misery and put an early end to <u>my</u> life. I did not get to sleep until about 3 o'clock, for I was coughing the whole night. I embrace you with all my heart and I am convinced that soon you will no longer <u>misjudge</u> me. I understand why you did what you did yesterday. Come round to see me at 1 o'clock today without fail. Do not cause me any more sorrow and anxiety. For the moment, farewell!

Your loving and true Father

The reconciliation did not last long, mainly due to the efforts of a mediocre musician who had attached himself to Beethoven by the name of Anton Schindler.* This man, undoubtedly the most sycophantic of all Beethoven's admirers – Beethoven himself wrote, 'I have long found this importunate hanger-on Schindler most repulsive', and after Beethoven's death the German poet Heinrich Heine described Schindler as 'a black beanpole with horrible

---

* Schindler made himself indispensable to Beethoven in the final period of the composer's life. After Beethoven's death, Schindler regarded himself as 'keeper of the flame'. He was Beethoven's earliest major biographer, but deliberately falsified facts to enhance Beethoven's image. He forged conversation-book entries to give the impression he had known Beethoven for much longer than he in reality had, and modern scholarship has established that around a hundred and fifty of his entries in the conversation books were made after Beethoven's death.

white tie and funereal expression who presents himself everywhere as *l'ami de Beethoven* and bores everyone to death with his fatuous chatter' – formed a dangerous aversion to Karl, for the sole reason that the youth was causing the great composer problems.

Schindler wrote in a conversation book of seeing Karl gambling with coachmen in coffee-houses, and of gambling with drinkers and cheating them out of money. He also wrote that Karl had said to his teachers, 'My uncle! I can do what I want with him. A little flattery and a few friendly gestures, and everything will be fine.' Holz didn't help, writing that Karl had said he could wrap his uncle round his finger.

Beethoven did not stop to ask how his confidants could have known these details. Instead it all fed his paranoia, and he took to going to the Polytechnic Institute at lunchtime to wait for his nephew and escort him home arm in arm.

Karl's behaviour, coupled with the build-up of threats, gossip, hints, and innuendo, led Beethoven to believe something dreadful was about to happen. If those close to him dismissed this as over-dramatic, he paid no attention. Why else would he personally turn up at the Institute to escort Karl home? No, some sixth sense told him to prepare for the worst.

He did not have long to wait. In the last days of July, when Karl should have been sitting exams at the Institute, he disappeared – but not before telling both Karl Holz and his landlord Schlemmer that he intended killing himself. He might have hinted that he was in possession of a pistol and gunpowder, hidden in his trunk, because after Holz reported the threat to Beethoven, Beethoven wrote in a conversation book, 'Trunk Karl'. The two words are written in a large scrawl, one underneath the other, on the top right-hand side of the page, the page then folded lengthways down the middle, as if as a sort of aide-memoire.

On Saturday, 5 August, Schlemmer went to see Beethoven and wrote in a conversation book:

> *I learned today that your nephew intended to shoot himself by next Sunday at the latest. All I could learn from him was that it was to do with debts he had accumulated from past misdeeds, though I cannot be certain of this as he would not tell me everything. I had a good search of his room, and found in his trunk a loaded pistol with bullets and gunpowder. I am telling you this so that you can take appropriate action as his father. I have the pistol safely locked away.*

If Beethoven had any suspicion that this was merely a melodramatic threat, since Karl had given enough hints to allow his plot to be foiled, he was swiftly disabused.

On the same day, Karl pawned his watch, and with the money bought two new pistols, bullets and gunpowder. He then took the coach south to Baden, one of his uncle's favourite locations, where Beethoven had spent many a summer, and Karl with him.

Karl checked into a boarding house for the night. The following morning he took one of his uncle's favourite walks, west out of the town towards Helenenthal. There he climbed a thickly wooded hill, on top of which stood the ruins of a medieval monastery, the Rauhenstein.

The derelict towers of the monastery today stretch up into the sky like broken fingers, as they did nearly two hundred years ago. Karl climbed into one of them, loaded the bullet into the first pistol, put it to his temple, and fired. The bullet missed. He loaded the second pistol, put it to his temple, and fired. The bullet tore across the skin, burning it and ripping it open, but failed to penetrate the skull.

Karl fell wounded to the ground, where he was later found by a hill walker. In pain but conscious, he asked to be taken ... to his mother.

Beethoven's world fell in. Not only had his nephew, his 'son', tried to kill himself, but he had then asked to be taken to his mother. Everything that Beethoven had fought for in that long exhausting court case – all the arguments, the successes, setbacks, and ultimate victory – had come to nothing. The wretched boy had cast it all aside, and in his moment of utmost desolation he had opted to be reunited with that immoral woman, his mother.

As soon as he heard what had happened, Beethoven went straight to Johanna's house. One can only imagine the frostiness between them, the tension in the air, as the two of them – mother and uncle – approached the bed on which lay the wounded Karl. Beethoven did not spare the boy. He berated him for what he had done. Karl wrote in a conversation book, 'Do not plague me with reproaches and lamentation. It's done. Later we can sort everything out.'

Beethoven asked, 'When did it happen?' It was Johanna – we can surmise cautioning her son not to strain himself by trying to write or speak – who wrote in the conversation book:

He has just come. The person who found him carried him down from a rock in Baden – I beg of you not to let the

doctor make a report, or they will take him away from here
at once, and we fear the worst.

Well might Johanna have been concerned. Attempted suicide was a crime. A doctor would be obliged to report it to the police, who would then take appropriate action. Beethoven was probably horrified to learn Johanna had already sent Karl Holz to get a doctor – she said she had no choice, since it seemed apparent from looking at Karl's wound that a bullet was lodged in his skull. There was no doubt some relief when Holz reported that the doctor was not at home.

Beethoven scribbled a quick note to Dr Carl von Smetana, who had operated on Karl's hernia some years before, and who he believed could be relied on to be discreet.

> *Most honoured Herr von Smetana,*
> *A great misfortune has happened, which Karl accidentally inflicted upon himself. I hope that he can still be saved, especially by you if you come quickly. Karl has a <u>bullet</u> in his head. How, you shall learn – But be quick, for God's sake, be quick.*
> *Yours respectfully,*
> *Beethoven*

Beethoven gave the letter to Holz and told him to be quick, but he returned with the news that another doctor had already been called in – it is not clear by whom – by the name of Dögl. Holz carried a message from Smetana that Dögl was a capable doctor, and that he would not intervene unless Dögl wished to consult him professionally.

Karl for once took the initiative, and declared himself satisfied with Dögl, and announced that was the end of the matter.

Beethoven left, distraught in the belief that his nephew had a bullet lodged in his skull, and was hovering between life and death.

As soon as his uncle had left, Karl's frustration poured out: 'If only I never had to see him again! If only he would stop blaming me for everything!' He even threatened to tear the blood-soaked bandage off if another word was spoken to him about his uncle.

Again we know this from Holz, who stayed to explain the situation to Johanna and her son. He said it would be impossible to hide what had happened from the authorities. The police would have to be told, and it was better it came from him, rather than somebody else.

Holz duly went to the police and explained what had happened. He returned with the depressing, but expected, news that Karl would be severely reprimanded, that he would have to be taken to hospital for treatment, and while there be subject to religious instruction from a priest into the wrong of what he had done. Only when the authorities were satisfied that he had been morally corrected, and he was able to pass a 'complete examination in religious instruction', would he be released from surveillance – if, that is, he survived.

The following day, Monday, 7 August, the case was reported to the criminal court and placed under the jurisdiction of a magistrate. It was up to the magistrate to appoint a priest to carry out the religious instruction. The same day, Karl was removed from his mother's home and admitted to hospital.

Beethoven was crushed. It would be charitable to say that his concern was entirely for Karl, but that appears not to be the case. He was aware the incident left him publicly humiliated. Crossing the Glacis to his apartment, he bumped into Stephan von Breuning's wife Constanze, who described him to her husband as 'completely unnerved'.

'Do you know what has happened to me?' he said to her. 'My nephew Karl shot himself!'

'Is he dead?' she asked.

'No, he only grazed himself, he is still alive. There is hope that he can be saved. But the disgrace this has caused me – and I loved him so much.'

Vienna was awash with the story. Within hours it seemed the entire city knew. In cafés, restaurants, in the back of fiacres, on street corners, there was only one topic of conversation. *Have you heard what happened to the Great Deaf One? His nephew, his son, tried to kill himself! What will this do to him? This'll tip him over the edge ...*

It is not difficult to imagine the effect of this trauma on Beethoven, himself in failing health and not far from mental collapse. Even Schindler, rarely known to utter any words about his master not in the form of a hagiography, wrote later that the strain of it all 'bowed the proud figure of the composer', and that he soon looked like a man of seventy.

Gerhard von Breuning, in his memoir, wrote, 'The news was shattering to Beethoven. The pain he felt at this event was indescribable. He was crushed, like a father who has lost his beloved son.'

Again, though, Beethoven seems as much concerned about himself as he does his unfortunate nephew, and is far from forgiving over what has happened. An eyewitness account graphically illustrates this. Breuning recounts how a certain Ignaz Seng, assistant in the surgical division at Vienna General Hospital, was doing his rounds in the late summer of 1826. A man in a grey coat who had the appearance of a 'simple peasant' came up to him. The man asked in a dull tone, 'Are you Assistant Dr Seng? The office referred me to you. Is my scoundrel of a nephew in your ward?'

Dr Seng asked the name of the patient, and on being told it was

Karl van Beethoven, he replied that yes, he was in a hospital ward, and he asked the man if he wanted to see him. Beethoven, realising that the doctor did not recognise him, said, 'I am Beethoven.'

As Dr Seng led Beethoven upstairs, he was harangued by Beethoven, who said, 'The truth is, I do not want to see him. He does not deserve it. He has caused me too much trouble.' Seng relates how Beethoven continued talking about the dreadful thing his nephew had done, how he had spoiled him by being too kind to him, and so on.

Dr Seng concludes his account – given verbally to Breuning – by saying the aspect that surprised him most about the whole encounter was the realisation that the plain individual he took to be a simple peasant was none other than 'the great Beethoven'. He promised the renowned composer that he would take the best possible care of the young man.

Karl spent a little over six weeks in hospital, and was discharged when his wound was considered to have healed sufficiently. In accordance with the law for would-be suicides, he was handed over to the police. In the afternoon, around three o'clock, a clergyman came to see him, examined him for evidence of improved morals and religious obedience, and wrote out an affidavit on his behalf.

That evening Karl's mother went to see him, and gave him a little money so he could send out for food. Johanna told Beethoven that Karl had to spend the night 'among common criminals and the scum of humanity ... without a bed'. Karl himself later told his uncle he was in total darkness during the evening, and couldn't sleep because of rats running around his cell. The following day a meal of meat was brought to him, but he was made to eat it without knife or fork, 'like an animal'.

It is possible there was a touch of exaggeration from both Karl and his mother, with the intention of making Beethoven feel guilty about his nephew's plight, because there now began something of a concerted campaign to persuade Beethoven to allow Karl to join the army. Stephan von Breuning wrote in a conversation book, 'A military life will be the best discipline for one who finds it hard to lead a purposeful life on his own. It will also teach him how to live on very little.'

Breuning also reminded Beethoven that through his position at the War Ministry he was on cordial terms with Field Marshal Joseph von Stutterheim, commander of the Eighth Moravian Infantry Regiment, and was sure he could persuade the Field Marshal to give Karl a place in his regiment. Both Schindler and Holz added their weight to Breuning's argument.

Karl himself was keeping up the pressure on his uncle. Even while in hospital he wrote in a conversation book:

> *I still wish to pursue a military career, and if allowed to do so I would be very happy. I am convinced it is a way of life that would suit me and which would make me happy. So please do what you think best, and above all please see to it that I get away from here as soon as possible.*

This was a subtle approach by Karl, which he calculated would resonate with Beethoven, because there was the issue of where he should go when he was discharged. Beethoven was adamant that he should not spend even a single day with his mother, and he told Karl as much. To join the army and move away from Vienna would solve that problem at least, even if a military career ran totally counter to Beethoven's wishes.

But Karl, after his suicide attempt, was newly emboldened. Maybe it was the knowledge that other people – Breuning, Holz, Schindler – supported him. Maybe it was a compulsion not to allow his act of desperation to fade without any clear benefit to him. For the first time in his life, Karl was beginning to stand up to his overpowering uncle. He wrote in a conversation book in the hours after being taken to his mother, clearly moments after Beethoven had ranted against Johanna in her absence:

> *I do not want to hear anything that is derogatory to her. It is not for me to be her judge. If I were to spend even a little time here with her, it would only be small compensation for all that she has suffered on my account. You cannot say it will be harmful for me to be here, if for no other reason that I will only be here for a short time.*

And moments later:

> *Under no circumstances will I treat her with any more coldness than I have before, whatever words you may care to say on the subject.*

Karl also knew that he had his mother on his side regarding his desire to be a soldier.

> *[Given her support] all the less can I deny her wish to be with me, since I am not likely to see her again for some time. There is no reason why this shouldn't stop you and me from seeing each other as often as you wish.*

Beethoven was seriously outnumbered. Reluctantly, in effect abandoning his long-held ambition for Karl to become a musician, the 'Beethoven' of the next generation, he agreed to let Karl join the army.

Hard to believe, then, that while agonising over his nephew's future, he was able to turn his mind to loftier matters, namely the dedication of the Ninth Symphony to accompany its publication.

He had drawn up an astonishingly glittering list of possible dedicatees, with one much lowlier name, indicating possibly that he recognised the extraordinary worth of the work. Potential dedicatees were the King of Prussia, the King of France, Emperor Alexander of Russia ... and his old friend and helper Ferdinand Ries, currently residing in London.

In April 1823, a full year before the first performance, Beethoven had written to Ries promising him the dedication. A year later, according to an entry in a conversation book, Ries was still a candidate, although joined now by the other more illustrious names. It appears that Beethoven decided on the Russian Emperor, but Alexander inconveniently died in December 1825.

In the spring of 1826 Beethoven decided finally that the symphony should be dedicated to the King of Prussia. The presentation copy was ready by September, and Beethoven hand wrote the title page containing the dedication – at just the time he was wrestling with the humiliation over Karl's suicide attempt, visiting him in hospital, fraught with worry over his condition and what to do with him when he was released from hospital.

There was a cordial exchange of letters between Beethoven and the Prussian monarch, and with his gracious acceptance of the dedication King Friedrich Wilhelm III enclosed a diamond ring 'as a token of my sincere appreciation'.

The actual ring that Beethoven received turned out to be set with a stone of 'reddish' hue, according to Schindler, which the court jeweller valued at a measly 300 florins. Beethoven was insulted and angry, and wanted to send it straight back. He was dissuaded from doing so. It was never established whether the

King had second thoughts, or whether the ring was stolen and substituted either in Berlin or Vienna.

While Karl was in hospital, Beethoven's brother Johann had suggested that when Karl had recovered sufficiently, Beethoven should bring him to the spacious, comfortable, quiet country estate he, Johann, had bought in Gneixendorf. Far from being grateful, Beethoven was appalled at the idea of spending any time with the brother he despised, and the woman he had tried to stop his brother marrying. To Johann's invitation he replied, 'I will not come. Your brother??????!!!! Ludwig.'

In late September, just days after Karl left hospital, Johann repeated the invitation, and this time there was a compelling reason to accept. Karl had a large visible scar on his temple where the bullet had torn open his skin. Stephan von Breuning was adamant that Karl could not go for interview with Field Marshal von Stutterheim until the scar was no longer visible, since the Field Marshal had told him he wanted there to be no mention of the affair.

It was therefore decided that Beethoven would take Karl to Gneixendorf for a short visit. It would allow the scar to heal, give time for his hair to grow long enough to cover it, as well as provide peace and relaxation after the trauma of the preceding weeks. It would also provide Beethoven himself with a much needed escape from the city, and might even have a beneficial effect on his health.

In the event the visit would last for a little over two months. It was to be fraught from the beginning, and by the time Beethoven returned to Vienna his health had collapsed completely, and he was only months from death.

Chapter 18

Frightening the Oxen

'The greatest composer of the century,
and you treated him like a servant'

Johann van Beethoven had led something of a charmed life.
He had trained as a pharmacist and it had been his ambition
early in life to acquire his own pharmacy, but he lacked the funds
to make his dream a reality. In 1808, at the age of thirty-one, he
scraped together enough money to buy a pharmacy in Linz, a city
on the Danube around a hundred miles west of Vienna. With a
down payment that left him practically penniless and a mortgage
he could not afford, together with the expenses of the purchase
and travel, he was barely able to afford the first payment.

The business yielded practically nothing, and rent from
rooms in the house that he let out was small. Within months
Johann was in danger of defaulting. In desperation he sold the
iron gratings on the windows, but it was nowhere near enough
to keep him going.

In an extraordinary stroke of luck, events over which he had
no control played into his hands. The Continental blockade that
Napoleon Bonaparte had imposed on British goods in 1806
caused the value of British merchandise to rise astronomically.

It just so happened that all the jars and pots on the shelves of Johann's pharmacy were made of English tin. He sold them all, replaced them with earthenware, and was able to forestall his financial crisis.

Then just when things were beginning to look ominous for him once again, a second totally fortuitous chain of events came to his rescue. The French Emperor, exasperated at Austria's continuing attempts to defeat him on the battlefield, decided to put an end to this precocity once and for all, and invaded Austria. He marched north-east, with the capital Vienna in his sights. This time there was to be no triumphal procession into a subdued city. Vienna, and the Viennese, needed to be taught a lesson. Napoleon established a base at Linz, and it was there that the Revolutionary Army's quartermasters placed orders for the supply of medical equipment – medicines, bandages, splints, and so on.

Who won the contract? One Nikolaus Johann van Beethoven. It was the making of him. It brought him wealth beyond his dreams. It also sealed his unpopularity – hatred, even – with his fellow Austrians for collaborating with the enemy, a stigma that was to follow him for the rest of his life. He brushed that off, and began to live the life of a wealthy and successful businessman.

As wealthy men do he acquired a mistress, and in late 1812 he married her, as we have seen against his elder brother's violent protestations. He sold the pharmacy in December 1816, buying another on the opposite bank of the Danube. And of crucial importance to our story, in August 1819 he bought a country estate in Gneixendorf.

Gneixendorf is a village lying on high ground just north of the town of Krems – dominated then as now by a huge medieval monastery – which sits on the banks of the Danube roughly halfway between Vienna and Linz. It was there that Johann, with his wife and her illegitimate daughter, whom he had adopted, lived the life of a country squire, and to where he invited his brother and nephew in late September 1826.

Delighted, finally, at Ludwig's acceptance of his invitation, Johann sent a carriage and driver to Vienna, and at nine o'clock on the morning of Thursday, 28 September 1826, Ludwig and Karl left Vienna for the two-day journey to Gneixendorf.

There is no question that Johann was looking forward to the visit. He gave his brother a small self-contained apartment of three rooms on the first floor of the south-west side of the house – a sundial on the outside wall testifying to the sunny aspect – and a personal manservant to tend to his needs.

The rooms consisted of bedroom, salon, and dining room. The salon, between the other two, had a mural of the River Rhine painted on its walls. Johann, homesick for the river on the banks of which he and his brothers had grown up in Bonn, commissioned an artist from his home town to paint the mural to remind him of his youth.*

He was obviously keen to show off the trappings of success to his brother. He might not have been a musician, but through his business acumen he had acquired considerable wealth. He also no doubt wanted to demonstrate to his brother that any reservations

---

* Johann's house still exists, is privately owned, and the small self-contained apartment in which Beethoven stayed is perfectly preserved. All the furniture is either genuine, or of the period. The murals of the Rhine are as vibrant today as they were when Beethoven saw them. The stove in the bedroom, the current owner told me when I visited, is the actual stove Beethoven filled with wood.

he might have had about the marriage to Therese Obermeyer had been ill founded.

Seen from Ludwig's perspective, things were very different. In fact they could hardly have been worse. A figure, if not of fun, certainly of gossip and some derision in Vienna, his extraordinary musical accomplishments – this was little over two years since the premiere of the Ninth Symphony – were in danger of being subsumed by the drama over Karl. He had never got on with his brother Johann, and had contempt for Johann's wife, and so the prospect of a stay in their house must have filled him with foreboding. The attempted suicide of a close family member would put a strain on the most rational of people, but one can only imagine its effect on Beethoven's already precarious mental state. His physical condition was pitiful: his stomach was now so swollen that he wore a belt around it to restrain it, and his ankles and feet were swollen to such an extent that he was in constant pain.

Johann did not help matters by charging his brother a small rent. When it became clear that Beethoven and his nephew were intending to stay well beyond the original two weeks, Johann pointed out that this would incur costs, and it was reasonable to expect a small contribution. Beethoven reacted furiously, but must have had something of a change of heart at one point, because an entry by Johann in a conversation book suggests Beethoven was considering moving in permanently, with Johann actually encouraging him with descriptions of how beautiful Gneixendorf was in spring and summer.

The manservant, Michael Krenn, was interviewed – along with other residents of Gneixendorf – by Thayer nearly forty years later. These accounts, together with many entries in conversation books, make it possible to build a picture of the fraught two months that Beethoven and Karl spent at Johann's country estate.

It seems as if the first few weeks of the stay were actually beneficial to Beethoven. The countryside in late autumn appealed to him, and he took pleasure from long walks. The fresh air might have been responsible for a slight improvement in his eye condition. The daily regime was a relaxed one. Beethoven would get up at half-past five in the morning to work, then join the family for breakfast at seven o'clock, after which, notebook and pencil in pocket, he would take a long walk across the fields. Local people grew used to seeing the famous composer, oblivious to anything around him, striding purposefully, shouting out loud and waving his arms in the air. They described how suddenly, in full stride, he would slow down, then stop, take out his notebook and scribble something down. They knew better than to interrupt him.

Beethoven would return to the house for lunch at half-past twelve, then go to his room until around three o'clock. After that he would again take a long walk across the countryside, return for supper at half-past seven, go to his room to write till ten o'clock, then go to bed. There was a piano in his small salon, which he played – although only occasionally, according to Michael – but no one was allowed to go near him when he was in his rooms. There were certainly no recitals, or musical soirées. The atmosphere, at all times, was tense.

Michael, son of one of the vineyard workers, was clearly frightened out of his wits to be assigned to the famous, eccentric, unpredictable composer. If he was apprehensive about unwittingly upsetting his master, he had good cause to be. And yet, as he was to discover, Beethoven had an unexpected soft side too.

We do not know what age Michael was, but can assume he was in his mid-teens, because in the early part of the stay at least he reacted with youthful mirth to Beethoven's eccentricities.

At first the cook was assigned the task of making Beethoven's bed each morning and sweeping the floor of the bedroom. But one morning, while she was doing this with Michael also in the room, Beethoven sat at a table, gesticulating with his hands, beating time with his feet, muttering under his breath and singing out loud. She tried to ignore it, but finally could no longer contain herself and burst out laughing. Beethoven saw this, leapt up from the table, and drove her angrily out of the room.

Michael, equally struggling to restrain his laughter, tried to hurry out of the room too, but Beethoven held him back, gave him a few coins, and told him that, from now on, he should make the bed and clean the floor each day. Beethoven told him to come early to get it done. Michael found he had to knock a long time, and increasingly loudly – no doubt worrying about waking the household – before Beethoven finally opened the door.

It took the boy a long time to become accustomed to Beethoven sitting at the table, banging, beating, waving his arms and singing, and for some time at least he had to hurry from the room, undetected if possible, and burst into laughter out of sight and safely protected by Beethoven's deafness.

On one occasion he panicked when Beethoven returned from a walk and could not find his precious notebook. He set Michael the task of finding it. 'Michael, hurry up, look everywhere, hunt for my notebook. I must have it back, whatever it takes!' he quotes Beethoven as saying. One can imagine the boy's relief when he found it, though he does not tell us where.

Beethoven – surprisingly, given his unsuccessful record with house servants – seemed to develop a liking for Michael, no doubt enhanced by the realisation of the boy's usefulness. He soon banned everybody from entering his rooms, with the exception of Michael. He instructed the boy to clean and tidy his rooms while he was out walking. On several occasions Michael found coins on the floor. He would gather them up, and when Beethoven returned hand them to him. Beethoven made Michael show him where he had found them, and then told the boy to keep them. This happened three or four times, but then stopped.*

Beethoven demonstrated – for him – exceptional loyalty to Michael when the boy's carelessness landed him in serious trouble. Therese gave him five florins with instructions to go into the village and buy fish and wine. Michael lost (or spent) the money. He returned to the house sullen and quiet. Therese asked him for the fish, and he confessed. Furious, she sacked him on the spot.

At dinner Beethoven asked where Michael was. Therese told him what had happened. Beethoven flew into a rage with her, gave her the five florins, and demanded she reinstate Michael – which she did.

After that there was clearly a bond between the composer and his manservant. From that point on, Beethoven refused to sit at the table for any meals with the family. He told Michael to bring his meals up to his apartment, and to prepare breakfast for him in his room. While eating, he would ask Michael to bring him up to date on what had been said around the table. He even let it be known that if he could, he would take Michael back to Vienna with him.

Beethoven was clearly undergoing some sort of mental collapse. Inside the house, his eccentricities, his unpredictability, were to some extent manageable – in fact, his desire to closet himself in his rooms and bar entry to everyone except Michael

---

* It would be nice to date the *Rondo a capriccio*, Op. 129, 'The Rage over the Lost Penny', to around this time. Although it was found, incomplete, after Beethoven's death, the evidence suggests it dates from much earlier.

might even have been welcomed. But outside the house, his erratic behaviour could hardly go unnoticed.

Again, nearly forty years later, an elderly resident of Gneixendorf recounted how the first time he had seen Beethoven striding
across the fields, arms waving, singing and shouting, he had taken
him for a madman. Once he realised who he was, that he was in
fact the brother of the estate's owner, he always greeted him politely, but his salutation was never reciprocated.

The same man, a farmer, recalled vividly how, before he knew
who Beethoven was, he was driving a pair of young oxen from
an outhouse towards Johann's manor house, when Beethoven approached, 'shouting and waving his arms in wild gesticulations'.
He said he gestured to Beethoven to be a little quieter, but was
met with a blank look. The oxen took fright, charged down a
steep hill, hotly pursued by the farmer who with a Herculean effort managed to restrain them and get them back up the hill.

The drama was not over. Beethoven was still outside, striding
along, shouting and gesticulating. The farmer, angry now, asked
him again to be quiet. Again there was no response. The oxen
panicked again, and this time charged straight for the house.
Fortunately another man, employed on the farm, managed to
stop them. Between them the two men calmed the beasts, while
Beethoven strode off, oblivious to what had happened.

The farmer asked the other man if he knew who the fool was
who had scared his oxen. On being told he was the landowner's
brother, the farmer replied, 'Fine brother, that's all I can say.'

Two other reported incidents are evidence of Beethoven's
precarious mental state. One day Johann decided to pay a visit
to a friend of his, a doctor, who lived with his wife in a neigh-
bouring village. He took his brother with him. Unfortunately the
doctor was out on a house call, but his wife, flattered to have

Gneixendorf's chief landowner in the house, poured him a glass of her husband's best wine and gave him delicacies to eat.

They were chatting convivially when the wife suddenly noticed a morose individual, sitting silently in the darkness on a bench by the stove. Taking the man for Johann's servant, she reached for a jug of rough open wine, poured a glass, and said, 'He shall have a drink too.'

Later that night, when the doctor returned home and his wife recounted the visit, he asked her some pertinent questions, then exclaimed, 'For goodness' sake, woman, what have you done? Do you have any idea who that was? The greatest composer of the century was in our house today, and you treated him like a servant!'

The anecdote is perhaps just as illuminating for the way it highlights the obviously frosty relationship between the two brothers – wouldn't you at least expect Johann to introduce his brother? – as it does Beethoven's anti-social behaviour.

The two brothers were together again when a similar occurrence happened. Johann took his brother with him when he went to call on a local government official to discuss some business. The official had his clerk with him. Johann sat opposite them, but Beethoven refused to move from the door, and stood there during the whole of the meeting, which took some time.

The official clearly treated the morose and silent Beethoven with enormous – albeit unreciprocated – respect throughout, because after the two brothers had left, he turned to his clerk and asked, 'Do you know who that man was who stood by the door?'

The clerk replied, 'Judging by the respect you showed towards him, sir, I would imagine him to be someone important. Otherwise I'd have taken him for an imbecile.'

Both stories are illuminating for showing that for those who did not know who Beethoven was, the figure he portrayed was about as diametrically removed from the genius we know him to be as it is possible to imagine.

Beethoven might have been fraught, tense, in ill-health, in pain, yet the eyewitness accounts of him waving his arms, singing and shouting – whether in the open countryside or at the table in his room – suggest musical ideas were forming in his mind. They were, but paradoxically – no surprise there – they were slightly at odds with his mental and physical state.

Two months before the trip to Gneixendorf, almost as soon as he had finished composing the String Quartet in C sharp minor, Op. 131, Beethoven had begun work on a new string quartet, which was to become Op. 135. Now, in Gneixendorf, sitting at a table in his small salon, a piano to the side, and no doubt gazing at the murals of the River Rhine, which he had once known so well, he worked on it for the whole of September and the first half of October – in other words, for the first half of his stay in Gneixendorf.

As I have already noted, the early part of the stay was relatively benign. Beethoven enjoyed the pleasant autumn weather, the long walks and fresh air. But things soon declined. He was difficult and uncooperative towards his brother and sister-in-law, constantly fretting over Karl and his bizarre decision to join the military, upsetting staff at the house and local people, and all the time struggling to cope with the terminal decline in his health.

One would have every reason, therefore, to expect the String Quartet in F, Op. 135, to be among his most dense, even impenetrable, works. It is quite the opposite. It is on a smaller scale than its immediate predecessors, and seemingly light years away from

Op. 133, the *Grosse Fuge*. In places it is carefree, even witty. The third movement is relatively short, and there seems to be none of the 'angst' that characterises the earlier quartets, in particular the *Cavatina* of Op. 130.

Beethoven finished the new quartet by mid-October, and if his behaviour away from the composing table was erratic, when working at his music he was clear-minded and methodical enough to copy out all the parts himself, before dispatching Johann to Vienna with them to deliver to the publisher.

That task completed, Beethoven turned his attention to a new final movement for the String Quartet in B flat, Op. 130, to replace the *Grosse Fuge*. This coincided with a deterioration on many levels, and yet again – as with Op. 135 – he worked rapidly, and after a few false starts completed the movement in around a month. Again like its predecessor there is a lightness to it, it is on a relatively small scale, and there is a pervading mood of optimism. All this in stark contrast to its creator.

Once the work was finished, Beethoven dispatched it to the publisher. It was to be the last complete piece of music he would ever compose.

The weather in Gneixendorf became increasingly cold as autumn gave way to winter, and Beethoven became a more and more un-cooperative guest, frequently complaining about the food and the coldness and damp in his quarters. There was also a further deterioration in his relations with Karl.

We do not know exactly how the twenty-year-old Karl occupied himself during the stay in Gneixendorf. We can only assume he was somewhat bored. There was nothing for him to do in the country, and he probably yearned for the student life with his friends in Vienna. It appears he played four-hand pieces at the piano with his uncle, because Therese remarks on this and writes in a conversation book, 'Karl plays very well.'

But this belies the underlying, indeed overt, tension between nephew and uncle, 'son' and 'father'. Beethoven continued to try to control Karl's activities, as he had done in Vienna. Therese writes pointedly in a conversation book, 'Do not be concerned. He will certainly come home by 1 o'clock. It seems he has some of your rash blood. I have not found him angry. It is you that he loves, to the point of worship.'

Beethoven certainly used Karl. He sent him frequently to Krems for writing materials, a task Karl welcomed, taking advantage of it to go drinking and play billiards – no doubt incurring Therese's reassurance to Beethoven in the conversation book.

Karl made repeated entries in conversation books, not attempting to restrain his frustration, even anger, at Beethoven's controlling attitude to him, which had clearly not been mollified by the suicide attempt. On one day, undated, Karl wrote:

> *You ask me why I do not talk ... Because I have had enough ... Yours is the right to command, and I must endure it all ... I can only regret that I can give no answer to anything you have said today, since I know of nothing better I can do than to listen and remain silent as is my duty. You must not consider this insolent.*

And on another, clearly in despair at Beethoven's suspicions:

> *Have you ever seen me speak a word? Not very likely, because I wasn't of a mind to speak at all. So nothing you have to say*

about intrigues even requires a rebuttal. Please, I beg of you, just leave me alone. If you want to leave, that's fine. If not, that's fine too. I only ask you once again to stop tormenting me as you do. In the end you may regret it, for I can take so much, but then it gets too much. You did the same thing to your brother today, completely without reason. You have to realise that other people are human beings too.

Johann – a target as well, judging by Karl's words – was clearly growing weary of having his difficult brother as house guest. The original stay of two weeks seemed to be stretching out with no finite end. By late November Johann decided to do something about it. Again, clear evidence of the tension between the two brothers, so great that a rational discussion was out of the question, is demonstrated by the fact that Johann chose to write his brother a letter, despite the fact they were both living under the same roof.

He began by touching a nerve, pointing out that Karl had been in Gneixendorf for so long that he had given up doing anything constructive at all, and the longer he stayed the more difficult he would find it to get back to anything like a normal life. Tactfully he says both of them, as the boy's uncles, are to blame, but that it is Beethoven's duty to allow Karl to fulfil his dream of entering the army as soon as possible.

After a few discursive lines, he comes straight to the point: 'I think [your departure] ought to be <u>by next Monday</u>.'

Karl, concerned about the scar on his temple, was clearly brought into the conversation, and suggests a small delay in departure:

I cannot argue against it since we have been here longer than was planned. But <u>Breuning</u> himself has said that I cannot

> *go to the Field Marshal until I am able to appear without*
> *any visible sign left of what happened to me, because he does*
> *not want the whole affair to be mentioned. This is almost*
> *accomplished now except for a little bit which really won't*
> *take much more time. Therefore I believe that we should stay*
> *until next week at the least. If I had hair ointment here then*
> *it would be unnecessary. Besides, the longer we remain here,*
> *the longer we can all be together. Once we return to Vienna,*
> *I will have to leave right away.*

Schindler (generally unreliable, but probably credible on this occasion) says Johann's forthright request to his brother to leave, and leave soon, upset Beethoven considerably, which probably accounted for Karl's rather diplomatic suggestion that they stay a little bit longer.

In any case there was a problem over transport. Johann, it appeared, had only one covered carriage (presumably the one he had sent to Vienna to pick up Beethoven and Karl two months earlier). It had recently been used to take Therese to and from Vienna, and Johann was planning to make a trip very soon.

It is likely that the brothers agreed on a date some time after the 'next Monday' referred to by Johann, which was 27 November, and after Johann's return from Vienna, which would mean the carriage was available. But an unexpected and dramatic turn of events brought the departure right forward.

On the night of Friday, 1 December, the two brothers had a blistering row. The subject, perhaps rather surprisingly, was Karl's future inheritance. Beethoven demanded of his brother that he make a new Will, cutting out his wife and her illegitimate daughter, and leaving everything to Karl. Johann refused point blank, and the brothers argued long and vociferously into the night.

Suddenly, in the early hours of the morning, Beethoven snapped. He had had enough. He said he and Karl would leave that instant, and he ordered Johann to get the carriage and a driver to take them back to Vienna.

Johann immediately saw the folly of this. He tried to reason with his brother that it was the middle of the night, it was bitterly cold, Beethoven was in no fit state with his poor health to undertake the journey without properly preparing himself, and so on.

Beethoven's mind was made up. He was leaving with Karl and leaving now. It was Johann's turn to snap. Two months of frustration and suppressed anger boiled up in him, and he exacted revenge by denying his brother the covered carriage. All he had, he said, was a rickety old open-top cart – impossible to make the two-day journey in.*

If he thought that would bring Beethoven to his senses, he miscalculated. *'Get it!'* was Beethoven's riposte.

Some time around three or four in the morning of Friday, 1 December, in the middle of a raw, damp, frosty, and bitterly cold night, Beethoven, dressed in entirely inadequate clothing, climbed into the open-top cart with his nephew Karl for the long journey back to Vienna.

They stayed the following night in a tavern on the north bank of the Danube river. The building was old and dilapidated, and Beethoven was given a room with no stove to heat it, and no shutters for the windows.

Towards midnight he broke out in a fever, accompanied by violent shaking, and a dry hacking cough that split his sides with

---

* Beethoven later described it to his doctor as a milk wagon (*Milchwagen*). It might well have been, or Beethoven might have been being deliberately pejorative.

pain. He was violently thirsty. He was given a glass of frozen water, which eased his thirst but increased the shivering.

At first light he stumbled outside, weak, exhausted, and barely able to stand. Uncomplaining, he allowed himself to be lifted into the cart, and it set off for Vienna. One imagines the landlord was grateful to get his guest off the premises without having a death on his hands.

Some time in the afternoon of Saturday, 2 December, Beethoven and his nephew arrived in Vienna. Beethoven could barely climb the stairs to his second-floor apartment in the Schwarzspanierhaus. He was still shivering from fever, had no strength, coughed at the smallest exertion, could scarcely walk on his swollen feet and ankles, and was in pain from his vastly distended stomach.

That he was close to death was not in doubt. The priority was to get a doctor as quickly as possible to try to ease his suffering. Easier said than done.

Chapter 19

Terminally Ill

'His face was damp, he spat blood'

The apartment that Beethoven moved into in the Schwarz-spanierhaus almost a year before the trip to Gneixendorf was, by any standards, stylish, in modern parlance well appointed. Beethoven was notoriously uncaring about where he lived, and there is no evidence he appreciated how suitable this apartment was for his needs.

The building that housed it was impressive. Abutting a church, it looked across open ground, affording light and fresh air for the monks whose bedrooms were on the top floor. Once converted into apartments, it was one of Vienna's more desirable residences, outside the city wall and across the Glacis, away from the noise and dust of the inner city. Beethoven's apartment on the second floor took up much of the middle section of the building, five windows – two in the bedroom – ensuring good views, as well as daylight.[*]

---

[*] Despite protestations from around the world, the building was pulled down in early 1904, after a small ceremony held on 15 November 1903 in the rooms once occupied by Beethoven.

The apartment was reached by a wide marble staircase. Immediately to the left a low wide door opened onto a spacious entrance hall.* Beethoven used the hall as a dining room. The portrait of his grandfather, the *Kapellmeister*, which his father had pawned and which he asked Wegeler to forward to him in Vienna, hung on a wall of this room.

From the hall, with all doors open, it was possible to see through all three of the front rooms. The first was the music room, with piles of disordered manuscripts and published music, which Stephan von Breuning named the 'junk room'. The next, the largest room in the apartment, with two windows facing out to the Glacis, contained two pianos – one given to Beethoven by the Viennese piano builder Conrad Graf,† the other the Broadwood shipped from London‡ – standing curve to curve with keyboards pointing in opposite directions. In the far right corner stood Beethoven's bed, next to it a small table with a bell for summoning his housekeeper, and a folded conversation book for friends to write their questions. The third room was the composition room, containing Beethoven's desk. The desk was angled so that, while working at it with all connecting doors open, Beethoven could see if any visitor came into the flat.

One other benefit, the Schwarzspanierhaus was directly across the road from the Rothes Haus, where his old friend Stephan von

---

* The door has been preserved, and is today in the museum that occupies the apartment that Beethoven lived in longer than anywhere else, in the Pasqualatihaus on the Mölkerbastei.

† Currently in the Beethoven Haus in Bonn, its keyboard protected by a perspex cover. It was last used for a recording of the Piano Sonata in A flat, Op. 110, and the Bagatelles, Op. 126, by the Austrian pianist Jörg Demus in 1967 – 'the last time its voice was heard', as I was told when I visited.

‡ Now in the Hungarian National Museum in Budapest.

Breuning lived with his family. Under different circumstances, Beethoven could have looked forward to many years of relative comfort in this apartment, as he continued to compose.

The reality was different. Supporting his gravely ill uncle on that chill Saturday afternoon, Karl staggered through the music room, mindless of precious compositions being trampled underfoot, no doubt clumsily negotiating the pianos, until with relief he allowed Beethoven to collapse onto the bed. We can imagine him trying to arrange the pillows under Beethoven's head, swinging his legs onto the bed and removing his boots.

Being late on a Saturday in the depths of winter, Karl did not immediately send for medical help, and was no doubt gratified to find that the following morning Beethoven had regained some strength. He continued to improve – it is possible his housekeeper Rosalie, known as Sali, came to cook for him – and after a few days it was Beethoven himself who decided on action.

He told Karl he wanted to pen some letters, but lacking the strength he would dictate them for Karl to write. The first was a short one-paragraph letter to his young friend and helper Karl 'Wooden' Holz. He explained that he had been taken ill and had confined himself to bed, and he asked Holz to call on him.

At that point he motioned for Karl to pass him the pen and paper, and underneath the letter he scribbled a four-bar canon on the words: *'Wir irren allesamt, nur alle irren anderst.'* ('We all err, but each one errs differently.')

They were the last musical notes he was to write.

The next letter was altogether different, very long and personal, to his old friends Franz and Eleonore Wegeler. They had written to him almost a year before, Wegeler addressing him as 'My dear old Louis!'; Eleonore beginning her letter more formally with 'For so long a time dear Beethoven!'

It is strange that Beethoven should choose this moment, a year later, to respond – or maybe it is not so strange. Both Wegeler and his wife separately implored Beethoven to make a return trip to Bonn and the Rhineland. He does not refer to this in his reply, but his words suggest little sign of a realisation that time for him was short:

> *If I let my Muse sleep, it is so that she may reawaken with renewed strength. I hope still to bring some great works into the world and then as an old child end my earthly course amongst kindly people … The beginning has now been made and soon you will get another letter, and the more often you write to me, the more pleasure you will give me …*

Holz came quickly in response to the letter, and on Beethoven's instructions set about trying to find a doctor. It was now that Beethoven's cavalier attitude to his doctors over the years came back to haunt him.

The first doctor to be contacted was Dr Braunhofer, he of 'no coffee or alcohol'. He said he could not come, because he lived too far away and the journey at that time of year would be too arduous. It is more than likely that his past knowledge of Beethoven's health was enough to tell him that the illness was terminal, and he did not want to be in charge of the composer at his death.

The next doctor approached was Dr Staudenheim, summarily sacked by Beethoven some years before. He said he would come, but did not do so. A third doctor was himself sick and unable to attend.

Finally Holz suggested a certain Dr Andreas Wawruch, Director of the Medical Clinic in Vienna and Professor of Pathology at Vienna General Hospital. Holz told Beethoven Wawruch was regarded as one of the ablest physicians in Vienna, and was also a keen music-lover, an admirer of Beethoven's compositions, and a competent cellist.

Beethoven did not demur; Wawruch agreed to attend, and so on 5 December he came to the Schwarzspanierhaus to care for a man he had never examined before, who was clearly terminally ill, and who was the most renowned and revered musician in Europe. It is to his eternal credit that Wawruch, knowing there was only one possible outcome, cared for his patient with kindness and diligence to the end, and left us a remarkable account of the final illness and its treatment.

On first meeting Beethoven, Wawruch wrote in a conversation book, 'One who greatly reveres your name will do everything possible to give you speedy relief. Prof. Wawruch.' Examination, given Beethoven's deafness, was not easy, and so Wawruch dictated questions for Karl to write down.*

Wawruch wrote up a report of the first few days that he treated Beethoven, and it makes difficult reading:

> *I found Beethoven afflicted with serious symptoms of inflammation of the lungs. His face was damp, he spat blood, his breathing so irregular that it threatened suffocation, and a stitch in the side so painful that it made lying on the back a torment. A strong counter-treatment for inflammation soon brought the desired relief. His constitution triumphed, and*

---

* Several pages of the relevant conversation book are missing, presumably removed and destroyed by Schindler as too intrusive for public knowledge.

by a fortunate outcome he was freed from apparent mortal danger. On the fifth day he was able, in a sitting position, to tell me, amid profound emotion, of the discomforts which he had suffered. On the seventh day he felt considerably better, so that he was able to get out of bed, walk about, read and write.

Wawruch visited Beethoven every day from 5 to 14 December, one day coming twice, but on the eighth day there was a dramatic deterioration. Wawruch wrote it up fully, and it merits quoting. Buried in his text is the suggestion of a furious row between Beethoven and Karl. Conversation book entries point to Beethoven accusing Karl of vacillating over his decision to join the military, and Karl arguing vociferously to the contrary. If these exchanges are what caused the crisis, it is evidence of the deterioration in Beethoven's condition, and his inability any longer to cope with emotional crisis.

On the eighth day I was considerably alarmed. I visited him in the morning and found him in great distress and jaundiced all over his body. A dreadful attack of vomiting and diarrhoea had threatened his life in the preceding night. A violent rage, a great grief caused by sustained ingratitude and undeserved humiliation, was the cause of this mighty explosion. Trembling and shivering, he was bent double because of the pains which raged in his liver and intestines, and his feet, which had been moderately bloated, were now massively swollen. From this time on dropsy developed, the passing of urine became more difficult, the liver showed plain indication of hard nodules, and there was an increase in jaundice. Gentle persuasion from his friends calmed the mental

tempest, and the forgiving man forgot all the humiliation
which had been put upon him. But the disease moved on-
ward with gigantic strides. Already in the third week he
threatened to suffocate in the night. The enormous accumu-
lation of fluid in his abdomen demanded speedy relief, and
I found myself compelled to advise tapping in order to guard
against the danger of his stomach bursting.

Things were critical. Beethoven's abdomen had swollen so much that Wawruch actually feared it would explode, and the only possible solution was to puncture it and drain it manually, a risky and painful procedure.

In the meantime, as Wawruch suggests, Beethoven's spirits were being kept up by friends, in particular by a thirteen-year-old boy named Gerhard von Breuning, son of his old friend Stephan. Beethoven instantly took to the boy, nicknaming him 'Hosenknopf' ('Trouser Button').* Gerhard frequently brought Beethoven soup made by his mother, and visited the composer every day either before, or after, school.

Wawruch took a second opinion, consulting Dr Stauden-heim, who had failed to visit as promised earlier, but who now examined Beethoven and concurred with the decision to drain the abdomen.

Only then was Beethoven told. Wawruch reported that 'after a few moments of serious thought, he gave his consent'.

To perform the risky procedure Wawruch brought in Dr Johann Seibert, chief surgeon at Vienna General Hospital.

---

* The same Gerhard von Breuning who left an invaluable record of Beethoven's final years in his book *Aus dem Schwarzspanierhaus*, and would in adult life become a distinguished physician.

On Wednesday, 20 December, with Wawruch, nephew Karl and brother Johann in attendance, the procedure was performed. Dr Seibert pierced Beethoven's side with the tube, and immediately fluid gushed out. Relief was instantaneous, even bringing humour from the patient: 'Professor, you remind me of Moses striking the rock with his staff.'

There were clearly smiling faces all round at the obvious relief Beethoven experienced. Wawruch quickly scribbled a series of questions and advice in a conversation book: 'Do you feel better? ... Was it painful? ... If you feel unwell you must tell me ... [In English:] God save you ... Lukewarm almond milk ... Are you beginning to feel pain now? ... Keep lying quietly on your side ... We shall soon measure off the fluid ... Five and a half measures were removed ... I hope you will be able to sleep more peacefully tonight ... You behaved like a brave knight.'

Shortly after the procedure the wound in Beethoven's side became infected, but it does not seem to have caused him much of a problem, and in any case his mood was considerably lightened by the arrival from a London admirer of a forty-volume edition of the works of Handel, whom he immediately declared to be 'the greatest, ablest composer that ever lived. I can still learn from him.'

With Beethoven bedridden, Karl went about his business of joining the army. He underwent a medical examination, and in the days following Christmas kitted himself out with uniforms, an overcoat and sabre.

On 2 January 1827, Karl bade farewell to his uncle, and embarked on the two-day journey to join his regiment in Iglau.* There is no record of what was said between them, no conversation book entry. He never saw his uncle again.

---

* Today Jihlava in the Czech Republic.

The following day Beethoven wrote to his lawyer declaring that Karl, 'my beloved nephew', should be the sole heir to all his property, including 'seven bank shares and whatever cash may be available'.

The relief from the draining of fluid was temporary. Beethoven's abdomen began to fill again. Wawruch believed a second procedure was necessary, but Seibert was reluctant, possibly because of the infected wound and an unwillingness to create a second puncture.

Beethoven, in a predictable pattern, was losing confidence in Wawruch. According to young Gerhard, when Wawruch's name was mentioned, Beethoven turned his face to the wall and exclaimed, 'The man's an ass.' But all around him urged him not to give up on the physician. Schindler wrote in a conversation book, 'He understands his profession, everybody knows that, and he is right in considering your well-being paramount.'

Gerhard, meanwhile, was taking an early interest in the career he was to follow, writing in a conversation book, 'How are you? ... Has your belly become smaller? ... You are supposed to perspire more ... How was your enema?' It is likely the dying composer was more willing to discuss his condition with Trouser Button than with a doctor in whom he was losing faith.

On Monday, 8 January, Dr Seibert repeated the procedure. There were no complications; the surgeon managed to draw off more fluid than before, and was pleased to find that it was clearer than the first time.

Three days later a meeting of doctors took place, with an interesting and somewhat unexpected addition to their number. As well as Wawruch, Staudenheim and Braunhofer, who had also now agreed to attend, there was present a name from Beethoven's past, Dr Johann Malfatti, uncle of Beethoven's one-time *inamorata* Therese Malfatti, and summarily dismissed by him ten years previously.

Schindler claims credit for the reconciliation, even saying he had to use all his powers of persuasion on Dr Malfatti, whose initial reaction was to say that as Beethoven was a master of harmony, 'so must I also live in harmony with my colleagues'.

But he was persuaded, and it seems the doctors were perfectly happy to involve him, all the more so since Beethoven too seemed pleased to see him and patch things up.

He was even more pleased with Dr Malfatti's recommendation. In effect Malfatti made it clear to the other doctors that the one thing that would bring Beethoven relief was alcohol. He was dying, and there was nothing any of them could do to stop that. So why not at least allow him to alleviate the pain by drinking alcohol? Furthermore, since Beethoven was suffering attacks that caused his skin to burn and brought him out in running sweat, why not make the drinks ice cold?

He prescribed an end to the medicines Beethoven was taking – '75 bottles plus powder,' wrote Schindler later with, no doubt, more than a touch of exaggeration – no intake for Beethoven other than frozen alcoholic fruit punch, accompanied by rubbing of the abdomen with blocks of iced water. He assured his colleagues he had thus completely cured another patient with a similar illness.

The doctors, no doubt assisted by Beethoven's willingness, concurred. As with the first abdominal procedure, the effect was instantaneous. Even Wawruch was stunned. 'I must confess that the treatment produced excellent results for a few days at least,' he wrote.

> *Beethoven felt himself so refreshed by the ice with alcoholic contents, that already in the first night he slept quietly throughout the night and began to perspire freely. He grew cheerful and was full of witty comments, and even dreamed of being able to complete the oratorio 'Saul and David'* which he had begun.*

But, again as with the abdominal draining, the relief was temporary, only this time it was largely Beethoven's fault. He liked drinking the punch so much that he drank more and more of it. In fact he repeatedly drank himself into a stupor. This did wonders for his mental state, successfully taking his mind off his dreadful illness, but had the opposite effect on his body.

Wawruch reported that the spirits soon caused a violent pressure of blood on the brain. Beethoven became comatose; his breathing was noisy and laboured as it would be if he was drunk; he began to slur his speech and talk nonsense, and occasionally, Wawruch noted, inflammatory pains in the throat were accompanied by hoarseness and even an inability to speak. His behaviour became more uncontrollable, and when the effect of the ice-cold drink caused havoc with his bowels, bringing on colic and diarrhoea, it was time 'to deprive him of this precious refreshment'.

Malfatti had another idea, and it was possibly the most bizarre of all the remedies inflicted on the dying composer. He was made to take a 'sweat bath'. Jugs filled with hot water were placed

---

* While we may trust Wawruch on medical matters, he is not so reliable when it comes to music. Beethoven never worked on such an oratorio – but Handel did, and given Beethoven had the forty-volume set of Handel's works, it is likely Wawruch confused the two.

in a bath and covered thickly with birch leaves. Beethoven – removed from his bed with enormous difficulty – was made to sit on the heated bed of leaves, and his body covered with a sheet up to the neck. The aim, said Malfatti, was to soften the skin and allow perspiration to flow freely.

The effect was disastrous. Beethoven's body absorbed the moisture 'like a block of salt', wrote Gerhard later, causing swelling all round. It became clear a third procedure to drain fluid from the abdomen would be required, even though the wound in Beethoven's side had not healed from the last puncture.

Dr Seibert carried out a third draining on 2 February, and the bath treatment was abandoned.

There was now a steady stream of visitors – friends and musical colleagues – anxious to see the great composer before it was too late. His old friend and drinking partner, Nikolaus Zmeskall, bedridden with gout, sent him greetings in a note. Beethoven himself, as if acknowledging time was short, dictated a number of letters.

Pleading financial hardship, as well as ill-health, he wrote to Sir George Smart in London asking the Philharmonic Society of London to make good their offer of payment for a future concert. They responded with a gift of £100, knowing full well the promised concert would never happen.

On a lighter note, he wrote to the publisher Schott of Mainz asking them to send him 'some very good old Rhine wine', which was unobtainable in Vienna.

Schuppanzigh and Linke, who had performed the Late Quartets, came to see him. Moritz Lichnowsky, brother of his great patron, came. Gleichenstein brought his wife, sister of Therese

Malfatti, who was disappointed that Beethoven did not recognise her, and their son.

Diabelli, for whom Beethoven had written the great set of piano variations, brought him a print he had published of Haydn's birthplace in Rohrau. Beethoven showed it to Trouser Button Gerhard, and said, 'Look, I got this today. See what a little house it is, and in it such a great man was born.'

Baron Pasqualati, in whose building on the Mölkerbastei Beethoven had lodged longer than anywhere else, sent provisions, including champagne, wine – and stewed apples, pears and peaches, which the composer particularly liked.

Three men called to see him, and when they sent word in to ask which of them Beethoven would care to see first, the answer came straight back 'Let Schubert come first.'* Earlier, Beethoven had said of the Viennese composer, who was to die so young, just twenty months after Beethoven, 'That man has the divine spark.'

As soon as the third procedure was carried out on Beethoven's abdomen, the swelling began again. There was no hesitation this time. On 27 February Dr Seibert inserted the tube into Beethoven's side for a fourth time. It seems that now everybody had given up hope, the medical team included.

Gerhard wrote that as the fluid flowed from Beethoven's body, it was allowed to run onto the floor and halfway across the room. In the conversation books there is mention of saturated

---

* There is no corroborative evidence that this meeting took place. If it did, it would be the only meeting – as far as we know – between the two great composers.

bedclothes, and a suggestion by one of the doctors that an oilcloth be procured and spread on top of the mattress.

Beethoven, finally, accepted that the end was near, and went into a deep depression. Dr Wawruch wrote later, 'No words of mine could brace him up, and when I promised him that he would certainly get better when the warm weather of spring arrived, he simply answered with a smile, "My day's work is finished. If there were a physician who could help me, 'his name shall be called Wonderful!'"' The allusion to Handel's *Messiah* was not lost on Wawruch.

On 23 March Johann Nepomuk Hummel, once Beethoven's rival in improvisation contests, arrived from Weimar with his wife and a musical colleague, Ferdinand Heller. They found Beethoven, as Heller wrote later, lying 'weak and miserable, sighing deeply at intervals. Not a word fell from his lips. Sweat stood upon his forehead.'

Hummel's wife took out her fine white linen handkerchief and wiped Beethoven's face several times. Heller wrote, 'Never shall I forget the grateful glance with which his broken eye looked upon her.'

Beethoven had one final onerous task, to append a codicil and signature to his Will, leaving his entire estate to Karl, which for some reason had not been done earlier. It was a difficult and laborious task. He tried several times to write his name correctly, but each time misspelling his surname – once he left out an 'h', the next time an 'e'.

Finally, in despair, and declaring he would not repeat it again, he wrote, 'luwig van Beethoven'.

When it was over, he turned to the small group gathered, and said, 'Plaudite, amici, comedia finita est.' ('Applaud, my friends, the comedy is over.')

Beethoven received the last rites. The following day, 24 March, the wine shipment from Schott arrived. He said, 'Pity, pity, too late.'

They were his final words.

While he could still swallow, a taste of the wine was put on his lips, but in the evening of the 24th he sank into a coma.

Gerhard von Breuning later wrote a graphic and deeply moving account of Beethoven's final forty-eight hours:

> *His delirium intensified with every sign of the death agony. This was at five in the afternoon, March 24th, 1827 … On the next day and the day after that the powerful man lay there unconscious, breathing heavily with a clearly audible rattle in the throat. His powerful frame and undamaged lungs fought like giants against approaching death. It was a fearful sight. Although we knew that the poor man was suffering no more, it was appalling to see this noble being so irrevocably disappearing and beyond all further communication. On 25th March it was not expected that he would survive the night, but on the 26th we found him still alive – breathing, if that was possible, even more laboriously than before. March 26th, 1827, was the sad day of Beethoven's death.*

In the late afternoon of 26 March, a storm blew up over Vienna. Gerhard described it as very violent, with driving snow and hail – unusual for late March.

There was a small group by Beethoven's bedside, but there is confusion over who exactly was there. One of those present, composer and pianist Anselm Hüttenbrenner, said later that Beethoven's sister-in-law, Karl's mother Johanna, was present. This is extremely unlikely, since she herself complained later that she had received no news of Beethoven's final illness until it was all over. Most likely the sole female present was the housekeeper Sali.

Beethoven's brother Johann was certainly there, and it was probable that Stephan von Breuning and Schindler were also present, though they left some time in the afternoon to choose a burial site. The portrait painter Joseph Teltscher was making a drawing of Beethoven, though he left the room when Stephan remonstrated with him. Gerhard, Trouser Button, left at a quarter past five to attend a lesson.

At around a quarter to six, there was an enormous clap of thunder, which startled everyone present. Beethoven opened his eyes, lifted his right hand, and looked up for several seconds with fist clenched, as if he wanted to say, 'Inimical powers, I defy you! Away with you! God is with me! Courage, soldiers! Forward! Trust in me! Victory is assured!' We owe this legendary, but exaggerated, account of Beethoven's last moments to Hüttenbrenner. If there is truth in it, the clenching of the fist was probably a muscle spasm brought on by the disease that almost certainly killed Beethoven, cirrhosis of the liver. But the legends had begun, within moments of his death.

What is fact is that at 6 p.m. on 26 March 1827 – at the age of fifty-six years and three months, and exactly forty-nine years to the hour and the day since he had first walked out to perform in public – the greatest composer the world had known died.

Chapter 20

The Last Master

'He was an artist, but a man as well'

The day after Beethoven's death, with his body still on the deathbed, Stephan von Breuning, Johann van Beethoven, and Anton Schindler carried out a comprehensive search of the apartment to try to find the seven bank shares Beethoven had left in his Will to Karl. They could not be found. Johann was angry, and suggested either that they had never existed or that Stephan and Schindler had hidden them. Breuning was distressed at this insinuation, and left.

He returned later, and asked Karl Holz to come as well. He asked Holz if Beethoven had a secret hiding place where he kept valuable documents. Holz said yes, there was a secret drawer in the writing desk. He went to it, and pulled out a protruding nail. The secret drawer fell out. Inside it were the bank shares, the letter to the Immortal Beloved, and no doubt to everybody's surprise a miniature portrait of Josephine Brunsvik.*

---

* The Heiligenstadt Testament, which must have been secreted in the same drawer for many years, was found among Beethoven's papers.

Later that day a post-mortem was performed by the pathologist Dr Johann Wagner. He made an incision across the front of Beethoven's forehead, lifted the top of his skull, and sawed out the temporal bones and auditory nerves. These were placed in a sealed jar of preserving fluid, which was held in the coroner's office for many years, before disappearing.

On examination of the auditory nerves, Dr Wagner found them to be 'shrivelled and lacking nerve impulses, with the arteries dilated to the size of a crow quill and covered in cartilage'.

Dr Wagner found Beethoven's liver to be 'shrunk up to half its proper volume, of a leathery consistence and greenish-blue colour, beset with knots the size of a bean on its tuberculated surface as well as in its substance. All its vessels were very much narrowed and bloodless.' In the cavity of the abdomen he found four quarts of an opaque greyish-brown liquid. The stomach and bowels were greatly distended with air, and both kidneys contained a thick brown fluid. The body in general was 'much emaciated'.

With all the danger inherent in attempting to make a diagnosis two centuries after the event, a modern reading of Dr Wagner's meticulous and carefully worded post-mortem report suggests the cause of Beethoven's death was alcohol-induced cirrhosis of the liver.

The following day there was a steady stream of visitors to the death chamber, many of whom cut off a lock of Beethoven's hair as a keepsake. Gerhard von Breuning, lamenting that his father had not allowed him to do this for himself until the body was ready to be placed into the coffin, found that by then there was no hair left to cut off, though that is likely to be an exaggeration.

Beethoven had remained unshaven during his final illness, and his beard had grown thick. A barber was brought in to shave his face, telling those present that he would dispose of the razor as it was customary not to re-use a razor that had shaved a corpse.

The weather was warm and springlike on 29 March 1827, encouraging those who might have been in any doubt to come out and witness the elaborate ceremonial. There was plenty of opportunity to do so. The funeral procession would wind its way northwest out of the city to the small village of Währing, after stopping for a Funeral Mass at the Church of the Holy Trinity. Vienna had never seen a funeral of such extended pomp and grandeur, not even for a Holy Roman Emperor.

The church was a mere five hundred paces from the Schwarzspanierhaus, but it took the procession more than an hour and a half to cover the short distance. As the cortege processed, a brass band played the funeral march from Beethoven's Piano Sonata Op. 26. On the steps of the church there was such a crush that soldiers had to keep order. Official mourners, risking exclusion, had to point to the crepe bands on their hats to gain entry.

The interior of the church was bathed in candlelight, all three altars, wall brackets and chandeliers flickering. Ignaz Seyfried had arranged two of the Trombone Equali that Beethoven had written on that fraught visit to his brother Johann in Linz, for voices, and these were now sung, accompanied by trombones. This was followed by the Funeral Mass.

The cortege then resumed its slow processional progress northwest out of the city. The route was on a steady upward incline, causing the four horses to take the strain, and bringing laboured breathing to musicians, pallbearers and crowds. It passed along the Währing stream and into the small parish church.

There, once again, the Equali were played and sung. After another Funeral Mass the coffin left the church, carried this time on the shoulders of a bearer party, and followed by the chief mourners, augmented by schoolchildren and the poor from the local almshouse. Bells rang out.

There was a downward slope to the small cemetery, and at the entrance gates the bearers laid the coffin down.

This was an unscheduled change of plan. The leading playwright of the day, Franz Grillparzer, had written a funeral oration to be declaimed at Beethoven's graveside by the foremost tragedian of the day, Heinrich Anschütz, as the coffin was lowered.* However, strict religious law forbade the declamation of any text that was not sacred on consecrated ground. And so Anschütz read the oration over the coffin at the gates.

Grillparzer described Beethoven, amidst lengthy and florid language, as 'The Last Master, the tuneful heir of Bach and Handel, Mozart and Haydn's immortal fame … He was an artist, but a man as well … Thus he was, thus he died, thus he will live to the end of time.'

The coffin was shouldered again, and carried to the open grave that abutted the outer wall of the small cemetery. The pallbearers stood around the grave with lighted torches. The coffin was lowered, and three garlands of laurel leaves were placed onto it. The priests consecrated the grave and gave Beethoven a final blessing. The pallbearers each threw a handful of earth onto the coffin, and then extinguished their torches.

Little of the dignity that characterised his funeral was accorded to the great composer in the months following his death. In early

---

* Both Grillparzer and Anschütz had been known to Beethoven personally.

April, in the same room in which he died, his personal effects were auctioned. According to Gerhard von Breuning, who attended with his father, 'a miserable collection of old-clothes dealers had found their way in, and the articles that came under the hammer were tugged this way and that, the pieces of furniture pushed and thumped, everything disarranged and soiled'.

On 5 November, Beethoven's musical effects, including sketches in his own hand, autographs of printed works, original manuscripts and copied parts, were auctioned in rooms in the Kohlmarkt. The total intake was 1140 florins and 18 kreuzer. Beethoven's total estate, including cash, bank shares and personal effects, was valued at 9885 florins and 13 kreuzer (approximately £1000, or slightly under).

Just over a year and a half after Beethoven's death, Franz Schubert – one of those pallbearers who had accompanied the coffin and stood at the graveside with lighted torch – was buried alongside the man he admired so much.

In October 1863, the bodies of both Beethoven and Schubert were exhumed, their skeletons cleaned and reburied in lead coffins.

During this process, Beethoven's skull was given to Gerhard von Breuning – by now a qualified doctor – for safekeeping. He kept it on the table by his bed, 'proudly watching over that head from whose mouth, in years gone by, I had so often heard the living word!'

Before reburial a team of physicians compared Beethoven's skull with Schubert's, noting that Beethoven's was 'compact and thick', whereas Schubert's was 'fine and feminine'.

In June 1888, when the decision was made to close the cemetery at Währing, the bodies of Beethoven and Schubert were again exhumed and removed to the recently opened Zentralfriedhof,

Vienna's main cemetery to the south of the city, where they lie today still side by side in the musicians' quarter.*

It is perhaps fitting that the wreaths placed on Beethoven's coffin were made of laurel leaves – since ancient time the symbol of achievement and success, of mystical powers and immortality. The legends surrounding this greatest of artists began with that raised fist on his deathbed, and continue to this day.

Most enduring is the image we have come to know of the leonine head, fixed and determined gaze, a huge sculpted figure in stone or bronze, determination in eyes and pose. In short, an image befitting the music.

In the years following his death, there was a campaign to have a monument to him erected in his home town, Bonn. Largely due to the efforts – and financial contribution – of Franz Liszt, this was finally achieved in August 1845.

A massive bronze statue, designed by an almost unknown sculptor, Ernst Julius Hähnel, showed Beethoven, one leg in front of the other, both feet planted firmly on the ground, holding a pen in his lowered right hand and a notebook in his left, standing upright and staring ahead, brow knitted and features concentrating, abundantly thick hair framing his head.

The statue was placed at the top end of the Münsterplatz, where it stands today, a little way in front of the house of Count von Fürstenburg, where the boy Beethoven used to go to give

---

* Währing is today a suburb of Vienna. The former cemetery is a small park, with tennis courts, named Schubertpark. The original graves with headstones of the two composers are still there.

piano lessons, when he was not having a 'raptus'.* A balcony was erected in front of the house for the guests of honour to witness the unveiling.

All Bonn turned out for the event. The small town on the Rhine had never seen anything like it. The guests of honour were no lesser figures than Queen Victoria and Prince Albert of Britain, King Friedrich Wilhelm and Queen Elizabeth of Prussia, and Archduke Friedrich of Austria.

The ceremony began with a speech from the Music Director at the university of Bonn, at the end of which, to the beating of drums, ringing of bells, firing of cannon, the statue was unveiled – and found to be facing down the square, its back to the guests of honour. Embarrassment all round.

Beethoven's music continues to resonate with each new generation. The opening motif of the Fifth Symphony was used as a single drumbeat in clandestine BBC broadcasts to the Free French under Nazi occupation. When the Berlin Wall fell in 1989, the first concert to be given in unified Berlin was the music of Beethoven. The European Union chose the theme of the final movement of the Ninth Symphony as its anthem.

Beethoven's music will, quite simply, endure for ever and all time. Hence the dedication of this book.

---

* The building is now the post office headquarters.

Postscript

K arl van Beethoven, although he must have been kept informed of his uncle's demise and would certainly have been allowed compassionate leave to attend the funeral, did not do so. He left the army in 1832 and married in the same year. He had four daughters and a son, whom he named Ludwig. That son had a son, who died childless. Karl died at the age of fifty-two of liver disease.

Johann van Beethoven lived prosperously on the proceeds of his pharmacy business for the rest of his life. He frequently attended concert performances of his brother's music, always sitting in the front row, according to Gerhard von Breuning, 'all got up in a blue frock-coat with white vest, loudly shrieking Bravos from his big mouth at the end of every piece, beating his bony white-gloved hands together importantly'. He was, wrote Gerhard with some malice, 'as preposterous after his brother's death as he had been contemptible during his brother's life'. Johann died at the age of seventy-one.

Johanna van Beethoven outlived her husband by more than fifty years, and her brother-in-law, with whom she had such a

346

volatile relationship, by forty-one years. She died in some poverty at the age of eighty-two. I am not aware that she ever, either in writing or interview, uttered a hostile opinion or critical word about Beethoven.

Stephan von Breuning, Beethoven's lifelong and most loyal friend, already in poor health in 1826, never recovered it, and died barely two months after Beethoven at the age of fifty-two. His son, Dr Gerhard von Breuning, attributed his father's early death to the trauma of caring for Beethoven in his final illness, and the distress of overseeing the disposal of his effects.

Ferdinand Ries, who made his home in London and did so much to further Beethoven's reputation in Britain, accumulated considerable wealth from composition and teaching, but lost much of it when the London bank in which he had invested failed. He moved with his family to Germany, but died after a short illness at the age of fifty-three.

Franz and Eleonore Wegeler returned to Bonn from Koblenz in 1837, and sat with Helene von Breuning reminiscing about the young Beethoven they had known, although 'Frau Breuning had to be largely left out of these discussions, her mind having become feeble with age'. She was eighty-seven at the time. Wegeler was eighty-three when he died; Eleonore died at seventy.

Antonie Brentano, candidate for the Immortal Beloved, had eleven grandchildren and thirteen great-grandchildren. At the age of forty-six she began to note down the names of her friends who had died. The first entry read: Beethoven, 26 March 1827. She died at the age of eighty-eight.

Archduke Rudolph, Beethoven's greatest patron and a composer in his own right, suffered a fatal stroke when he was only forty-three. In accordance with his wishes, his heart was removed from his body and placed in a niche in the walls of the Cathedral of St Wenceslas in Olmütz. His body lies with other members of the Habsburg dynasty in the family crypt in Vienna.

This book, as I said in the Preface, is for lovers of Beethoven's music rather than academics, and so I have not crowded the narrative with source references. The musicologists know where the source material is.

For those who want to read further, the essential biography remains Thayer's *Life of Beethoven*, revised and edited by Elliott Forbes. It is a weighty tome, and there is a lot in it that the average reader might want to skip, but it is the biography which all subsequent biographers acknowledge, since it is the result of interviews carried out by Thayer with people who actually knew Beethoven.

Two contemporary books providing unique and first-hand insights are *Remembering Beethoven* by Franz Wegeler and Ferdinand Ries, and *From the House of the Black-Robed Spaniard* by Gerhard von Breuning.

The American musicologists Maynard Solomon and Lewis Lockwood have both written comprehensive biographies of Beethoven, though some of Solomon's theories – particularly with regard to identifying the Immortal Beloved – have been superseded, and Lockwood openly acknowledges that in his portrait the music looms larger than the life.

The Beethoven Compendium, A Guide to Beethoven's Life and Music, edited by the British musicologist Professor Barry Cooper of Manchester University, is an invaluable guide to all aspects of Beethoven's life, music, and the times in which he lived. Similarly, Professor Cooper's *Beethoven*, in the Master Musicians series, is a comprehensive and accessible account of the life, seamlessly integrating the music, though a knowledge of music and ability to read it is useful.

There are hundreds of books, if not thousands, but you would be hard-pressed to find one which does not contain musical examples, notes on staves. My belief that there are many lovers of Beethoven's music who cannot read a note of music, and have no desire to do so, was a spur to writing this book.

As with books, there are hundreds, if not thousands, of recordings of his works. I am regularly asked, in person or in letters or emails to Classic FM, to recommend recordings. It is, of course, impossible. It depends on how you like your Beethoven. Authentic or modern instruments? Chamber ensemble or full symphony orchestra? Rigid adherence or flexible approach?

I have dozens of recordings of a single work. I suspect most people will want just one. Pick from these:

Symphonies: Toscanini for hard driving speeds, Furtwängler for more flexibility. Riccardo Chailly and the Leipzig Gewandhaus for the modern symphony orchestra in all its glory. Emmanuel Krivine and La Chambre Philharmonique for authentic chamber-sized ensemble. Nikolaus Harnoncourt and the Chamber Orchestra of Europe.

Piano Concertos: Howard Shelley and the Orchestra of Opera North, with bonus of Choral Fantasia and Triple Concerto. Pierre-Laurent Aimard with Nikolaus Harnoncourt and the Chamber Orchestra of Europe. Paul Lewis with Jiří Belohlávek and the BBC Symphony Orchestra.

String Quartets: The Lindsays, in the earlier of their two sets, recorded in the late 1970s, passion suffusing every note. The

Endellion String Quartet more recently, using the edition prepared by the Beethoven scholar and editor Jonathan Del Mar. The
Busch Quartet for something different – recorded in the 1930s,
with a veil of hiss, the benefit of hindsight pouring the forthcoming tragedy of Europe into every note.

Piano Sonatas: Daniel Barenboim for modern virtuosity on a
concert grand. Paul Lewis for a young virtuoso's freshness. I still
love the Hungarian pianist Jenö Jandó on Naxos, recorded in
1988 in Budapest in what sounds like a bare-walled studio with
a single microphone. Beethoven can sometimes be over-sanitised.
Not here. For authenticity, eccentricity, and that hiss again, Ar-
tur Schnabel. As this book goes to the printer, the French pianist
Jean-Efflam Bavouzet has issued the first of a complete set, as has
the young Korean pianist HJ Lim.

Fidelio: Christa Ludwig and Jon Vickers, with the Philharmonia
Chorus and Orchestra under Otto Klemperer. Never bettered.
More recently, Claudio Abbado with the Lucerne Festival Or-
chestra, Nikolaus Harnoncourt with the Chamber Orchestra of
Europe.

My desert island disc: Piano Sonata Op. 110, recorded by Jörg
Demus on Beethoven's last piano, the Graf. Close your eyes and
imagine…

Beethoven's Music

Beethoven's music, is, I believe, the greatest body of work ever produced by a classical composer.

As will have become clear from reading this book, Beethoven did things differently. He obeyed no rules. He set new standards. He changed music for ever. What follows is an account of how he achieved that, with an introduction to the main areas of composition in which he worked, together with a brief analysis of each piece within that area.

My aim is to guide you through the most important compositions, in the hope that this will lead you to explore the music further. Whether you are new to Beethoven's music, or you know only a few of the better-known compositions, a magnificent voyage of discovery awaits you. If you are already familiar with the music, I hope you might find a revelation or two in what follows.

Beethoven said he was composing for all mankind. If you allow him into your life, his music will become your lifelong companion. To quote him: 'Music is a higher revelation than all wisdom or philosophy.'

Selection of compositions

The Symphonies

Beethoven's nine symphonies are the starting point for any exploration of his work. They are perhaps his most familiar body of compositions, the opening of the Fifth being regularly described as the best-known bars in all classical music. The theme of the final movement of the Ninth is used as the anthem of the European Union. The 'Pastoral' is regularly voted as the most popular of Beethoven's symphonies in the Classic FM Hall of Fame. The 'Eroica', for its sheer power and unpredictability, is my personal favourite.

In the early nineteenth century, the symphony was regarded as the purest form of musical expression, but Beethoven came to it relatively late in life, perhaps concerned about unfavourable comparisons with Mozart and Haydn. It was not until Beethoven was almost thirty years of age that he produced his Symphony No. 1.

Again rather surprisingly, he produced his symphonies somewhat irregularly. The first eight were composed within a dozen or so years; there was then a gap of twelve years before he produced his Ninth, although he had first made sketches for it some decades earlier.

However, as with so many forms of musical expression, Beethoven would transform the symphony – after he had composed the 'Eroica', it would never be the same again.

His Ninth Symphony, the 'Choral', is usually regarded as the pinnacle of his achievements, and indeed it is, but perhaps only because he died before completing another symphony. He had firm plans beyond the Ninth and had made sketches for a Tenth Symphony when he became terminally ill. Who knows what Beethoven's genius might have gone on to create had he not died at the age of fifty-six?

These are the six symphonies I consider to be the most essential.

Symphony No. 3, Op. 55, 'Eroica'

Background: This symphony was the first major work Beethoven composed after returning from his stay in Heiligenstadt, where he wrote his Last Will and Testament, acknowledging that he was incurably deaf. It can be seen as a monumental act of self-will, even defiance. It is generally regarded as ushering in Beethoven's 'Heroic' period.

By now, at thirty-two years of age in 1803, he was well known in musical circles in Vienna, and already had a reputation for eccentricity, both in composition and performance. This new symphony cemented that view. The sophisticated Viennese audience had simply never heard anything like it.

Form: Not just Beethoven's most monumental work to date, but far and away the most monumental of its kind – at least twice as long as any symphony hitherto composed by anyone else. It is conventional only in that it consists of four movements, but each one departs from what an audience had come to expect.

Listen out for: Its sheer length, anything up to an hour in performance, is not the only innovation. The two opening chords demand your attention – they have none of the politeness of other composers. There is the 'wrong' note in bar seven, the 'false' horn entry before the recapitulation, the rarity of a funeral march, and in the final movement possibly the most unexpected occurrence of all: after a furious run from top to bottom on strings, the music then fragments, and we have variations and theme, rather than the conventional theme and variations. In a masterstroke, that theme is a sibling of the opening theme of the first movement, with the emphasis on beats 2 and 4 rather than 1 and 3.

It is a work that, no matter how well you know it, takes you by surprise at every turn. As you listen, remember Beethoven's original dedicatee was Napoleon Bonaparte, a hero to him until the First Consul declared himself Emperor. The 'Eroica' is indeed heroic, in one form or another, from first note to last. Although Beethoven angrily scratched Napoleon's name off the title page, he could never quite rid himself of admiration for the French ruler, still dedicating the work to the memory 'of a great man'.

Symphony No. 5, Op. 67

Background: Undoubtedly the best-known orchestral work Beethoven composed. Who does not know the opening bars, that famous motif of three short notes and a long one? It achieved immortality when used as the call sign for the BBC's clandestine broadcasts to the French Resistance during the Second World War. It was an inspired choice – short, instantly recognisable, dramatic, and in Morse code those opening notes represent the letter V, for Victory.

The symphony has become inextricably identified with Fate. This is entirely due to Beethoven's secretary and (unreliable) biographer Anton Schindler describing it as 'Fate knocking at the door'. It is a small step to believe that they were the words of Beethoven himself, though there is no evidence he ever uttered them. He once wrote that we should not read anything into his music, nor look for hidden messages, just listen to the music.

He wrote his Fifth Symphony in 1807–8, when his life was in some turmoil. His younger brother had married his mistress, who was already pregnant with their child. Beethoven was utterly horrified. His own attempts at an amorous liaison – with Josephine Deym – had been rebuffed, and his application for regular work as an opera composer had been rejected by theatre directors. But an offer of 500 florins from an aristocrat for a new symphony was enough to persuade him.

Form: The symphony consists of four movements, which was the convention of the time. However, what was very much not the convention was to run movements together. This Beethoven does, with no break between the third and fourth movements. It is the first time trombones, contra bassoon and piccolo have ever been used in a symphony. And it is the first time that the opening motif is carried on throughout the work. It permeates, in one form or another, every movement. The highly regarded critic E. T. A. Hoffmann described it as a journey from dark night into radiant sunlight, and that description has stuck.

Listen out for: In the first place, there is that opening motif, present in so many different ways throughout the symphony. The passage that links the third and fourth movements is one of the most mysterious Beethoven wrote in any work. Beginning low, with steady beat on the timpani, it slowly builds until exploding in a blaze of light at the start of the fourth movement. It is for the opening chord of the final movement that Beethoven brings in trombones for the first time in the work.

Inspired, to an extent, by music that had emanated from the French Revolution, this work is revolutionary in every aspect, from first note to last.

Symphony No. 6, Op. 68, 'Pastoral'

Background: The year in which Beethoven composed this work, 1808, was frenetically busy. He directed a concert of his own music in April, performed new works, and planned a new opera (which he abandoned). But he spent most of the year waiting to be given a date for a benefit concert he was promised, which would allow him to present new compositions, and also earn a good financial return.

He composed the 'Pastoral' in the spring and summer, inspired by long walks in the countryside. It received its first performance, along with the Fifth Symphony, Fourth Piano Concerto, and several other works, at the benefit concert which was finally scheduled for 22 December.

Form: The only orchestral composition by Beethoven in which he tells us exactly what to listen out for. Uniquely in his symphonies, he gives each movement a verbal description: Awakening of happy feelings on arrival in the country; Scene by the brook; Merry gathering of country folk; Tempest, storm; Shepherds' song: Happy and thankful feelings after the storm. It is also the only symphony by Beethoven that runs to five movements.

Listen out for: The mood of the first movement is carefree, as befits its title. In the second movement we hear the babbling brook. Famously, towards the end of this movement Beethoven imitates bird calls in the orchestra – nightingale on flute, quail on oboe, cuckoo on clarinet. The merry dancing of country folk Beethoven will have witnessed for himself in one of the villages of the Vienna Woods. In the middle section of this movement the bassoon interrupts with downward notes, inspired by a drunken musician Beethoven saw playing in a musical group in a tavern. Gathering clouds herald the storm, which causes the dancers to flee inside for shelter. Then, with one of his loveliest melodies, Beethoven has the shepherds give thanks for coming through the storm unscathed.

The symphony is unique in Beethoven's work for its carefree and joyful mood throughout, reflecting his love of the countryside and the long walks he enjoyed taking.

Symphony No. 7, Op. 92

Background: Beethoven suffered a bout of ill health in the first half of 1811, and took his doctor's advice to leave Vienna and recuperate in the spa town of Teplitz in Bohemia. His general wellbeing was not improved by a devaluation of the currency fivefold, drastically reducing the annuity he was being paid by three wealthy patrons. Matters were made worse when one of the patrons was declared bankrupt and another was killed in a fall from his horse, although the third, Archduke Rudolph, increased his payments to cover the losses to Beethoven.

After visits to Prague and Silesia, he returned to Vienna, still not fully restored to good health, and wrote an angry letter to his publisher complaining that they had mistranslated the title of one of his Piano Sonatas.

In a not particularly good frame of mind, he began work on a new symphony, which would be characterised by the sheer exuberance that runs through three of the four movements.

Form: The symphony is in four movements of which the second, similarly to the 'Eroica', has the character of a funeral march, although he does not name it as such. It conjures in my mind heavy military boots trudging through mud and snow. After a slow opening to the first movement, full of portent, the symphony takes flight. The frenetic pace of the first, third and fourth movements does not let up. It is normal to see the conductor and orchestra players exhausted after the final chord sounds!

Listen out for: The sheer intensity of this symphony is exhilarating, and at the same time, to an extent, terrifying. Beethoven conducted a performance of it to celebrate the victory of the British army over the French at Vitoria in northern Spain. It is the only eyewitness description we have of him conducting, given by a member of the violin section, the composer Louis Spohr. It stands alone among Beethoven's symphonies for sudden changes of pace and dynamics – slow then fast, soft then loud. Unsettling maybe at first, but once you are familiar with the piece it carries you along on a wave of passion and power.

Symphony No. 9, Op. 125, 'Choral'

Background: Beethoven composed his Ninth Symphony in 1823–4, but the idea for it had been germinating for many years. Since his university days in Bonn he had kept a volume of poetry by Friedrich Schiller, with the aim of setting the poem 'An die Freude' to music. Finally, in 1822, he decided this should be in the form of a symphony. When, in response to a letter from him, the London Philharmonic Society offered him £50 (a paltry sum) for a new symphony, he had the incentive he needed.

Form: Four movements, but each one longer and unlike any symphonic movement he had written before. Sketches show that his decision to have solo bass bring in voices in the fourth movement was one he came to after trying out, and rejecting, several other ideas. However well we may know it, that solo bass entry pleading with friends to change their tone – 'O Freunde, nicht diese Töne!' – remains one of the most dramatic in all symphonic music.

Listen out for: The misty veiled opening prepares us for mystery and drama. What follows is unrelenting tension and sheer power. The driving rhythm creates a momentum that does not let up. The second movement has solo timpani right at the start, heightening the sense of drama. Towards the end we have a foreshadowing of the main theme that will take flight in the fourth movement.

The third movement, with two main themes, is in complete contrast. It is utterly serene. The briefest of pauses ushers in the fourth and final movement, and the drama returns. A long orchestral passage contains a quotation from each of the three preceding movements, but none of them is allowed to finish. They are each in turn cut off. When, finally, the solo bass voice enters, it seems entirely natural, as if everything has been moving towards this point – even though it is unprecedented. The main theme, one of the most famous in all music, finally appears, and it is at this point that the listener understands that every step in the journey has been leading to this moment.

Beethoven's Ninth Symphony set the bar for symphonic composition at a new level. There is not a symphonist since who has not acknowledged Beethoven's achievement. The greatest of them have understood that it is only possible to be different to Beethoven, not to surmount him. Beethoven's Ninth remains the supreme achievement in Western music.

Wellington's Victory, Op. 91

Background: This is a true 'curiosity' piece. Correctly entitled *Wellingtons Sieg oder die Schlacht bei Vitoria* (*Wellington's Victory or the Battle of Vitoria*, sometimes known as the Battle Symphony), Beethoven composed it in 1813 for the Panharmonicon, a mechanical instrument that produced the sounds of the orchestra. He was persuaded to do it by the man credited with inventing the metronome, Johann Nepomuk Mälzel, who wanted a piece of music to celebrate Wellington's famous victory over the French in northern Spain. Beethoven, surprisingly, obliged. The piece was instantly popular, so much so that Mälzel persuaded Beethoven to orchestrate it. Beethoven himself conducted the first performance. It remained popular in the years following Napoleon's ultimate defeat, earning Beethoven considerable amounts of money, but is not often heard today.

Form: Here is Beethoven doing something very rare for him – writing programmatic music in response to demand. This 'symphony' tells a story. It is in two distinct sections (rather than movements). The first depicts the Battle of Vitoria and is militaristic in tone, beginning with drum rolls, fanfares and anthems representing the two opposing armies. They confront each other and fight, and cannon and muskets can be heard. The second is a 'Victory Symphony'. This is more in the style of the Beethoven we know – upbeat, driving and victorious. It resembles the Victory Symphony that closes the overture to Egmont.

Listen out for: The British army is represented by 'Rule Britannia', the French by 'Marlborough s'en va-t-en guerre', a traditional French tune that resembles the English 'For He's a Jolly Good Fellow'. The Marseillaise was considered treasonous in Vienna, which is probably why Beethoven did not use it. The first section is a vivid depiction of warfare, and it is not far-fetched to speculate that Tchaikovsky knew it and referred to it when composing his '1812 Overture'. The second section, the Victory Symphony, has the British 'God Save the King' triumphing over the defeated French army.

The Piano Concertos

Given that the piano was Beethoven's instrument, his principal means of expressing himself, it is no surprise that when it comes to concertos, he concentrated mainly on works for piano and orchestra. In fact, they occupied him almost to the exclusion of any other. Apart from the five piano concertos, there is one single violin concerto, a Triple Concerto (for piano, violin and cello) and nothing else. Beethoven wrote no concerto for any other of the instruments one might expect, such as cello, French horn, clarinet, flute or trumpet.

However, given that the piano was his voice, it is curious that we only have five piano concertos, and that the last of them was composed when he was just thirty-eight years of age. We can be fairly certain that the main reason for this was his encroaching deafness.

Like Mozart before him, Beethoven's calling card on the concert stage was to perform his own piano concertos. Mozart was the first composer of importance to do this, and it earned him a significant amount of money and considerable prestige. Beethoven's first public performance in Vienna was as soloist in his own Piano Concerto No. 1 (or possibly No. 2). Some months later he appeared at another concert performing his Piano Concerto No. 2 (or possibly No. 1).

The sophisticated Viennese audiences were delighted to find they had another extraordinarily talented composer/performer in their city, so soon after losing Mozart. And so Beethoven was again the soloist at the premiere of the Third and Fourth Piano Concertos. By the time of the Fifth, the 'Emperor', though, his deafness had made it impossible for him to perform. It is the only one of the five that he did not perform himself, and no further piano concertos were to follow. A sixth was begun but abandoned.

The catastrophic effect of his deafness did not extend to solo works for piano, and he continued to compose piano sonatas until almost the end of his life.

The first two piano concertos, composed when Beethoven was in his late teens to mid-twenties (although both were later revised), show him attempting to come to grips with the form.

With the Third he found his distinctive voice. It, along with the two that follow, show Beethoven as master of the form.

Piano Concerto No. 3, Op. 37

Background: In a period of great creativity between 1799 and 1801, when Beethoven was in his late twenties, he composed his First Symphony, completed his first set of String Quartets, began work on his Second Symphony, and composed his Piano Concerto No. 3. He also performed several times on the concert stage. It was around this time that he realised he was having a problem with his hearing, which might have led him to work as hard as he could while he was still able.

Form: This work is in the traditional three movements, as are all the Piano Concertos. Beethoven has now truly found his own voice. The orchestral introduction is the longest of any of the five, with a gradual building of tension. When the piano enters, it is as if it has to. And how does it enter? With two simple upward scales. This is the springboard for the most complex of any piano concerto movement he has so far composed. The slow movement is solemn and almost hymn-like. Towards the end, that simple scale reappears, but with a flattened seventh note. Beethoven repeats it immediately, lest we should be in any doubt. The final movement alternates between exuberance and drama.

Listen out for: As will be the case in all Beethoven's compositions featuring piano and orchestra from now on, the piano is the equal of the orchestra. In fact, it drives the orchestra. Those opening scales are a statement of intent. Never have such simple scales carried such portent. The first time I ever heard the work I thought the pianist had made a dreadful mistake when the scale returns towards the end of the second movement. But Beethoven knows we will think that, which is why he repeats it.

Beethoven was the soloist at the premiere of the work, but had not had time to write out his part fully. He asked a musical colleague, Ignaz Seyfried, to turn for him. Seyfried later said that the pages in front of him looked as if they contained nothing but Egyptian hieroglyphics. He had to wait for a jab in the ribs or a glance from Beethoven to know when to turn the page. At the jovial dinner afterwards Beethoven teased him for being so scared.

Piano Concerto No. 4, Op. 58
Background: Beethoven composed his Fourth Piano Concerto in the first half of 1806, at a time of turmoil in his life, both creative and personal. The previous autumn his opera *Leonore* (later to become *Fidelio*) had failed, more or less shut down by Napoleon's army officers occupying the city. Beethoven had learned that his younger brother Carl was expecting a child with his mistress, whom he intended to marry. Beethoven was in despair. So grim was his mood that his patron Prince Lichnowsky took him away to his country estate in Silesia for rest and quiet. In the months preceding this trip, Beethoven had composed his Fourth Piano Concerto and his Fourth Symphony.

Form: Three movements, but once again unlike anything Beethoven – or anyone else – had ever composed. No one had begun a piano concerto with solo piano. In the second movement the piano and orchestra are almost like two distinct voices, until the close when they are reconciled. The second movement leads into the third without a break.

Listen out for: The concerto opens in a totally new way: solo piano, with a soft, gently turning phrase just five bars long. After the piano states the phrase, the orchestra enters in the 'wrong' key for a lengthy passage during which the piano is silent. The piano finally re-enters, and a dialogue begins. That opening phrase on piano, in one form or another, dominates the first movement. The second movement, where piano and orchestra are separated until the close, when the piano 'overcomes' the orchestra's objections, was described by a nineteenth-century Beethoven biographer as Orpheus taming the Furies. I prefer to describe it as a married couple having an argument – two separate voices, one aggressive (orchestra), the other placatory (piano), until finally the latter voice overcomes and quells the anger in the other. Without a break, the third movement provides a lively rondo, reinforcing the impression of a reconciliation between two previously argumentative forces.

Piano Concerto No. 5, Op. 73, 'Emperor'

Background: Beethoven's final piano concerto. Far and away the best loved of the five, it is regularly voted the most popular of all his works in the Classic FM Hall of Fame. Beethoven began composing it weeks after the huge concert of December 1808, at which he premiered his Fourth Piano Concerto and Fifth and Sixth Symphonies. That was the culmination of a traumatic year for him, but early in the new year he received a guarantee of an annuity from three aristocrats, giving him peace of mind and financial security.

Form: Written in three movements, with no pause between the second and third – a form Beethoven had come to favour for concertos. By far the longest of his piano concertos, it begins with chords from the orchestra interspersed with huge virtuosic runs on the piano. It is the most arresting opening of any piano concerto written to date. The second movement, by contrast, is sublime and almost hymn-like. Unusually, the main theme is taken by the orchestra rather than the soloist. A descending semitone leads directly into the third movement, which is in the form of a lively rondo.

Listen out for: From the opening chord on full orchestra, interrupted by a huge run on piano, Beethoven has our attention. The movement is vigorous, progressing through several unexpected key changes, before a climactic ending in the home key. The second movement has passages on piano intertwining with the main melody expressed by full orchestra, strings muted. This is one of the best loved movements of any concerto Beethoven was to write – a world away from the anger and tension so often associated with his works.

At the end of the movement, Beethoven pulls off a masterstroke. As the music becomes quieter and quieter, falling in pitch, the bassoon alone drops a single semitone, launching the third movement into an effervescent, syncopated rondo. In characteristic Beethoven style (he does something similar in both the Ninth Symphony and the *Missa Solemnis*) towards the end of the third movement he brings the entire work to an almost complete stop, the beats accentuated by timpani. A moment's pause, and furious runs on the piano with orchestral accompaniment bring the work to a triumphant conclusion.

Violin Concerto, Op. 61

Background: Composed in late 1806, after a traumatic start to the year, during which Beethoven stayed at the country estate of Prince Lichnowsky, learned his brother's wife had given birth, and stormed out into the rain after the Prince asked him to play for

French soldiers. The concerto was intended for the violinist Franz Clement, but word reached Beethoven that Clement had shown off at the first performance by playing the violin upside down between movements. By the time of publication Beethoven had given the dedication instead to Stephan von Breuning. He did not write another violin concerto, although he adapted this one for piano and orchestra, sometimes called Piano Concerto No. 6.

One further performance of the Violin Concerto is recorded in Beethoven's lifetime, after which it fell into obscurity. Only when the thirteen-year-old Joseph Joachim performed it in London in 1844, with Mendelssohn conducting, did it begin to gain in popularity, eventually becoming a staple of the violin repertoire.

Form: Three movements, and as with all Beethoven's concertos from Piano Concerto No. 3 onwards, the second movement leads directly into the third. The opening of the entire work, four solo beats on the timpani, was an entirely new way of beginning any composition. Beethoven did not write a cadenza for this concerto.

Listen out for: Those four opening beats on solo timpani, although played softly, attract our attention immediately. The great violinist Yehudi Menuhin wrote in his memoirs that on one occasion, performing the Beethoven violin concerto in the American Midwest, he knew from those beats that the performance would be a disaster. A long orchestral introduction precedes the first violin entry, a simple rising and falling theme. The serene slow movement is one of his most beautiful while the final movement is a rondo in a similar spirit to that of the 'Emperor' Concerto. Brahms conspicuously borrowed from it for the final movement of his own Violin Concerto.

Triple Concerto for piano, violin and cello, Op. 56

Background: My candidate for the most neglected of Beethoven's works. Seldom heard in the concert hall, probably because of the cost of engaging three soloists, as well as full orchestra and conductor. Beethoven composed this in 1804 shortly after his contract with the Theater an der Wien was terminated. Weeks later he learned that Napoleon had declared himself Emperor and angrily scratched his name off the title page of the 'Eroica' Symphony. Beethoven moved in with his friend Stephan von Breuning, with whom he had a serious – and almost terminal – disagreement. Yet during this period he composed the Triple Concerto, which is almost lighthearted in manner. It is dedicated to the Habsburg emperor's younger brother Archduke Rudolph, who was Beethoven's pupil and only in his mid-teens at the time.

Form: Although this is a concerto for three solo instruments – unknown before Beethoven and rare afterwards – the part for cello is considerably more virtuosic than the other two. Beethoven probably had the young Archduke's capabilities in mind when he wrote the piano part, similarly with the violin part, which suggests the cellist was the most competent of the three soloists.

Listen out for: Given the virtuosity of its part, the cello, unsurprisingly, is the first instrument to enter after the orchestral introduction, followed by the violin and finally the piano. The interplay between the three solo instruments in this lengthy movement is exquisite, with Beethoven clearly writing to show off the particular capabilities of the soloists he knew would be performing it. The slow movement is, I think, one of Beethoven's finest – a yearning theme on violin and cello which rises to heights almost of eroticism. The third movement is a jaunty rondo, reminiscent once again of the Violin Concerto and the 'Emperor' Concerto.

To dismiss the work, as many have, as a kind of 'warm-up' for the piano concertos which would follow is, in my view, thoroughly wrong. This is a work that deserves far more credit – and many more performances – than it gets.

The Overtures

Beethoven wrote eleven overtures. Some served as introductions to his own work, such as *Die Geschöpfe des Prometheus* (*Creatures of Prometheus*) and *Fidelio*. Others were written to introduce other works (*Egmont, Coriolan*) or for other reasons: *Die Weihe des Hauses* (*Consecration of the House*) marked the opening of a theatre while *Namensfeier* (*Name-day*) celebrated a prince's name-day.

The overture that caused him most trouble was for his opera *Fidelio*. He wrote no fewer than four versions, of which only one is regularly used today. Of the remaining three, one makes an appearance here, albeit in an unusual way (see *Leonore/Fidelio* Overture, p. 372).

Fidelio aside, Beethoven's best known and most often heard overtures are *Egmont* and *Coriolan*. They differ from each other in that the overture to *Egmont* precedes incidental music that Beethoven composed for Goethe's play – nine pieces in all, from which only Klärchen's aria is performed today, and that only rarely. The overture to *Coriolan*, on the other hand, is simply that. Beethoven composed it as a curtain-raiser for the tragedy *Coriolan* by the Austrian dramatist Heinrich Collin.

Coriolan Overture, Op. 62

Background: Beethoven returned to Vienna in October 1806 after a traumatic stay with his patron Prince Lichnowsky at his country estate in Silesia. Within weeks of returning he completed his Fourth Symphony. In December his newly composed Violin Concerto received its first performance. Around this time he was asked to compose an overture to Heinrich Collin's play *Coriolan*, based on the legendary Roman general. Beethoven composed the overture in early 1807, and it received its first performance at a private concert given by Prince Lichnowsky in March 1807.

Form: The overture consists of two basic themes. The first is the war-like theme attached to Coriolanus; the second is a more tender melody that represents his mother. The overture follows the basic plot of Collin's play – the bellicose Coriolanus being urged by his mother to restrain himself. In the end, unable to achieve his ambitions, Coriolanus takes his own life (unlike the Shakespearean tragedy of the same name, in which he is murdered).

Listen out for: After success on the battlefield Coriolanus seeks political office, but his natural antagonism towards the ordinary citizen leads to him being opposed and then exiled. From the opening chords we are made aware of Coriolanus's aggressive behaviour. By contrast the theme of his mother is full of tenderness. The two are in dialogue throughout the overture and it becomes evident from the music that Coriolanus will not respond to his mother's pleas. The quiet ending represents Coriolanus's death.

Egmont Overture, Op. 84

Background: Beethoven was commissioned in late 1809 to write incidental music for Goethe's play *Egmont*. He did not hesitate to accept. The plot of *Egmont* was close to Beethoven's heart: the struggle for liberty over oppression, in this case the fight for the freedom of the Netherlands led by Count Egmont against the Spanish occupier led by the tyrannical Duke of Alba. It was not just the subject matter that appealed to Beethoven. He was himself of Flemish descent – this was the struggle of his ancestors.

Form: By far the best known and most popular of Beethoven's stand-alone overtures, it is a regular on the concert platform. As with *Coriolan*, there are two easily identifiable strands. There is the oppression of Spanish rule and the trumped-up charges against Count Egmont as he faces trial; and there is the pleading of his family and supporters for mercy and justice. We hear the trial, the evidence, the pleading, the delivery of the guilty verdict (a foregone conclusion), the execution of Count Egmont, and then, at the end, a glorious Victory Symphony representing the ultimate success of the fight for freedom over the Spanish.

Listen out for: This overture is programmatic music by Beethoven. It tells a story. The opening portentous chord and the minor key chords which follow it represent the Spanish court and the grave charges against Count Egmont. A lone oboe represents Egmont's innocence and the longing of his family and supporters for his freedom. The oboe was Beethoven's instrument of choice to depict freedom in the face of oppression, most notably in the dungeon scene in *Fidelio*.

The chords return as the prosecution outlines the case against Egmont, punctuated by gentle phrases on wind and strings, representing Egmont's defence. This interaction continues until the trial is abruptly halted – dotted chords on high French horns – and the judges deliver their guilty verdict: a series of dotted chords from full orchestra. Egmont's execution is depicted by a plunging motif – we 'hear' the executioner's axe fall.

There then follows an extraordinary passage. We are in the major key. Beginning softly and slowly building, this is the Victory Symphony. It ends in triumphant chords, including high ascending runs on piccolo. Count Egmont's death has not been in vain. The people will ultimately rise and force the Spanish out of their homeland.

Leonore / Fidelio Overtures, Op. 72

Background: As I mentioned in the Introduction, four overtures for a single opera! The first, known as Leonore No. 1, was written either just before the first performance of *Leonore* in 1805, or soon after. There is no record of it ever being performed in Beethoven's lifetime. It was published many years after his death and was probably rejected as too slight for the drama which followed. The second overture, Leonore No. 2, was used before the first performance of the opera. It was then rejected as being too 'meaty', with large orchestra at full stretch. A quotation from Florestan's main dungeon aria and an ornamented version of the trumpet call towards the end were considered to give away too much of the plot. Leonore No. 3 is essentially a rewrite of No. 2. It was used before the revised version of *Leonore* five months after the premiere. More dramatic, with more light and shade but retaining the Florestan quotation and trumpet call, it was rejected as being too long and again giving too much away. Today it is often played between the dungeon scene, with husband and wife reunited, and the final triumph scene in the town square, where its inherent drama fits well.

The fourth overture, composed for the second and final revision (which produced *Fidelio*, the opera we know today), is the one always now used as the overture, as well as being a frequent concert piece.

Form: The overture to *Fidelio*, the final version of Beethoven's only opera, is half the length of Leonores 1 and 2. There is no quotation from any part of the opera, nor any trumpet call. As such it gives away nothing of the plot and serves as an ideal curtain-raiser for the drama that is to follow.

Listen out for: Dramatic opening chords are followed by a tender sequence on French horns. Drumbeats herald a largely joyous passage in the major key. As he does in the opera itself, Beethoven used oboe to soar above the orchestra, signalling freedom. There is drama in the overture but always it yields to tenderness, constantly presaging the happy outcome to the plot. From the first performance of the newly revised opera, it was seen as the perfect overture to what is about to unfold.

Opera

We know that Beethoven excelled in practically every form of music he turned to, setting new standards for the symphony and other orchestral works as well as smaller forms, such as the piano sonata and string quartet. But one major musical form continually eluded him, until at last he produced just a single work – one that to this day his critics say falls below his usual standards. I could not disagree more. But the fact remains that it is Beethoven's only successful foray into this particular musical form: the opera.

Why did Beethoven struggle – that is the right word – with opera? For a start, he had the extraordinary legacy of Mozart to contend with. Mozart found writing opera as straightforward and uncomplicated as any other type of composition. More than twenty operas or musical dramas in his short life attest to that.

By comparison, even a cursory glance at Beethoven's sketches or manuscripts shows crossings out, corrections, ideas later abandoned, even expletives in the margin! This goes for most forms Beethoven composed in, but as we know he triumphed in many of them. The same cannot be said for opera.

This did not prevent him from trying. In 1803 he was commissioned to write an opera, to be called *Vestas Feuer*. He spent six months working intermittently on it, by which point he had made over twenty pages of sketches and written out the first scene in full score. He then abandoned it, blaming the poor quality of the libretto. Five years later he sketched out ideas for an opera based on Shakespeare's *Macbeth*. In the following four years five more subjects were considered as possible operatic projects. Much later, in 1823, he entered into discussions with the Austrian playwright Franz Grillparzer (who would later write Beethoven's funeral oration) about two possible subjects. Not one of these numerous projects ever came to fruition.

Beethoven did, however, compose one completed opera, and it is an acknowledged masterpiece (though, as I said, it has its detractors). But the journey from the beginning to the completed work was long and tortuous.

Fidelio, Op. 72

Background: From early 1803 to spring 1804, Beethoven was composer-in-residence at the Theater an der Wien – literally in residence, in a suburb of Vienna outside the city wall. It was during this period that he worked on *Vestas Feuer*. He abandoned it at the end of the year, which may have been a contributory factor to his contract being terminated shortly thereafter.

By the time he was reinstated in late summer 1804, he was already working on a new libretto, *Leonore*. This was completed, and given an unsuccessful performance a year later. The following spring it was extensively revised, but Beethoven withdrew it. Eight years later, after a series of successful concerts, Beethoven was asked to revive his opera. He agreed to do so on the condition that he was allowed to revise it. The revision became *Fidelio*, the opera we know today.

Form: Both earlier versions of *Leonore* were overlong – three full acts in its first incarnation. *Fidelio* is in two acts, and packed with drama. The new librettist, Georg Friedrich Treitschke, tightened up the action, rewriting Florestan's all-important aria at the start of Act II. In the final scene he moved the action into the town square, thus taking the characters – and the audience – literally from darkness into light.

Listen out for: After a dramatic overture, the curtain rises on a scene of unexpected domesticity (fuel for critics). Soon, though, four characters join to sing a quartet, a miracle of writing with each character expressing a different emotion. From this moment, drama takes over from domesticity. The Prisoners' Chorus, a staple of male choruses to this day, is clearly written from the heart – Beethoven's natural empathy with people who find themselves at the wrong end of corrupt justice. Florestan's impassioned cry from the dungeon floor at the start of Act II is accompanied by soaring oboe as he remembers his adored wife and their idyllic life together (the same soaring oboe phrase Beethoven wrote many years earlier for the unperformed Cantata on the Death of Emperor Joseph II). Again we can imagine Beethoven pouring his heart into 'O namenlose Freude' ('O nameless joy'), the love duet sung by the reunited husband and wife of Florestan and Leonore, at a time in his personal life when he had finally accepted he would never find true love.

Fidelio has two main themes: the love of a husband and wife, one so strong that the wife will risk her life to free her husband; and the triumph of freedom over oppression, a political creed that imbued Beethoven's being. Given *Fidelio*'s ultimate success, it might seem odd that Beethoven never tried his hand at opera again. But when you consider the monumental struggle involved – three different versions over eight years – it is not really surprising. We should simply be grateful for this one undoubted masterpiece.

The Choral Works

By his own admission Beethoven found it difficult to write for voices. When he heard sounds in his head, he said, they were the sounds of an orchestra. The few works that he did write for voices and orchestra were religious in nature, including the Ninth Symphony with its references to the 'spark of divinity' and the 'Creator'.

Beethoven was not particularly religious – I have found no evidence of him ever going to church to pray or worship. Of his three purely religious compositions (excluding the ninth, which is instrumental until the final movement), only two are overtly so. The early oratorio, 'Christus am Ölberge' (Christ on the Mount of Olives'), takes an incident from the New Testament, but the libretto is secular. The two entirely religious works works are both settings of the Mass. In 1807 he composed a setting to a commission from Prince Esterházy. This setting is rarely heard today, considered slight in comparison to the great work of Beethoven's late years, the *Missa Solemnis*. This setting of the Mass testifies to a deepening spirituality as Beethoven entered his fifties.

Choral Fantasia, **Op. 80**

Background: My candidate for Beethoven's second most neglected and underrated composition (after the Triple Concerto). Beethoven composed it hastily in 1808 for a benefit concert on 22 December. It was the final piece to be performed and it was a disaster. Beethoven had not prepared the opening piano solo properly, so that the orchestra did not know where to come in. He had also agreed a cut with the orchestra leader, which he failed to observe. Today it is rarely performed and generally considered an inferior work (particularly in comparison to the Ninth) and an expensive one, requiring a full orchestra, solo pianist, chorus and six solo singers (a very unusual line-up of two sopranos, one mezzo-soprano, two tenors, one bass).

Form: The piece is in three distinct parts, albeit running into each other without pause, and is unique in Beethoven's output in that it begins with solo piano performing a lengthy 'improvisation' (for that is what it most certainly was at the first performance). The orchestra then joins in, and the theme is very similar to the main theme of the later Ninth Symphony – and suffers from the comparison, since it is slighter. Finally solo singers and chorus join in for a unison finale.

Listen out for: That central theme, introduced by full orchestra after the piano introduction, presages the final movement of the Ninth Symphony but turns back on itself rather than 'taking off'. It is thus considered an inferior, early 'try out' of what would become the famous theme of the Ninth. This is entirely wrong. It is a beautifully balanced theme, perfectly fitting under the pianist's hands, and allowing expansion and variation. The soloists and chorus join in for the final section in what seems an entirely natural progression from darkness to light, chaos (not too strong a word for the first performance) to order. The final section, clearly the inspiration for the future Ninth, is infectious and joyous from first note to last.

Missa Solemnis, Op. 123

Background: The *Missa Solemnis* is far and away Beethoven's greatest piece for orchestra and voices. Although a setting of the Mass, from his day to our own it has been considered more of a concert piece than a religious work. In fact it was for its symphonic character, not its religious qualities, that the censor banned a full performance for its premiere in a theatre – just three out of five sections were allowed. The composition of the *Missa Solemnis* caused Beethoven huge problems. It took him almost four years, missing the enthronement of his patron Archduke Rudolph as Bishop of Olmütz, for which it was intended, by three whole years. Evidence that Beethoven intended the work for a wider audience – for humanity, in fact – lies in the words he wrote at the head of the Kyrie: '*Vom Herzen – Möge es wieder – zu Herze gehen!*' ('From the heart – may it return to the heart'!)

Form: Set to the traditional words of the Roman Catholic Mass, the work consists of the standard five parts: Kyrie, Gloria, Credo, Sanctus, Agnus Dei. Unusually for Beethoven there is no development of themes but rather a continuous narrative with almost no repetition. The work makes enormous demands on players and singers alike, requiring virtuosity from all performers.

Listen out for: From the opening chords from full orchestra, the singing of 'Kyrie' by the chorus, this is an affirmative work. If faith is wrestling with doubt, then doubt is vanquished in the very first bar, and remains so till the end. Beethoven gives extraordinary colour to individual words, such as 'omnipotens' and 'descendit' in the Credo. And of all settings of the Mass, only Beethoven gives importance to the little word 'et'. Possibly the most beautiful passage comes in the Benedictus, in effect a full symphonic movement, when a solo violin, beginning in the high register, slowly descends. It was this intimate, ethereal passage that led to the censor's ban – the Holy Spirit depicted by an earthly violin!

At roughly an hour and a half in performance, the *Missa Solemnis* is the longest and most intense of all Beethoven's compositions (excepting *Fidelio* with which, as an opera, it cannot be compared). Its greatest accomplishment, in my view, is that it can be loved, admired and enjoyed by those of all faiths and none. That is surely what Beethoven intended.

The Piano Variations

The piano was Beethoven's instrument, so it is hardly surprising that he wrote more compositions for that particular instrument, in one form or another, than any other. The major form, of course, was the piano sonata but Beethoven also wrote numerous sets of piano variations and bagatelles, almost as though using the piano to relax.

Many individual pieces also merit a listen. 'The Rage over the Lost Penny' Op. 129 is clearly giving vent to a particular frustration, with a dash of humour thrown in. The *'Andante favori'* WoO 57, originally intended as the slow movement for Piano Sonata Op. 53, became so popular it acquired its enduring nickname. Beethoven complained he could hardly walk down the street without hearing it emanating from one front room or another.

There are rondos, allegrettos, waltzes and fugues. Beethoven gave opus numbers to three sets of bagatelles, but not – ironically – to the one that would become the single best known piece of music he would ever write, known by the dedication written at the top of the title page: 'Für Elise'.

If the Bagatelle was his second-best method of 'relaxing' at the piano, by far his favourite was taking a theme – not necessarily one of his own – and playing variations on it. The very first composition he published, at the age of twelve, was a set of variations. He produced no fewer than thirteen sets of piano variations before 1800, eleven of them based on operatic themes – none of which he considered worthy of an opus number.

There are fewer sets of piano variations after 1800, as Beethoven became more absorbed in other forms of composition, but two in particular rank among his most important works for piano.

Eroica Variations, Op. 53

Background: In 1802, when Beethoven was thirty-one years old, he spent six months in the village of Heiligenstadt, where he slowly came to terms with his deafness and where he wrote his Last Will and Testament. While there he put the finishing touches to the Second Symphony, composed a set of three piano sonatas (Op. 31), and wrote a set of piano variations (Op. 35).

That set of variations has a main theme with which Beethoven was obsessed. He used it first as a country dance, then as the finale of his ballet, *The Creatures of Prometheus*. It then formed the main theme for Op. 53, and Beethoven went on to use it as the main theme of the final movement of the Symphony No. 3, the 'Eroica'. Beethoven named the new composition *The Prometheus Variations*, though once the Symphony No. 3 was published, the name 'Eroica' was applied instead and thus it has remained.

Form: Beethoven wrote fifteen variations and a fugue on the theme but in a remarkable twist on the form he opens not with the main theme, but the bass line. He then presents three variations of this bass line, before finally – fully three minutes in – stating the main theme. Fifteen variations follow, with nearly all marked to be repeated, culminating in a mighty fugue.

Listen out for: Beethoven weaves musical miracles based on the simple 'Eroica' theme. Each variation is different, yet always the main theme is discernible. Variation 13 is nothing short of a series of discords – grace notes a semitone below the staccato quaver. Beethoven is pushing the boundaries of anything that has been heard before. You can almost see him smiling as he writes dissonances intended to shock the listener. In this set of variations he is palpably enjoying himself. The final variation, with its huge semidemisemiquaver runs, is a foretaste of the late piano sonatas to come.

And then comes the closing fugue, beginning with the same four base notes that opened the whole work. There follows a furious fugue, as if Beethoven were letting himself go – while never losing sight of the underlying theme, those four notes repeated in octave bass chords. As with the opening, it is some time before we hear the main theme. And as in the 'Eroica' Symphony, we hear variations and theme, rather than the conventional theme and variations.

This is Beethoven transforming what was conventionally known as the piano variation. I rate the *Eroica Variations* as one of his very best pieces for piano.

Diabelli Variations, Op. 120

Background: In March 1819 the music publisher Anton Diabelli asked fifty of Vienna's most prominent composers to provide a single variation each on a waltz he had himself composed. The timing for Beethoven could hardly have been worse. He was already working on the *Missa Solemnis* and he was embroiled in two court cases. He also felt insulted to have been treated by Diabelli on the same level as the other composers (Schubert and Franz Xaver Mozart, son of Wolfgang Amadeus, among them), considering himself to be superior to them all. Nevertheless he began work on a more extensive set of variations than Diabelli had asked for, only to put them aside and not look at them again for another four years.

Form: Having been asked for a single variation, Beethoven composed no fewer than thirty-three, composing his greatest, most wide-ranging set of piano variations. The opening waltz composed by Diabelli has been dismissed as trite and banal. In fact it is a lively waltz, with off-beat accents and changes of dynamics, the melody carried in the bass line, offering ample scope for variation. The thirty-three variations cover a multitude of forms, as with the *Eroica Variations* (almost) every variation containing passages to be repeated.

Listen out for: Diabelli's waltz is essentially upbeat and bright, and this characterises practically all the variations Beethoven writes. The first is a march, and the thirty-second variation is an extensive fugue. As with the *Eroica Variations* we expect this fugue to close the work. But Beethoven has a surprise for us. He adds a final variation, in the form of a simple minuet. It has almost an air of resignation about it. Beethoven marks it to be played softly, 'with grace and sweetness'. The closing passage of this final variation alternates between soft, very soft, and only occasionally loud. The penultimate chord is marked *pianissimo*. The final chord is loud. It is as if Beethoven is willing himself to stop. Thirty-three variations is enough! But he leaves us with the impression he could have written thirty-three more.

Diabelli had asked for a single variation on his little waltz. The other composers were happy to oblige. Beethoven, meanwhile, had always intended his composition to be a major set of variations. He did not change his mind in the years that he had set it aside. When he returned to it, he produced a piano masterpiece that stands alone among the twenty sets of variations he composed in his lifetime. It is described, along with J. S. Bach's *Goldberg Variations*, as one of the greatest sets of variations ever written for the piano.

The Piano Sonatas

As with the concerto, Beethoven wrote few sonatas for instruments other than the piano – twelve for violin, of which the mighty 'Kreutzer' and the lighter 'Spring' are the best known, five for cello, and one for horn. But his thirty-five sonatas for piano stand supreme as the greatest of their kind: they completely transformed the piano sonata post-Mozart. More than any other form, they chart Beethoven's life as a composer from his boyhood years until his death.

I like to refer to Beethoven's piano sonatas as his autobiography. There is documented evidence that, rather than get involved in intense discussion or debate, he would go to the piano to deliver his opinion on something, particularly once his deafness became acute. The piano was, in effect, his voice.

It is therefore not surprising that, of all the musical forms in which Beethoven composed, the piano sonata was the only one without a significant gap in composition. The first eight symphonies, for example, were composed in around thirteen years, there is then a gap of more than a decade before he composed the Ninth (even if sketches and ideas were noted earlier). The string quartets were composed in three distinct blocks, to the extent that they are known today as the Early, Middle and Late Quartets.

The piano sonatas, by contrast, encompass Beethoven's life. He wrote the first set of three, the 'Kurfürsten' Sonatas, when he was around twelve years old. He composed his final sonata five years before his death. There is no significant gap in the creation of the intervening thirty-one sonatas. Even in the most fallow creative period of his life, the draining four and a half years of the court case against his sister-in-law, he produced not just 'a' piano sonata but the longest, most complex one of his entire life: the 'Hammerklavier'.

In the piano sonatas Beethoven is telling us about his life. He tells us of his joy, his anger, his frustration, his passions, his pain, his triumph. The descent into deafness is there in the sonatas. Of all his compositions, none are as deeply personal. In these thirty-five works Beethoven bares his soul and tells us his story.

Thirty-five? If you have a set of Beethoven piano sonatas on CD, the likelihood is there are thirty-two. But I believe those three early piano sonatas, composed when he was just a boy, should be counted with those that followed. He may not have given them an opus number but (with his teacher Neefe's guidance) he had them published. Listen carefully and the seeds of the mature Beethoven are there.

Beethoven's piano sonatas hold a special place in his output. They are, in my view, his greatest achievement.

Piano Sonata No. 8, Op. 13, 'Pathétique'

Background: In 1798 Beethoven was twenty-seven years old. He had been in Vienna for five years and was establishing himself as a composer of formidable talent. He had written and performed two piano concertos and had composed a set of string quartets, as well as several other chamber works, including piano trios, string trios, cello sonatas, piano quintet, and sextet. He had also written seven piano sonatas, which he had performed in aristocratic salons to great acclaim.

Then came Piano Sonata No. 8, which really made his audiences sit up and listen, given the radically new elements it contained. Beethoven was, by this time, great friends with Andreas and Nanette Streicher, who ran a piano-building firm. They developed pianos specially to Beethoven's liking, as well as holding soirées at which he performed. We can be in no doubt that they built a stronger instrument, with wider keyboard, to accommodate the demands of this new piano sonata.

Form: For the first time by any composer, Beethoven began the first movement with a huge sustained chord, which he marked with the very unusual *fortepiano*. In bar 11, just before the first main theme which rushes upwards, he writes a huge downward run of semihemidemisemiquavers – rarely seen notes, which have five tails. The second movement is a gloriously perfect melody and the final movement is a Rondo, picking up a theme from the first movement.

Listen out for: From that massive opening chord, Beethoven takes us into new territory. The opening movement drives forward relentlessly, ending in a series of *fortissimo* chords. The second movement – used by American singer Billy Joel as the theme of his song 'This Night' – is placid and calming, so perfect that Beethoven simply states it, counter-states it, then restates it. It is as though it emerged from him fully formed, with none of the usual struggle we associate with Beethoven's music. The name 'Pathétique' was given to the work by the publisher, who found in it a mournful quality. Beethoven apparently approved.

Piano Sonata No. 14, Op. 27, No. 2, 'Moonlight'

Background: Beethoven composed a set of two piano sonatas – of which the second would become known as the 'Moonlight' Sonata – in 1801. It was a pivotal year for him. Aged thirty, he wrote in June of that year to his old childhood friend Franz Wegeler, by then a qualified doctor in Bonn, that he was having trouble with his hearing. He had fallen in love with one of his pupils, Countess Giulietta Guicciardi, telling Wegeler in the same letter of 'a dear charming girl who loves me and whom I love', and he made a last-minute decision to dedicate the 'Sonata Quasi Una Fantasia' (the name the 'Moonlight' was published under) to Giulietta.

Form: The sonata consists of three movements but Beethoven subverts – and revolutionises – the form by placing the slow movement first. It is this movement that will later give the sonata its name, when a critic described it as being 'like the moon setting over Lake Lucerne'. It consists almost entirely of triplets in the right hand and sustained chords in the left. The dynamic marking is never louder than *piano*. The second movement is a bridge to a furious third movement, which takes the opening triplets and transforms them into stormy semiquaver runs.

Listen out for: The first movement is the best known of Beethoven's piano sonatas, largely thanks to music critic Ludwig Rellstab's description, made some years after Beethoven's death. There is thus no reason to believe Beethoven had any thought of moonlight when he was composing it. It is, however, a perfect depiction of stillness in the night: his direction to hold the sustaining pedal down creates a certain blur of sound, which had never been heard before in this form.

The opening movement became instantly popular in Beethoven's day and has remained so ever since. Its universal popularity rather irritated Beethoven. 'Surely I have written better things,' he said to his pupil Carl Czerny.

Piano Sonata No. 21, Op. 53, 'Waldstein'

Background: On his return from Heiligenstadt in autumn 1802, Beethoven launched himself into furious composition. The most ambitious of the pieces he brought to fruition was the 'Eroica' Symphony, which has led to this stage in Beethoven's life being called his 'heroic period'. Several more works were published in 1803 and in the following year he began work on the Fifth Symphony and the Fourth Piano Concerto. He continued to produce piano sonatas though. At the end of 1803 he composed a new piano sonata, named for and dedicated to Count Waldstein, who had done so much to help and encourage him in his early years in Bonn. With its brightness and memorable themes, the 'Waldstein' Sonata became instantly popular, and remains so to this day.

Form: Three movements, with no break between the second and third. Beethoven begins the sonata in a way that was totally different to anything that had gone before: furiously fast block chords, which yield to juxtaposed semiquaver runs in both hands. Block chords return and form the essential character of the first movement. The original second movement was deemed by Beethoven to be too weighty, so he hived it off and published it separately – it was to become the enormously popular *Andante Favori*. He replaced it with a shorter movement, almost ghostly in the way it leads directly into the final movement, which by contrast is bright and airy, with a gloriously memorable and soaring main theme.

Listen out for: Although the opening of the sonata is fast and furious, Beethoven marks it to be played *pianissimo*. The virtuosity demanded of the performer is made all the more difficult by the need to play the chords as quietly as possible – Beethoven once more subverting normal practice. The replacement second movement is cleverly calculated to create a feeling approaching bewilderment. Where is this going? After the *fortissimo* chords at the end of the first movement, we are back in *pianissimo* territory, with little coordination between left and right hands and the emphasis off the beat. Stability returns with the third movement, its 'airborne' theme soaring above semiquaver broken chords. Beethoven achieves an especially ethereal effect by having the main theme in the left hand but played with hands crossed over. Again he marks this *pianissimo*. An extraordinary piano sonata, in that it creates enormous difficulties for the pianist to play as Beethoven wanted, yet provides the listener with a work of exquisite, almost unearthly, beauty. By virtue of this sonata alone, Count Waldstein is assured of immortality.

Piano Sonata No. 23, Op. 57, 'Appassionata'

Background: Within a year or so of composing the 'Waldstein' Piano Sonata, Beethoven set about composing the largest and most complex piano sonata he had yet produced. The name 'Appassionata' was ascribed to it some years after Beethoven's death but we can imagine he would have approved, since he himself described it as the most 'tempestuous' of his piano sonatas, at least until the 'Hammerklavier' of a decade or so later. Beethoven was enormously busy while composing the 'Appassionata', bringing the 'Eroica' before the public for the first time and preparing his opera *Leonore* for its first (unsuccessful) performance.

Form: Composed in the conventional three-movement format, but there is nothing conventional about it. The *pianissimo* descending phrase of the opening of the first movement gives no hint of the turbulence to come. The movement's main theme rises from the depths – which reportedly made this Richard Wagner's favourite Beethoven piano sonata – and, with sudden changes between *pianissimo*, *fortissimo*, even *sforzando*, gives the movement an essential driving quality. The second movement brings some peace, with almost hymn-like block chords. This leads, via two sustained chords (one *pianissimo*, the next *fortissimo*!), into a driving final movement in which the turmoil returns, and remains unresolved.

Listen out for: The 'Appassionata' demands greater virtuosity from the pianist than any of his previous sonatas. But – and this is the genius of Beethoven – that does not make it in any way inaccessible, or even difficult, for the listener. That rising, turning theme of the first movement is immediately beguiling, demanding attention and carrying you along with every note. It is Beethoven's clear intention in the second movement to restore some calm and stability, with the chords regular and on the beat. But even here he marks one chord *fortepiano*, unusually. The chords soon yield, though, to semiquavers and demisemiquavers, presaging the turbulence that follows, without a break, in the third movement. The latter moves at a frenetic pace, with furious movement in both hands. That ascending and descending theme of the first movement has been deconstructed. A brief period of calm intersects the movement, but it does not last. Ultimately there is no relief from what could almost be described as a sense of desolation. Suddenly, when you expect the movement to continue, Beethoven brings it – and the work – to an end with two final chords. Yet the listener is left with a feeling of accomplishment and triumph, which to me is the essence of Beethoven's compositions.

Piano Sonata No. 26, Op. 81a, 'Das Lebewohl' / 'Les adieux'

Background: This piano sonata is unique in Beethoven's sonata output in that he gave it a title telling us exactly what it was intended to represent, as well as titles for each movement explaining their purpose. It stands alone with the 'Pastoral' Symphony in this respect, which also has representative headings for each movement. In 1809 Archduke Rudolph, youngest brother of the emperor and Beethoven's most loyal and generous patron, was forced to flee from Vienna, along with the royal family, in the face of the advancing French army under Napoleon. Beethoven dedicated the work to the Archduke, with the first movement marked 'Das Lebewohl' ('The Farewell'), the second 'Abwesenheit' ('Absence'), the third 'Das Wiedersehen' ('The Return'). The publisher gave it a French title, 'Les adieux', which Beethoven disliked.

Form: The sonata is in the conventional three movements, but with the second and third running together, as was customary for Beethoven by this stage in his output. Unlike any other piano sonata – or indeed any other composition barring the 'Pastoral' Symphony – the mood he creates specifically matches the headings given to each movement.

Listen out for: The first movement, 'Das Lebewohl', begins with a three-chord descending motif, above which Beethoven writes

'Le – be wohl!', so we can be in no doubt as to his intention. This aching motif leads into a brief quiet passage, before exploding into what can only be described as uncontrolled sadness. The three-chord motif reappears throughout the movement. Extreme quietness in the closing bars is interrupted by two *forte* chords, as though expressing anger at being unable to prevent the Archduke's departure. The relatively short second movement, 'Abwesenheit', is full of pain, even despair. A fragmented introduction leads into a sorrowful main theme that has no resolution until the final movement, which explodes with joy. Beethoven gives this movement the highly unusual marking of '*Vivacissimamente*'. However lively '*Vivace*' might be, this is altogether on a different level. For the avoidance of doubt, he adds: '*Im lebhaftesten Zeitmasse*' ('in the liveliest time measurements'). Beethoven rarely gives such detailed instruction. This is truly a movement of unconfined joy, demanding the utmost technical virtuosity from the performer.

Beethoven kept his promise to Archduke Rudolph to compose only the first movement before the Archduke's departure, the second during his absence, the third once he was safely back in Vienna. Without doubt this enhanced the emotional integrity of each movement. Archduke Rudolph returned after an absence of eight months. It was not unusual for Beethoven to set aside a work during its composition, but never before (or after) was that dictated by external events.

Piano Sonata No. 29, 'Hammerklavier'

Background: The 'Hammerklavier' is the longest, most complex piano sonata Beethoven wrote, using more keys than any other piano composition before it. It is the sole work of importance he composed during the dreadful and taxing four-and-a-half-year court battle against his sister-in-law Johanna for custody of her son Karl, his nephew. It launched Beethoven into his 'Late Period', when his compositions became more complex, more deeply personal, literally more inexplicable. He had begun work on a new piano sonata in 1817 and was undoubtedly inspired by the arrival of a gift: a new piano from John Broadwood & Sons of London. The heavier English action suited – and may well have encouraged – the tempestuous nature of the new sonata, particularly its *fortissimo* opening. Beethoven himself gave the sonata the name 'Hammerklavier' but it is hardly descriptive (unlike *Das Lebewohl*), meaning simply 'hammer-keyboard'.

Form: Unusually for Beethoven the sonata is in four movements: three huge outer movements, with a short *Scherzo* as the second movement. The final movement is preceded by an introduction. At a late stage, following publication in Vienna and just before it was published in London, Beethoven added a single opening bar of two rising dotted crotchet octave chords to the slow movement: musical pillars to balance the huge *adagio* that follows. He gives unusually explicit instructions for how it should be played: *Appassionata e con molto sentimento* (passionately and with much feeling).

Listen out for: We are straight into turbulence in the opening bars. At Beethoven's metronome marking, the two-octave leap in the left hand at the very start is almost physically impossible – it was considered so in his day. By bar 34 we are in new territory: Beethoven uses the extremes of the keyboard, with notes more than four octaves apart. The pianist's hands are as far apart as they can be. The *fortissimo* chords that form the two-bar opening dominate the movement. Beethoven composed the work for Archduke Rudolph's name-day and this almost fanfare-like opening could be described as a birthday greeting, though that seems rather a pedestrian characterisation given the complex development that follows. At times the chords seem to 'splash' onto the keys, with intentional discords. One can imagine Beethoven playing with abandon as he pushes the boundaries of what has gone before. The relatively brief *Scherzo* seems almost like light relief with its 'skipping' rhythm, but moves into more shadowy territory with a theme that echoes the opening movement of the 'Eroica' Symphony, albeit inverted. It ends suddenly, leading directly into the huge, almost painfully emotional slow movement, beginning with that extra bar Beethoven added later. It is the longest, most intense, slow movement of any of his piano sonatas. This is Beethoven pouring out his heart. A slow connecting section of huge semiquaver and demisemiquaver chords and runs leads into the final movement, *pianissimo* trills and a *fortissimo* run beginning the greatest fugue Beethoven would ever write for his instrument.

The 'Hammerklavier' was immediately recognised as – and remains – the summit of works for solo piano, influencing all the great composers who followed, from Liszt and Chopin to Schumann and Brahms.

Piano Sonata No. 30, Op. 109

Background: Beethoven's last three piano sonatas, Opp. 109, 110 and 111 (neither Beethoven nor his publisher gave names to any of them) were composed within a short period of eighteen months to two years. Today virtuoso pianists nearly always record all three together. This is understandable, not simply because they were composed so closely in time, but because they represent the most intimate of Beethoven's compositions for solo piano. The publisher Adolf Schlesinger asked Beethoven for a set of three piano sonatas, and Beethoven agreed to write them. Opus 109 was begun in the aftermath of the Court of Appeal ruling that finally gave Beethoven guardianship of his nephew Karl.

Form: The sonata is in three movements, but Beethoven now begins to break down the conventional division between movements. It could just as easily be described as being in two movements, with the first flowing directly into the second. The third movement is by far the most expansive, comprising a theme and six variations.

Listen out for: Beethoven himself wrote in a conversation book that he was working on a 'small new piece'. Certainly the first movement is like a one-sided conversation – and we feel we are arriving in the middle of it, almost as though Beethoven were in mid-sentence. There are huge demisemiquaver runs, unusual dynamic markings of *fp*, and *piano* diminishing to sudden *fortissimo* in the space of two semiquavers. This is Beethoven using the piano as his voice. The second movement continues the conversation, with evident moments of frustration – as though the composer was irritated at having to repeat himself. And then the beautiful third movement, in which he has regained his composure. A simple theme opens it, which Beethoven explores in different ways with each variation. The first variation, played an octave higher, is redolent with warmth and emotion. The second is more fragmented, recalling the opening of the first movement. In variation three Beethoven seems to liberate himself, the words pouring from his mouth – it is the only variation to end loudly, as if emphatically making his point. The fourth variation is slower and quieter, and in the unusual time signature of 9/8. With the fifth we are back to Beethoven in determined mood, while the sixth is Beethoven composing almost in free form. Bar divisions serve no purpose; they almost get in the way. Marked '*cantabile*', the movement ends with the original theme but, as at the beginning of the whole work, it seems almost to be cut off.

At the end it feels as though Beethoven is still talking. It is we who have chosen to walk away. With this sonata Beethoven has begun the process of speaking to us of his innermost thoughts. This will continue with the remaining two piano sonatas – and, most conspicuously of all – in the Late String Quartets still to come.

Piano Sonata No. 31, Op. 110

Background: Beethoven composed the middle piano sonata of the final set of three in the spring and summer of 1821, at a time when it is hard to believe he was able to compose anything at all. He fell ill towards the end of the previous year; barely recovered he then contracted rheumatic fever and spent six weeks confined to his bed in January and February. At the end of March he learned that his former pupil Josephine Brunsvik, the woman to whom he had at one time written passionate letters of love, had died after a long illness. Barely had he started work on the new piano sonata when he was once again taken ill, this time with jaundice. By autumn, he had been quite seriously ill for much of the year. Small wonder that the new sonata was not completed until December.

Form: As with the other two sonatas of this final set, it is almost irrelevant to talk of movements. Technically this is in three movements but there is only a single break, between the first and second. The long final movement consists of two slow linking passages, each followed by a fugue. This is the heart of the sonata.

Listen out for: It is quite extraordinary, given his ill health and emotional strain, that the opening movement of this piano sonata is so full of warmth and optimism. But this does not endure.

After a fleeting second movement the mood changes. Beethoven writes on the score '*Arioso dolente*' and '*klagender gesang*' ('doleful song' in Italian and German). The first time it leads into a fugue, which is then cut off by its return. After sounding this mournful passage (one of the saddest themes he wrote) for a second time, Beethoven produces a chord repeated nine times, getting gradually louder with each repeat. He then launches into a large, complex double fugue – the only such fugue he would write for piano. At the end it becomes almost a 'splash' of sound. Sadness has become triumph. I read this extraordinary final movement as Beethoven telling us about his deafness and the pain it has caused him. This is the *klagender gesang*. But he interrupts it, breaking it off in mid-flow. Those chords symbolise his resolute determination not to allow deafness to overwhelm him, to force him to abandon the only occupation he is capable of pursuing – music.

This piano sonata, I believe, is Beethoven truly using the piano as his voice. It is his legacy to us. 'You want to know how deeply deafness affected me, and how I was able to overcome it? Then listen to this piece.' And from that I extrapolate that he is sending us a message of hope, of optimism. On a very personal level, the Piano Sonata Opus 110 remains my single favourite piece of Beethoven's music, the one I turn to more than any other.

Piano Sonata No. 32, Op. 111

Background: No sooner had Beethoven completed the previous piano sonata than he began work on the next. It would be his last. In January 1822 he was once again seriously ill, with what was described as 'gout in the chest'. This time he did not allow illness to interrupt composition. In February he sent the completed sonata, and the one before it, to his publisher. Maybe he knew he had been too hasty. He immediately revised the finale of Op. 111 and sent the revised version to Schlesinger in early April. It would be another year before the sonata was published, by which time he was working intensively on the Ninth Symphony.

Form: The work consists of two movements, the first relatively short, the second more than double the length. This led to much speculation in Beethoven's time as to why he did not write a third movement, as was normal. 'I did not have time,' he replied, almost certainly facetiously. Today the work is seen as perfectly balanced. The turbulent first movement has been described as portraying life's hard struggle; the second represents the transcendental, in which details have become unimportant.

Listen out for: If the first movement depicts struggle, this is evident from the very opening chord, *forte* and *sforzando*, leading to *piano*. The opening is disjointed, with no clear rhythm. We have no idea what to expect. A deep rumble in the bass leads into a passage of furious activity, which scarcely relents throughout the whole movement. By total contrast, the second movement begins with a gentle theme, played softly, followed by five variations and a final coda. In this movement, the last Beethoven would write for solo piano, it is as though he has abandoned all rules; he is composing almost in free form. The opening theme is simple enough, no more than a statement mostly in chords. Its descending motif has a finality about it, as if Beethoven somehow knew this would be his last statement. He then proceeds to deconstruct, reconstruct, unpick and rebuild the theme in ways that no other composer could have contemplated.

In the third variation he produces syncopated rhythm that is pure jazz – though jazz itself would not be born for seventy or more years. Today's virtuosos have described it as boogie-woogie and ragtime, and that is accurate. Beethoven has taken music into the twentieth century. The final coda is redolent with high trills, testing the performer to the limit, the theme sounding in the bass register. For the listener this is piano music unlike any that had hitherto been written. After pages of demisemiquaver runs in both hands, suddenly the sonata ends with soft chords, diminishing to a pianissimo final bar. Beethoven composed thirty-five piano sonatas throughout his lifetime, and he has surprised us right to the very last note.

The String Quartets

In all Beethoven wrote sixteen string quartets, and he composed them, broadly, in three fairly distinct blocks, so that they are conveniently referred to today as his Early, Middle and Late Quartets. If Haydn is known as the 'father' of the string quartet, and Mozart took the form to new heights, Beethoven – characteristically – completely transformed it.

He was a slow starter. In fact he composed the Early Quartets, a set of six, when he was around twenty-seven to thirty years of age, but after he sent them to a friend, he then wrote to him to ask for them back, since he had 'only now' learned how to write quartets properly! These early quartets are anything but lightweight – Beethoven himself named the fourth movement of No. 6 *La Malinconia* (Melancholy). Already we have portents of what is to come many years later.

The Middle Quartets, composed when Beethoven was between thirty-five and forty years old, are made up of three Razumovsky Quartets (commissioned by the Russian ambassador in Vienna), the *Harp* (because of the plucked strings in the first movement), and the *Serioso* (named thus by Beethoven on the manuscript). The first of the Razumovskys is relatively light and instantly accessible. The first movement begins with a wonderfully lively melody, and the second movement opens with a single note repeated so often on the cello that cellists of the day thought Beethoven was playing a joke on them and refused to play it!

Aware that his health was failing, his deafness total, at odds with his nephew, drained physically and emotionally, Beethoven retreated into himself. The Late Quartets – five in all and unnamed except for opus numbers – are the most profound compositions of his entire life.

For the last two years of his life, as far as major works were concerned, he concentrated exclusively on the string quartet. With his deafness now total, it was as if he knew that this form alone was left to him, and those five quartets therefore represent his final, and deepest, pronouncements. In intensity and complexity they stand alone.

String Quartet No. 12, Op. 127

Background: When Beethoven decided to write a string quartet in 1824, it had been more than a decade since he had last composed in such a form (the last of his Middle Quartets, the *Serioso*). There were two major factors behind his return to the string quartet. He had just premiered his Ninth Symphony, a bruising experience in which his deafness had prevented him from hearing his greatest orchestral triumph, and he needed the intimacy of the quartet. No need for audience approval; this was Beethoven in conversation, essentially, with himself. The second, more practical reason, was that a Russian nobleman, Prince Galitzin, had written to him from St Petersburg asking him to compose up to three string quartets, and to name his price. Not for the first time in his career, an idea of his own was given life by the coincidence of a commission and the opportunity to earn money. Three of his late quartets were composed for the Prince, Opp. 127, 132 and 130. The final two, Opp. 131 and 135, were written to no commission.

Form: This quartet consists of four movements, but Beethoven had initially planned two additional movements: one between the first and second, and another between the third and fourth – a sign that, as with the late piano sonatas, the traditional three- or four-movement work had essentially become a thing of the past.

Listen out for: There is something of a grand opening to this quartet, marked *maestoso*, but Beethoven soon moves into more intimate territory. By far the longest movement is the second, which Beethoven marks to be played in a singing manner. It consists of six variations and a coda, a form which Beethoven has used in his late piano sonatas. There are many *pianissimo* passages; turbulence, when it is there, gives way to quieter utterances. Beethoven is clearly satisfied with the result, even if neither the players nor the audience were pleased with the first performance.

String Quartet No. 13, Op. 130

Background: This is the third of the quartets commissioned by Prince Galitzin. As I have said, the Late Quartets are Beethoven at his most intimate, describing his life to us – and how full of pain it is. This quartet he began to write almost as soon as he had completed the 'Heiliger Dankgesang' of the previous one. Still recovering, he is burdened with responsibility for his nephew Karl, following that tortuous court case. The self-inflicted turmoil he feels, and the irrational behaviour of which he must have been aware, inform this work from start to finish.

Form: This quartet consists of no fewer than six movements. No composer had written a string quartet with six movements before, but why should that stop him? The quartet takes around forty-five minutes to perform. The two dominant movements are the fifth, the *Cavatina*, and the sixth, the *Grosse Fuge*.

Listen out for: The tone of the whole work is set with a portentous opening, played *piano*. We are in mysterious uncharted territory from the opening bars. An *Allegro* follows, but is never allowed to introduce 'lightness'. The alternation between these two contrasting ideas forms the bulk of the movement. A brief and swift *Presto* leads into a movement that is almost in free form, dominated by melancholic *piano* and *pianissimo* passages. The mood lifts – slightly – for a German dance. The fifth movement is one of the most extraordinary pieces of writing in all Beethoven's works. Although the title, *Cavatina*, suggests a short simple song, it is redolent with pain and sadness. A rising interval of a seventh is balanced by falling intervals of a fifth and a sixth. Then, in a remarkable passage, above which Beethoven writes '*Beklemmt*' ('anxious' or 'oppressed' – no single-word translation is adequate), the first violin 'weeps'. It makes fragmented sounds, musical sobs. Beethoven is baring his soul as he has never done before. Small wonder that he later wrote that he had shed tears writing the *Cavatina*. We hear them. The final movement, marked *Grosse Fuge*, is Beethoven pulling himself together, sheer defiance from beginning to end. It is a long piece, around twenty minutes, a furious fugue in which there is no respite from first note to last. The virtuosity demanded of the players is beyond anything anyone had written before. Similarly the demands on the audience are heavy and the effect draining. It is hardly surprising Beethoven agreed to suggestions that he should hive the movement off and publish it separately. The replacement final movement, written a year later, after his nephew's attempted suicide and amid his own terminally failing health, is remarkably lightweight, at least when compared to the *Grosse Fuge*. That is Beethoven – always ready to confound expectations. The replacement final movement is the last complete piece of music he would write.

String Quartet No. 14, Op. 131

Background: Beethoven began work on what is considered to be the greatest of all his string quartets in December 1825, having just moved into a new apartment in Vienna, which would be his last. No sooner had he begun than he fell ill with eye and abdominal complaints. His worries over his nephew Karl – who had announced his intention to join the military – had worsened inexorably. He was arguing with performers and publishers about his two previous string quartets: all wanted changes. In the midst of this, the unthinkable occurred. Karl attempted suicide by shooting himself in the head. With all this strife in Beethoven's life, it is extraordinary that he was able to compose at all, yet this work is musically the most complex of all his late quartets.

Form: Beethoven now abandons convention altogether. This string quartet consists of seven movements, played without a break. Which is to say it consists of a single movement. Either description is correct.

Listen out for: The first movement is redolent with melancholy, Richard Wagner calling it 'the most melancholy sentiment expressed in music'. The mood lifts slightly in the second, with an almost cheerful turning phrase, but you are aware the melancholy is never far away. A very short introduction leads to the central movement, a set of variations on a simple theme shared by first and second violins over *pizzicato* in the cello. The variations cover a variety of moods ranging from sadness to exuberance (almost). Joy is never unconfined in any single passage of the late quartets. Beethoven uses runs in the deep register of the cello to remind us that serious matters are here to intrude on any happiness we may feel. Even the *Presto*, which follows the variations, and which seems at first to take flight, remains anchored. In one extraordinary passage, Beethoven has all four instruments playing in the high register on the bridge – an eerie sound unheard before. Was Beethoven, now profoundly deaf, remembering something he had heard many years before, or was he inventing a new sound? We return to an echo of the sombre opening as Beethoven leads us, via a gentle introduction, into a swift final movement. Here he alternates a subject consisting of a violent rhythm with a contrasting lyrical second theme. Beethoven has, once again, poured his heart out to us, with his private life in turmoil and his health failing. Other composers recognised the greatness of this work. Schubert, after hearing a performance, is said to have remarked, 'After this, what is there left for us to write?' Schumann said of this work and Op. 127 that they had 'a grandeur which no words can express . . . standing on the extreme boundary of all that has hitherto been attained by human art and imagination.'

String Quartet No. 15, Op. 132

Background: Beethoven began writing this string quartet, actually the thirteenth in order of composition, towards the end of 1824. In mid April of the following year he fell very seriously ill. It was a recurrence of the abdominal complaint that had plagued him the previous winter. This time he was so severely debilitated, and the abdominal pain so severe, that he feared he would die. Although he had begun work on the quartet before his condition became severe, and was to continue composition after his recovery, the whole work needs to be listened to with this sharp decline in his health in mind – in particular, for obvious reasons, the huge slow movement – and his unexpected recovery.

Form: Again, in this quartet, Beethoven blurs the line between movements. The third movement, marked *Molto adagio – Andante*, dominates the work. The brief fourth movement leads directly into the fifth. Five movements in a string quartet is unheard of, even from Beethoven. The whole work can run to forty minutes or more, the duration of a (lengthy) symphony.

Listen out for: The opening of the first movement consists of *pianissimo* block chords, giving no intimation of the *Allegro* which will soon follow. As has now become customary with Beethoven and the string quartet, there are no longer rules; surprises exist at every turn. The centrepiece of the work is the huge slow movement, around twenty minutes in length – the length of an entire string quartet by Haydn or Mozart. Here Beethoven tells us exactly what he is expressing, and how it should be played. At the top of the movement he writes: '*Heiliger Dankgesang eines Genesenen an die Gottheit, in der lydischen Tonart*' ('Holy song of thanksgiving from a convalescent to the deity, in the Lydian mode'). This is Beethoven expressing thanks to a divine being for allowing him to recover from an illness that he feared would kill him. The use of *Gottheit* rather than the plainer *Gott* shows, I believe, a spirituality rather than a religious attachment. The Lydian mode refers to a medieval style of organ playing, using block chords. The opening bars of this movement have the four strings playing chords without *vibrato*, reproducing the sound of an organ. When the livelier *Andante* begins, Beethoven writes '*Neue Kraft fühlend*' ('Feeling new strength'). The only other times in his entire output that Beethoven tells us what his music represents are in the movement headings for his 'Pastoral' Symphony, but there he is describing scenes, and in the *Lebewohl* Piano Sonata, depicting activity. This is altogether more personal and ethereal – he is asking us to try to imagine his feelings. Towards the end of this huge movement, with the return of the Lydian mode, albeit varied this time, he writes twice in the space of three bars '*Mit innigster Empfindung*' ('With innermost feeling'). This is Beethoven truly baring his soul, confiding his innermost emotions to us. A change of mood and the brief *Alla Marcia* leads into a passionate finale. Against even his expectations, Beethoven has recovered his health, and celebrates it in music.

String Quartet No. 16, Op. 135

Background: In the aftermath of Karl's attempted suicide, and with his own health failing, Beethoven began work on a new string quartet. Having begun it, he left for his brother's house in Gneixendorf, west of Vienna, taking Karl with him to recuperate from the head wound he had suffered. You would expect the new composition, therefore, to be even more intense, more deeply emotional, than the one he had only recently finished. But this string quartet is almost light in character, certainly when compared to its predecessors. It is especially unexpected given that, as soon as he arrived in Gneixendorf, he seemed to be arguing constantly with his brother, he did not get on with his sister-in-law, and Karl remained a constant source of worry.

Form: The surprise does not end with the relative lightness of the piece. After composing string quartets in six and seven movements, or one single monumental movement, Beethoven now reverts to the traditional four movements. It is as though, knowing he has gone as far as it is humanly possible for a composer to go, he returns to safer territory.

Listen out for: A quizzical opening to the first movement leads into a passage that borders on the joyful. This is an entirely different Beethoven to the composer of the preceding four Late Quartets. You would (almost) be tempted to believe he is enjoying a relaxed period in his life. In fact his health is worsening daily, and he is only months away from the end. The second movement he marks *Vivace* and it has a carefree feel to it, in direct contradiction to the turmoil in his life. The third movement, the slow movement, Beethoven marks '*Lento assai, cantante e tranquillo*' ('Fairly slowly, in a singing and tranquil way'). This opens with a truly beautiful turning theme. It is possible to read sadness into it, but I prefer to think of Beethoven seeking refuge in music. Here he is almost accepting his fate. He must know he will not live for much longer, and that his life's work is done. This movement shows us that Beethoven, even as the end approaches, can still produce music of divine beauty. Nothing earthly, nothing that life can throw at him, not even his deafness, can prevent him creating everlasting art. But Beethoven is not finished yet. For reasons only he knows, he writes above the final movement '*DER SCHWER GEFASSTE ENTSCHLUSS*' ('the most difficult decision'). And then underneath the opening notes he writes '*Muss es sein? . . . Es muss sein! . . . Es muss sein!*' ('Must it be? . . . It must be! . . . It must be!'). What was the decision? What must be? The music soon breaks away from its portentous opening to bask, it seems, in contentment. It offers no answer.

That is Beethoven: contradictory, enigmatic, and the creator – in my opinion – of the greatest body of music ever written.

Cast of Characters

Arnim, Bettina, *née* Brentano (1785—1859). Half-sister of Franz Brentano, she had met Goethe several times. She sent Beethoven's score of *Egmont* to him and set up a meeting between the two in Bohemia in 1812.

Beethoven, Caspar Carl van (1774–1815). Elder of Beethoven's two younger brothers. Followed Ludwig to Vienna in 1794. Tried to earn a living teaching music, but eventually took a job as a clerk in the Finance Department of the Hofburg Palace.

Beethoven, Johann van (c.1740–92). Beethoven's father. Tenor at the Electoral court at Bonn, but failed to succeed his father as *Kapellmeister*. Became an alcoholic and was dismissed from court service in 1789.

Beethoven, Ludwig van (1712–73). Beethoven's beloved grandfather. Born in Mechelen (Malines), Flanders. As a bass singer he moved to Bonn in 1733 where he became *Kapellmeister* in 1761. Beethoven was only three when he died, but remained devoted to him for the rest of his life.

Beethoven, Maria Magdalena van (1746–87). Beethoven's mother. Her first husband died soon after the wedding and the child she bore him died in infancy. She married Johann van Beethoven on 12 November 1767. Three of their children survived into adulthood. She died of consumption at the age of forty.

Beethoven, Nikolaus Johann van (1776–1848). Beethoven's youngest brother. Trained as a pharmacist in Bonn. Followed Beethoven to Vienna in 1795, where he worked as a pharmacist's assistant. In March 1808 he bought an apothecary shop in Linz in Upper Austria.

Bonaparte, Jérôme (1784–1860). Younger brother of Napoleon, who appointed him King of Westphalia. In 1808 he invited Beethoven to become *Kapellmeister* in the capital Kassel.

Bonaparte, Napoleon (1769–1821). French First Consul and later Emperor. Beethoven's initial admiration for Bonaparte's rise from humble origins and belief in equality for all led to his dedication of the *Eroica* Symphony to him. But when Napoleon crowned himself Emperor, Beethoven angrily withdrew the dedication.

Braun, Baron Peter von (1758–1819). Director of the Imperial Court Theatres. In 1804 he purchased the Theater an der Wien, ending Beethoven's contract there, but making the theatre available for his opera *Leonore* in 1806. Baron von Hartl became Director in 1807 and angered Beethoven by repeatedly postponing his promised benefit concert.

Braunhofer, Dr Anton. Physician who attended Beethoven during the last years of his life, after the rupture in relations with Dr Malfatti.

Brentano, Antonie, *née* Birkenstock (1780–1869). Undoubtedly the great love of Beethoven's life. Born in Vienna, she married Franz Brentano in 1798 and reluctantly moved with him to Frankfurt. The relationship with Beethoven developed when she returned to her native city in 1809 on learning that her father was dying. She stayed for three years, selling her father's huge collection of antiquities, and in 1812 travelled with her husband and youngest daughter to Prague and Bohemia. The dates and locations make her a candidate for identification as the Immortal Beloved.

Breuning, Eleonore von (1771–1841). Daughter of Helene. Childhood friend of Beethoven's in Bonn. He taught her piano. She married Franz Gerhard Wegeler in 1802.

Breuning, Gerhard von (1813–92). Son of Beethoven's lifelong friend Stephan von Breuning by his second marriage. As a young teenager Gerhard became close to Beethoven during his final illness. Beethoven nicknamed him '*Hosenknopf*', 'Trouser Button'. In adulthood he qualified as a doctor.

Breuning, Helene von (1750–1838). Head of one of Bonn's most prominent families, after her husband died in the palace fire of 1777. Made her house and piano available to young Ludwig and employed him to teach piano to two of her children.

Breuning, Stephan von (1774–1827). Beethoven's closest friend in Bonn, a friendship which was renewed in Vienna when Stephan moved there. Outside musical circles, Stephan remained Beethoven's closest friend – with periodic interruptions caused by arguments – for the whole of Beethoven's life. Stephan at first worked for the Teutonic Order, then as an official in the War Department at the Hofburg Palace.

Bridgetower, George Augustus Polgreen (1779–1860). Violinist, son of an African father and Polish mother who settled in London. His virtuosity brought him to the attention of the Prince of Wales, who retained him. He came to Vienna in 1803 and Beethoven composed the famous Violin Sonata Op. 47 (later known as the *Kreutzer*) for him, and gave its first performance with him.

Broadwood, Thomas. Member of the British family of piano-makers. He met Beethoven in Vienna and sent the composer a magnificent six-octave instrument with the heavier British action, which suited his playing. The piano undoubtedly provided inspiration for the most monumental of all Beethoven's piano sonatas, the *Hammerklavier* Op. 106.

Czerny, Carl (1791–1857). Taken on as a pupil by Beethoven in 1801, later becoming close to him. He was renowned for his intimate knowledge of Beethoven's piano works, particularly the sonatas, and his ability to play them as Beethoven had instructed.

Deym, Countess Josephine, *née* Brunsvik (1799–1821). A member of the Hungarian Brunsvik family. Beethoven fell in love with her, composing the song *An die Hoffnung* for her, but she rejected him. Widowed in 1804, she then married her children's tutor, Count von Stackelberg, in 1810. A candidate for identification as the Immortal Beloved.

Dragonetti, Domenico (1763–1846). Italian virtuoso double-bass player. Made Beethoven aware of the potential of the double-bass when he performed one of Beethoven's Cello Sonatas on it, accompanied by the composer. The result was a more important role for the instrument in Beethoven's symphonies (particularly in nos 3, 5 and 9) than any other composer had hitherto given it.

Galitzin, Prince Nikolas Borisovich (1794–1866). Russian prince and great admirer of Beethoven's music. He commissioned three string quartets from the composer, which became Opp. 127, 130 and 132, and together with Opp. 131 and 135 form the Late Quartets.

Gleichenstein, Ignaz (1778–1828). A native of Freiburg on the Upper Rhine, he took over the handling of Beethoven's financial affairs after Ferdinand Ries left Vienna. In 1811 he married Anna Malfatti, younger sister of Therese.

Glöggl, Franz Xaver (1764–1839). *Kapellmeister* in Linz. During Beethoven's fraught visit to his brother Johann in Linz in 1812, Glöggl became well acquainted with him and asked him to compose a set of *Equali* for trombones.

Goethe, Johann Wolfgang von (1749–1832). Germany's greatest poet and playwright. Beethoven set many of his poems and texts to music, the best known being the incidental music to *Count Egmont*. The two met only once, in Teplitz in July 1812, and the relationship was uneasy. Beethoven felt Goethe was in thrall to the Imperial Court; Goethe wrote to his wife that Beethoven was 'an absolutely untamed personality'. In later years Beethoven tried to rekindle the relationship, but Goethe did not respond.

Grillparzer, Franz (1791–1872). As a boy he met Beethoven in Heiligenstadt in the summer of 1808, and was destined to become Austria's greatest playwright.

Guicciardi, Countess Giulietta (1784–1856). Pupil of Beethoven with whom he fell in love and intended marrying. He composed the 'Moonlight' Sonata for her and dedicated it to her. In 1803 she married Count Gallenberg.

Haydn, Joseph (1732–1809). Beethoven first met Haydn in Bonn, when Haydn was on his way to England. Generally regarded as Europe's greatest living composer after Mozart's death, Haydn agreed to take on the young Beethoven as a pupil on his return to Vienna. Relations between the two were variable. Haydn criticised the Op. 1 Piano Trios, which angered Beethoven, but Beethoven dedicated the three Piano Sonatas Op. 2 to Haydn, and always held him in high regard.

Holz, Karl (1798–1868). Government official and accomplished violinist, often playing second violin in Schuppanzigh's quartet. For a period in Beethoven's final years he acted as assistant and secretary. The canon *Wir irren allesamt*, which Beethoven sent to Holz from his deathbed, was the last complete work he composed. In performance it lasts barely thirty seconds.

Hummel, Johann Nepomuk (1778–1837). Composer and pianist. He and Beethoven were rivals, but soon developed a mutual respect. Friends noted how different their styles of composition and playing were: Hummel's delicate and refined, Beethoven's stormy and unpredictable.

Kinsky, Prince Ferdinand (1781–1812). Professional soldier. Still in his teens when he first met Beethoven and heard his music. Instantly became an admirer and supporter of the composer and advocate of his music. One of three aristocrats – along with Archduke Rudolph and Prince Lobkowitz – who agreed in 1809 to pay Beethoven an annuity for life.

Lichnowsky, Prince Karl (1756–1814). One of Beethoven's earliest and most influential patrons in Vienna. For a while, shortly after his arrival in Vienna, Beethoven lived with the Prince and Princess in their apartment. The Prince retained his own string quartet and gave regular Friday matinées at which Beethoven often performed his music. Beethoven dedicated his Piano Trios Op. 1 to the Prince, as well as the Second Symphony and several piano pieces, though he later fell out with him.

Liszt, Franz (1811–86). Hungarian pianist and composer. Liszt played for Beethoven when he was just eleven years old and Beethoven predicted a great future for him. It was Liszt who led the campaign for a monument to be erected to Beethoven in the Münsterplatz in Bonn, where it still stands.

Lobkowitz, Prince Franz Joseph (1772–1816). Great music lover, capable violinist and patron of the arts. He converted a room of his Vienna palace into a concert hall and retained his own orchestra. An early admirer of Beethoven's music, he made his concert hall and orchestra available to him. Among Beethoven's dedications to him were his first String Quartets Op. 18, as well as the Third, Fifth and Sixth Symphonies. The Prince was born with a deformed hip and walked all his life with the aid of a crutch. Along with Archduke Rudolph and Prince Kinsky, he agreed in 1809 to pay Beethoven an annuity for life.

Malfatti, Dr Johann (1775–1859). Italian physician who settled in Vienna in 1795 and became Beethoven's doctor after the sudden death of Dr Schmidt in 1809.

Malfatti, Therese (1792–1851). Pupil of Beethoven with whom he fell in love and to whom he intended proposing marriage, but she became engaged to Baron Drosdick. Beethoven almost certainly composed the famous Bagatelle WoO 59, 'Für Elise', for her.

Maximilian, Franz (1756–1801). Elector of Cologne and Archbishop of Cologne and Münster. Youngest son of Empress Maria Theresa, brother of two Habsburg Emperors and uncle of a third, brother of Marie Antoinette. He ruled his principality from Bonn, where he fostered the musical career of the young Beethoven. He made possible Beethoven's first visit to Vienna to meet Mozart. An enlightened ruler and great patron of the arts.

Milder-Hauptmann, Anna (1785–1838). Fine soprano admired by both Haydn and Beethoven. She took the title role in the first performance of *Leonore*.

Mozart, Wolfgang Amadeus (1756–91). From as early as he could remember Beethoven admired Mozart's music, studying the scores as soon as they reached Bonn. He achieved his ambition to meet Mozart when he travelled to Vienna in 1787, played for him, and Mozart agreed to take him on as a pupil.

Neefe, Christian Gottlob (1748–98). First full-time teacher of the young Beethoven in Bonn. He recognised Beethoven's extraordinary talent, securing for him the post of assistant organist, as well as instrumentalist, with the court theatre orchestra. He was the first to compare Beethoven to Mozart, and he worked hard to persuade the Elector to allow Beethoven to travel to Vienna to meet Mozart.

Oppersdorff, Count Franz von (1778–1818). Aristocrat who retained his private orchestra at his estate in Upper Silesia, which Beethoven visited with Prince Lichnowsky in 1806. The Count commissioned the Fourth and Fifth Symphonies, receiving the dedication of the Fourth.

Palffy, Count Ferdinand (1774–1840). Court Theatre director who purchased the Theater an der Wien in 1813. Instrumental in persuading Beethoven to resurrect his opera *Leonore / Fidelio*.

Pasqualati, Baron Johann (1777–1830). Property owner in Vienna. Beethoven lived in the top-floor apartment of the building the Baron owned on the Mölkerbastei for longer than he lived anywhere else, albeit with interruptions.

Razumovsky, Count Andreas Kirillovich (1752–1836). Russian ambassador in Vienna. He retained a permanent string quartet led by Schuppanzigh in which he often played second violin. He commissioned the set of quartets which came to be known as the Razumovsky Quartets to commemorate the opening of the sumptuous new palace he built in the Landstrasse suburb.

Ries, Ferdinand (1784–1838). Pupil of Beethoven in Bonn who then worked tirelessly as Beethoven's assistant in Vienna, until he was forced to return to Bonn to be conscripted into the occupying French army. On his return to Vienna he resumed his attachment to Beethoven, before leaving the city for good. In 1813 he settled in London. He became a leading figure in the London Philharmonic Society, and was instrumental in persuading the Society to commission a new symphony from Beethoven, which became the Ninth, the 'Choral'. He was a prolific composer in his own right. Ries was blind in one eye and wore an eye patch all his life.

Röckel, Joseph August (1783–1870). Fine tenor, he took over the role of Florestan in Beethoven's opera *Leonore*, after the first disastrous performances.

Rudolph, Archduke of Austria (1788–1831). Brother of Emperor Franz. First heard Beethoven's music at the composer's benefit concert at the Burgtheater in Vienna, in the company of his mother the Empress. He was a devotee of Beethoven's music from that moment on, and became his only composition pupil. An excellent pianist and accomplished composer, he was to become Beethoven's leading and most influential patron. Beethoven dedicated far more compositions to him than to anyone else, including the *Missa Solemnis*, the Emperor Piano Concerto, numerous Piano Sonatas and other chamber music. Rudolph was instrumental in persuading Princes Kinsky and Lobkowitz in 1809 to join him in paying Beethoven an annuity for life – and continued to do so even after the princes defaulted.

Schikaneder, Emanuel Johann (1751–1812). Manager of the Theater an der Wien, best known as librettist of Mozart's *The Magic Flute*. He appointed Beethoven as composer-in-residence at the Wien in 1803 and wrote a libretto, *Vestas Feuer*, for him. Beethoven began to set it, but quickly abandoned it.

Schiller, Johann Christoph Friedrich von (1759–1805). Renowned German poet and playwright. Beethoven never met him but greatly admired his poetry. He knew Schiller's lyric poem *An die Freude* while still in Bonn, harbouring ambitions to set it to music, which he finally accomplished in the Ninth Symphony.

Schindler, Anton (1795–1864). Lawyer and violinist. He was in very close contact with Beethoven during the composer's final years, acting as assistant and secretary with more zeal than any of his predecessors. After Beethoven's death he sanitised much documentary evidence to preserve his master's reputation, destroying many of the Conversation Books and falsifying others. Beethoven did not admire him as a man, but came to rely on his dedication and efficiency.

Schmidt, Dr Johann Adam (1759–1809). Beethoven's doctor, whose advice to him regarding his deafness largely consisted of going to the country to rest his ears, which was welcome after the drastic and failed remedies of earlier doctors. It was on his recommendation that Beethoven spent the fateful summer of 1802 in Heiligenstadt. Beethoven had a high regard for him.

Schubert, Franz Peter (1797–1828). Austrian composer. Given that the bulk of his output was composed before Beethoven's death, it is inconceivable that the two did not know each other, at least by sight, though there is no absolute proof that they met. Schubert's natural shyness and Beethoven's unpredictable attitude towards other composers probably mitigated against it. Nevertheless on his deathbed Beethoven studied the scores of many of Schubert's songs and professed admiration for them. Schubert was a pallbearer at Beethoven's funeral, and his own deathbed wish was to be buried alongside him, a wish that was fulfilled.

Schuppanzigh, Ignaz (1776–1830). Violinist and leader of Prince Lichnowsky's String Quartet. Great friend of Beethoven and admirer of his music. Regularly the first to play his compositions for violin and string quartet. Beethoven made much fun of his fatness, composing a small musical 'joke' for him for chorus and male voices entitled 'In Praise of the Fat One'.

Sebald, Amalie (1787–1846). Singer from Berlin. Beethoven met her in Teplitz in 1812 and grew very fond of her. Amalie looked after him during his illness there, and the intimate nature of their notes to each other led, at one time, to her being considered as a candidate for the Immortal Beloved.

Seibert, Dr Johann (1782–1846). Chief surgeon at Vienna General Hospital. Brought in by Dr Wawruch to perform the abdominal operations on Beethoven during his final illness.

Seyfried, Ignaz Xavier (1776–1841). *Kapellmeister* at the Theater an der Wien. He turned pages for Beethoven at the premiere of the Third Piano Concerto, and on a number of occasions conducted performances of Beethoven's music.

Sonnleithner, Joseph Ferdinand (1766–1835). Co-founder of the publishing house Kunst-und Industrie Comptoir, and librettist of the first version of Beethoven's opera *Leonore*.

Treitschke, Georg Friedrich (1776–1842). Playwright and poet engaged by the Kärntnertor Theatre. Beethoven was to ask him to write the third and definitive version of *Leonore / Fidelio*.

Umlauf, Michael (1781–1842). Viennese conductor and *Kapellmeister* at the Kärntnertor Theatre. He conducted *Fidelio* during the Congress of Vienna and the first performance of the Ninth Symphony, with Beethoven at his side to give him the *tempi*.

Unger, Karoline (c. 1803–77). Contralto at the Kärntnertor Theatre. She sang in the first performance of the Ninth Symphony, and turned Beethoven around to see the applause that greeted it.

Waldstein, Count Ferdinand von (1762–1823). Friend of Elector Maximilian Franz in Bonn and leading patron of the young Beethoven. He was instrumental in securing Beethoven's second and conclusive trip to Vienna, writing prophetically in Beethoven's autograph book that he would receive 'Mozart's spirit from Haydn's hands'. Beethoven was to immortalise his name with the Waldstein Sonata.

Wawruch, Dr Andreas Ignaz (1773–1842). Beethoven's principal doctor during his final illness, who wrote a detailed report on its progression. Given that Beethoven died in his care, it was inevitable he would be criticised for his treatment in the years following Beethoven's death. Seen from today's perspective his treatment was not inappropriate, given that Beethoven was already terminally ill when Dr Wawruch first attended him.

Wegeler, Dr Franz Gerhard (1765–1848). Close friend of the young Beethoven in Bonn, introducing him to the Breuning family. The two met again when Wegeler came to Vienna. It was in a letter to Wegeler in 1801 that Beethoven first mentioned his problem with hearing. Wegeler married Eleonore von Breuning in 1802.

Weissenbach, Dr Alois (1766–1821). Surgeon and poet from Salzburg who wrote the text for the cantata *Der glorreiche Augenblick* which Beethoven composed for the Congress of Vienna. Beethoven's relationship with him was short but highly amicable, no doubt influenced by the fact that Weissenbach too was deaf.

Zmeskall, Nikolaus von (1759–1833). Official in the Hungarian Chancellery in Vienna, and capable amateur cellist. Became a close friend of Beethoven, often providing him with distractions when problems with work – and his hearing – threatened to overwhelm him. Zmeskall was very short-sighted. Beethoven composed the Duet 'Obligato for two pairs of spectacles' WoO 32 in 1796–7 for viola and cello for Zmeskall and him to play together when he too had begun to wear spectacles.

Timeline

1770

17 December: Beethoven is baptised in the church of St Remigius, Bonn. The date of his birth is not recorded, but since it was customary for baptisms to take place within 24 hours of birth, it is likely he was born on 16 December.

1773

24 December: Beethoven's beloved grandfather, *Kapellmeister* Ludwig van Beethoven, dies.

1774

8 April: Beethoven's brother Caspar Carl baptised.

1776

2 October: Beethoven's brother Nikolaus Johann baptised.

1778

26 March: Beethoven's first known public performance, in Cologne.

1780

Beethoven begins lessons with Christian Gottlob Neefe.

1783

Beethoven composes his first piece, *Nine Variations on a March by Dressler,* aged 12.

14 October: Beethoven publishes the three Kurfürsten Piano Sonatas, dedicated to the Elector of Cologne and Münster, Maximilian Friedrich.

1784

Beethoven appointed assistant court organist alongside Neefe.

1787

April: Beethoven travels to Vienna to meet Mozart, who agrees to take him on as a pupil, but Beethoven has to return to Bonn where his mother is dying of consumption.

17 July: Beethoven's mother, Maria Magdalena, dies.

1790

Beethoven composes the Cantata on the Death of Joseph II, and the Cantata on the Elevation of Leopold II. The musicians of the electoral orchestra refuse to perform the first, claiming it is unplayable.

December: Beethoven meets Haydn who promises he will take him on as a pupil if he comes to Vienna.

1791

Beethoven composes the Ritterballet, allowing his patron Count Waldstein to claim it as his own composition.

1792

November: Beethoven leaves Bonn for Vienna to study with Haydn.
18 December: Beethoven's father dies.

1793

Beethoven begins lessons with Haydn and quickly establishes his reputation as the finest piano virtuoso in Vienna.

1794

Caspar Carl moves to Vienna.
Beethoven begins composing Piano Trios Op. 1.

1795

29 March: Beethoven's first public performance in Vienna, where he premieres either his First or Second Piano Concerto.
Beethoven composes Piano Sonatas Op. 2.
Beethoven performs the Piano Trios before Haydn, who is critical of No. 3, advising against publication. Beethoven is furious, but he heals the rift with his teacher when he dedicates the Piano Sonatas to him.
Nikolaus Johann moves to Vienna.

1796

Beethoven composes the Cello Sonatas Op. 5 in Berlin while travelling with Prince Lichnowsky.

1797

Beethoven gives the first performance of Quintet Op. 16 at Jahn's restaurant in the Himmelpfortgasse.

In the summer of this year he falls seriously ill. It is possibly typhus and may have been the beginning of his deafness.

1798

Beethoven completes the Piano Sonatas Op. 10, composes the three string Trios Op. 9, the Trio Op. 11, and the three Violin Sonatas Op. 12. Later in the year he begins work on the Septet Op. 20 and composes the huge Pathétique Sonata Op. 13.

1799

Beethoven composes his first String Quartets Op. 18, and begins work on Symphony No. 1.

1800

Beethoven defeats the celebrated Prussian piano virtuoso Daniel Steibelt in an improvisation contest at the palace of Prince Lobkowitz. His position as Vienna's greatest piano virtuoso is secure and remains unchallenged for the rest of his life.

2 April: Beethoven's first benefit concert, at the Burgtheater in Vienna. He premieres the Septet and the First Symphony. At the concert he meets Archduke Rudolph, accompanied by his mother, Empress Theresa.

Beethoven begins work on Symphony No. 2.

1801

Beethoven composes music for *The Creatures of Prometheus.*

Beethoven's great friend from his childhood in Bonn, Stephan von Breuning, moves to Vienna.

29 June: Beethoven mentions his deafness for the first time in a letter to his old friend Dr Franz Wegeler in Bonn.

26 July: Elector Max Franz dies at Hetzendorf, Vienna. Beethoven subsequently changes the dedication of his First Symphony to Baron van Swieten.

October: Ferdinand Ries, son of Franz Ries the leader of the electoral orchestra in Bonn, arrives in Vienna. Beethoven welcomes him and takes him on as secretary.

Beethoven falls in love with Countess Giulietta Guicciardi, and dedicates the Sonata 'Quasi una fantasia' to her. Many years later, after his death, it acquires the nickname Moonlight Sonata.

1802

Baron Braun refuses Beethoven his anticipated benefit concert.

April: Beethoven moves to Heiligenstadt north of Vienna for the summer to relieve his hearing. There he composes the Prometheus ('Eroica') Variations Op. 35 and the three Piano Sonatas Op. 31. He completes Symphony No. 2.

6 October: Beethoven writes the Heiligenstadt Testament, his last will and testament, publicly acknowledging his deafness for the first time.

1803

January: Beethoven appointed composer at the Theater an der Wien, moving into lodgings there with his brother Caspar Carl.

February to March: Beethoven composes the oratorio, Christus am Ölberge.

5 April: Beethoven's benefit concert in the Theater an der Wien. He premieres the Second Symphony and the Third Piano Concerto, playing the solo part himself. The First Symphony is also premiered.

24 May: Beethoven gives the first performance of the Violin Sonata Op. 47, with the English virtuoso George Bridgetower as soloist.

Summer: Beethoven composes the 'Eroica' Symphony in the village of Döbling, south of Vienna.

Beethoven composes the 'Waldstein' Sonata, with Andante Grazioso as second movement.

1804

Beethoven begins work on his opera *Leonore*, with Sonnleithner as librettist.

April: Beethoven's contract at the Theater an der Wien is terminated, after Baron Braun buys the theatre.

20 May: Napoleon proclaimed Emperor of France. Beethoven tears up the title page of the Eroica bearing the dedication to him.

June: Beethoven moves into Stephan von Breuning's apartment, but the arrangement ends after a serious disagreement between them.

The 'Eroica' Symphony is performed at Prince Lobkowitz's palace.

October: Beethoven becomes acquainted with Josephine Deym, née Brunsvik, and begins giving her piano lessons. He composes the song 'An die Hoffnung' for her.

1805

Beethoven composes the Piano Sonata Op. 57, 'Appassionata'. He completes composition of his opera *Leonore*.

September: The censor bans the projected performance of *Leonore* at the Theater an der Wien.
5 October: The censor lifts the ban on *Leonore*.
20 November: First performance of *Leonore*.

1806

29 March: Revised version of *Leonore* performed at the Theater an der Wien.
25 May: Caspar Carl van Beethoven marries Johanna Reiss.
Beethoven works on the set of three String Quartets commissioned by Count Razumovsky and the Fourth Symphony.
4 September: Beethoven's nephew Karl is born.
Count Oppersdorff, a near neighbour of Lichnowsky in Silesia, buys the Fourth Symphony. Beethoven begins work on the Fifth Symphony.

1807

February: 'Appassionata' Sonata published
April: Muzio Clementi in London secures the rights to publish several works in Great Britain for the sum of £200.
13 September: Beethoven's Mass in C is performed at Prince Esterházy's castle chapel in Eisenstadt.
Beethoven completes work on the Fifth Symphony.

1808

27 March: Performance of Haydn's Creation in honour of the composer's seventy-sixth birthday.
Summer: Beethoven composes the 'Pastoral' Symphony while staying in Heiligenstadt.
10 August: Beethoven publishes Fourth Piano Concerto and Violin Concerto.
October: Beethoven is offered the post of *Kapellmeister* to King Jérôme of Westphalia (Napoleon's younger brother) in Kassel, at a salary of 600 ducats.
22 December: Beethoven gives his much-postponed and long-awaited benefit concert at the Theater an der Wien, which sees the first performance of the Fifth and 'Pastoral' Symphonies.

1809

7 January: Beethoven accepts the offer of *Kapellmeister* in Kassel.
Beethoven begins work on the Fifth Piano Concerto, the 'Emperor'.
26 February: Archduke Rudolph, Prince Lobkowitz and Prince Kinsky agree to pay Beethoven an annuity for life on the sole condition that he remain in Vienna.

4 May: Beethoven composes the beginning of the Piano Sonata Op. 81a, 'Les adieux'.

31 May: Joseph Haydn, Beethoven's former teacher, dies at the age of 77.

23 November: Beethoven agrees to set forty-three folksongs for the Scottish publisher George Thomson.

1810

13 February: Josephine Deym marries Baron von Stackelberg, her children's tutor.

Beethoven becomes acquainted with the Malfatti family. He composes the Bagatelle WoO 59 for Therese Malfatti; Dr Giovanni Malfatti becomes Beethoven's doctor.

July: The critic E. T. A. Hoffmann's famous review of Beethoven's Fifth Symphony is published in the *Allgemeine Musikalische Zeitung*.

1811

15 March: Austria's currency is devalued fivefold under a Finanz-Patent, drastically reducing the amount Beethoven receives under his annuity.

Beethoven completes the 'Archduke' Trio.

28 May: Ignaz Gleichenstein, who has been acting as Beethoven's secretary, marries Anna Malfatti, Therese's sister.

Beethoven begins the Seventh Symphony.

During a long period of illness, Antonie Brentano is regularly visited by Beethoven. He sets the poem 'An die Geliebte' to music for her.

1812

Beethoven begins the Eighth Symphony.

Beethoven composes the Piano Trio WoO 39 for Maximiliane Brentano.

1 July: Beethoven arrives in Prague, on his way to Teplitz in northern Bohemia.

2 July: Beethoven sees Prince Kinsky concerning his annuity.

5 July: Beethoven arrives at Teplitz in the early morning.

6 July: Beethoven begins a passionate letter to an unnamed woman. In it he calls her his 'Immortal Beloved' [*unsterbliche Geliebte*].

July: Beethoven and Goethe meet several times.

25 July: Beethoven leaves Teplitz for Karlsbad to join the Brentano family.

Beethoven returns to Teplitz, where he meets Amalie Sebald. She looks after him when he falls ill.

September: Beethoven travels to Linz, determined to stop his brother Johann from marrying his housekeeper, Therese Obermayer.

October: Beethoven composes three equali for trombones for the Linz *Kapellmeister* Glöggl.

2/3 November: Prince Kinsky dies after being thrown from his horse while hunting.

8 November: Johann van Beethoven marries Therese Obermayer.

1813

8 March: Karl Brentano is born.

8 April: Minona von Stackelberg is born.

12 April: Caspar Carl van Beethoven, seriously ill with consumption, declares that in the event of his death he wants Beethoven to be guardian of his son Karl.

21 June: The English army under Wellington defeats the French at the Battle of Vitoria in Spain. Mälzel persuades Beethoven to write a piece in celebration of the victory for his mechanical instrument, the Panharmonicon. In return Mälzel constructs the first of several ear trumpets for Beethoven. The piece is later orchestrated and becomes known as the Battle Symphony Op. 91.

July: Prince Lobkowitz leaves Vienna in disgrace after going bankrupt.

28 August: Gerhard von Breuning is born.

8 December: Beethoven and Mälzel give a charity concert at the Hofburg at which the Battle Symphony and the Seventh Symphony are heard in public for the first time.

1814

January: Beethoven agrees to revive his opera *Leonore/Fidelio*, asking Treitschke to provide a new libretto.

11 April: Beethoven gives the first public performance of the Archduke Trio Op. 97 with Schuppanzigh and Linke; his deafness makes it a traumatic experience.

15 April: Beethoven's old patron Prince Lichnowsky dies.

18 July: Fidelio performed for the first time in its final form.

26 September: Fidelio performed before several heads of state assembled for the Congress of Vienna.

29 November: Beethoven attends the first performance of *Der glorreiche Augenblick*, a cantata he composed for the Congress, at the Hofburg.

31 December: Count Razumovsky's magnificent palace is destroyed by fire.

1815

May: Beethoven abandons attempts to compose a Sixth Piano Concerto.

June: Philharmonic Society of London commission three overtures from

Beethoven for 75 guineas; he sends them the already composed Opp. 113, 115 and 117.

14 November: Beethoven's brother Caspar Carl makes his will, appointing his wife Johanna and Beethoven co-guardians of his son Karl.

15 November: Caspar Carl van Beethoven dies of consumption.

22 November: Caspar Carl's widow Johanna and Beethoven are appointed joint guardians of Karl, now aged nine.

28 November: Beethoven appeals to the Landrecht, the court of the nobility, for sole custody of Karl.

1816

9 January: The Landrecht rules in Beethoven's favour over the guardianship of Karl.

19 January: Beethoven is legally appointed sole guardian of Karl.

2 February: Karl is removed from his mother, and Beethoven enrols him in a boarding school run by Giannatasio del Rio.

April: Beethoven composes the song cycle *An die ferne Geliebte.*

Carl Czerny, on Beethoven's instructions, begins giving Karl piano lessons.

18 September: Karl undergoes a hernia operation. The Giannatasios take him to recuperate with Beethoven in Baden.

15 December: Prince Lobkowitz dies at his estate in Bohemia.

1817

9 June: Ferdinand Ries writes on behalf of the London Philharmonic Society, inviting Beethoven to London.

Beethoven begins work on what is to become the gigantic Hammerklavier Sonata, Op. 106.

27 December: Thomas Broadwood dispatches to Beethoven a new grand piano with the heavier English action.

1818

Karl runs away

24 January: Karl leaves Giannatasio's boarding school and begins living with Beethoven, studying with a private tutor.

Beethoven's planned trip to London is cancelled; he blames poor health.

February: Beethoven begins to use conversation books, due to his increasing deafness.

Beethoven begins sketches for the Ninth Symphony.

19 May: Beethoven takes Karl to Mödling for the summer months, enrolling him in the local school run by the village priest, Pater Fröhlich.

August: Beethoven completes the Hammerklavier Sonata.

18 September: Johanna van Beethoven petitions the Landrecht to obtain guardianship of Karl. Her petition is rejected.

Beethoven makes more sketches for a new symphony, which he decides will have voices.

3 October: Another appeal by Johanna is dismissed.

3 December: Karl runs away to his mother; Beethoven calls in the police to bring him back.

7 December: Johanna again petitions the Landrecht.

11 December: Beethoven admits to the Landrecht that he is not a member of the nobility. The Landrecht transfers the case to the lower court, the Magistrat.

1819

11 January: Beethoven loses guardianship of Karl.

March: Beethoven begins a set of variations for the publisher Diabelli.

April: Beethoven begins the *Missa Solemnis*, intended for the enthronement of Archduke Rudolph as Archbishop of Olmütz the following year.

22 June: Karl enters Blöchlinger's institute.

2 August: Johann van Beethoven buys a large estate at Gneixendorf bei Krems on the Danube.

November: Beethoven works on the Gloria and Credo of the *Missa Solemnis*.

1820

7 January: Beethoven petitions the Court of Appeal over the guardianship of Karl.

9 March: Archduke Rudolph is enthroned as Archbishop of Olmütz; the *Missa Solemnis* is not ready for the occasion.

8 April: The Court of Appeal makes a final ruling in Beethoven's favour over the guardianship of Karl; Johanna appeals directly to the Emperor, who refuses to intervene.

31 May: Beethoven agrees to compose three Piano Sonatas for the publisher Adolf Schlesinger; they are to become Opp. 109–11.

1821

Beethoven falls seriously ill with rheumatic fever.

31 March: Josephine Deym-Stackelberg (née Brunsvik) dies.

July: Barely recovered from fever, Beethoven develops jaundice.

Beethoven completes the *Missa Solemnis* by the end of the year.

1822

January: Beethoven again becomes unwell, suffering for several months with 'gout in the chest'.

Beethoven makes sketches setting Schiller's poem 'An die Freude' to music for use in the new symphony with voices.

Autumn: Beethoven meets the young Franz Liszt, a pupil of Czerny, who plays for him. Beethoven is impressed and anoints him his 'successor'.

9 November: Prince Galitzin commissions three String Quartets from Beethoven; they are to become Opp. 127, 130 and 132.

10 November: The Philharmonic Society of London offers Beethoven £50 for a new symphony.

Beethoven is elected to the Royal Academy of Music of Sweden.

1823

Spring: Beethoven composes a canon, Falstefferel, to mark Schuppanzigh's return to Vienna from Russia.

August: After a sudden deterioration in his health, Beethoven goes to stay in Baden, where he works intensively on the Ninth Symphony.

6 August: Wenzel Schlemmer, Beethoven's favourite copyist, dies.

29 August: Karl leaves Blöchlinger's institute and visits his uncle in Baden, before enrolling at the university in Vienna.

1824

Beethoven decides to dedicate the Diabelli Variations to Antonie Brentano.

February: Vienna's leading musical names petition Beethoven – successfully – to hold the first performance of the *Missa Solemnis* and Ninth Symphony in Vienna. But the censor bans any performance of the Missa, a religious work, in a theatre.

7 May: The *Missa Solemnis* and Ninth Symphony are given their premieres at the Kärntnertor theatre.

May: Beethoven dismisses Schindler; Karl Holz, a young Chancellery official and violinist, takes his place.

June: Beethoven begins work on the String Quartet Op. 127, and later in the year the String Quartet Op. 132.

1825

21 March: First London performance of the Ninth Symphony, directed by Sir George Smart. Ill health forces Beethoven to cancel his intended trip to London to conduct the performance.

April: Beethoven falls ill with a serious abdominal complaint.

Karl informs his uncle of his decision to join the army.

May: Beethoven, in Baden again, works on the Galitzin Quartets, composing the *Heiliger Dankgesang*, the Holy Song of Thanks, for Op. 132 as his health appears to improve.

June: Beethoven begins work on the String Quartet Op. 130.

July: String Quartet Op. 132 completed.

23 August: Beethoven begins work on the Grosse Fuge, intended as the finale for Op. 130 but later published separately as Op. 133.

Johann van Beethoven invites Ludwig and Karl to stay at his estate in Gneixendorf.

Beethoven composes the Cavatina of Op. 130.

15 October: Beethoven moves to his final lodgings in Vienna, the Schwarzspanierhaus.

Beethoven attempts a reconciliation with Karl, informing him he has purchased bank shares in his name.

15 December: Beethoven begins work on String Quartet Op. 131.

1826

21 March: Schuppanzigh and his quartet give the first public performance of the String Quartet Op. 130. Beethoven agrees to compose a new final movement to replace the Grosse Fuge.

27 July: Karl buys a pistol intending to commit suicide. His intentions become known to his landlord, who contacts Beethoven.

29 July: Karl pawns his watch to buy another pistol and disappears with it.

30 July: Karl attempts suicide at the Rauhenstein ruins in the Helenenthal Valley outside Baden. He is found and taken to his mother to recuperate.

July: Beethoven begins his last String Quartet, Op. 135.

7 August: Karl is admitted to hospital for further treatment.

August: Ninth Symphony is published.

25 September: Karl leaves hospital.

28 September: Beethoven and Karl leave Vienna to stay with Johann at Gneixendorf.

In Gneixendorf Beethoven composes a new finale for Op. 130.

1 December: After a furious row with Johann, Beethoven and Karl leave in the middle of the night in an open-top carriage for Vienna. Beethoven falls ill en route.

20 December: Beethoven undergoes an operation to reduce his abdominal swelling.

1827

2 January: Karl departs for military service in Iglau in Bohemia.

8 January: Beethoven undergoes a second operation to drain fluid.

2 February: A third operation, as Beethoven's health rapidly deteriorates.

27 February: A fourth operation, by which time the wound in Beethoven's side has become infected.

March: Beethoven makes sketches for a Tenth Symphony.

22 March: Beethoven receives the last rites.

26 March: Beethoven dies.

29 March: Beethoven's funeral takes place; he is buried at the Währinger cemetery.

4 June: Stephan von Breuning dies.

5 November: Beethoven's musical effects are auctioned. His total estate is estimated at 9885 florins and 18 kreuzer, approximately £988 / $1,620.

Acknowledgements

It was Darren Henley, Managing Director of Classic FM, who picked up the telephone in the summer of 2010 and gave me a new career in radio. And it was Darren who, when I told him I had embarked on a biography of Beethoven, said immediately he wanted it to be a Classic FM publication.

He introduced me to Lorne Forsyth, Chairman of Elliott & Thompson, Classic FM's publisher, and Olivia Bays, Publisher at Elliott & Thompson. Both were excited at the prospect of a new, full-length biography of the great artist, and encouraged me from our first meeting.

Olivia was a knowledgeable and sympathetic editor, infinitely patient with my corrections and amendments, and long suffering to a fault with the many changes of mind over the front cover. She is one of the few people I have ever worked with who responds as rapidly to emails as I do myself – exactly what a writer with more than forty years of journalism behind him is used to and needs.

I am grateful to Jennie Condell and James Collins at Elliott & Thompson for tracking down all the illustrations I asked for, and for making my own photographs look far more professional than they originally were.

The most important Beethoven research centre outside Europe is the American Beethoven Society at San José State University in California. I have been a member for many years. I have lauded the efficiency and dedication of the Society in previous publications on Beethoven. I once needed the words to an obscure musical jest by Beethoven. It was on my fax from San José within twenty four hours. My grateful thanks, once again, to Director William Meredith and Curator Patricia Stroh.

Thanks too to Boris Goyke at the Beethoven-Haus in Bonn, and Marian Hochel, Director of Chateau Duchcov-Dux in the Czech Republic, for their help in tracking down rare material.

Finally – and most importantly, for without her encouragement from the day I first said I was undertaking this enormous project, I might have fallen at the first of many hurdles – my eternal thanks to Nula.

About Classic FM

Classic FM is the UK's most popular classical music brand, reaching 5.1 million listeners every week. Classic FM's programmes are hosted by a mix of classical music experts and household names including John Suchet, Alexander Armstrong, Moira Stuart, John Humphrys, Myleene Klass, Bill Turnbull, Alan Titchmarsh, Charlotte Hawkins, Aled Jones and Margherita Taylor. Since its launch in 1992, Classic FM has aimed to make classical music accessible and relevant to everyone and in doing so, introduce an entirely new audience to the genre. ClassicFM.com is the UK's biggest classical music website and has 2.7 million unique monthly web and app users. Classic FM is owned by Global. It is available across the UK on 100–102 FM, DAB digital radio and TV, the Classic FM app, at ClassicFM.com and on Global Player.

Source: RAJAR / Ipsos-MORI / RSMB, period ending December 18th 2016.

Index

About the Author

John Suchet presents Classic FM's flagship morning programme, from 9am every weekday. His informative style of presentation, coupled with a deep knowledge of classical music, has won a wide spectrum of new listeners to the station. Before turning to classical music, John was one of the UK's best-known television journalists. As a reporter for ITN he covered world events, including the Iran revolution, the Soviet invasion of Afghanistan and the Philippines revolution. He then became a newscaster, regularly presenting ITN's flagship *News at Ten*, as well as all other bulletins, over a period of nearly twenty years.

John has been honoured for both roles. In 1986 he was voted Television Journalist of the Year, in 1996 Television Newscaster of the Year, and in 2008 the Royal Television Society awarded him its highest accolade, a Lifetime Achievement Award. John has been given an honorary degree by his old university, the University of Dundee, and in 2001 the Royal Academy of Music awarded him an Honorary Fellowship in recognition of his work on Beethoven, having written six books on the composer. He is also the author of *Mozart: The Man Revealed*, *Verdi: The Man Revealed*, *Tchaikovsky: The Man Revealed*, and the *Sunday Times* bestselling *The Last Waltz: The Strauss Dynasty and Vienna*.